the SCIENCE of COOKING

the SCIENCE of COOKING

DR. STUART FARRIMOND

Senior Editors
Bob Bridle, Claire Cross

Senior Art Editors
Alison Gardner, Kathryn Wilding

Editors
Alice Kewellhampton, Shashwati Tia Sarkar
Toby Mann

US Editors
Cheri Clark, Lori Hand

Designers
Vicky Read, Rehan Adbul

Illustrators
Peter Bull, Nick Radord, Andy@KJA-artists

Jacket Designer
Steven Marsden

Jackets Assistant
Laura Bithell

Senior Pre-production Producer
Tony Phipps

Senior Producer
Ché Creasey

Creative Technical Support
Sonia Charbonnier, Tom Morse

Managing Editor
Dawn Henderson

Managing Art Editor
Marianne Markham

Art Director
Maxine Pedliham

Publishing Director
Mary-Clare Jerram

First American Edition, 2017
Published in the United States by DK Publishing
345 Hudson Street, New York, New York 10014

Copyright © 2017 Dorling Kindersley Limited
DK, a Division of Penguin Random House LLC
17 18 19 20 21   10 9 8 7 6 5 4 3 2
002—261482—Sept/2017

A catalog record for this book is available from
the Library of Congress.

ISBN 978-1-4654-6369-2

NOTE: The author and publisher advocate sustainable food
choices, and every effort has been made to include only
sustainable foods in this book. Food sustainability is, however,
a shifting landscape, and so we encourage readers to keep up
to date with advice on this subject, so that they are equipped
to make their own ethical choices.

DK books are available at special discounts when purchased
in bulk for sales promotions, premiums, fund-raising, or
educational use. For details, contact: DK Publishing Special
Markets, 345 Hudson Street, New York, New York 10014
SpecialSales@dk.com

Printed and bound in China

All images ©
Dorling Kindersley Limited
For further information see:
www.dkimages.com

A WORLD OF IDEAS:
SEE ALL THERE IS TO KNOW
www.dk.com

CONTENTS

FOREWORD 8

TASTE AND FLAVOR 10

KITCHEN ESSENTIALS 20

An Essential Guide to **KNIVES** 22
An Essential Guide to **POTS AND PANS** 24
An Essential Guide to **UTENSILS** 26

MEAT AND POULTRY 28

In Focus: **MEAT** 30
The Process of **GRILLING** 44
The Process of **SLOW COOKING** 54

FISH AND SEAFOOD 64

In Focus: **FISH** 66
The Process of **PAN-FRYING** 76
The Process of **SOUS VIDE** 84

EGGS AND DAIRY 92

In Focus: **EGGS** 94
In Focus: **MILK** 108
In Focus: **CHEESE** 120

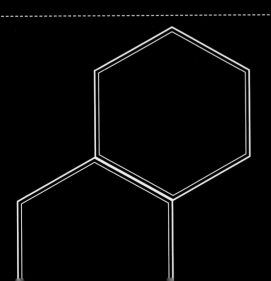

RICE, GRAINS, AND PASTA 126

In Focus: RICE 128

The Process of PRESSURE COOKING 134

VEGETABLES, FRUITS, NUTS, AND SEEDS 146

The Process of STEAMING 152

In Focus: POTATOES 160

The Process of MICROWAVING 164

In Focus: NUTS 174

HERBS, SPICES, OILS, AND FLAVORINGS 178

In Focus: HERBS 180

In Focus: CHILES 188

In Focus: OIL AND FAT 194

BAKING AND SWEET THINGS 206

In Focus: FLOUR 208

The Process of OVEN BAKING 222

In Focus: SUGAR 230

In Focus: CHOCOLATE 236

ACKNOWLEDGMENTS AND INDEX 244

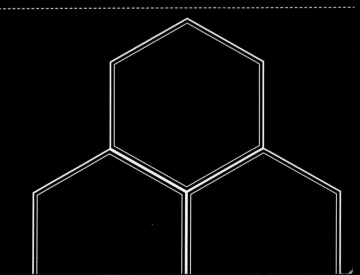

Dr. Stuart Farrimond
FOREWORD

Every cook knows that preparing food for others can bring a joy that is even more fulfilling than eating.

Cooking is termed an "art" and is steeped in rituals and processes that chefs throughout the ages have followed blindly. Many of these "rules," however, serve to confuse and stifle creativity. Science and logic show us that often customs are simply wrong. For example, beans do not need to be soaked for hours before cooking, meat does not need to be rested to seal in juices, and marinated meat can taste better if left for one hour, rather than five.

In this book, I answer more than 160 of the most common culinary questions and conundrums, drawing on the latest research to give meaningful and practical answers. I show that science can be a vehicle for fully appreciating the wonders that we see in the kitchen every day. With the aid of a microscope, we can see how a whisk transforms the yellow slime of egg white into a snow-white cotton-like meringue. And a

sprinkling of chemistry shows why a steak left to sizzle on a hot grill evolves from a bland and chewy hunk of flesh into a mouthwatering, meaty delight.

With striking imagery and diagrams, this book delves into the most commonly used cooking processes and techniques; shines a spotlight on core ingredients, such as meat, fish, dairy, spices, flour, and eggs; and offers a guide on how to equip your kitchen with the best gear.

Writing in informal language and with minimal jargon, my aim is for you, the reader to understand more of the science of food and cooking to help lift the lid on their creativity. No longer shackled by the rules of a recipe, cooks can use science to invent dishes and experiment. After you read this book, I sincerely hope that you feel inspired and equipped to cook in a new way that will both delight and surprise.

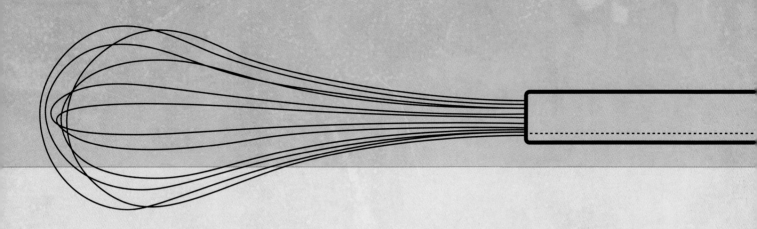

"**My aim** *is for you, the reader*
to understand more of
the **science of food and**
cooking, *to help lift the lid*
on your **creativity.**"

TASTE & FLAVOR

Why do we
COOK?

To think of cooking as purely functional would be to look at just one aspect of it.

There are various reasons to cook food, but essentially our very existence pivots on our ability to cook. Cooking makes food more edible and, in so doing, cuts down on the time it takes to digest it. Great apes, our primate ancestors, spend 80 percent of their day chewing food. Learning to grind, purée, dry, or preserve food helped us to digest it more speedily, but it was the advent of cooking, at least one million years ago, that enabled us to spend less time chewing and digesting food and more time thinking and focusing on other pursuits. Today, we spend just five percent of our day eating. So how else does cooking food benefit us?

It makes food safe Cooking destroys bacteria, microbes, and many of the toxins these produce. Raw meat and fish can be rendered safe, and heat destroys many plant toxins, such as the deadly substance, phytohemagglutinin, in kidney beans.

Flavors multiply Cooking makes food taste incredible. Heat browns meats, vegetables, breads, and cakes; caramelizes sugars; and releases locked-in flavors from herbs and spices in a process known as the Maillard reaction (see pp16–17).

Cooking helps digestion Fat melts, chewy connective tissue in meat softens into nutritious gelatin, and proteins unravel, or "denature," from their tightly coiled structure into ones that digestive enzymes can break down more easily.

Starches are softened When heated in water, clustered granules of hard-to-digest carbohydrates unravel and soften. This "gelatinization" of energy-dense starches transforms vegetables and cereal flours so the intestines can easily process them.

Nutrients are released Without cooking foods to break down their starches, significant amounts of a food's nourishment are locked up in "resistant" starch that cannot be digested. Heating also forces some of the vitamins and minerals that are confined inside cells to be liberated, increasing how much of these essential substances the body can absorb.

It helps us socialize The ritual of cooking and sharing is entrenched in our psyche, bringing families and friends together. Research shows that regularly eating with others improves well-being.

"Cooked food tastes incredible. *Cooking* releases locked-in flavors *and brings new* textures *to foods."*

TO ENHANCE
FLAVOR

TO AID
DIGESTION

TO MAKE
FOOD SAFE

TO HELP US
SOCIALIZE

TO SOFTEN
STARCHES

TO RELEASE
NUTRIENTS

How do we
TASTE?

Taste is a surprisingly complex process.

A multisensory experience, taste involves aroma, texture, and heat, all combining to create an overall impression.

As you lift food to your lips, before any food actually reaches the tongue, aromas flood the nostrils. Teeth then break down food, releasing more aromas, and the food's texture, or "mouthfeel," becomes critical to its appreciation. In the mouth, more flavor-carrying particles waft to the back of the oral cavity, up to the smell receptors, but now they are experienced as if coming from the tongue. Sweet, salty, bitter, sour, umami, and fatty taste receptors (see opposite) are stimulated, and a cascade of messages filters to the brain. As you chew, hot food cools, increasing taste intensity: at 86–95°F (30–35°C), taste receptors are most active.

Taste signals are relayed to the thalamus, which passes signals to other regions of the brain.

As you inhale, airborne molecules of food are vacuumed up into the nose.

When signals reach the frontal lobe, we become aware of what we are smelling and tasting.

THALAMUS

FRONTAL LOBE

TONGUE

Taste receptors on the tongue register basic tastes.

Nerves carry taste messages to the brain.

NERVE PATHWAYS FOR TASTE

Aroma molecules pass to the smell sensors at the back of the nose. Here the brain interprets them as taste from the mouth.

MYTH BUSTER

——— *Myth* ———

DIFFERENT TONGUE REGIONS DETECT DIFFERENT TASTES

——— *Truth* ———

In 1901, German scientist D. P. Hänig promoted the idea that different tastes were stronger in different parts of the tongue. This research was later used to create a "taste map." Now, we know that all tastes are sensed across the tongue and difference in sensitivity across the tongue is negligible.

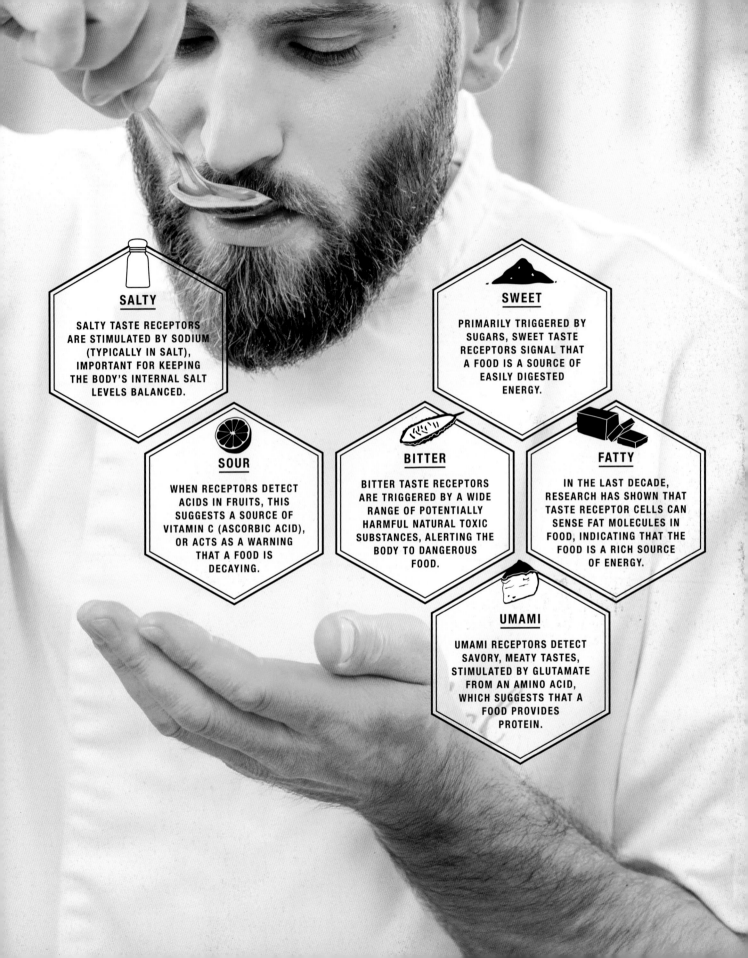

SALTY

SALTY TASTE RECEPTORS ARE STIMULATED BY SODIUM (TYPICALLY IN SALT), IMPORTANT FOR KEEPING THE BODY'S INTERNAL SALT LEVELS BALANCED.

SWEET

PRIMARILY TRIGGERED BY SUGARS, SWEET TASTE RECEPTORS SIGNAL THAT A FOOD IS A SOURCE OF EASILY DIGESTED ENERGY.

SOUR

WHEN RECEPTORS DETECT ACIDS IN FRUITS, THIS SUGGESTS A SOURCE OF VITAMIN C (ASCORBIC ACID), OR ACTS AS A WARNING THAT A FOOD IS DECAYING.

BITTER

BITTER TASTE RECEPTORS ARE TRIGGERED BY A WIDE RANGE OF POTENTIALLY HARMFUL NATURAL TOXIC SUBSTANCES, ALERTING THE BODY TO DANGEROUS FOOD.

FATTY

IN THE LAST DECADE, RESEARCH HAS SHOWN THAT TASTE RECEPTOR CELLS CAN SENSE FAT MOLECULES IN FOOD, INDICATING THAT THE FOOD IS A RICH SOURCE OF ENERGY.

UMAMI

UMAMI RECEPTORS DETECT SAVORY, MEATY TASTES, STIMULATED BY GLUTAMATE FROM AN AMINO ACID, WHICH SUGGESTS THAT A FOOD PROVIDES PROTEIN.

Why does cooked FOOD TASTE SO GOOD?

Taste is a surprisingly complex process.

In 1912, French medical researcher Louis-Camille Maillard made a discovery that would leave a lasting impact on cooking science. He analyzed how the building blocks of proteins (amino acids) and sugars react together, and uncovered a complex family of reactions that begin to take place when protein-containing foods, such as meats, nuts, cereals, and many vegetables, reach around 284°F (140°C).

We now call these molecular changes the "Maillard reaction," and they help us make sense of the many ways in which food browns and takes on flavor as it cooks. Seared steak, crispy fish skin, the aromatic crust on bread, and even the aroma of toasted nuts and spices are all thanks to this reaction. The interplay of the two components creates enticing aromas unique to each food. Understanding the Maillard reaction helps the cook in many ways: adding fructose-rich honey to a marinade fuels the reaction; pouring cream into simmering sugar provides milk proteins and sugars for butterscotch and caramel flavors; and brushing pastry with egg provides extra protein for the crust to brown.

THE MAILLARD REACTION

Amino acids—the building blocks of proteins—clash with nearby sugar molecules (even meats contain traces of sugar) to fuse into new substances. Fused molecules fling themselves apart and crash into others to combine, separate, and reform in countless ways. Hundreds of new substances are born, some brown in color and many carrying aromas. As the temperature climbs, more changes occur. The exact flavors and aromas generated by browning depend on a food's unique combination of protein types and sugars.

	BEFORE

WHAT'S GOING ON?

UP TO 284°F 140°C

The start of cooking
The temperature needs to reach about 284°F (140°C) before sugar molecules and amino acids have enough energy to react together. While the outer layers of the food are damp, it will not warm above the boiling point of water (212°F/100°C), so surface moisture must be driven off by dry heat first.

WHAT'S GOING ON?

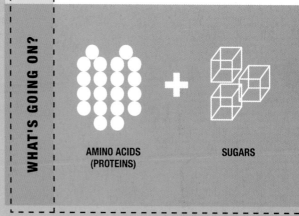

AMINO ACIDS (PROTEINS)   +   SUGARS

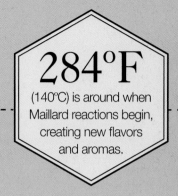

284°F

(140°C) is around when Maillard reactions begin, creating new flavors and aromas.

DURING THE MAILLARD REACTION	AFTER
284–320+°F 140–160+°C	**356°F >** 180°C >

284°F (140°C)
At around 284°F (140°C) protein-containing foods start to turn brown in the Maillard reaction. This is also called the "browning reaction," but color is just part of the story. At 284°F (140°C), proteins and sugars clash and fuse, creating hundreds of new flavor and aroma substances.

302°F (150°C)
Maillard reactions intensify as the temperature rises. As food reaches 302°F (150°C), it generates new flavor molecules twice as quickly as it did at 284°F (140°C), adding more complex flavors and aromas.

320°F (160°C)
As the temperature increases, molecular changes continue and more enticing new flavors and aromas are created—the flavor enhancement peaks at this point. There are now cascades of malty, nutty, meaty, and caramel-like flavors.

356°F (180°C)
When food reaches 356°F (180°C), another reaction called pyrolysis, or burning, begins and food starts to char, destroying aromas and leaving acrid, bitter flavors. Carbohydrates, proteins, and then fats, break down, producing some potentially harmful substances. Watch food closely and remove from the heat before it begins to blacken.

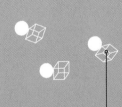

Amino acids and sugars start to combine to create new flavors.

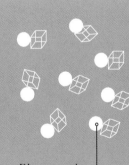

Flavor reactions double in speed.

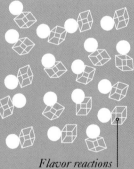

Flavor reactions accelerate to a peak.

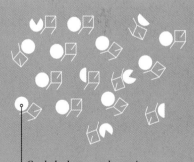

Carbohydrates and proteins form black, acrid substances.

Why do some flavors go together SO WELL?

Taste is a surprisingly complex process.

Each food has characteristic flavor compounds, the chemicals that lend it its aroma, pungency, and taste. The names and chemical formulas of these varied substances include fruity esters, spicy phenolics, flowery and citrusy terpenes, and piquant sulfur-containing molecules. Until recently, discovering foods that worked together well was largely trial and error, but a rise in experimental chefs has seen a new "science" of food pairing. Researchers have cataloged the flavor compounds of hundreds of foods, showing that classical food combinations do share many flavor compounds, while also revealing more unusual matches. However, the theories do not account for a food's texture and don't always hold true for Asian and Indian cuisines, where spice combinations have very few or no flavor links.

Here we look at which foods pair well with beef based on shared flavor compounds. The thicker the line, the more shared flavor compounds there are.

COLOR KEY

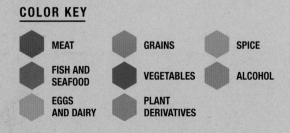

- MEAT
- FISH AND SEAFOOD
- EGGS AND DAIRY
- GRAINS
- VEGETABLES
- PLANT DERIVATIVES
- SPICE
- ALCOHOL

RED WINE

The nutty aromas from benzaldehyde, oak aromas from lactones, and smoky and tobacco flavors, interplay with roasted beef flavors.

BEER

Strong-tasting, dark beers ca[rry] spicy notes along with broth[y] flavor compounds that link t[o] flavors created when beef undergoes Maillard brownin[g] (see pp16–17).

COFFEE

Many of coffee's 200-plus complex, rich flavors are due to the roasting of beans, which share compounds created when beef is seared or roasted.

MILK

Grass-fed beef pairs well with heated milk flavors, owing to pasture-raised cattle's higher concentration of fatty-flavored, fragrant lactone chemicals present in the meat.

BUTTER

Two highly potent flavor molecule[s] that convey butter's buttery and creamy aroma, diacetyl and acetoin, are shared by beef. These rich notes are greatest in prime cuts.

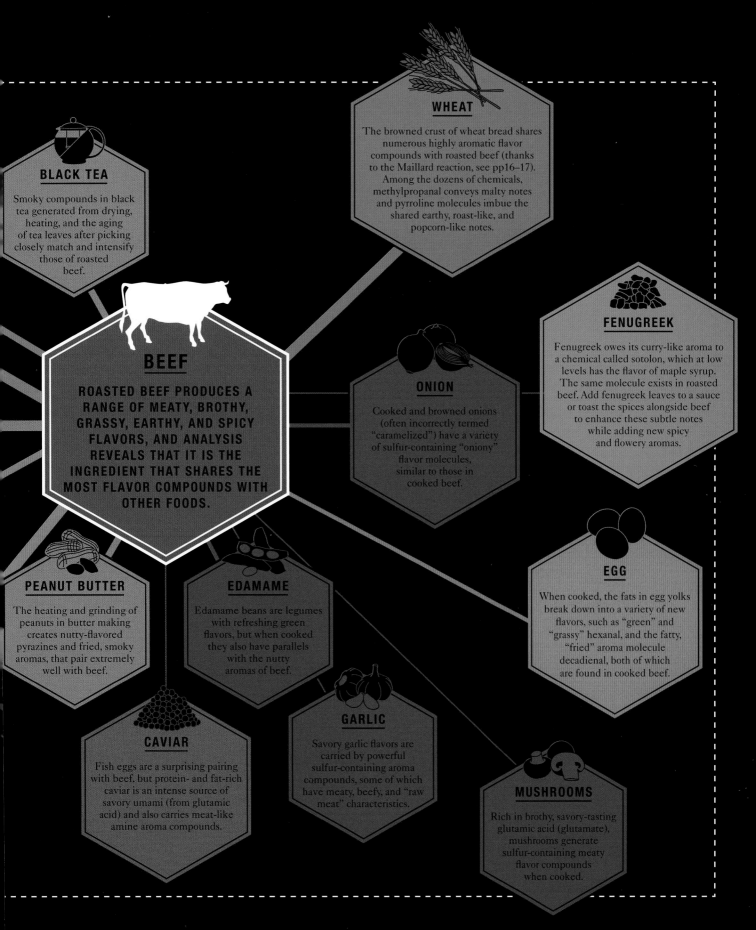

WHEAT

The browned crust of wheat bread shares numerous highly aromatic flavor compounds with roasted beef (thanks to the Maillard reaction, see pp16–17). Among the dozens of chemicals, methylpropanal conveys malty notes and pyrroline molecules imbue the shared earthy, roast-like, and popcorn-like notes.

BLACK TEA

Smoky compounds in black tea generated from drying, heating, and the aging of tea leaves after picking closely match and intensify those of roasted beef.

FENUGREEK

Fenugreek owes its curry-like aroma to a chemical called sotolon, which at low levels has the flavor of maple syrup. The same molecule exists in roasted beef. Add fenugreek leaves to a sauce or toast the spices alongside beef to enhance these subtle notes while adding new spicy and flowery aromas.

BEEF

ROASTED BEEF PRODUCES A RANGE OF MEATY, BROTHY, GRASSY, EARTHY, AND SPICY FLAVORS, AND ANALYSIS REVEALS THAT IT IS THE INGREDIENT THAT SHARES THE MOST FLAVOR COMPOUNDS WITH OTHER FOODS.

ONION

Cooked and browned onions (often incorrectly termed "caramelized") have a variety of sulfur-containing "oniony" flavor molecules, similar to those in cooked beef.

EGG

When cooked, the fats in egg yolks break down into a variety of new flavors, such as "green" and "grassy" hexanal, and the fatty, "fried" aroma molecule decadienal, both of which are found in cooked beef.

PEANUT BUTTER

The heating and grinding of peanuts in butter making creates nutty-flavored pyrazines and fried, smoky aromas, that pair extremely well with beef.

EDAMAME

Edamame beans are legumes with refreshing green flavors, but when cooked they also have parallels with the nutty aromas of beef.

CAVIAR

Fish eggs are a surprising pairing with beef, but protein- and fat-rich caviar is an intense source of savory umami (from glutamic acid) and also carries meat-like amine aroma compounds.

GARLIC

Savory garlic flavors are carried by powerful sulfur-containing aroma compounds, some of which have meaty, beefy, and "raw meat" characteristics.

MUSHROOMS

Rich in brothy, savory-tasting glutamic acid (glutamate), mushrooms generate sulfur-containing meaty flavor compounds when cooked.

KITCHEN ESSENTIALS

The cutting edge is called the bevel, where the metal narrows to a fraction of a millimeter.

An essential guide to
KNIVES

A few select knives meet most kitchen needs.

Many chefs consider good-quality, durable, sharp knives among their most prized possessions.

How knives are constructed

Knives are either stamped or forged. The most widely sold are lightweight stamped blades, made by punching a hole out of a sheet of steel. Forged blades are made by beating, heating, and cooling metal, which forces metal atoms into minute crystal clusters, creating a more durable "fine-grained" metal. The following is a guide to the basic knives every cook should own.

Carbon steel
This metal is a simple blend of iron and carbon (unlike other steels that have extra elements added). A well-cared-for blade can stay sharp longer than stainless steel, but carbon steel is prone to rust; so knives require careful maintenance, cleaning, drying, and oiling.

Stainless steel
Chromium is added to the iron–carbon mix to produce a more flexible, rust-resistant steel. Good-quality stainless steel has a fine grain for sharpness, and it can be alloyed with other metals for durability. Easy to sharpen and strong, stainless steel is often most practical for the home cook.

Ceramic
Very sharp, light, and hard, ceramic blades are a good choice for cutting through meat. The blades are usually made of zirconium oxide, ground to a razor-sharp edge. The blades don't rust, but are hard to sharpen and don't flex like steel, so they can easily break or chip if they hit bone or are dropped.

SERRATED KNIFE

Use for
Foods that have a tough crust or smooth, delicate skin, such as bread, cake, or large tomatoes where precision isn't required.

What to look for
A long blade, a comfortable handle, and deep, pointed serrations.

A carving knife should be thinner than a chef's knife as it is used to make the finest of cuts.

Comfort and grip are more important than the actual handle material.

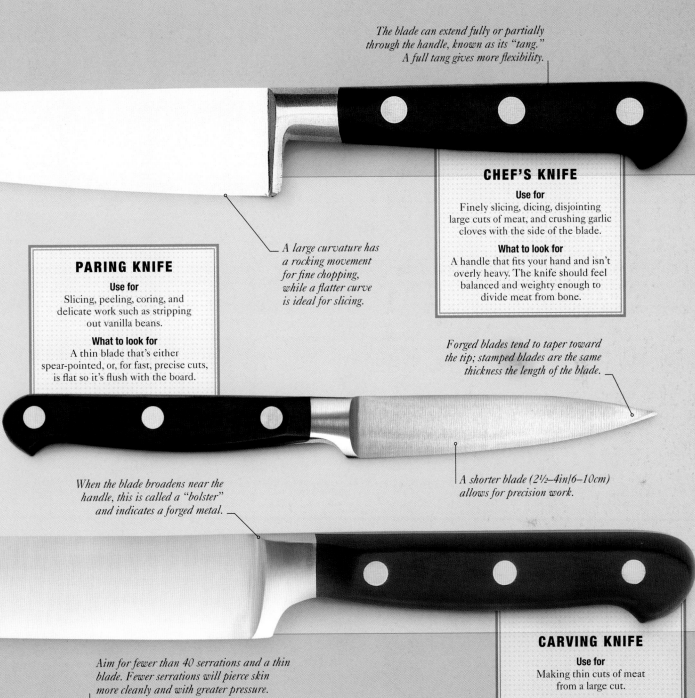

The blade can extend fully or partially through the handle, known as its "tang." A full tang gives more flexibility.

CHEF'S KNIFE

Use for

Finely slicing, dicing, disjointing large cuts of meat, and crushing garlic cloves with the side of the blade.

What to look for

A handle that fits your hand and isn't overly heavy. The knife should feel balanced and weighty enough to divide meat from bone.

A large curvature has a rocking movement for fine chopping, while a flatter curve is ideal for slicing.

PARING KNIFE

Use for

Slicing, peeling, coring, and delicate work such as stripping out vanilla beans.

What to look for

A thin blade that's either spear-pointed, or, for fast, precise cuts, is flat so it's flush with the board.

Forged blades tend to taper toward the tip; stamped blades are the same thickness the length of the blade.

When the blade broadens near the handle, this is called a "bolster" and indicates a forged metal.

A shorter blade (2½–4in|6–10cm) allows for precision work.

CARVING KNIFE

Use for

Making thin cuts of meat from a large cut.

What to look for

A long, thin, very sharp cutting edge with a pointed tip. It should have less curvature than the chef's knife as it's for slicing rather than rocking.

Aim for fewer than 40 serrations and a thin blade. Fewer serrations will pierce skin more cleanly and with greater pressure.

Sawlike points exert intense pressure over a tiny area to puncture the surface, then the scalloped blades slide into the crevices to slice food open.

4 quart (20cm) saucepan for large portions of rice or pasta, and soups, stews, and stocks.

Stainless steel–clad aluminum is easy-care and heat-efficient.

3 quart (18cm) saucepan for cooking small meals and boiling vegetables.

An essential guide to
POTS AND PANS

A good core collection helps to give great results.

The type of metal you choose for your cookware affects how food cooks, but more important is a pan's thickness: the thicker the base, the more evenly the heat from the burner spreads across it. Corrodible metals such as carbon steel and cast iron should be "seasoned" before first use by heating with oil three or four times to form a nonstick "patina." Store-bought nonstick pans have a waxy resin, but this degrades above 500°F (260°C), so they suit delicate foods that stick, such as fish.

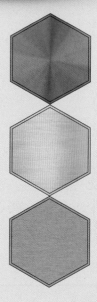

Stainless steel
Heavy, durable stainless steel is good for everyday saucepans, but conducts heat poorly (unless clad around aluminum or copper), and food sticks easily. The shiny surface makes it easy to see when food is browning when deglazing or making a sauce.

Copper
Heavy and expensive but responsive to temperature changes, a thick-based copper pan conducts heat faster than other materials. It reacts to acid and may be coated to avoid discoloring food and leaving a metallic taste. It's too heavy to suit sauté pans or woks.

Aluminum
Conducts heat quickly, making it very responsive to temperature changes, but loses heat rapidly off the stove. It is lightweight, so good for frying pans, sauté pans, and saucepans. "Anodized" aluminum has a coating to keep it from reacting with acidic foods.

Carbon steel is sturdy but heat-responsive.

WOK
Use for
Stir-frying over the hottest flame, steaming, and deep-fat frying.

What to look for
A tight-fitting lid, a thin base, and long sturdy handle. Avoid nonstick, which won't tolerate high stir-frying heats. Carbon steel is ideal; to season it, scrub off the existing oil coat, heat to blacken, add oil to smoke, then rub off the oil when cool. Do this 3–4 times before use.

CAST-IRON SKILLET
Use for
Root veg, meats, sticky foods (if seasoned), putting under the broiler and in the oven.

What to look for
A long, heat-proof handle (cast iron retains heat) and a grip handle to aid in lifting.

2 quart (16cm) saucepan for melting butter, caramelizing sugar, making sauces, and poaching eggs.

ROUND CASSEROLE DISH

Use for
Slow-braising meats.

What to look for
A tight-fitting lid and easy-to-grasp handles. Although heavy, cast iron is ideal because it keeps a steady temperature, and an enamel interior is durable and doesn't react with acids.

Cast iron retains heat for slow cooking.

A round base, rather than oval, heats evenly over the burner.

SAUCEPANS

Use for
Sauces, stews, soups, stocks, boiling vegetables, rice, and pasta.

What to look for
Lids to retain moisture, and an extra small-grip handle on large pans to aid in lifting. Heat-proof handles are oven-friendly.

10IN (24CM) NONSTICK FRYING PAN

Use for
Delicate fish, eggs, and crêpes.

What to look for
A thick base and thick nonstick coat—choose from a reputable supplier.

Long handle

Carbon steel
This heats up faster than stainless steel, but like iron, it rusts and reacts with foods, so it needs to be seasoned to make it as durable as stainless steel. It is best for woks, frying pans, and skillets.

Cast iron
Very heavy, cast iron is dense and heats slowly, but, once heated, it retains heat well and is ideal for browning meat in a skillet or casserole. Bare cast iron rusts and reacts with acidic foods, so season it to form a protective nonstick seal and clean carefully.

Lightweight stainless steel-clad aluminium makes it easy to toss food.

A thick base spreads heat and avoids hot spots.

Curved sides are ideal for whisking and gravies.

When seasoned, cast iron is nonstick, but avoid abrasive cleaners.

Small grip handle

12IN (30CM) SAUTÉ PAN

Use for
Searing and frying large batches; creating sauces and large meals.

What to look for
A tight-fitting lid to hold moisture, a long handle, and a moderately heavy base.

◄ MEASURING CUP

A clear tempered glass jug accurately judges liquid volumes. Because of water's surface tension, it is tricky to judge its natural downward bulge in a cup.

DIGITAL SCALES ►

Good-quality ones are more precise than analogue. Look for a base that accommodates a large bowl, a weight capacity of at least 11lb (5kg), a clear display, and accuracy to a tenth (0.1) of a unit.

An essential guide to
UTENSILS

Different models and materials will suit particular cooking needs.

It's difficult to make good food without the appropriate tools. A handful of key utensils will enable you to craft fantastic dishes.

What you need

There are more materials and varieties of kitchen tools and utensils than ever before, but when choosing, carefully consider the pros and cons of each piece of equipment. Not every invention is a step forwards—pay attention to how versatile it is and how the material works with different ingredients.

HONING STEEL ▲

Metal steels realign and straighten a worn knife edge, rather than sharpen it. Choose a heavy steel, 10in (25cm) long. Diamond-coated and ceramic steels grind some metal off, so can partially sharpen knives.

ROLLING PIN ▲

Wood holds flour well and doesn't conduct heat from the hands. Opt for a handleless, long pin with a tapered shape for pivoting and tilting.

OTHER USEFUL ITEMS

- A Y-shaped peeler can be used by left- and right-handed cooks. Choose a sharp blade with a 1in (2.5cm) gap between blade and handle to prevent clogging.
- For turning and lifting food, look for tongs with a firm spring action and scalloped fingers. Heat-resistant silicone ends can be used on all surfaces.
- Look for a food processor with sharp, sturdy blades, a dough blade, slicing and shredding disks, and a motor housed under the work bowl (rather than a belt).
- Choose a masher with a long, rigid metal handle and a mashing disk with small, round, rather than wavy, holes.
- Useful cake-pan features include a quick-release clasp and removable base.
- For a mortar and pestle, opt for a hard, slightly rough surface, such as granite.

BALLOON WHISK ▲

Choose a balloon-shaped whisk with at least 10 wires for versatility and efficiency. Metal gives whisks a hard edge that aerates well and breaks up fat globules. Silicone whisks are an alternative for nonstick surfaces.

◄ GRATER

Choose one with a large grating surface. A sturdy-based four-sided box grater has holes for coarse shredding, fine grating, zesting, and powdering.

SLOTTED SPOON ▲

Look for a long-handled, deep-bowled spoon. Stainless steel is thin and rigid so more adept at sliding under floating morsels than bulkier plastic or silicone.

◄ METAL SIEVE

Metal wires produce a very fine-mesh sieve to keep the smallest particles from passing through. A hook opposite the handle lets a sieve rest over a pan.

LADLE ▲

A long-handled, stainless steel ladle skims fat and froth from a stew or stock. A ladle made from one piece of metal will last longer than one with a welded-on bowl.

METAL SPATULA ▲

A broad, long, slotted spatula that is thin and flexible is ideal for sliding under delicate foods. For nonstick cookware, use a sturdy plastic or silicone one.

THERMOMETER ▲

Look for one with a probe that can rest in a pan. Those that read to 410°F (210°C), can also be used for caramelizing sugar.

RUBBER SPATULA ▲

A rubber spatula is ideal for delicate work, such as folding in whipped egg whites or tempering chocolate. A heat-proof silicone spatula is best for hot foods.

WOODEN SPOON ▲

Wood is easy on nonstick surfaces and metal and is a poor conductor of heat, so the handle stays cool in hot food. A porous material, it absorbs food particles and flavors so it needs thorough cleaning.

MIXING BOWLS

Stainless steel lasts a long time, but can't be put in a microwave. Tempered glass is heat-resistant and microwave-friendly. Ceramic and stoneware can chip, are slow to warm, so ideal for working with dough.

CHOPPING BOARD

Durable and good for all foods, wooden boards have "give" so they don't dull knives, unlike granite and glass. Plastic traps bacteria in grooves, while wood has bacteria-killing tannins, making it a hygienic choice.

MEAT & POULTRY

In focus
MEAT

Meat forms the centerpiece of most traditional cooking. Understanding its structure and composition helps you make the most of your cut.

As varied as meats can appear, they are all made of the same three tissues: muscle, fat, and connective tissue. The varying proportions of these tissues and the type of muscle tissue in the cut determine the flavor and texture of a piece of meat, and therefore its best culinary purpose. Muscle, which powers movement in the living animal, is red or pink in color and makes up the bulk of most cuts of meat. It is 70 to 85 percent water—moisture that needs to

be conserved to keep cooked meat juicy. Connective tissue forms sheathes around muscle fibers and connects muscles to bone— it slowly breaks down during cooking, imparting rich flavor to meat dishes. However, at higher temperatures, connective tissue shrinks and squeezes moisture out of the meat. Fat is chewy and bland uncooked, but imparts huge amounts of flavor when the fat cells burst open during cooking.

KNOW YOUR MEAT

The components of different meats—the relative proportions of fat to muscle, the quantity of connective tissue, and the type of muscle in the cut—determine their ratios of fat and protein. All meats are great sources of protein; here we compare them.

WHITE MEAT

Chicken
Pale-colored chicken meat is not high in fat, so it has a dry mouthfeel if overcooked. Cooking it in a sauce can help to introduce moisture.

FAT: MEDIUM
PROTEIN: HIGH

Duck
Rich, dark duck meat has a thick layer of fat under the skin. Roasting, frying, or grilling works best; prick or score the skin first to help the fat melt.

FAT: MEDIUM
PROTEIN: MEDIUM

Turkey
With lots of muscle and little fat, white turkey meat is good for stir-frying and grilling. The dark leg meat contains more connective tissue and can be stewed.

FAT: LOW
PROTEIN: HIGH

SCIENCE
CONNECTIVE TISSUE IS MADE OF PROTEINS THAT SOFTEN AND BREAK DOWN WHEN HEATED TO 126°F (52°C).

COOKING
LONG, SLOW COOKING TRANSFORMS CONNECTIVE TISSUE INTO VELVETY GELATIN, GIVING MEAT ITS SUCCULENCE.

CONNECTIVE TISSUE

Tough connective tissue joins muscle fibers together, and connects muscle to the bone.

Bone-in cuts
In this T-bone steak, a section of bone divides the lean fillet meat from the higher-fat sirloin, offering a range of textures.

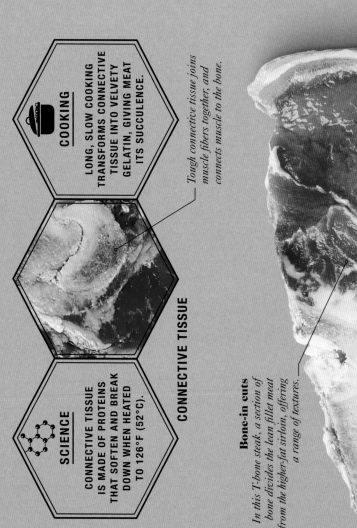

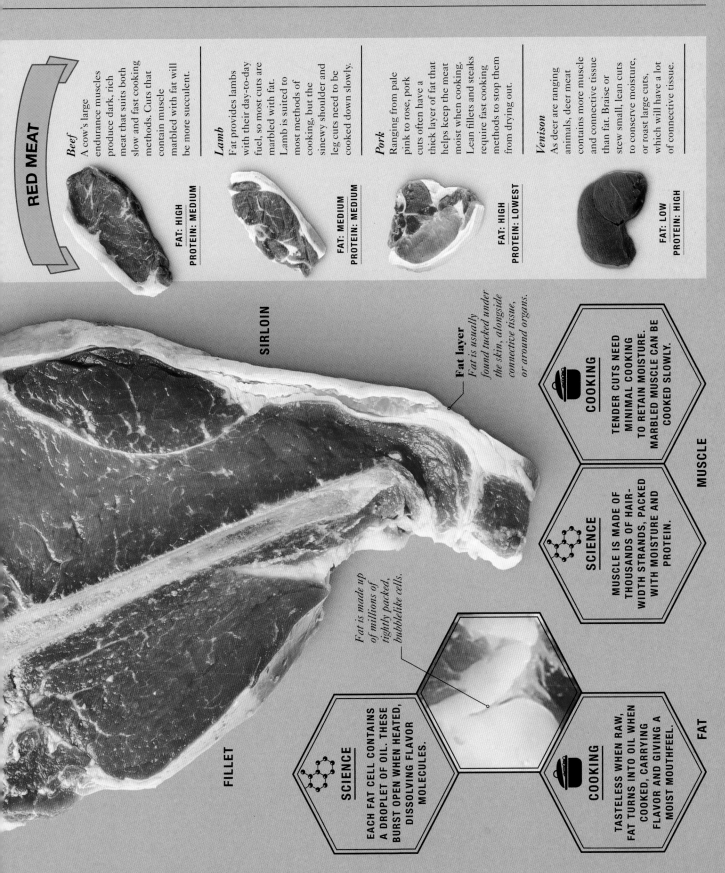

RED MEAT

Beef
A cow's large endurance muscles produce dark, rich meat that suits both slow and fast cooking methods. Cuts that contain muscle marbled with fat will be more succulent.

FAT: HIGH
PROTEIN: MEDIUM

Lamb
Fat provides lambs with their day-to-day fuel, so most cuts are marbled with fat. Lamb is suited to most methods of cooking, but the sinewy shoulder and leg cuts need to be cooked down slowly.

FAT: MEDIUM
PROTEIN: MEDIUM

Pork
Ranging from pale pink to rose, pork cuts often have a thick layer of fat that helps keep the meat moist when cooking. Lean fillets and steaks require fast cooking methods to stop them from drying out.

FAT: HIGH
PROTEIN: LOWEST

Venison
As deer are ranging animals, deer meat contains more muscle and connective tissue than fat. Braise or stew small, lean cuts to conserve moisture, or roast large cuts, which will have a lot of connective tissue.

FAT: LOW
PROTEIN: HIGH

SIRLOIN

FILLET

Fat layer
Fat is usually found tucked under the skin, alongside connective tissue, or around organs.

Fat is made up of millions of tightly packed, bubblelike cells.

MUSCLE

COOKING
TENDER CUTS NEED MINIMAL COOKING TO RETAIN MOISTURE. MARBLED MUSCLE CAN BE COOKED SLOWLY.

SCIENCE
MUSCLE IS MADE OF THOUSANDS OF HAIR-WIDTH STRANDS, PACKED WITH MOISTURE AND PROTEIN.

FAT

SCIENCE
EACH FAT CELL CONTAINS A DROPLET OF OIL. THESE BURST OPEN WHEN HEATED, DISSOLVING FLAVOR MOLECULES.

COOKING
TASTELESS WHEN RAW, FAT TURNS INTO OIL WHEN COOKED, CARRYING FLAVOR AND GIVING A MOIST MOUTHFEEL.

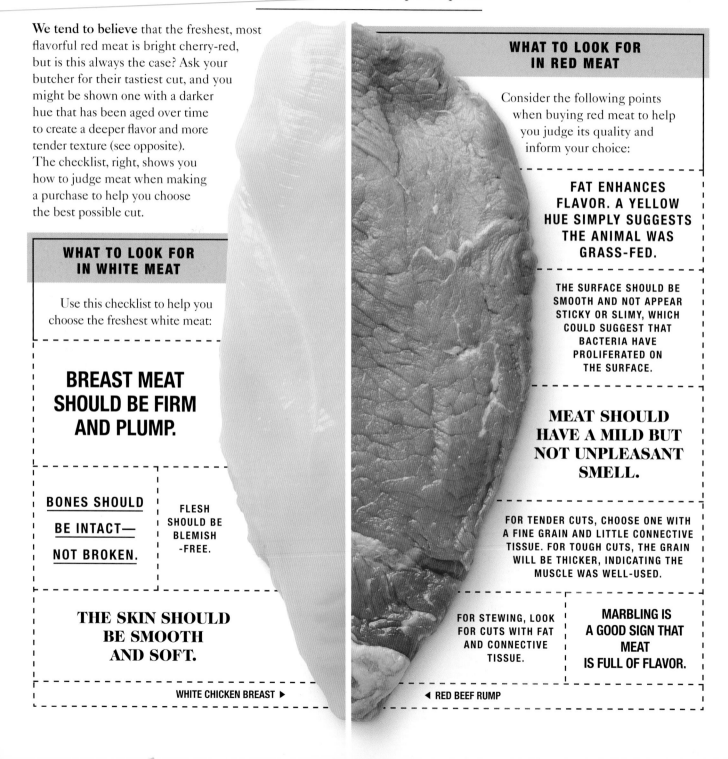

How can I tell
IF MEAT IS GOOD QUALITY?

With so much meat plastic-wrapped and displayed under harsh supermarket lighting, it can be hard to spot a top cut.

We tend to believe that the freshest, most flavorful red meat is bright cherry-red, but is this always the case? Ask your butcher for their tastiest cut, and you might be shown one with a darker hue that has been aged over time to create a deeper flavor and more tender texture (see opposite). The checklist, right, shows you how to judge meat when making a purchase to help you choose the best possible cut.

WHAT TO LOOK FOR IN WHITE MEAT

Use this checklist to help you choose the freshest white meat:

BREAST MEAT SHOULD BE FIRM AND PLUMP.

BONES SHOULD BE INTACT— NOT BROKEN.

FLESH SHOULD BE BLEMISH -FREE.

THE SKIN SHOULD BE SMOOTH AND SOFT.

WHITE CHICKEN BREAST ▶

WHAT TO LOOK FOR IN RED MEAT

Consider the following points when buying red meat to help you judge its quality and inform your choice:

FAT ENHANCES FLAVOR. A YELLOW HUE SIMPLY SUGGESTS THE ANIMAL WAS GRASS-FED.

THE SURFACE SHOULD BE SMOOTH AND NOT APPEAR STICKY OR SLIMY, WHICH COULD SUGGEST THAT BACTERIA HAVE PROLIFERATED ON THE SURFACE.

MEAT SHOULD HAVE A MILD BUT NOT UNPLEASANT SMELL.

FOR TENDER CUTS, CHOOSE ONE WITH A FINE GRAIN AND LITTLE CONNECTIVE TISSUE. FOR TOUGH CUTS, THE GRAIN WILL BE THICKER, INDICATING THE MUSCLE WAS WELL-USED.

FOR STEWING, LOOK FOR CUTS WITH FAT AND CONNECTIVE TISSUE.

MARBLING IS A GOOD SIGN THAT MEAT IS FULL OF FLAVOR.

◀ RED BEEF RUMP

Should I avoid buying
MEAT THAT HAS TURNED BROWN?

The color of meat alone is not a reliable indicator of its freshness or quality.

The natural color of meat comes from a red oxygen-carrying pigment, myoglobin, stored in the muscle tissue (see p34). Different animals have varying levels of myoglobin, with red meat containing more than white and older animals having higher levels, giving their meat a darker hue. Vacuum-packed meat deprived of oxygen has a natural purple tinge. Once in contact with air, myoglobin changes color, turning meat bright red. If it stays purple, this suggests that the animal may have been stressed at slaughter and its meat will be dry and firm. When meat is dry-aged by butchers, it darkens, its taste intensifies, and it loses moisture and shrinks. So brown meat may not be spoiled—use your senses of touch and smell to judge whether it is okay to eat (see left).

JUST BUTCHERED
Meat vacuum-packed after slaughter can have a natural purple hue.

0hr

Vacuum-packed meat is deprived of oxygen, so is dark in color.

3 HOURS
Exposed to oxygen, meat changes to a bright red color.

3hr

Once a package has been opened and oxygen comes into contact with the myoglobin, the tissue becomes bright red.

7 HOURS
If continuously exposed to oxygen, meat gradually darkens.

7hr

After a week, meat turns a deeper red as the oxygen reacts with the myoglobin.

COLOR ENHANCER
CARBON MONOXIDE IS SOMETIMES ADDED TO VACUUM PACKS—IT REACTS WITH MYOGLOBIN, TURNING MEAT RED.

9 DAYS
Myoglobin browns the longer it is exposed to oxygen, giving the meat a red-brown color.

9d

How oxygen transforms the color of meat
When exposed to oxygen, myoglobin in the muscles turns red and then brown. When butchers dry-age meat, the surface gradually darkens, while enzymes in the meat slowly soften the texture and enhance the flavor.

When meat is dry-aged in temperature-controlled conditions, it gradually darkens and may start to gray around the edges.

Why do different meats
LOOK AND TASTE SO DIFFERENT?

Variations in meat color between animals make a difference in how each meat is best cooked.

The color of meat is related to the levels of a red-colored, oxygen-supplying protein, myoglobin, in an animal's muscles. The higher the levels of myoglobin, the darker and redder the meat, while lower levels of myoglobin result in paler meat.

Some animals have varying levels of myoglobin in different muscles, depending on how that muscle is used, so an animal can have both light and dark areas of meat. Dark "slow-twitch" muscles, like those in a leg, are for endurance and need a steady oxygen supply, so have more myoglobin. Whiter "fast-twitch" muscles, for short bursts of energy, need less oxygen, such as chicken breast muscles, designed for flapping wings.

Proportions of light and dark meat affect flavor and texture. Darker, well-exercised muscles tend to have more protein, fat droplets, iron, and flavor-generating enzymes.

HOW DIFFERENT-COLORED MEATS COMPARE

Myoglobin levels in different animals
This chart compares myoglobin levels in different animals and explains how these levels affect the meat, with higher levels intensifying flavor and lower levels creating a blander-tasting meat.

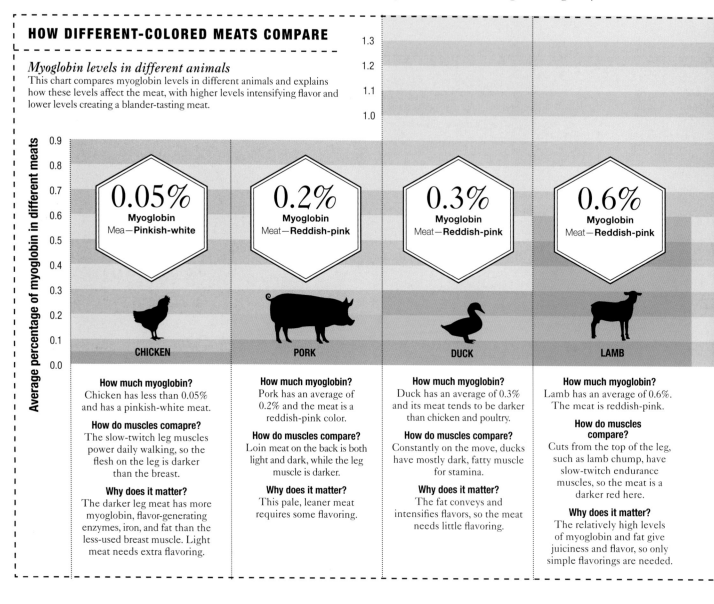

Average percentage of myoglobin in different meats

0.05%
Myoglobin
Mea—**Pinkish-white**
CHICKEN

0.2%
Myoglobin
Meat—**Reddish-pink**
PORK

0.3%
Myoglobin
Meat—**Reddish-pink**
DUCK

0.6%
Myoglobin
Meat—**Reddish-pink**
LAMB

How much myoglobin?
Chicken has less than 0.05% and has a pinkish-white meat.

How do muscles comapre?
The slow-twitch leg muscles power daily walking, so the flesh on the leg is darker than the breast.

Why does it matter?
The darker leg meat has more myoglobin, flavor-generating enzymes, iron, and fat than the less-used breast muscle. Light meat needs extra flavoring.

How much myoglobin?
Pork has an average of 0.2% and the meat is a reddish-pink color.

How do muscles compare?
Loin meat on the back is both light and dark, while the leg muscle is darker.

Why does it matter?
This pale, leaner meat requires some flavoring.

How much myoglobin?
Duck has an average of 0.3% and its meat tends to be darker than chicken and poultry.

How do muscles compare?
Constantly on the move, ducks have mostly dark, fatty muscle for stamina.

Why does it matter?
The fat conveys and intensifies flavors, so the meat needs little flavoring.

How much myoglobin?
Lamb has an average of 0.6%. The meat is reddish-pink.

How do muscles compare?
Cuts from the top of the leg, such as lamb chump, have slow-twitch endurance muscles, so the meat is a darker red here.

Why does it matter?
The relatively high levels of myoglobin and fat give juiciness and flavor, so only simple flavorings are needed.

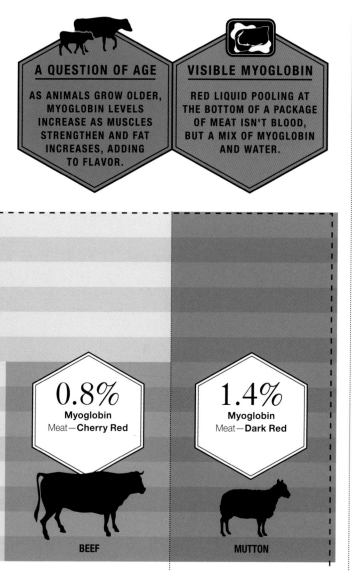

A QUESTION OF AGE

AS ANIMALS GROW OLDER, MYOGLOBIN LEVELS INCREASE AS MUSCLES STRENGTHEN AND FAT INCREASES, ADDING TO FLAVOR.

VISIBLE MYOGLOBIN

RED LIQUID POOLING AT THE BOTTOM OF A PACKAGE OF MEAT ISN'T BLOOD, BUT A MIX OF MYOGLOBIN AND WATER.

0.8%
Myoglobin
Meat—**Cherry Red**

BEEF

1.4%
Myoglobin
Meat—**Dark Red**

MUTTON

How much myoglobin?
Beef has an average of 0.8%. The meat is bright cherry-red.

How do muscles compare?
Cows roam great distances, so they have mostly dark, slow-twitch muscle.

Why does it matter?
Endurance muscles with higher levels of myoglobin tend to have a more intense taste and flavorful fat, so they often need minimal flavoring.

How much myoglobin?
Mutton (sheep older than 1 year) has around 1.4%. The meat is an intense red color.

How do muscles compare?
The muscles in older sheep have been worked more, so they have stronger connective tissue and denser meat.

Why does it matter?
With plenty of fat, mutton has a more intense flavor than lamb, which some prefer. The strong taste can be offset with herbs and spices.

Is it better to choose ORGANIC MEAT?

Organic meat is sold as a tastier, healthier, and more ethical alternative, but what are the facts?

Science shows us that animals that have had enough exercise, have been well fed, and have been spared undue stress produce meat that has lots of well-textured muscle and flavorsome fat. Organic-status meat should help guarantee all of these things; however, several other factors come into play (see box below) that mean it's important to check the provenance of your meat.

What we know about organic meat

Buying organic status means you can be satisfied that a key set of standards has been met in rearing an animal.

- Organically reared animals have been well looked after, with outdoor access and a stress-free existence, so they tend to be healthier overall and have good-quality meat.

- Animals are raised on organic land and eat organic feed; however, this has little bearing on the quality of meat.

- Animals reared organically aren't given antibiotics or growth-promoting hormones, although this is already the case for all cattle in many countries.

- Organic farmers are encouraged to look after the environment the animals are reared in.

- Organic stock are more likely to have been slaughtered humanely, which produces better-quality meat. If an animal is stressed preslaughter, adrenaline levels surge, burning energy and producing dry, firm, dark meat.

Factors beyond organic

There are some factors beyond whether or not an animal has been raised organically that can affect meat quality.

Being fed grass or grain (see p.32) has more impact on flavor. Grain-fed muscle has more flavorful fat, is less acidic, and contains pleasant-tasting substances called lactones, while grass-fed cows' meat can have a bitter, grassy flavor.

If meat isn't stored or transported with care, this affects quality. High demand for organic means it can travel far and be stored for a long period of time. A nonorganic farm rearing humanely treated animals slaughtered and sold locally is likely to be superior.

Are purebred and heritage
CATTLE BREEDS TASTIER?

Meat from traditional, purebred animals comes at a premium, but you may wonder what you're really getting for your money.

Traditional heritage breeds have declined since meat farming became a global industry. A hundred years ago, dozens of breeds, such as North Devon and Galloway, roamed pastures; today there are just a handful, such as Angus, favored in North America for its bulky frame and well-marbled meat, and, in the UK, the less tender Limousin.

A superior taste?

Beef has a complex flavor, yet genetic differences lead to only subtle taste variations. Research consistently shows that the amount of marbling in any given cut is more important than the actual breed. If handled and butchered well, carefully stored after slaughter, and carefully cooked, research shows that heritage breeds tend to have a stronger flavor and a juicier mouthfeel, so you might choose to buy a premium cut for this subtle distinction.

On the whole, premium breeds are likely to have been well cared for and the meat will have been properly handled, stored, and aged, all of which improve the taste and texture of the meat on your plate.

MEAT FROM GRASS-FED COWS

Leaner grass-fed cows store their fat just under the skin.

Do larger chickens
LACK FLAVOR?

The size of the chicken you purchase can be an indication of its breed and, in turn, the depth of flavor.

The modern "broiler" chicken, which is the most commonly bred chicken today, is the result of decades of aggressive selective breeding.

Broilers are a hybrid of various species, all chosen for their very large size or fast-growing nature. The bird that is industrially farmed today is four times the size of those bred 50 years ago, reaches slaughter weight in just 35 days (less than half the time of traditional breeds), and is plagued with health problems due to its abnormal proportions. Modern broiler breeds make meat affordable, but there's no denying it: the taste is bland. Heritage breeds of chicken take longer to grow and are considerably more expensive, but research shows that the meat has a significantly richer flavor and better mouthfeel than intensively farmed chickens.

SUPER-SIZE CHICKENS

INDUSTRIALLY FARMED CHICKENS ARE NOW FOUR TIMES LARGER THAN THEY WERE FIFTY YEARS AGO.

The meat of grain-fed cows tends to be well-marbled throughout.

MEAT FROM GRAIN-FED COWS

How can an animal's feed affect
THE TASTE AND TEXTURE OF ITS MEAT?

Whether cattle are fed on grass or grain affects their calorie intake and their lifestyle, and both of these factors influence the type of meat produced.

Most cattle eat grass for some, if not all, of their lives, with grain supplements sometimes given in cold months and preslaughter—the finishing period—when cattle may be fattened up on a high-energy diet. Grain-fed meat has a "beefier" flavor, which many prefer, but research suggests that tastes are changing to prefer less beefy, grass-fed meat. The box, right, shows how grass and grain diets affect the texture and flavor of the meat you buy.

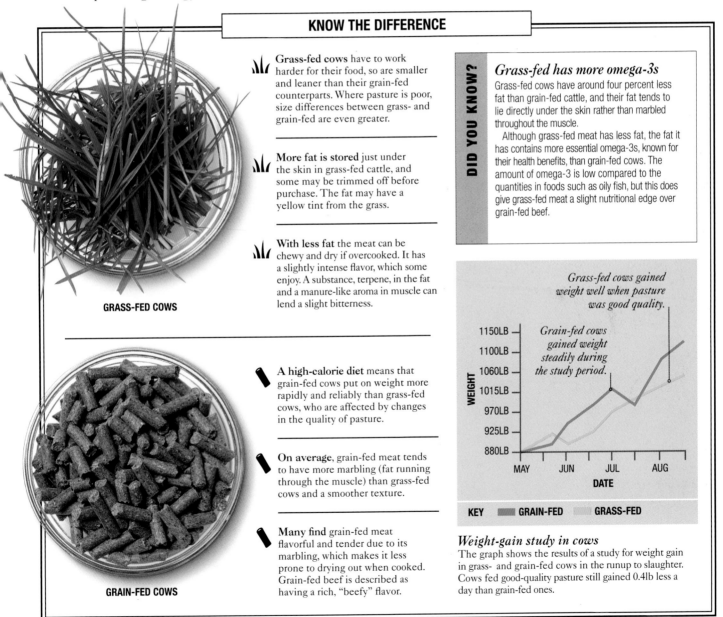

KNOW THE DIFFERENCE

Grass-fed cows have to work harder for their food, so are smaller and leaner than their grain-fed counterparts. Where pasture is poor, size differences between grass- and grain-fed are even greater.

More fat is stored just under the skin in grass-fed cattle, and some may be trimmed off before purchase. The fat may have a yellow tint from the grass.

With less fat the meat can be chewy and dry if overcooked. It has a slightly intense flavor, which some enjoy. A substance, terpene, in the fat and a manure-like aroma in muscle can lend a slight bitterness.

GRASS-FED COWS

A high-calorie diet means that grain-fed cows put on weight more rapidly and reliably than grass-fed cows, who are affected by changes in the quality of pasture.

On average, grain-fed meat tends to have more marbling (fat running through the muscle) than grass-fed cows and a smoother texture.

Many find grain-fed meat flavorful and tender due to its marbling, which makes it less prone to drying out when cooked. Grain-fed beef is described as having a rich, "beefy" flavor.

GRAIN-FED COWS

DID YOU KNOW?

Grass-fed has more omega-3s
Grass-fed cows have around four percent less fat than grain-fed cattle, and their fat tends to lie directly under the skin rather than marbled throughout the muscle.

Although grass-fed meat has less fat, the fat it has contains more essential omega-3s, known for their health benefits, than grain-fed cows. The amount of omega-3 is low compared to the quantities in foods such as oily fish, but this does give grass-fed meat a slight nutritional edge over grain-fed beef.

Grass-fed cows gained weight well when pasture was good quality.

Grain-fed cows gained weight steadily during the study period.

WEIGHT

1150LB
1100LB
1060LB
1015LB
970LB
925LB
880LB

MAY | JUN | JUL | AUG

DATE

KEY — **GRAIN-FED** — **GRASS-FED**

Weight-gain study in cows
The graph shows the results of a study for weight gain in grass- and grain-fed cows in the runup to slaughter. Cows fed good-quality pasture still gained 0.4lb less a day than grain-fed ones.

Is fillet steak from the tenderloin really
THE BEST CUT OF BEEF?

With different cuts commanding a range of prices, a cow is like a stock market on four legs.

Fillet steak, or filet mignon, is a scarce, highly sought-after commodity. Part of the reason for the demand is that it comes from the least-worked section of the least-worked muscle on a cow—the tenderloin along the back. It is extremely tender and is in short supply because it is small, fueling demand. But is fillet worth the hype?

How fat flavors meat

Fillet steak is low in fat because the tenderloin muscle doesn't need much energy. We think of saturated fat as bad, but fat helps us to enjoy meat's full flavor and texture, melting when

A THICKER CUT

A THICKER FILLET—ABOUT 1.5IN (4CM)—ALLOWS THE OUTSIDE TO BE WELL BROWNED WITHOUT OVERDOING THE MIDDLE.

cooked to make meat juicy and tender, and chemically reacting (or oxidizing) in heat to generate flavors. Fat dissolves flavor molecules, carrying them to our palate.

A lack of fat means that fillet requires very careful cooking to ensure it doesn't dry out and lose its silky-smooth consistency. If you enjoy meat no more than medium done, a properly cooked fillet is indeed the best cut. However, if you prefer meat medium to well done, other cuts are often more delicious; the information opposite details the texture and flavor of six different cuts and how best to cook them.

"Fillet steak, *from one of the least-worked muscles on the cow*, is extremely tender *and highly sought after.*"

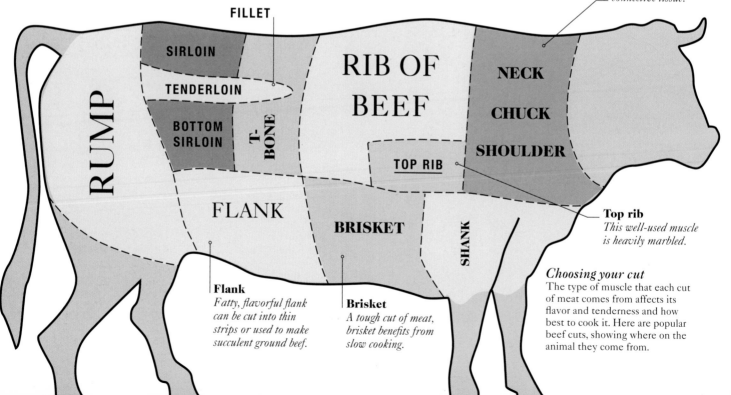

Neck, chuck, shoulder
These cheaper cuts have plenty of tough connective tissue.

FILLET

SIRLOIN

TENDERLOIN

RUMP

BOTTOM SIRLOIN

T-BONE

RIB OF BEEF

NECK

CHUCK

SHOULDER

TOP RIB

FLANK

BRISKET

SHANK

Top rib
This well-used muscle is heavily marbled.

Flank
Fatty, flavorful flank can be cut into thin strips or used to make succulent ground beef.

Brisket
A tough cut of meat, brisket benefits from slow cooking.

Choosing your cut
The type of muscle that each cut of meat comes from affects its flavor and tenderness and how best to cook it. Here are popular beef cuts, showing where on the animal they come from.

OTHER TOP CUTS

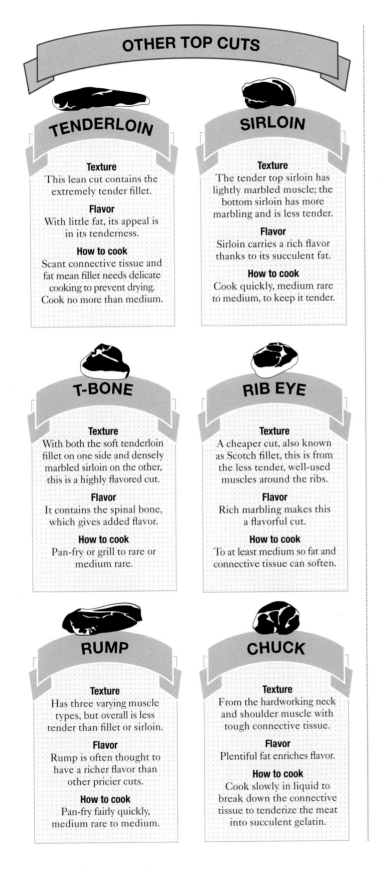

TENDERLOIN

Texture
This lean cut contains the extremely tender fillet.

Flavor
With little fat, its appeal is in its tenderness.

How to cook
Scant connective tissue and fat mean fillet needs delicate cooking to prevent drying. Cook no more than medium.

SIRLOIN

Texture
The tender top sirloin has lightly marbled muscle; the bottom sirloin has more marbling and is less tender.

Flavor
Sirloin carries a rich flavor thanks to its succulent fat.

How to cook
Cook quickly, medium rare to medium, to keep it tender.

T-BONE

Texture
With both the soft tenderloin fillet on one side and densely marbled sirloin on the other, this is a highly flavored cut.

Flavor
It contains the spinal bone, which gives added flavor.

How to cook
Pan-fry or grill to rare or medium rare.

RIB EYE

Texture
A cheaper cut, also known as Scotch fillet, this is from the less tender, well-used muscles around the ribs.

Flavor
Rich marbling makes this a flavorful cut.

How to cook
To at least medium so fat and connective tissue can soften.

RUMP

Texture
Has three varying muscle types, but overall is less tender than fillet or sirloin.

Flavor
Rump is often thought to have a richer flavor than other pricier cuts.

How to cook
Pan-fry fairly quickly, medium rare to medium.

CHUCK

Texture
From the hardworking neck and shoulder muscle with tough connective tissue.

Flavor
Plentiful fat enriches flavor.

How to cook
Cook slowly in liquid to break down the connective tissue to tenderize the meat into succulent gelatin.

Why is it so expensive to buy WAGYU BEEF?

Fat-rippled beef from Wagyu cattle is some of the most sought-after in the world—with good reason.

Wagyu means "Japanese beef" (*Wa* means "Japan" and *Gyu* "cow") and refers to a small group of breeds that have highly marbled beef—up to 40 percent in some cuts—which makes their meat wonderfully flavorful and very rich. Enzymes called calpains, which break down and tenderize meat, are particularly active in Wagyu breeds.

In Japan, these cattle have a no-expense-spared existence to ensure the meat meets the highest standards of excellence (see below). Some farmers massage their cows to keep the muscles tender, and feed them cold beer to increase fat levels. Such labor- and time-intensive work, along with the superior taste and texture of the meat, enables the highest-grade Wagyu beef to command up to $275 per pound.

*"Some farmers **massage** their cows to keep the muscles tender, and feed them **cold beer**."*

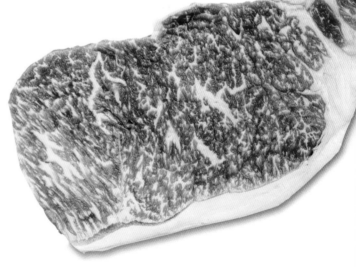

Wagyu grading system
Wagyu (see above) is classified by its marbling, color, and texture. A-grade Wagyu is the highest quality available, and is graded from 1 to 5, with A5 being the cream of the crop. A5 Wagyu is ruby red and densely textured with glistening ribbons of fat and a smooth, velvety texture.

What is the difference between ORGANIC, FREE-RANGE, AND INDOOR CHICKENS?

The way in which a chicken is raised impacts the quality and flavor of its meat.

Of all the animals bred for industrial-scale meat production, chickens are the most poorly treated. Most broiler chickens (the name of the hybrid species reared for meat, see p36) live short lives tightly packed in hangar-like sheds. Improvements in animal welfare have been slow, so labels help us to understand how a chicken lived. However, whether free range or organic guarantees improved flavor, nutrition—or (for free-range), better levels of welfare—is debatable.

What's the reality?

Feed, space, stress levels, and lifespan all have an impact on what chicken meat tastes like. Labeling can be misleading, but knowing about the conditions in which chickens were raised will give you an idea of the quality of their meat (see right). Free-range chickens may live longer lives, but have only limited access to the outdoors, which can result in the high stress levels that cause dry, acidic meat. In contrast, indoor-farmed chickens are killed at a young age to produce more tender meat. Overall, slow-growing breeds from small farms who are fed a range of foods have firmer, more flavorful meat.

THINK ORGANIC

OF CHICKENS RAISED IN THE US, FEWER THAN 2 PERCENT ARE ORGANIC. IN THE UK, THE FIGURE IS 1 PERCENT.

FREE-RANGE

Conditions on the farm
Free-range chickens must have access to the outdoors. While the birds are kept in better conditions than indoor-farmed ones, "pop hole" exits can be difficult for the chickens to reach, so many birds never actually reach the outside.

What this means
Chickens with access to outdoors have more protein. However, stress levels are high in many free-range farms, which can affect the quality of the meat.

DID YOU KNOW?

Corn-fed chickens
Chickens that have been fed a diet of corn (maize) are raised in various different farm conditions. The label is no guarantee of meat quality.

Impact on taste
The chickens' diet gives their meat a brothy flavor, but taste and texture depend on farming conditions. Corn-fed chickens are usually indoor-farmed, but can also be free-range or organic; always check the label.

INDOOR-FARMED

Conditions on the farm
In industrial-scale farming, chickens are kept in large, hangar-like sheds and do not have access to the outdoors. There may be a density of 19–20 birds per square yard, and birds may never see natural light.

What this means
The chickens are killed at a young age, and get little exercise, which means meat is quite tender, but it is also paler and has less flavor.

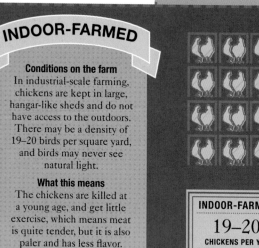

INDOOR-FARMED
19–20
CHICKENS PER YD²

FREE-RANGE
13–15
CHICKENS PER YD²

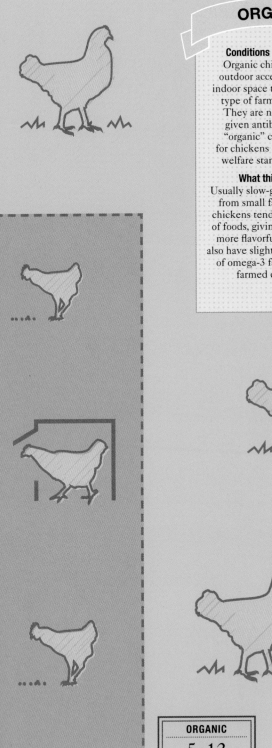

ORGANIC

Conditions on the farm
Organic chickens have outdoor access and more indoor space than any other type of farmed chicken. They are not routinely given antibiotics. The "organic" classification for chickens is the highest welfare standard in use.

What this means
Usually slow-growing breeds from small farms, organic chickens tend to eat a range of foods, giving them firmer, more flavorful meat. They also have slightly higher levels of omega-3 fats than other farmed chickens.

ORGANIC
5–12
CHICKENS PER YD²

How can I tell if meat has been
INJECTED WITH WATER?

Water-plumped meat is common, and can have varying effects on taste and texture.

Large-scale meat producers often bulk up products with water, claiming this improves the quality of the meat instead of just increasing its weight for sale. Roasts and whole birds can be physically injected with small needles via pumps, bacon and ham can be "wet-cured" by injecting or soaking meat in brine, and meat can be "vacuum tumbled" in briny water.

Undoubtedly, the texture of some meat, such as chicken, can be improved with brine-soaking because engorged muscle fibers become softer, but injecting meat with water can also affect the intensity of the flavor, resulting in a blander meat.

Signs that water has been added
Pooling at the bottom of a package is an unreliable indicator that water has been added, as dripping is inevitable for even unplumped meat. Instead, check the ingredients to see if there is a percentage for the amount of meat, if "water" is high up on the list, or if the label says "added" or "retained" water.

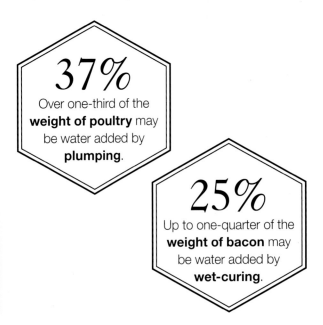

37%
Over one-third of the **weight of poultry** may be water added by **plumping**.

25%
Up to one-quarter of the **weight of bacon** may be water added by **wet-curing**.

If I freeze meat, will it destroy the
TASTE AND TEXTURE?

Undeniably convenient, freezers allow us to store food for months, but low-powered home freezers are far less efficient than industrial ones, which "flash freeze" meats very quickly.

Meat freezes from the outside inward. In home freezers this is a slow process, giving time for sharp-edged ice crystals to form, which gradually get bigger and pierce the muscle's delicate structure. When thawed, damaged cells lose water and the meat is less juicy and tender.

A phenomenon called "freezer burn," whereby patches of ice evaporate in the dry freezer air leaving hard "burnt" spots, is also more likely the longer meat is frozen. Storing meat in an airtight wrapper helps to prevent this. The chart, right, recommends maximum freezing times for meats before fats degrade and quality drops.

CUTS OF MEAT		RECOMMENDED MAXIMUM FREEZING TIMES
CHICKEN	Pieces	
	Whole	
BEEF, VEAL, LAMB, AND PORK	Steaks	▓▓▓▓▓▓
	Roasts	▓▓▓▓
	Chops	▓▓▓▓
	Ground	▓▓▓
SAUSAGES		▓▓
BACON		▓
MONTHS		1 2 3 4 5 6 7 8 9 10 11 12

Recommended freezing times
This chart provides recommended maximum freezing times before texture and taste significantly decline. Some meats, such as steaks and roasts, can survive a while longer, but because the fats gradually degrade (they "oxidize") and turn rancid, it is best not to exceed these freezing times.

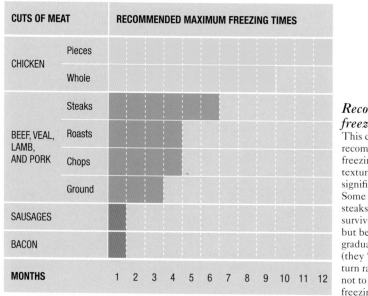

Flatten meat to ⅛–¼in (3–5mm) thick.

Do I really need to
POUND MEAT?

Preparing meat prior to cooking by pummelling it with a tenderizer may feel counterintuitive, but can have surprising benefits.

Striking a cut of meat with a tenderizing hammer crushes and damages muscle fibers, creating tiny rips in the connective tissue that binds the fibers together. This may sound worrying, but puncturing the muscle fibers and tissues in this way actually means that the meat retains 5–15 percent more moisture during cooking because the pounded muscle fibers shrink less, and the damaged proteins in the fibers soak up moisture, giving the meat succulence.

Tough steaks and cuts of meat in particular benefit from tenderizing. Lean chicken breasts don't need tenderizing, just gentle pounding with the smooth side of a mallet to flatten them and help them cook more evenly: if not, the thin, tapering end of a chicken breast cooks before the core of the thick end.

How to pound meat
It isn't necessary to use a great deal of force when tenderizing meat, but do make sure that you pound the meat on both sides to keep it even.

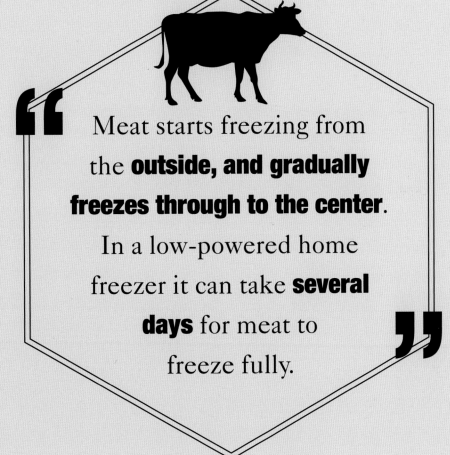

"Meat starts freezing from the **outside, and gradually freezes through to the center**. In a low-powered home freezer it can take **several days** for meat to freeze fully."

The Process of
GRILLING

The unique flavors and aromas produced when food is grilled are only partly due to the flavor molecules that are released when meat browns.

Grilling over an open flame feels simple, but it requires a dollop of science for the best results. How charcoal is positioned, when cooking starts, and the distance between the coals and the food all help to cook food thoroughly and create an intense taste. When you grill over charcoal, drips of fat from meat vaporize when they hit the coals, erupting into flavor-filled molecules, which rise with the heat to coat the underside of the meat. Fattier cuts, such as chops or ribs, drip even more juices, creating an abundance of heady, flavored particles. Gas grills are efficient, though flavors can lack the intensity of food cooked over charcoal.

THE BEST COLOR

A SILVER SURFACE IS IDEAL FOR THE INTERIOR OF A GRILL. SILVER REFLECTS THE HEAT (RADIATION) RAYS, INTENSIFYING THE HEAT.

WOOD CHIP EFFECT

COOKING OVER WOOD ADDS A LAYER OF FLAVOR. ABOVE 752°F (400°C), LIGNIN IN WOOD BREAKS DOWN INTO AROMATIC PARTICLES.

A SMALL EFFECT

DOUBLING THE DISTANCE OF FOOD FROM THE COALS FROM 4 TO 8IN (10 TO 20CM) REDUCES HEAT STRIKING THE FOOD BY A THIRD.

POSITION THE FOOD
Keeping food about 4in (10cm) above the coals of a medium-sized grill ensures that the food is bathed in heat. Moving it any closer will simply burn the surface.

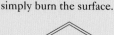

#3

HEAT THE CHARCOAL
Once the coals are lit, wait until the flames die before adding the food. At this point, a coating of white ash will cover the coals, which steadies the rate at which they burn and allows heat to diffuse evenly across the grill.

#2

Fat and liquid drip down.

Flavour molecules rise in the smoke.

Air vents help to control how quickly air enters the grill.

Agitating the coals so more air reaches them helps them burn hotter.

Ash collects on the base of the grill.

#1

SPREAD THE CHARCOAL
Spread the coals across the lower grill rack. Raising the coals above the base allows air to circulate so the coals burn hotter, and ash can fall to the grill base.

See inside

As meat heats, a crust forms on the surface where moisture evaporates. Above this, a "boiling zone" develops, where the temperature remains at 212°F (100°C). The meat in this part remains moist and heat moves from here to the center of the meat.

The boiling zone.

The surface of the meat dries out and a crust forms via the Maillard reaction (see pp16–17).

Key

◁◁•••• Heat traveling from surface of food

▬▬▬ Dehydrated crust

Cuts thicker than 4cm (1½in) will be slow to heat through so are best cooked with a lid on.

Without a lid, heat escapes from the food's surface, cooling the side of the meat not facing the heat source.

For medium-sized barbecues, 4in (10cm) is the ideal distance between the food and the charcoal.

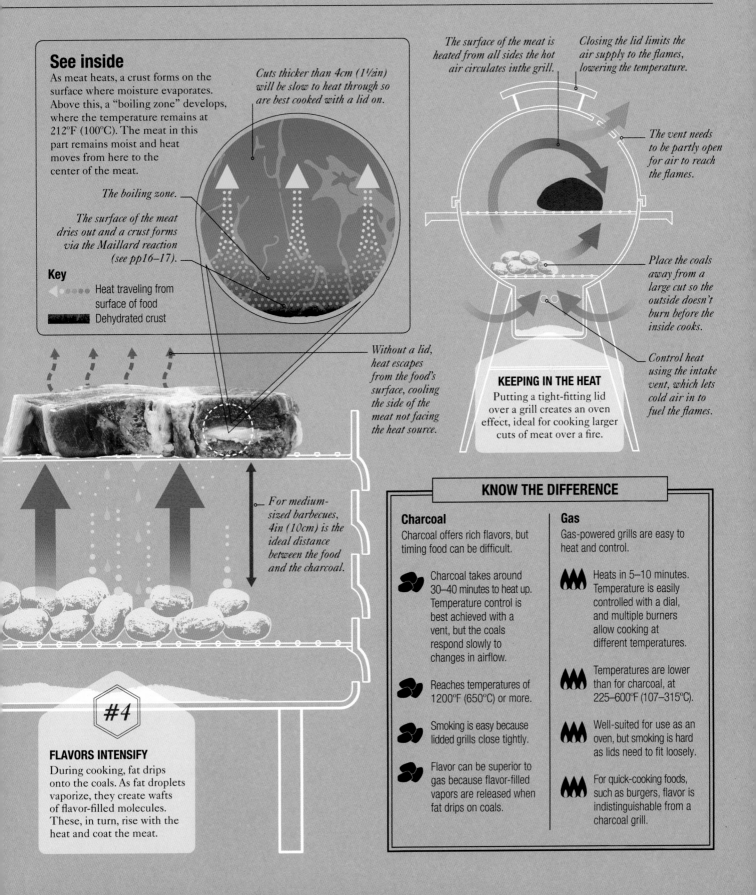

#4

FLAVORS INTENSIFY

During cooking, fat drips onto the coals. As fat droplets vaporize, they create wafts of flavor-filled molecules. These, in turn, rise with the heat and coat the meat.

The surface of the meat is heated from all sides the hot air circulates in the grill.

Closing the lid limits the air supply to the flames, lowering the temperature.

The vent needs to be partly open for air to reach the flames.

Place the coals away from a large cut so the outside doesn't burn before the inside cooks.

Control heat using the intake vent, which lets cold air in to fuel the flames.

KEEPING IN THE HEAT

Putting a tight-fitting lid over a grill creates an oven effect, ideal for cooking larger cuts of meat over a fire.

KNOW THE DIFFERENCE

Charcoal
Charcoal offers rich flavors, but timing food can be difficult.

- Charcoal takes around 30–40 minutes to heat up. Temperature control is best achieved with a vent, but the coals respond slowly to changes in airflow.

- Reaches temperatures of 1200°F (650°C) or more.

- Smoking is easy because lidded grills close tightly.

- Flavor can be superior to gas because flavor-filled vapors are released when fat drips on coals.

Gas
Gas-powered grills are easy to heat and control.

- Heats in 5–10 minutes. Temperature is easily controlled with a dial, and multiple burners allow cooking at different temperatures.

- Temperatures are lower than for charcoal, at 225–600°F (107–315°C).

- Well-suited for use as an oven, but smoking is hard as lids need to fit loosely.

- For quick-cooking foods, such as burgers, flavor is indistinguishable from a charcoal grill.

What are the benefits of
MARINATING MEAT?

The word "marinate" literally means to "pickle in sea salt brine."

Marinades are often misunderstood. Historically, this was a salty soup that was used to preserve meat, but nowadays, we think about steeping meat in a rich-tasting "marinade" to infuse it with flavors. However, this is largely a myth (see below). This doesn't mean that meat won't benefit from a marinade, because with the right ingredients a marinade can give meat an aromatic, flavorful coating and mildly tenderized outer layers.

How long should meat be marinated for?

Marinate meat for no longer than 24 hours, and ideally less. If you marinate meat for too long, the salt in the marinade will actually start to cure the outside of the meat and the outer layers will be mushy when cooked. Marinating meat for just 30 minutes before cooking will have an impact on flavor.

Tender and tasty

The ingredients in a marinade work together to enhance the flavor of meat and tenderize its outer layers. During cooking, the sugars and proteins in a marinade help to brown the meat, creating a crisp, flavorful crust.

WELL SEARED

ALKALINE INGREDIENTS, SUCH AS EGG WHITES AND BAKING SODA, CAN ACCELERATE THE BROWNING REACTION.

MYTH BUSTER

——— *Myth* ———
MARINADES INFUSE MEAT WITH FLAVOR

——— *Truth* ———
It is physically impossible for marinades to penetrate far into meat. Most flavor molecules are too large to squeeze into the muscle tissue cells in meat, which are around 75 percent water and packed tightly like a sodden sponge. Oil molecules, which disperse most of the flavor molecules, are also unable to enter muscle cells. This means that oil and flavor molecules infuse no further than a few millimeters into the meat, and instead pool on the surface.

Marinating ingredients

Marinades can have myriad flavor combinations, but certain key components are needed for success. A marinade should include most of the following: salt, a fat, such as oil, an acid ingredient (optional, because it can slow browning), and flavorings, such as sugar, herbs, and spices.

MARINADE BASICS

- **Salt** This is the most important marinade ingredient because as well as enhancing overall flavor it also disrupts the structure of the proteins in the top layers of the meat (see opposite), allowing a little moisture to enter and giving meat a more tender texture.

- **Fats** Oils, such as olive oil, serve as a base for a marinade, spreading other flavour molecules and helping meat to brown and crisp. Yogurts are traditionally used in Indian marinades. The dairy sugars and proteins interact with those on the meat during cooking to create unique aromatic substances.

ACIDIC INGREDIENTS (OPTIONAL)

- **Lemon juice** Lemon juice adds a tangy flavor to marinades, triggering the bitterness taste buds. It also helps to tenderize the outer layers of meat.

- **Vinegar** Vinegar helps tenderize meat and brings a tartness to a marinade that helps to offset the naturally rich flavor of the meat and the oil or fat in the marinade.

- **Wine** This provides tartness and the alcohol helps to disperse other flavors in a marinade. Wine can soften the outer layers of the meat.

FLAVORINGS

- **Sugar** This reduces the tongue's sensitivity to bitterness. As well as enhancing flavor, sugar helps to speed browning and also caramelizes. Use honey or corn syrup rather than table sugar.

- **Herbs and spices** Aromatic herbs and spices are used to add a range of flavor accents, helping to distinguish a marinade as sweet, spicy, sharp, or fresh-tasting. The flavours are extracted when carried in the marinade's oil.

LEMON   **CHILES**

Should I season meat with
SALT WELL IN ADVANCE OR JUST BEFORE COOKING?

It may seem a trivial distinction, but choosing the right time to sprinkle makes a real difference.

If salting meat before cooking was just about adding flavor, the question of when to add it wouldn't matter. However, salt does far more than enhance flavor. If you've poured salt over spilled red wine, you'll know that salt has an incredible ability to soak up moisture, a quality known as "hygroscopy." Rubbing salt on uncooked meat has a similar effect, drawing water out of the muscle, creating a layer of surface brine.

Enhancing texture

The diagrams, right, show the effects of salting meat just before cooking and some time before. Salting meat just before cooking creates a brine layer that can be dabbed off to dry the meat and help it brown more quickly. Salting meat well in advance of cooking has added benefits. Left for longer, salt starts to tenderize meat by "denaturing" the surface proteins; after about 40 minutes, meat is noticeably softer. You can still dab the surface, too, before cooking to enhance browning.

The salting exception

While salt helps to tenderize whole cuts of meat, ground meat should not be presalted. This softens the fine "grains" of the grind, making them stick together. A presalted burger will become rubbery, and a cooked burger prepared in this way will actually bounce if dropped on the floor.

Salt draws the water out of the muscle to the surface of the meat.

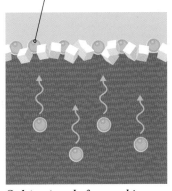

Salting just before cooking
Within a couple of minutes of salting, salt draws moisture out of the meat. This combines with the surface layer of salt to form a thin, sweat-like covering of brine.

Over time, salt diffuses into the meat, pulling water with it.

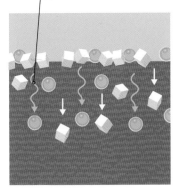

Salting well in advance
After about 15 minutes, salt and water start to draw back into the meat. The salty brine disrupts, or "denatures", proteins, causing them to unwind, which softens and tenderizes meat.

How do I
SMOKE MEAT AT HOME?

An age-old practice, smoking was originally used to preserve meat. Today we smoke food to transform its aroma and create enticing flavors.

OAK

There are two techniques for smoking: cold and hot smoking. Cold smoking up to 86°F (30°C), bathes food in vapors from wood chips without cooking it. Hot smoking, at 131–176°F (55°–80°C), also gives meat a cooked texture (see below), but does not impart as many sweet and spicy flavor notes as cold smoking does.

The science behind smoking

When wood heats up, a substance called lignin within wood breaks apart, dispersing into an array of fragrant flavor molecules, which waft up and adhere to the meat's surface. Lignin begins to break down and release smoke when the wood reaches 338°F (170°C). At around 392°F (200°C), the smoke starts to thicken and darken, and the lignin readily fractures to release plumes of caramel, flowery, and bread-like aromas. When the wood turns black and the smoke thickens further, at about 752°F (400°C), the molecular reactions are in full swing, adding further layers of aroma to the meat. If the smoke thins, this indicates that the wood is too hot or has been used up.

IN PRACTICE

HOT SMOKING MEAT

Specialized smoking equipment is available for hot and cold smoking, but it's also easy to smoke food with basic cookware. A wok or pan can be used for hot smoking, shown here, ideal for small portions of meat, such as chicken breasts or wings, or pork ribs. This method can also be used for hard cheese and fish, such as salmon fillets.

#1

#2

#3

PREPARE FLAVORINGS
Cover the side of a wok with a large piece of heavy-duty aluminum foil, leaving a 2½in (5cm) hole at the bottom. Evenly sprinkle 2 tbsp culinary wood chips—such as pecan, oak, or beech—into the bottom of the lined wok. You can also add other flavorings, such as tea leaves or spices. Position the rack in the wok.

RELEASE FLAVOR MOLECULES
Place the wok over high heat, and heat for about 5 minutes, until the chips are smoking well. Heating the chips until they are smoking (this starts at around 338°F/170°C) frees flavorful molecules from the wood, which which are deposited on the surface of the meat.

SEAL IN THE SMOKE
Place the meat onto the rack, leaving space around each piece to allow smoke to circulate. Put the lid on and carefully fold the overhanging foil up around the edge of the lid. This will help to keep the flavorful smoke inside the wok.

APPLE

Wood chips
Choose culinary wood chips made from hardwood, as these are packed with flavorful lignin.

SWEET CHESTNUT

Is it possible to AGE MEAT AT HOME?

Aging lends meat complexity of flavor and aroma, but ready-aged meat can be very expensive.

Dry-aging meat is a time- and space-consuming process that causes cuts to lose volume, which is why aged meat is expensive. Leaving meat in cool, humid conditions gives time for enzymes to break down collagen and muscle fibers, tenderizing meat and fragmenting large, flavorless molecules into aromatic, flavorful, smaller ones. In specialized facilities, large cuts are aged in temperature- and humidity-controlled rooms for months, but a similar effect can be created at home with a standard beef roast and a fridge. The timeline below shows how meat transforms during the aging process.

338°F
(170°C) is the temperature that **wood** must reach to release its **flavor**.

#4

BATHE IN THE SMOKE
Leave the meat to smoke in the wok for 10 minutes over high heat, then remove the wok from the heat and leave the meat to bathe in the smoke for a further 20 minutes, or longer for a stronger flavor. Finish the meat by grilling, or slicing and stir-frying to give it a browned crust.

AGING TIMELINE
Dry-aging meat develops complex flavors and tenderizes meat. Below is a summary of the changes happening to beef as it ages.

TIME	WHAT HAPPENS
DAYS 01–14	**Starting to tenderize** Place a large joint of beef on a rack above a drip tray containing a little water. Place in a cool fridge (37–41°F/3–5°C). Enzymes begin to tenderize the meat; at 14 days, meat has reached 80 percent of its maximum tenderness.
DAYS 15–28	**Flavors begin to develop** As enzymes continue to break down tissues, sweet and nutty flavors begin to develop in the meat. Keep the water in the tray topped off to help the air in the fridge stay humid, and thereby limit how much the meat dries out.
DAYS 29–42	**Optimum tenderness and flavor** The longer meat is left, the more time the enzymes have to work and the more flavors will develop. Fat breaks down to create complex cheese-like flavors. Before cooking, slice off any mold and the charcoal-colored crust to reveal a deep-red meat.

Should I trim
ALL THE FAT OFF MEAT?

Health-wise, the message is to avoid saturated animal fat, but fat has other roles in cooking.

We're aware of how saturated fats in red meat impact cholesterol and calories. But fat also carries much of the flavor of meat, so from a culinary standpoint it's generally better to leave fat on.

There are a couple of exceptions. When flash-frying a steak Diane, there isn't enough time for the strip of fat to cook, so this remains semi-raw. And large lumps of fat in stewing steak should be cut out as there may not be enough cooking time for the collagen to break down and the fat to melt.

MEAT ENHANCING

WHEN HEATED, FAT OXIDIZES, CREATING NEW FLAVORS, AND MELTS, MAKING MEAT MORE TENDER.

Does it matter if you cut meat
ACROSS THE GRAIN OR ALONG IT?

You can spot the direction of the muscle fibers on meat by inspecting the fibers on its surface.

Whether you cut meat "across the grain" or "along it" has profound effects on tenderness and juiciness. The "grain" is the direction in which the muscle fibers run. On a piece of meat, look for the direction of the fibers and lines of connective tissue on the surface. If you tore the muscle, it would split along these grains. When you cut meat for serving, it should be cut across, not along, the grain. Biting into meat cut this way allows your teeth to exert maximum force on the tough sheaths of connective tissue that envelop each strand. The meat breaks apart in the mouth easily and any soft gelatin or fat is released onto the palate. Biting into meat cut along the grain takes ten times the biting force as chewing across the grain.

What is the secret to
PERFECTLY CRISPY PORK CRACKLING?

Golden pork crackling is prized by many meat eaters.

Turning the pale, rubbery skin on pork into light and airy crackling is a challenge, but with the right preparation and cooking stages, this is actually fairly easy to master.

How do I create crackling?
Many believe that pork crackling is just fat, but it is actually made from the whole layer of pork skin and contains connective tissue and protein, which give it strength, in addition to an underlying layer of fat—nearly half of which is unsaturated. Follow the method below for a perfectly cooked roast with delicious crackling.

IN PRACTICE

COOKING PORK CRACKLING
Several key stages are needed to create crunchy, golden crackling. Before cooking, skin needs to be dried and scored. Cooking is then done in two stages. Roasting a

#1

SALT AND DRY
For successful pork crackling, the skin of the meat needs to be dried before cooking. Rub salt into the roast well in advance. The salt quickly draws moisture out—pat the moist surface dry, then place the roast in the cold air of the fridge to dry out.

> "Crackling is made up *of the whole layer* of pork skin and contains *strong connective tissue* and protein."

belly of pork at a low temperature gives juicy meat, but the skin will be chewy. For crunchy crackling, a final cooking stage at a high heat is needed (see below).

#2

INCREASE THE SURFACE AREA

Scoring the surface of the skin is crucial to increase the surface area and allow the hot oven air to penetrate further into the skin. Score across the skin, placing the scores a finger's width apart. Make sure you score down well into the fat, but not right through to the meat. During cooking, moisture escapes through the cuts and fat will bubble up and fry on the surface.

#3

COOK SLOWLY, THEN REST

Cook the pork on a lower heat, around 375°F (190°C), allowing 35 minutes for each pound until the flesh is nearly cooked—a knife should have little resistance when twisted in the meat. At this point, the meat will be juicy, but the fat will be chewy and flabby. Remove from the oven, cover in foil, and leave to rest, while turning up the oven to 475°F (240°C).

#4

INCREASE THE HEAT

Once the temperature has increased, baste or drizzle oil over the resting roast to increase heat transfer to the skin, then return the meat to the oven for about 20 minutes, rotating the meat regularly to avoid hot spots. The remaining moisture in the skin will evaporate, bubbles of steam will expand, and the surface will brown.

Should I cook meat from room
TEMPERATURE?

Many cooks take meat out of the fridge early with the aim of reducing cooking time.

Bringing meat to room temperature before cooking seems sensible for speeding up cooking. In reality, this makes little difference and could even pose a health risk. The core of a medium-thickness steak takes 2 hours to increase just 41°F (5°C), and in this time infection-causing bacteria may have grown on the surface. Searing meat kills off germs on the surface, but won't eradicate all the toxins that have infused the meat.

The only time it is worth warming meat precooking (but not to room temperature) is when using a thin skillet: a cold steak could drop the pan's temperature to below the minimum 284°F (140°C) needed for browning.

Does searing a steak really
"SEAL IN" JUICES?

Searing steak is a well-known practice, but the benefits might not be quite those you were expecting.

It's often thought that cooking meat rapidly at a high temperature "seals" the outside into a crisp, impermeable crust that stops moisture from escaping. Science shows us that the opposite is true—the crust that forms when steak is cooked rapidly at a high heat isn't waterproof; in fact, a seared steak dries out faster than an unseared one, as the high heat needed to brown the meat's outer layers dries out the inside more rapidly.

However, a seared brown crust does make for a far tastier steak, as the high heat triggers the Maillard reaction (see pp16–17), releasing myriad mouthwatering flavor molecules.

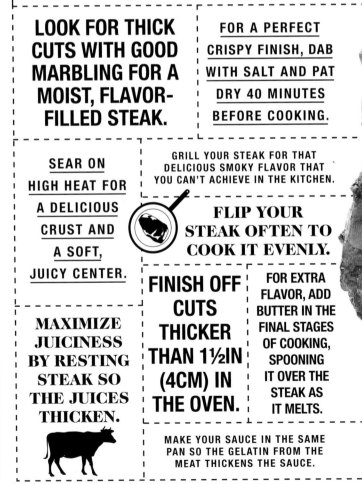

SEARED STEAK

How do I cook the
PERFECT STEAK?

The "perfect" steak may mean different things for different people, but some key principles hold true.

While the perfectly flavored steak is partly dependent on personal taste, some core guidelines and tips can help you to hone your steak-making skills and make the most of your prime cut. Ensure the pan or grill is hot and follow the tips below and guide opposite for steaks up to 1½in (4cm) thick.

TOP TIPS FOR COOKING STEAKS

Keep the following points in mind when cooking your steak to optimize flavor and texture:

LOOK FOR THICK CUTS WITH GOOD MARBLING FOR A MOIST, FLAVOR-FILLED STEAK.

FOR A PERFECT CRISPY FINISH, DAB WITH SALT AND PAT DRY 40 MINUTES BEFORE COOKING.

SEAR ON HIGH HEAT FOR A DELICIOUS CRUST AND A SOFT, JUICY CENTER.

GRILL YOUR STEAK FOR THAT DELICIOUS SMOKY FLAVOR THAT YOU CAN'T ACHIEVE IN THE KITCHEN.

FLIP YOUR STEAK OFTEN TO COOK IT EVENLY.

MAXIMIZE JUICINESS BY RESTING STEAK SO THE JUICES THICKEN.

FINISH OFF CUTS THICKER THAN 1½IN (4CM) IN THE OVEN.

FOR EXTRA FLAVOR, ADD BUTTER IN THE FINAL STAGES OF COOKING, SPOONING IT OVER THE STEAK AS IT MELTS.

MAKE YOUR SAUCE IN THE SAME PAN SO THE GELATIN FROM THE MEAT THICKENS THE SAUCE.

WHEN IS IT DONE?

A meat thermometer is the most accurate way to test meat, but you can also gauge red meat by color and texture. The finger test, below, together with how the meat looks, helps you to judge when steak is done.

"BLUE"/EXTRA-RARE

Seared briefly, for about 1 minute on each side, the texture and internal chemistry of meat will be similar to raw. An extra-rare steak will be soft to the touch, feeling like the relaxed fleshy muscle at the base of the thumb. The center of the steak will reach about 129°F (54°C).

RARE

A rare steak feels like the base of the thumb when the thumb and index finger touch. It has a juicy texture; while muscle fibers have firmed and the color is more pink, much of the moisture remains. Cooked for about 2.5 minutes on each side, it reaches 135°F (57°C).

MEDIUM–RARE

A medium rare steak has a similar texture to rare, but is pinker and firmer, feeling like the base of the thumb when the thumb and middle finger touch. Cooked around 3.5 minutes on each side, the internal temperature is around 145°F (63°C).

MEDIUM

At about 160°F (71°C), most of the proteins clump together and meat is a light brown color. Firm and moist, it feels like the base of the thumb when the thumb and ring finger touch. Cook for around 5 minutes on each side.

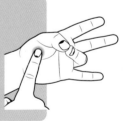

WELL DONE

At 165°F (74°C), meat is tougher, drier, and darker as more proteins coagulate and force moisture from cells. Meat feels like the base of the thumb when the thumb and little finger touch. Cook for about 6 minutes on each side.

DATA

How it works
Food is cooked for
an extended period of time,
immersed in liquid.

Best for
Tough cuts of meat with
white connective tissue,
root vegetables, dried beans
and other pulses.

What to consider
Low temperatures mean you
must preboil dried kidney
beans (see p140). Brown
onions and meat beforehand
to give roasted flavors.

The Process of
SLOW COOKING

*Cooking at low to moderate temperature over
a long period of time will convert a tough cut
of meat into a melt-in-the-mouth delight.*

Low-temperature cooking gives
ample time for chewy collagen in
tough meat to be converted into
velvety gelatin, a reaction that takes
place at above 149–158°F (65–70°C).
Gelatin breaks down in the
cooking liquid, thickening it
and emulsifying flavor-rich
fats to create a rich, luscious
gravy. Allow the meat to cool
in its liquid after
cooking—any
remaining gelatin will
pull cooking liquid into
the meat, making
it extra moist. Lean
cuts with minimal
connective tissue will
dry out if slow cooked.

LOWER IS BETTER

**KEEP HEAT LOW. MUSCLE
FIBRES COOK FROM
140°F (60°C); AS THE
TEMPERATURE RISES,
MOISTURE IS
LOST.**

154°F

or 68°C is the
temperature at which
collagen starts to break
into gelatin.

THICKENING

**IF THE SAUCE NEEDS
THICKENING AFTER SLOW
COOKING, REMOVE THE
MEAT BEFORE BOILING ON
A STOVETOP.**

ADD THE INGREDIENTS
Put the ingredients in the
inner cooking pot. Slow
cookers don't reach the high
temperatures needed for the
Maillard reaction (see p16),
so brown onions and meat
in a pan first, if needed.

#1

HEAT IS TRAPPED INSIDE
Unless adding flavorings,
avoid removing the lid to
look inside during cooking
because this causes steam
and heat to escape, so the
liquid will need topping up.

#6

HEAT RADIATES UPWARD
Heat from the base unit
spreads across the bottom
and sides of the inner pot.
The heat then passes into the
cooking liquid and directly
into food resting on the base.

#5

*A heating element is in the
base or around the sides
(some models have both).*

ADD LIQUID

Slow cookers are heated from the bottom, like a pan on the stovetop, so can burn if the pot is dry. Add enough liquid just to cover the food, but not too much as the sauce will be too thin and lack flavor.

#2

SECURE THE LID

Put the lid on. This will stop heat and steam from escaping, allowing the temperature inside the inner pot to reach a steady temperature and prevent the liquid evaporating away.

#3

See inside

White, chewy connective tissue is made of collagen and elastin proteins. Collagen begins to denature at 126°F (52°C), then contracts and shrinks at 136°F (58°C), squeezing moisture out. At around 154°F (68°C), however, collagen breaks apart and reforms into soft gelatin, giving succulence to the dehydrating meat (see below). However, elastin does not break down at normal cooking temperatures, so remains as inedible gristle.

Key

Collagen molecules
Gelatin molecules

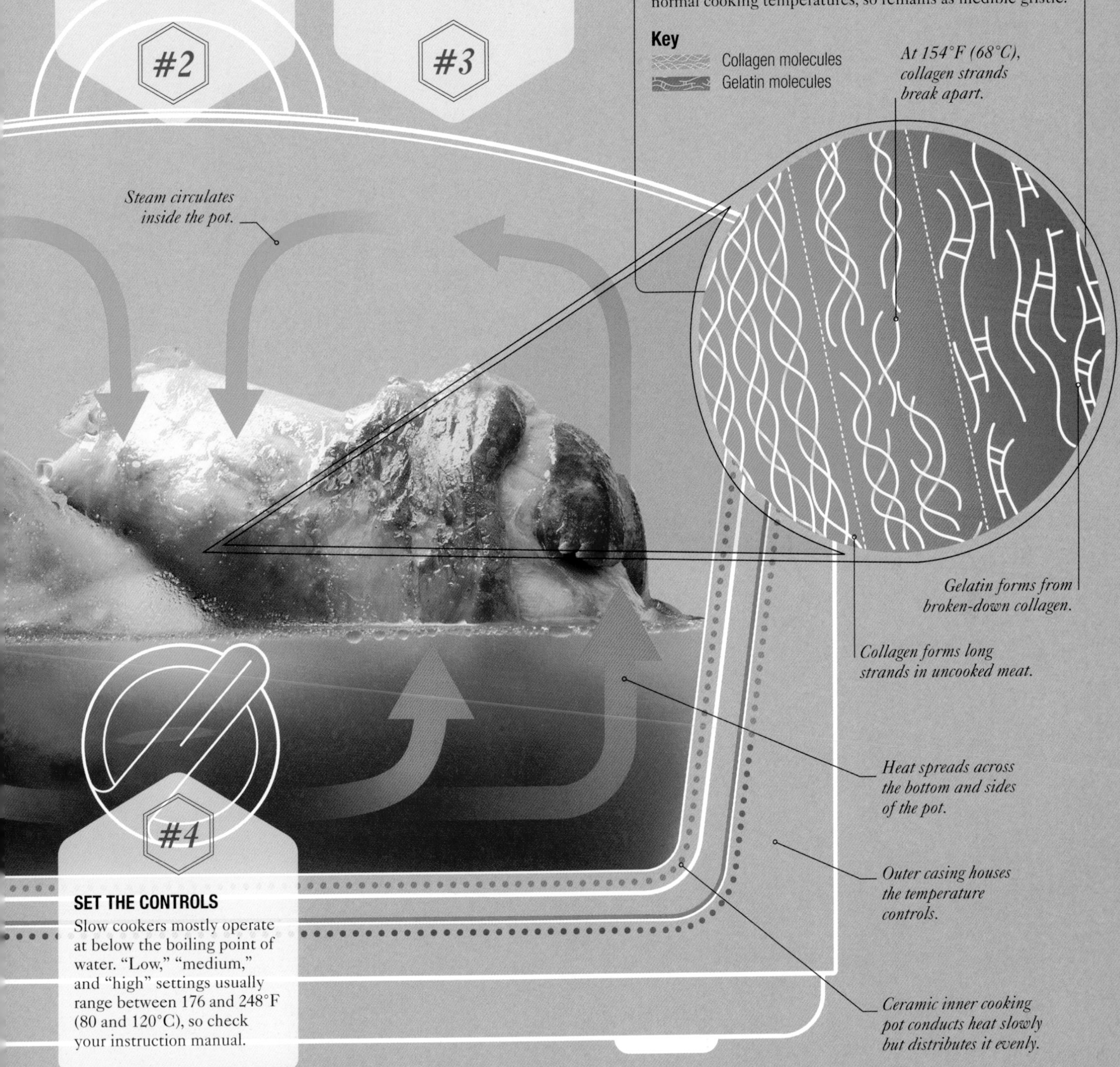

At 154°F (68°C), collagen strands break apart.

Steam circulates inside the pot.

Gelatin forms from broken-down collagen.

Collagen forms long strands in uncooked meat.

Heat spreads across the bottom and sides of the pot.

#4

Outer casing houses the temperature controls.

SET THE CONTROLS

Slow cookers mostly operate at below the boiling point of water. "Low," "medium," and "high" settings usually range between 176 and 248°F (80 and 120°C), so check your instruction manual.

Ceramic inner cooking pot conducts heat slowly but distributes it evenly.

How can I keep
CHICKEN OR TURKEY FROM DRYING OUT?

Different preparation and cooking techniques offer some useful ways to keep these lean meats moist.

Poultry's delicate white meat is abundant in bulky and tender "fast-twitch" muscle (see p34), used for quick, powerful actions, which tends to cook rapidly. There is very little fat in the breast meat and almost no connective tissue, both of which are important for ensuring that meat has a juicy, succulent mouthfeel.

A LEAN CUT

THE LEANEST PART OF A CHICKEN, MOST PRONE TO DRYING OUT WHEN COOKED, IS THE PALE BREAST MEAT.

Cooking a chicken or turkey in a conventional home oven is convenient, but the blasting-hot oven air quickly dehydrates this fragile meat. The preparation and cooking methods outlined below, for both whole chickens and smaller pieces, offer a range of solutions for ensuring that chicken and turkey remain moist and succulent during cooking.

OPEN FIRE	SOUS VIDE	SPATCHCOCKING	BRINING

OPEN FIRE

The method
Known as "spit roasting," this involves skewering a whole bird on a spit and roasting it over an open flame while it rotates.

How this helps
As the spit rotates, heat rays coming from the flames cook all sides of the meat evenly. Cooking in this way is less dehydrating than the hot, dry air from a conventional oven.

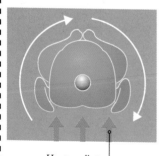

Heat radiates evenly over the rotating meat.

SOUS VIDE

The method
Most practical for smaller cuts of meat, this involves placing the cuts an airless bag and immersing it in a hot-water bath set at a controlled temperature.

How this helps
This is the most foolproof way to keep poultry moist. Surrounded by precisely heated water, there is not much danger of overcooking. However, sous vide doesn't brown meat, so for Maillard flavors (see pp16—17), it needs searing in a pan or with a blowtorch afterward.

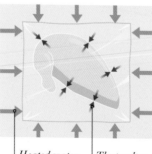

Heated water cooks from all sides.

The poultry retains moisture.

SPATCHCOCKING

The method
This can be done when oven-roasting a whole bird. The backbone is removed so that the butterflied bird can lie flat, with the breast in the center and the legs on either side.

How this helps
Flattening the bird in this way helps the meat to cook more evenly throughout, in a similar way that pounding a chicken breast does (see p42). Speeding cooking in this way means that the outer layers are less likely to dry out.

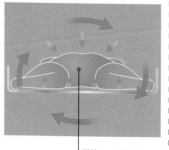

When laid flat, the center cooks more quickly and dries out less.

BRINING

The method
A whole bird is submerged in salty water overnight.

How this helps
The aim of brining is to force water into uncooked meat. Left for several hours, salt penetrates into the meat (in a process called diffusion), pulling water with it as it does so (a process known as osmosis), drawing the water toward the center. This is an imperfect method because the salt travels slowly and may not reach all the muscle.

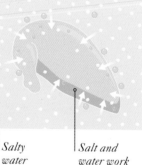

Salty water

Salt and water work into the meat.

What does BASTING DO?

Bathing meat in its own cooking juices is an effective way to enhance your meat.

Conventional wisdom is that basting meat during cooking adds moisture, resulting in a succulent dish; however, this is not the case (see Myth Buster, below). Regularly ladling meat with its own oily juices does, however, add flavor and texture because it increases the surface temperature to hasten the Maillard reaction (see pp16—17), releasing rich, meaty flavors and crisping the skin. The shiny glaze suggests that the meat is moist, but bear in mind that oil speeds up cooking, so care is needed to avoid drying out the outer layers.

ADDING FATS

The method
Combine slices of breast meat with other fat-containing, moist foods.

How this helps
Even when cooked in ideal conditions, breast meat can still taste dry, which is due to its lack of fat. Combining thinly cut or shredded meat with moist, fattier foods and meaty, gelatinous sauces offsets the dryness, giving a succulent mouthfeel.

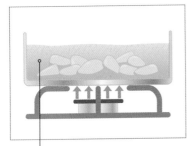

Fat- and gelatin-containing liquid helps the meat taste less dry.

SEPARATING A BIRD

The method
Break up a whole bird into individual pieces.

How this helps
Similar to spatchcocking, breaking up a bird, or buying separate cuts, is an easy way to avoid overcooking the meat. Fast-cooking breast can be cooked independently of the darker, slow-cooking legs and thighs. A whole bird is broken down into eight pieces: two drumsticks, two thighs, two breasts, and two wings.

Heat cooks separated parts at an even rate if they are of a similar type of meat.

GRAVY BASE

SOME OF THE COOKING JUICES, TOGETHER WITH MEAT FRAGMENTS IN THE PAN, CAN BE USED IN A RICH GRAVY.

Basting tool
Meat basters can be used to draw up juices, which are then squirted evenly over meat.

MYTH BUSTER

——— *Myth* ———
BASTING MEAT KEEPS IT MOIST

——— *Truth* ———
Oven-roasted meat is prone to drying out. Traditional teaching states that basting meat in its juices moistens meat and increases succulence. However, little or none, of the basting liquid soaks into meat; instead it dribbles off or forms a glaze. The muscle tissue has no capacity to absorb liquid because it is already saturated with juices and furthermore is being squeezed by collagen fibers as they shrink in the heat.

How can I tell
WHEN MEAT IS DONE?

Some foods, such as eggs, can be cooked to a timer, whereas the art of cooking meat is knowing when to stop.

Each piece of meat is different: its thickness, water content, fat density, amount of stringy connective tissue it has, and position of bones all affect cooking times. Fat conducts heat poorly, so fatty cuts take time to cook properly; meat with tough white connective tissue also needs slower cooking to break tough tissue down into succulent gelatin; and bones transfer heat quickly to the core of the meat, speeding up

cooking times. A fast-read digital meat thermometer is the easiest way to test whether meat is cooked. You can also gauge red meat by its appearance and feel (see below and p53), cooking it to your preferred level of doneness. White meat, such as chicken, needs to be cooked completely, while pork needs to be cooked well, but can have a little pinkness. Use the guidelines below to check that meat is cooked correctly.

Poultry

Pork

Red meat

WHEN IS RED MEAT DONE?

Red meat, such as lamb and beef, can be cooked to be rare, medium, or well done, depending on your preference.

COOKED RARE, RED MEAT WILL BE RED LIKE BLOOD IN THE CENTER AND ITS TEXTURE SOFT.

FOR MEDIUM DONENESS, MEAT IS FIRMER, MOIST, AND LIGHT BROWN.

WELL DONE RED MEAT IS DARKER AND FIRM TO THE TOUCH.

WHEN IS POULTRY DONE?

Pierce the flesh with the tip of a thin, sharp knife or a skewer to see if the juices run clear. If there is no pinkness, the myoglobin pigment has unraveled and the core temperature has exceeded the safe minimum of 165°F (74°C).

WHEN COOKED OVER WOOD OR CHARCOAL, GASES FROM BURNING FUEL CAN PASS INTO THE SURFACE OF CHICKEN MEAT TO TRIGGER A SERIES OF REACTIONS THAT FIX THE RED SUBSTANCE, MYOGLOBIN, IN THE OUTERMOST LAYERS OF THE MEAT INTO A PERMANENTLY PINK STATE, BUT THE MEAT IS PERFECTLY COOKED.

IMMATURE BONE MARROW IS RED, SO RED ON BONES CAN JUST MEAN THAT A CHICKEN WAS KILLED YOUNG.

WHEN IS PORK DONE?

Unlike chicken, pork does not need to be cooked until white throughout. This pale meat is cooked when a quick-read digital thermometer reads 145°F (62°C).

PORK MEAT SHOULD BE MOSTLY WHITE, WITH A HINT OF PINK.

Why do I need to rest
MEAT AFTER COOKING?

Resting meat is a concept we are all familiar with, but some confusion surrounds the reasons for doing this.

Leaving meat to rest has real benefits—meat "bleeds" less on the plate, slices more cleanly, and tastes juicier. There are no set rules on how long meat should rest for— a few minutes at room temperature can be enough for a medium-sized steak. In this time, heat from the outer layers spreads into the core, and moisture from the cooler core diffuses outward, giving a more even temperature and juiciness. Most importantly, resting lets the meat's "internal gravy" thicken as water between the muscle fibers mingles with broken-down proteins. As the steak rests and cools, these thickened internal juices form a delicious jus.

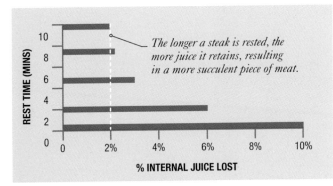

The longer a steak is rested, the more juice it retains, resulting in a more succulent piece of meat.

% INTERNAL JUICE LOST

Meat weight loss after cooking
The table above shows weight loss through "bleeding" in identically sized beef steaks cut into at different times after cooking. At 2 minutes, 6 percent of weight is lost, while after 10 minutes just 2 percent is lost.

MYTH BUSTER

——— *Myth* ———
RESTING MEAT LETS TENSE MUSCLES RELAX

——— *Truth* ———
After slaughter, muscles go through a period of rigor mortis, degrading muscle proteins so they are no longer able to contract and relax. In addition, muscle proteins heated above 122°F (50°C) will have unraveled permanently. Resting thickens juices and allows some fluid to be reabsorbed into muscle fibers, but does not actually "relax" the muscles.

What can I do with
OVERCOOKED MEAT?

Like spilled milk, there is no undoing overcooked meat.

When meat is overcooked, the proteins have coagulated and the fibers have lost their moisture and shriveled, resulting in tough, dry meat. However, all is not lost. The most effective way to salvage overcooked meat is to recreate the slow-cooking effect used for stews. Slow-cooked meat tastes succulent because tough cuts become surrounded by smooth gelatin (see pp54–55), so try shredding overcooked lean cuts and mixing them with a gravy made from meat stock, fats or butter, and silky gelatin. Another way to reintroduce succulence is to add dry meat to dishes with other sources of moisture, as shown below.

Oil used for frying gives impression of juiciness.

Thick sauces add succulence.

Add to a fritter
Finely dice meat to use in a fritter with onions and oils.

Mince for a sauce
Dry meat can be minced and used in a pasta sauce.

Vegetables add a variety of textures.

Fats reintroduce moisture to blended meat.

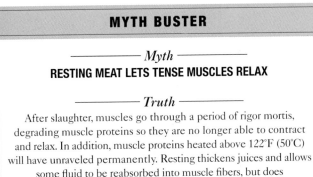

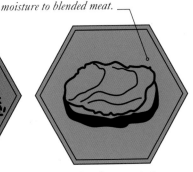

Use in a stir-fry
Thinly slice overcooked meat and use it in a stir-fry.

Blend in a pâté
Meat can be blended and added to fats in a succulent pâté.

What's the secret of a TASTY SAUCE?

The artistry of sauce making is harmonizing flavors and perfecting texture.

For a great sauce or jus, the taste, aroma, mouthfeel, and flavor pairings all need to work together. A sauce can intensify a main ingredient, such as the rich sauce of a beef bourguignon, complement and accentuate other flavors, or even salvage overcooked meat.

Building a sauce

The aim of a sauce is to achieve a smooth consistency that is thicker than water but less dense than the main ingredient. The diagram, right, shows how sauces are built from liquids and thickening agents. Starches are the most often used thickeners, but despite their versatility, they can be heavy and starch molecules cling to flavor molecules tightly, making them relatively bland and in need of additional flavoring. Oil- and fat-based sauces are more intense because flavor molecules dissolve more successfully in fats.

> **"A sauce** *can help to intensify a main ingredient, such as the* **rich red wine sauce** *of a beef bourguignon."*

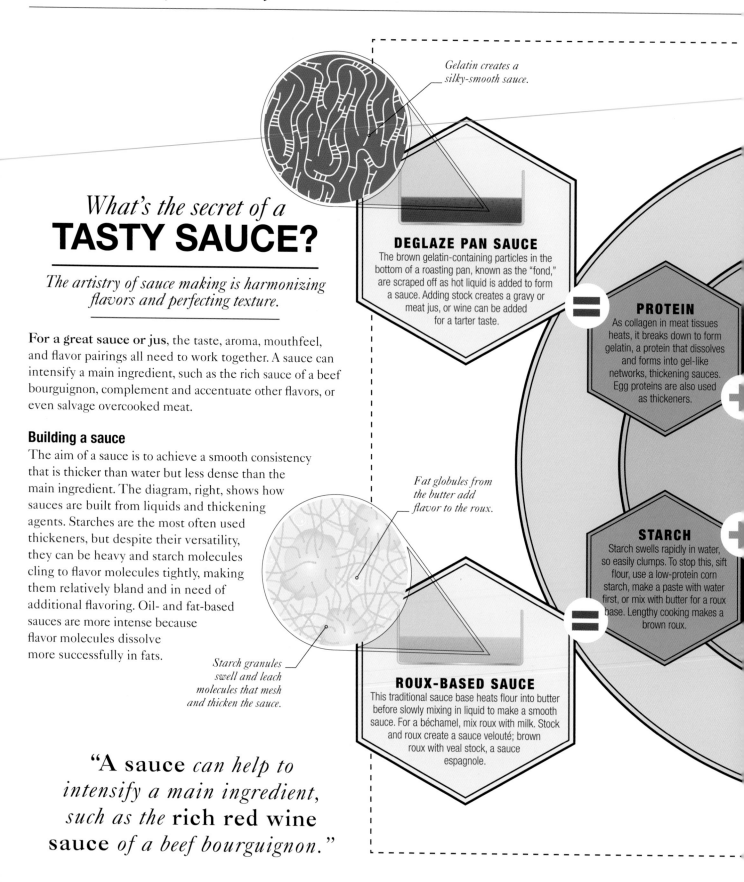

Gelatin creates a silky-smooth sauce.

DEGLAZE PAN SAUCE
The brown gelatin-containing particles in the bottom of a roasting pan, known as the "fond," are scraped off as hot liquid is added to form a sauce. Adding stock creates a gravy or meat jus, or wine can be added for a tarter taste.

PROTEIN
As collagen in meat tissues heats, it breaks down to form gelatin, a protein that dissolves and forms into gel-like networks, thickening sauces. Egg proteins are also used as thickeners.

Fat globules from the butter add flavor to the roux.

Starch granules swell and leach molecules that mesh and thicken the sauce.

STARCH
Starch swells rapidly in water, so easily clumps. To stop this, sift flour, use a low-protein corn starch, make a paste with water first, or mix with butter for a roux base. Lengthy cooking makes a brown roux.

ROUX-BASED SAUCE
This traditional sauce base heats flour into butter before slowly mixing in liquid to make a smooth sauce. For a béchamel, mix roux with milk. Stock and roux create a sauce velouté; brown roux with veal stock, a sauce espagnole.

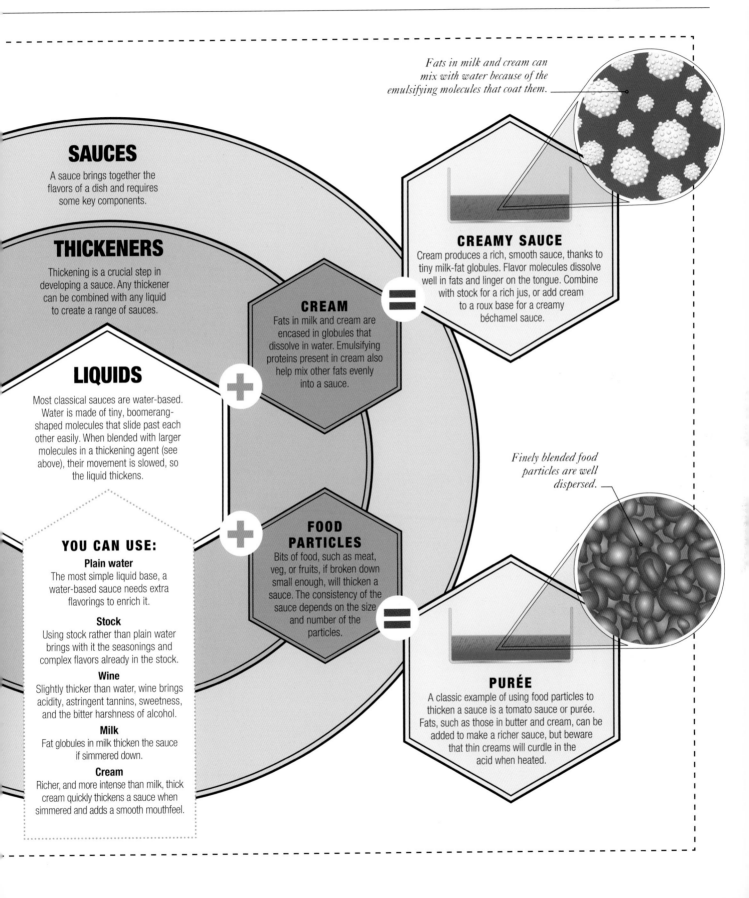

Fats in milk and cream can mix with water because of the emulsifying molecules that coat them.

SAUCES

A sauce brings together the flavors of a dish and requires some key components.

THICKENERS

Thickening is a crucial step in developing a sauce. Any thickener can be combined with any liquid to create a range of sauces.

CREAM

Fats in milk and cream are encased in globules that dissolve in water. Emulsifying proteins present in cream also help mix other fats evenly into a sauce.

=

CREAMY SAUCE

Cream produces a rich, smooth sauce, thanks to tiny milk-fat globules. Flavor molecules dissolve well in fats and linger on the tongue. Combine with stock for a rich jus, or add cream to a roux base for a creamy béchamel sauce.

LIQUIDS

Most classical sauces are water-based. Water is made of tiny, boomerang-shaped molecules that slide past each other easily. When blended with larger molecules in a thickening agent (see above), their movement is slowed, so the liquid thickens.

+

+

FOOD PARTICLES

Bits of food, such as meat, veg, or fruits, if broken down small enough, will thicken a sauce. The consistency of the sauce depends on the size and number of the particles.

Finely blended food particles are well dispersed.

=

YOU CAN USE:

Plain water
The most simple liquid base, a water-based sauce needs extra flavorings to enrich it.

Stock
Using stock rather than plain water brings with it the seasonings and complex flavors already in the stock.

Wine
Slightly thicker than water, wine brings acidity, astringent tannins, sweetness, and the bitter harshness of alcohol.

Milk
Fat globules in milk thicken the sauce if simmered down.

Cream
Richer, and more intense than milk, thick cream quickly thickens a sauce when simmered and adds a smooth mouthfeel.

PURÉE

A classic example of using food particles to thicken a sauce is a tomato sauce or purée. Fats, such as those in butter and cream, can be added to make a richer sauce, but beware that thin creams will curdle in the acid when heated.

Is it worth all the effort to
MAKE MY OWN STOCK?

Ask a classically trained chef what raises a good dish into a phenomenal one and they will tell you it is the stock.

The benefits of making your own stock are undeniable: homemade stock lends dishes a depth of flavor that no powder or cube comes close to. The French chef Auguste Escoffier, who pioneered classical French cooking, insisted that without a good stock prepared from fresh ingredients, food would never be better than distinctly average.

Using and making stocks

A stock is an extraction of flavors from fresh ingredients. In near-boiling water, flavor molecules diffuse out of vegetables and meat as they slowly cook.

There are no absolute rules, although it's best not to salt stock, and keep flavorings simple and subtle so that the stock can be used for a variety of dishes—you can add strong herbs and spices later. A basic meat or vegetable stock forms the foundation of many dishes: it can be thickened with flour into a "roux"; mixed with wine, herbs, and spices; reduced into a concentrated, intense jus; enriched with cream or butter; or bulked into a soup.

WHAT IS BOUILLON?

SIMPLY THE FRENCH WORD FOR "BROTH", BOUILLON HAS BECOME WIDELY USED AS A NAME FOR PREMADE STOCK POWDER.

IN PRACTICE

MAKING CHICKEN STOCK

Chopping ingredients into small pieces speeds flavor release as it increases their surface area, liberating flavor molecules and the gelatin from meat and bones. You can use a pressure cooker in place of a saucepan—it allows water to reach high temperatures without boiling (see p134), speeding flavor extraction and keeping liquid clear.

#1

BROWN THE CHICKEN
Break up one whole chicken carcass into pieces and roast in a preheated oven for 20 minutes at 400°F (200°C). Alternatively, cook the pieces in a little oil in a frying pan over a medium heat until golden-brown. Browning the chicken creates the Maillard reaction (see p16), which will add intensity of flavor to the stock.

#2

ADD VEGETABLES AND AROMATICS
Place the chicken bones in a large pan. Add one diced onion, 2 diced carrots, 2 sticks of celery (chopped), 3 cloves of garlic, ½ tsp whole black peppercorns, and a large handful of aromatic herbs, such as parsley, fresh thyme, or bay leaves. Cover with cold water to about 1in (2.5cm) above the level of the stock ingredients.

#3

HEAT ON THE STOVE
Bring to a boil, then reduce the heat. Simmer gently for at least 1½ hours (ideally 3–4 hours). Skim off scum that rises to the surface. If using a pressure cooker, cook for 30 minutes to 1 hour. Remove the stock from the heat and allow it to cool, then skim off the fat and pour through a fine sieve. Use immediately, store in the fridge for up to 3 days, or freeze for up to 3 months.

Why is it safe to eat
RARE BEEF, BUT NOT CHICKEN OR PORK?

If you enjoy a rare steak, you may wonder why you can't cook other meats in the same way.

Risk of food poisoning affects some meats more than others, and depends on the way an animal is kept, fed, and handled when it is butchered.

Take care with chicken

Fears of eating undercooked chicken are well-founded. Chickens often harbor dangerous bacteria such as *Salmonella* and *Campylobacter*. Most bacteria live on, rather than inside, meat, and come from contact with animal feces. In an industrial setting, carcasses of chickens killed on conveyor lines are often piled together, easily contaminating all parts of the meat with bacteria. Larger animals, such as cows and pigs, are usually handled with more care, so are less likely to be cross-contaminated with infected material; searing the outside should kill any bacteria. Pork, in particular from pigs fed on garbage and other animals, can carry worms that lay their eggs deep inside muscle. However, improved feeding practices mean that most experts believe slightly pink, cooked pork is safe to eat. Cook poultry and pork to minimum temperatures to kill bacteria (see box).

> **OFFICIAL GUIDELINES**
>
> POULTRY SHOULD BE COOKED TO AT LEAST 165°F (74°C) AND PORK TO 145°F (62°C) TO KILL HARMFUL BACTERIA.

Why do so many foods
TASTE LIKE CHICKEN?

Goose, frog, snake, turtle, salamander, pigeon… all taste a bit like chicken! There is a logical explanation.

Red meats taste distinctive to us, but when we try a white meat for the first time, we often compare it to chicken. The clue is in the type of muscle the animal has.

A type of muscle

Chickens don't do a great deal of endurance exercise, so their meat is mostly pale "fast-twitch" muscle, designed for brief, powerful movements, such as flapping. Fast-twitch muscle is soft, lean, and lacks flavor-giving fat, so it tastes bland. Most of the animals that taste like chicken, such as pigeons or frogs, have a similar ratio of paler muscle. In contrast, darker, red "slow-twitch" endurance muscle, found more in red meats, has more fat and distinctive flavor-giving substances, making it easier to tell these meats apart. The flavor molecules in each meat vary between species, but scientists have charted how meat flavors have been inherited. They have found that many of the animals that we eat today (except pork, beef, and venison) descend from one common chicken-flavored ancestor.

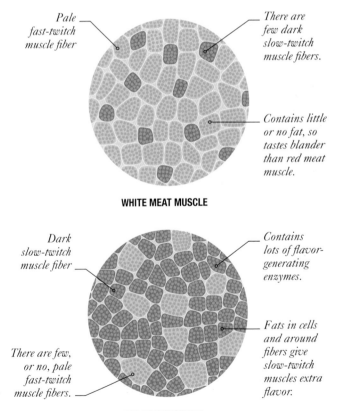

Pale fast-twitch muscle fiber

There are few dark slow-twitch muscle fibers.

Contains little or no fat, so tastes blander than red meat muscle.

WHITE MEAT MUSCLE

Dark slow-twitch muscle fiber

Contains lots of flavor-generating enzymes.

There are few, or no, pale fast-twitch muscle fibers.

Fats in cells and around fibers give slow-twitch muscles extra flavor.

RED MEAT MUSCLE

Muscle types and meat flavor
The two muscle types above show how the composition of muscle in red and white meats affects the appearance and flavor of the meat.

FISH & SEAFOOD

In focus
FISH

If you want to experience a wide variety of flavor sensations, look to the seas. There are about five times more species of animals living underwater than there are mammals on the land.

High in protein and essential nutrients, but low in saturated fat, fish is a nutrient powerhouse. Its subtle flavor profile and delicate texture means it requires careful cooking. Like meat from land-based animals, fish is comprised of muscle, connective tissue, and fat, but its tissues are quite different. Its flesh is mostly muscle, suited for short, powerful bursts of acceleration, and

designed to work in the cool temperatures of the sea and rivers. This means that proteins in fish unfold and coagulate and cook at a lower temperature than land animals. Fish shouldn't be kept in the fridge for as long as meat for similar reasons: the muscle-digesting enzymes in fish thrive at ocean-like temperatures (40°F or 5°C), rapidly spoiling the meat. Putting fish in a container of ice (32°F or 0°C) will slow down these enzymes, making fresh fish last twice as long.

KNOW YOUR FISH

Rich in protein and fats, how relatively lean or fatty a fish is determines how you cook it. Fatty fish such as salmon suit a variety of methods, while leaner white fish and more delicate fish such as trout require gentle cooking methods, such as poaching.

OILY FISH

Salmon
With its oily flesh and meaty texture, salmon works well with a range of cooking methods. Wild salmon is leaner and firmer in texture than farmed salmon.

FAT: HIGH
PROTEIN: MEDIUM

Mackerel
This small fish has a creamy, slightly salty flavor. Sturdy and firm-fleshed, it can be grilled or broiled whole. Store it on ice as it spoils quickly.

FAT: HIGH
PROTEIN: MEDIUM

Tuna
As a warm-blooded, active carnivore, tuna has dense, flavourful meat. However, its flaky flesh dries out rapidly, so thick slices cooked rapidly help keep the silky texture.

FAT: LOW
PROTEIN: HIGH

Eyes
Bright, clear, bulging eyes are a sign of freshness in a fish. If eyes are dull, a fish is past peak freshness. The eyes are edible and are prized in some cuisines.

Gills
These threadlike filaments are the organ that lets fish extract oxygen from water. Gills have a red tinge due to high blood flow, but taste bitter as a result so are always best removed.

Fillets
These are cut from either side of the fish's body, removing the spine. This cut offers the most meat.

Head
Mostly made of bone and connective tissue, which cooks down into gelatin, fish heads add flavor and texture to stocks and stews.

Trout
Closely related to salmon, trout has an earthy flavor and flaky, delicate flesh with moderate fat, so it is best gently baked or steamed.

FAT: MEDIUM
PROTEIN: HIGH

WHITE FISH

Cod
This mild flavored, white-fleshed fish is lean—cod has just 0.3 percent fat. Cook gently and serve with fat-containing foods to add succulence.

FAT: LOW
PROTEIN: MEDIUM

Haddock
Similar to cod, haddock is low in fat and has a high water content of up to 80 percent, so it can be fragile when cooked. Poach it or bake it.

FAT: LOW
PROTEIN: MEDIUM

Monkfish
The tight, meaty white flesh of monkfish tail can withstand the high temperatures used in stir- and pan-frying. The large head is usually discarded.

FAT: LOW
PROTEIN: MEDIUM

Sea bass
This covers a range of species characterized for their thick coat of scales. The slightly sweet, flaky flesh can be baked, broiled, or pan-fried.

FAT: LOW
PROTEIN: MEDIUM

MUSCLE STRUCTURE

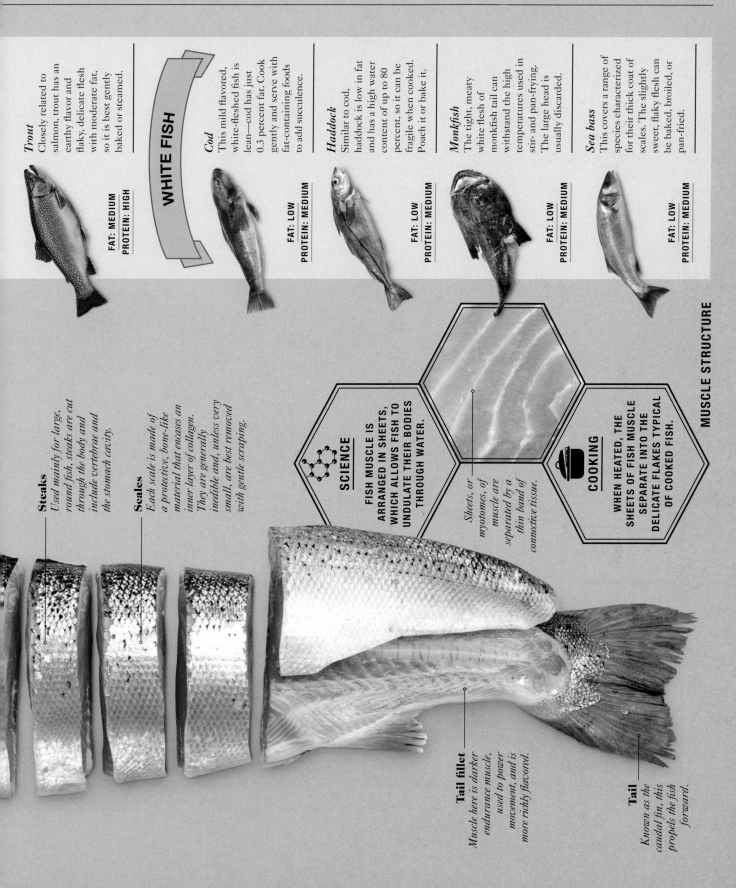

Steaks
Used mainly for large, round fish, steaks are cut through the body and include vertebrae and the stomach cavity.

Scales
Each scale is made of a protective, bone-like material that encases an inner layer of collagen. They are generally inedible and, unless very small, are best removed with gentle scraping.

SCIENCE
FISH MUSCLE IS ARRANGED IN SHEETS, WHICH ALLOWS FISH TO UNDULATE THEIR BODIES THROUGH WATER.

Sheets, or myotomes, of muscle are separated by a thin band of connective tissue.

COOKING
WHEN HEATED, THE SHEETS OF FISH MUSCLE SEPARATE INTO THE DELICATE FLAKES TYPICAL OF COOKED FISH.

Tail fillet
Muscle here is darker endurance muscle, used to power movement, and is more richly flavored.

Tail
Known as the caudal fin, this propels the fish forward.

How do I know if FISH IS FRESH?

Fresh fish has a short shelf life, so knowing how to spot-check for freshness can be useful.

Once a fish dies, its digestive enzymes continue to work and bacteria that is naturally present on the fish start breaking down its flesh. Because bacteria in fish breed well at lower temperatures, and the unsaturated oils turn rancid more rapidly than other animal fats, fish should ideally be eaten within one week of being caught. Use the indicators below to help you identify the freshest fish.

Skin and scales
These will be metallic-looking and bright on fresh fish, rather than dull, and there should be no patchy or broken scales.

Smell
A fresh, slightly briny smell is ideal. Avoid fish that have an unpleasant, or especially strong, fishy aroma.

Eyes
Look for fish with bright, shiny, bulging eyes and avoid those with milky, sunken eyes.

SALMON

Feel
The freshest fish have a firm consistency and are springy to the touch, rather than inelastic, soft, or squishy.

Gills
In fresh fish, the gills are moist, bright red, and clean-looking, rather than dull or slimy.

MYTH BUSTER

—— *Myth* ——
ALL FISH SMELL "FISHY"

—— *Truth* ——
Freshly landed fish actually have a pleasant grassy smell, but after 2–3 days this sweet smell vanishes. In saltwater fish, the foul-smelling odor comes from the breakdown of urea and trimethylamine oxide (TAMO). Freshwater fish don't have TAMO, but start to smell over time as bacteria produce rancid-smelling gases. So a freshly caught fish doesn't smell "fishy," but fishy smells evolve the less fresh it becomes.

Why is fish called "BRAIN FOOD"?

Our prehuman ancestors started fishing around two million years ago. Today, researchers believe that fish nutrients fuelled our rapid brain growth.

Fish is a rich source of iodine and iron, essential minerals for healthy brain development in childhood. In addition to these brain-fortifying minerals, the oils in fish also contain essential omega-3 fats, which act as building blocks for the fatty sheaths that surround nerve cells, coating the nerves and allowing them to function properly. Oily fish, such as salmon, anchovies, sardines, mackerel, trout, and tuna, have the most plentiful supply of brain-fortifying omega-3 fats.

The way in which fish is prepared or cooked can affect its levels of essential fats. Canning fish destroys a large proportion of omega-3s, and cooking at high temperatures, for example, frying, can break down, or oxidize, omega-3s. Delicate cooking methods, such as baking and steaming, are best for preserving these oils.

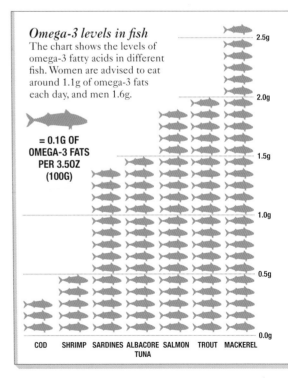

Omega-3 levels in fish
The chart shows the levels of omega-3 fatty acids in different fish. Women are advised to eat around 1.1g of omega-3 fats each day, and men 1.6g.

= 0.1G OF OMEGA-3 FATS PER 3.5OZ (100G)

							2.5g
							2.0g
							1.5g
							1.0g
							0.5g
COD	SHRIMP	SARDINES	ALBACORE TUNA	SALMON	TROUT	MACKEREL	0.0g

FISH & SEAFOOD

In focus FISH

If you want to experience a wide variety of flavor sensations, look to the seas. There are about five times more species of animals living underwater than there are mammals on the land.

High in protein and essential nutrients, but low in saturated fat, fish is a nutrient powerhouse. Its subtle flavor profile and delicate texture means it requires careful cooking. Like meat from land-based animals, fish is comprised of muscle, connective tissue, and fat, but its tissues are quite different. Its flesh is mostly muscle, suited for short, powerful bursts of acceleration, and

designed to work in the cool temperatures of the sea and rivers. This means that proteins in fish unfold and coagulate and cook at a lower temperature than land animals. Fish shouldn't be kept in the fridge for as long as meat for similar reasons: the muscle-digesting enzymes in fish thrive at ocean-like temperatures (40°F or 5°C), rapidly spoiling the meat. Putting fish in a container of ice (32°F or 0°C) will slow down these enzymes, making fresh fish last twice as long.

KNOW YOUR FISH

Rich in protein and fats, how relatively lean or fatty a fish is determines how you cook it. Fatty fish such as salmon suit a variety of methods, while leaner white fish and more delicate fish such as trout require gentle cooking methods, such as poaching.

OILY FISH

Salmon
With its oily flesh and meaty texture, salmon works well with a range of cooking methods. Wild salmon is leaner and firmer in texture than farmed salmon.

FAT: HIGH
PROTEIN: MEDIUM

Mackerel
This small fish has a creamy, slightly salty flavor. Sturdy and firm-fleshed, it can be grilled or broiled whole. Store it on ice as it spoils quickly.

FAT: HIGH
PROTEIN: MEDIUM

Tuna
As a warm-blooded, active carnivore, tuna has dense, flavourful meat. However, its flaky flesh dries out rapidly, so thick slices cooked rapidly help keep the silky texture.

FAT: LOW
PROTEIN: HIGH

Head
Mostly made of bone and connective tissue, which cooks down into gelatin, fish heads add flavor and texture to stocks and stews.

Eyes
Bright, clear, bulging eyes are a sign of freshness in a fish. If eyes are dull, a fish is past peak freshness. The eyes are edible and are prized in some cuisines.

Gills
These threadlike filaments are the organ that lets fish extract oxygen from water. Gills have a red tinge due to high blood flow, but taste bitter as a result so are always best removed.

Fillets
These are cut from either side of the fish's body, removing the spine. This cut offers the most meat.

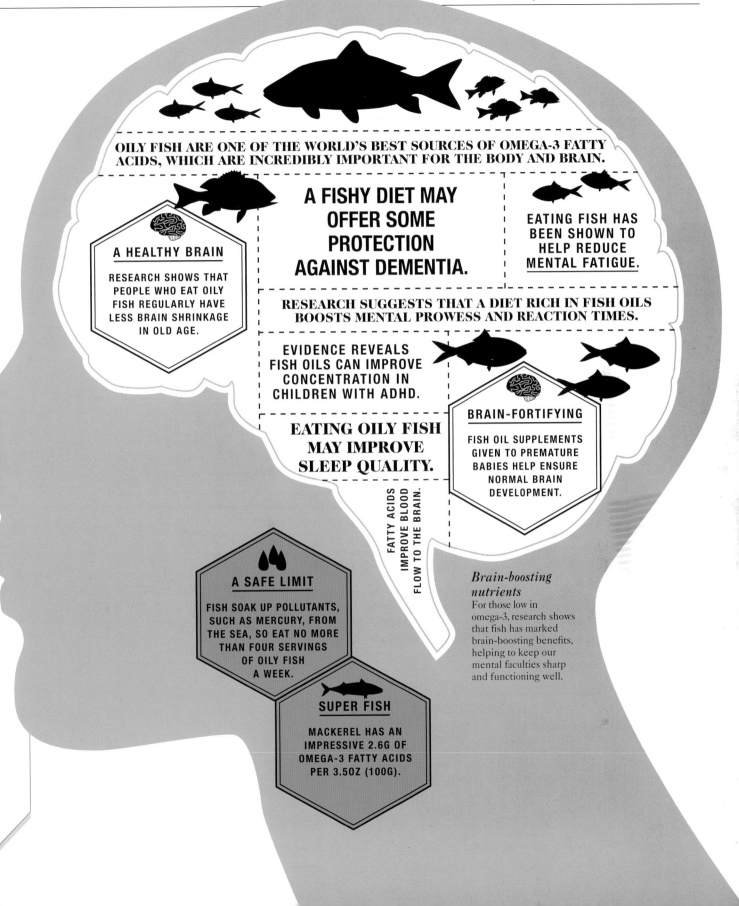

OILY FISH ARE ONE OF THE WORLD'S BEST SOURCES OF OMEGA-3 FATTY ACIDS, WHICH ARE INCREDIBLY IMPORTANT FOR THE BODY AND BRAIN.

A FISHY DIET MAY OFFER SOME PROTECTION AGAINST DEMENTIA.

A HEALTHY BRAIN

RESEARCH SHOWS THAT PEOPLE WHO EAT OILY FISH REGULARLY HAVE LESS BRAIN SHRINKAGE IN OLD AGE.

EATING FISH HAS BEEN SHOWN TO HELP REDUCE MENTAL FATIGUE.

RESEARCH SUGGESTS THAT A DIET RICH IN FISH OILS BOOSTS MENTAL PROWESS AND REACTION TIMES.

EVIDENCE REVEALS FISH OILS CAN IMPROVE CONCENTRATION IN CHILDREN WITH ADHD.

EATING OILY FISH MAY IMPROVE SLEEP QUALITY.

BRAIN-FORTIFYING

FISH OIL SUPPLEMENTS GIVEN TO PREMATURE BABIES HELP ENSURE NORMAL BRAIN DEVELOPMENT.

FATTY ACIDS IMPROVE BLOOD FLOW TO THE BRAIN.

A SAFE LIMIT

FISH SOAK UP POLLUTANTS, SUCH AS MERCURY, FROM THE SEA, SO EAT NO MORE THAN FOUR SERVINGS OF OILY FISH A WEEK.

SUPER FISH

MACKEREL HAS AN IMPRESSIVE 2.6G OF OMEGA-3 FATTY ACIDS PER 3.5OZ (100G).

Brain-boosting nutrients

For those low in omega-3, research shows that fish has marked brain-boosting benefits, helping to keep our mental faculties sharp and functioning well.

Why does salmon come in
VARYING SHADES OF ORANGE?

It's a natural assumption that the color of a salmon is an indicator of its quality.

If you've ever eaten too many carrots, you'll appreciate how the color of the food you eat can affect the color of your skin. The pigment in carrots—a substance called carotene—can turn skin orange. In just the same way, a natural pigment, astaxanthin, in the food that salmon eat, which also comes from the carotene family, turns their flesh orange (see below).

Shades of orange

The color of wild salmon can vary, depending on the food that they are able to hunt. Some types of King Salmon are an exception as these are unable to process the red astaxanthin pigment, giving them unusally pale flesh compared to other wild salmon.

Farmed salmon are consistently brighter and more orange than their wild counterparts. Although farmed salmon don't have the chance to hunt shellfish, fish farmers add astaxanthin to their pellet feed, to give them a striking pink-orange glow. This is intended to appeal to consumers, where the commonly held belief is that the redder the salmon, the fresher, better tasting, and higher quality the fish will be. The delicious pale-fleshed King salmon disproves this belief.

A COMMON COLOR

THE PIGMENT ASTAXANTHIN, WHICH GIVES SHELLFISH THEIR ORANGE COLOR, ALSO GIVES FLAMINGOS THEIR PINK PLUMAGE.

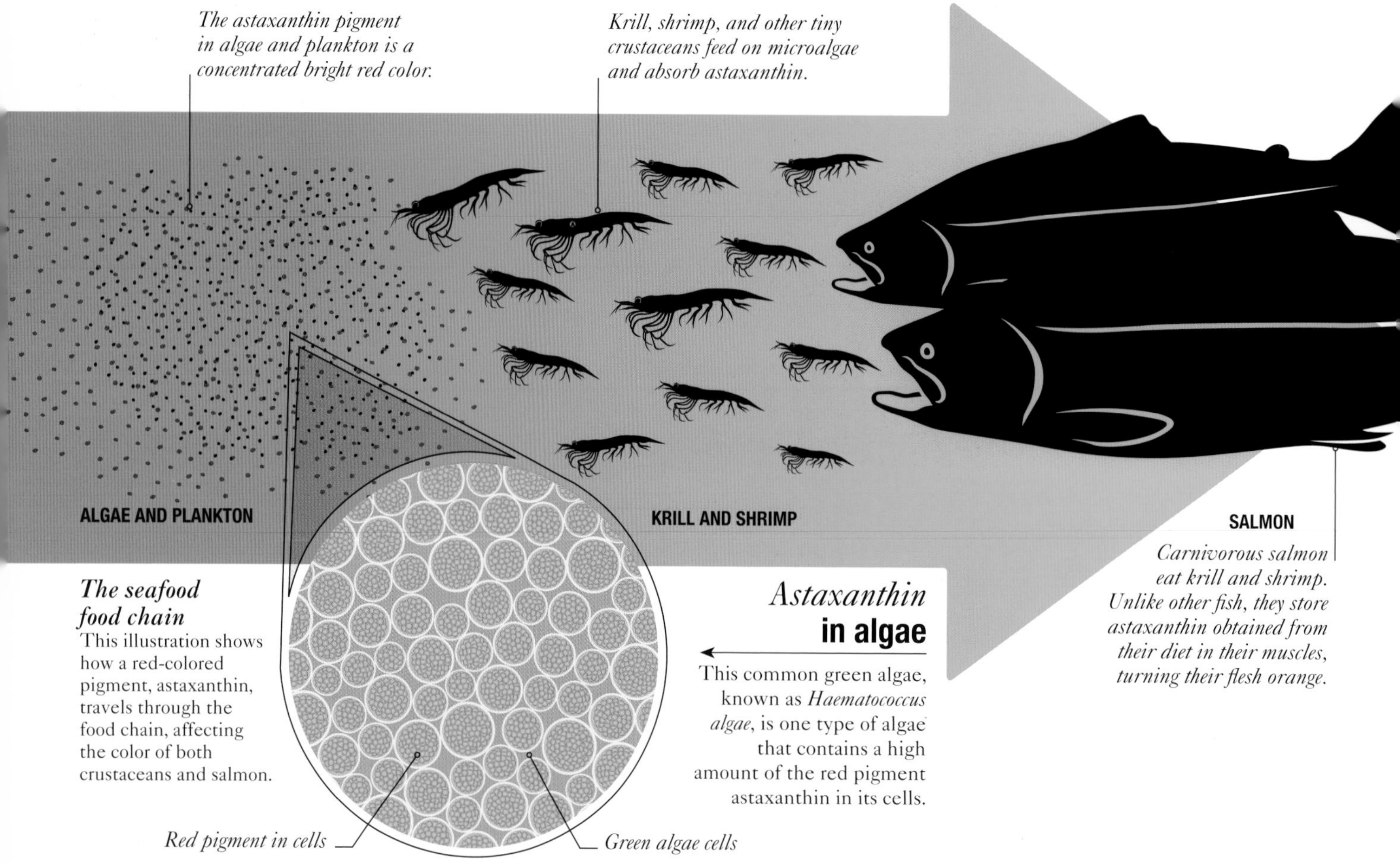

The astaxanthin pigment in algae and plankton is a concentrated bright red color.

Krill, shrimp, and other tiny crustaceans feed on microalgae and absorb astaxanthin.

ALGAE AND PLANKTON

KRILL AND SHRIMP

SALMON

Carnivorous salmon eat krill and shrimp. Unlike other fish, they store astaxanthin obtained from their diet in their muscles, turning their flesh orange.

The seafood food chain
This illustration shows how a red-colored pigment, astaxanthin, travels through the food chain, affecting the color of both crustaceans and salmon.

Astaxanthin **in algae**

This common green algae, known as *Haematococcus algae*, is one type of algae that contains a high amount of the red pigment astaxanthin in its cells.

Red pigment in cells

Green algae cells

Is farmed fish
AS GOOD AS WILD?

Feeding practices, lifestyle, and slaughter conditions all need to be considered when assessing fish.

While rearing cattle, sheep, pigs, and chicken on farms seems quite normal, there's a tendency to feel that breeding fish in a pen is less natural. Fish are one of the last major foods that are mostly caught from the wild, and wild fish are believed to be tastier, more natural, and healthier compared to fish that do not have free access to the seas. However, while there are small differences in taste and texture (see below), these can be hard to discern. Stories of farmed fish being given antibiotics, doused in

CHANGING TIDES

BY 2030, NEARLY TWO-THIRDS OF ALL SEAFOOD WILL BE FARMED RATHER THAN CAUGHT IN THE WILD.

pesticides, and fed artificial dyes to make their flesh brighter (see opposite) raise concerns, but many salmon farms are leading the way in raising standards. In terms of ethical practices, wild salmon has drawbacks, with other fish sometimes being injured and killed in nets, and sustainability is uncertain. Looking for "responsibly sourced" wild fish and purchasing farmed fish that are certified as meeting the highest standards can help to counter concerns and ensure a quality purchase.

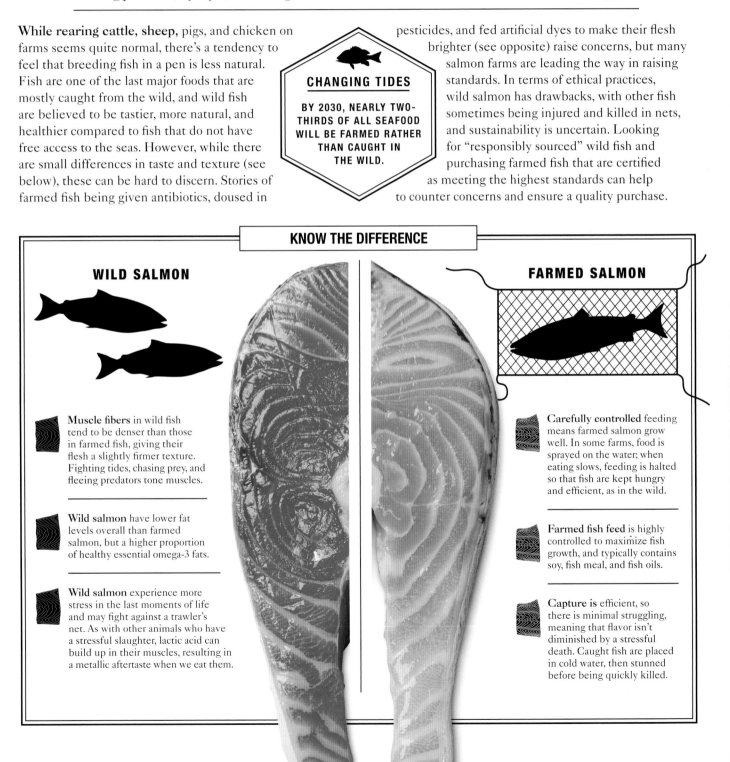

KNOW THE DIFFERENCE

WILD SALMON

Muscle fibers in wild fish tend to be denser than those in farmed fish, giving their flesh a slightly firmer texture. Fighting tides, chasing prey, and fleeing predators tone muscles.

Wild salmon have lower fat levels overall than farmed salmon, but a higher proportion of healthy essential omega-3 fats.

Wild salmon experience more stress in the last moments of life and may fight against a trawler's net. As with other animals who have a stressful slaughter, lactic acid can build up in their muscles, resulting in a metallic aftertaste when we eat them.

FARMED SALMON

Carefully controlled feeding means farmed salmon grow well. In some farms, food is sprayed on the water; when eating slows, feeding is halted so that fish are kept hungry and efficient, as in the wild.

Farmed fish feed is highly controlled to maximize fish growth, and typically contains soy, fish meal, and fish oils.

Capture is efficient, so there is minimal struggling, meaning that flavor isn't diminished by a stressful death. Caught fish are placed in cold water, then stunned before being quickly killed.

Is it better to buy shrimp
WITH THEIR HEADS ON?

Shrimp are the most widely eaten seafood in the world, and are available to buy in many different forms.

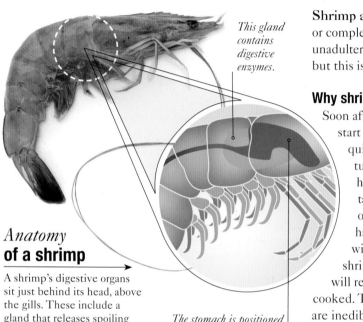

This gland contains digestive enzymes.

Anatomy of a shrimp

A shrimp's digestive organs sit just behind its head, above the gills. These include a gland that releases spoiling enzymes after death.

The stomach is positioned at the base of the head.

Shrimp are sold whole, with the head removed, the shell split, or completely peeled. Normally, we would assume that a whole, unadulterated fish offers the fullest, freshest flavor experience, but this is not necessarily the case with shrimp.

Why shrimp heads affect taste

Soon after death, substances from a shrimp's digestive system start to leak out into its flesh. Enzymes in these juices quickly begin to eat away at the flesh, causing it to turn mushy. Most of these enzymes come from the hepatopancreas, a small gland in the base of the head, so taking off the head as soon as possible slows the degradation of the shrimp. Unless they are very fresh, shrimp that have had their heads removed before shipping to the store will have the best meat. If you are eating freshly caught shrimp, however, those with their heads on will retain more moisture and flavor when cooked. The shells and most of the head are inedible, but can be used to make a flavorful stock.

Is it better to buy shrimp
RAW OR PRECOOKED, FRESH OR FROZEN?

When shrimp are caught, whether in the ocean or on a shrimp farm, time is of the essence—they can spoil within just a few hours.

Because shrimp spoil quickly (see above), they are often processed in the moments after being caught. They may be rapidly frozen at sea, chilled on ice for processing on shore, or cooked at sea by briskly boiling them in seawater. Shrimp that are cooked on shore, or are harvested from shrimp farms, are simmered more gently, but nevertheless tend to be overdone and dry. Unless your shrimp are freshly caught, choose frozen, shell-on shrimp with the head off for the best flavor and freshness. Shrimp that are "individually quick frozen" (IQF) are the best quality.

−4°F (−20°C) is the **maximum** temperature at which shrimp are **rapidly frozen** after catch.

SHRIMP CURRY

" Called "insects of the sea" because of their **segmented body** and "exoskeleton" shell, shrimp are the **baby-sized relatives** of lobsters and crabs. They are the most **widely eaten** seafood in the world. "

Why do we EAT OYSTERS RAW?

Cooking breaks down proteins in animal flesh, but this is a bad thing when it comes to molluscs, such as oysters.

The flavor of most foods improves with cooking: proteins break down into their component parts (amino acids) to stimulate the taste buds, starches break down into sweeter sugars, tough fibers weaken, textures firm, and excess moisture is driven off. This is not true for shellfish such as oysters and razor clams; their flavor ebbs away with each minute of cooking.

Molluscs, unlike most fish (see pp66–7), use flavor-containing amino acids, especially glutamate, to help them survive the dehydrating effects of the salty sea. Glutamate stimulates the umami taste receptors on the tongue (see pp14–15), giving them a savory, meaty flavor. Cooking oysters

and clams traps these tasty molecules in the tangle of cooking, coagulating muscle proteins, masking them from the taste buds. The only way to release them again would be by cooking for long enough to break apart the proteins. But by that time, the shellfish would have the consistency of rubber.

Common oysters

Each oyster species has a specific flavor profile, but this can vary depending on where they were farmed. The species below are the most commonly available to buy.

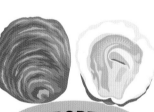

ATLANTIC

A commonly cultivated variety in the US, Atlantic oysters are the only species native to the East Coast of North America. They have a distinctive, teardrop-shaped shell.

Taste
They have a salty, clean flavor with savory and mineral notes. Crisp texture.

EUROPEAN

Native to Europe and distinguished by their flat, shallow shape, numbers have depleted in natural breeding grounds over the 19th and 20th centuries. Hard to find outside Europe.

Taste
They have a mild, slightly metallic flavor, and are almost crunchy in texture.

KUMAMOTO

These oysters originate in Japan, but are now popular around the world. They are smaller than most other oysters, and take longer to reach maturity. Their shells are deep and fluted.

Taste
Milder than other varieties, they have melon aromas and a soft texture.

PACIFIC

Now cultivated around the world, Pacific oysters are native to the Asian Pacific. They were introduced to the US and then Europe as native stocks in these depleted areas.

Taste
Flavor varies, but Pacific oysters are generally less salty than other species.

When is the best
SEASON FOR OYSTERS?

Many people argue that oysters should not be eaten in summer, and this may have once been prudent advice.

There is an adage that oysters should not be eaten during the summer months (May until August). This saying may be rooted in a desire to avoid food poisoning. Algae are in their most vigorous growth during summer, flooding the water with toxins that can cause food poisoning if ingested—summer "red tides" are when large numbers of algal blooms discolor coastal waters.

Another traditional reason to avoid oysters in summer is because it is their breeding season. During this part of the year, oysters expend all of their energy reserves producing eggs, making them small, soft, and flimsy, and dramatically reducing their flavor.

Oyster farming

Thankfully, this advice can now be cast out to sea. Most oysters purchased in stores today are farmed oysters that come from well-maintained waters. Commercial farms will also select oyster breeds that have a very short spawning period—or are sterilized so that they never spawn. Oysters can now be savored year round—regardless of whether or not you decide to cook them.

> "*While* cooking improves the flavor of most foods, *this is not true for* oysters and clams."

Eating raw safely

Raw oysters and clams are far from risk-free. Molluscs, such as oysters and clams, are filter feeders, drawing in water and filtering it for plankton and algae. This process can also trap harmful microbes, creating a small, infectious cesspool.

Many of these microbes come from sewage contamination, but most store-bought oysters are from protected, inland waters that are monitored for bacteria and harmful chemicals. Oysters are also "purged" before sale—kept in a tank of clean saltwater so they can naturally cleanse themselves.

To avoid risk, eat molluscs from a reputable source. They should be stored very cold (ideally on ice) and eaten promptly. Avoid eating raw fish if you have immune system problems.

MYTH BUSTER

— *Myth* —
OYSTERS ARE AN APHRODISIAC

— *Truth* —
Those looking to explain this myth often point to the high zinc content of oysters, a mineral used to create the key sex-drive hormone, testosterone. By this logic, oysters may help the zinc deficient, but no more than any other zinc-rich foods. There are two other substances in oysters rarely found in other foods that help create sex hormones: aspartic acid and NMDA. However, experiments on mice using these substances have been inconclusive, and, in any case, an excess of zinc could dampen libido by causing a surge in the "hormone of satisfaction", prolactin.

How it works
A hot frying pan, glazed with oil, transfers heat quickly and evenly into food. High temperatures create a crisp, browned exterior.

Best for
Fish fillets; thin cuts of meat, such as steak, pork chops, or chicken breasts; potatoes.

What to consider
Timing is key. As heat travels through food slowly, the outside can easily burn before the center cooks.

The process of
PAN-FRYING

Heating food in a frying pan glazed with a little oil is one of the simplest and most effective ways to cook meat or fish—but how does it work?

Frying is great for cooking flavorful food quickly. Liquid fats heat up twice as quickly as water and reach higher temperatures. These high heats let food develop a crisp, aromatic crust via the Maillard reaction (see pp16–17). Oils lubricate food and let flavor molecules from food seep across the pan, while adding their own buttery or fresh notes. This diagram puts a spotlight on the process to help you fry food to perfection.

A THICKER CUT

AS HEAT TRAVELS SLOWLY THROUGH MEAT AND FISH, FILLETS THICKER THAN 1½IN (4CM) SHOULD BE FINISHED IN THE OVEN.

75%
hotter cooking temperatures are used for **pan-frying** compared to **boiling**.

SPEEDY TECHNIQUE

OIL REACHES HIGHER TEMPERATURES THAN THE BOILING POINT OF WATER, SO PAN-FRYING IS A QUICK COOKING METHOD.

OIL THE PAN
Add at least 1 tbsp sunflower oil or other oil or fat with a high smoke point (see pp192–193) to the pan. Oil transfers heat to the food and prevents it from directly bonding with the metal of the frying pan. Heat until the oil begins to shimmer.

#2

PLACE FOOD IN THE PAN
Add the food to the pan. It should sizzle right away, as surface moisture evaporates from the food, indicating the oil is above 212°F (100°C). For an aromatic crust, water must be driven off quickly so that food cooks above 284°F (140°C).

#3

Do not overcrowd the pan; otherwise the temperature of the pan will drop and the fish will steam in its own moisture rather than fry.

TURN ON THE HEAT
Place a heavy-bottomed frying pan over medium-high heat, and heat for at least 1 minute without oil to allow the metal to warm up.

#1

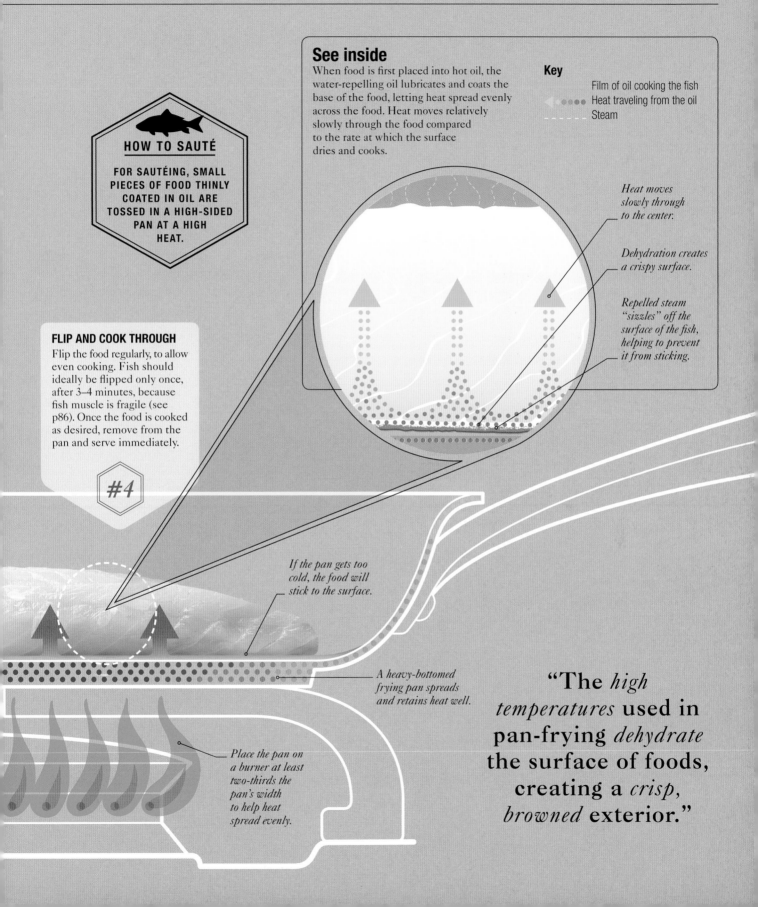

HOW TO SAUTÉ

FOR SAUTÉING, SMALL PIECES OF FOOD THINLY COATED IN OIL ARE TOSSED IN A HIGH-SIDED PAN AT A HIGH HEAT.

See inside

When food is first placed into hot oil, the water-repelling oil lubricates and coats the base of the food, letting heat spread evenly across the food. Heat moves relatively slowly through the food compared to the rate at which the surface dries and cooks.

Key

Film of oil cooking the fish
Heat traveling from the oil
Steam

Heat moves slowly through to the center.

Dehydration creates a crispy surface.

Repelled steam "sizzles" off the surface of the fish, helping to prevent it from sticking.

FLIP AND COOK THROUGH

Flip the food regularly, to allow even cooking. Fish should ideally be flipped only once, after 3–4 minutes, because fish muscle is fragile (see p86). Once the food is cooked as desired, remove from the pan and serve immediately.

#4

If the pan gets too cold, the food will stick to the surface.

A heavy-bottomed frying pan spreads and retains heat well.

Place the pan on a burner at least two-thirds the pan's width to help heat spread evenly.

"The *high temperatures* used in pan-frying *dehydrate* the surface of foods, creating a *crisp*, *browned* exterior."

How can I
PRESERVE FISH AT HOME?

Curing is one of the oldest methods of preserving fish—and it's simple to achieve in your own kitchen.

The best fish is tender and moist, but if we don't have a freezer and want to save fresh fish for eating another day by refrigerating it, the moisture that gives it a smooth mouthfeel soon turns the flesh into a damp breeding ground for bacteria. Before refrigerators, salting and drying seafood was the norm for keeping microbes at bay. Norwegian *tørrfisk* (stockfish) keeps this historical tradition alive today: whole, gutted cod are simply hung on racks and left out to dry. This method is impractical for the home cook, as it requires outdoor drying space, takes months to complete, and can be very smelly. Preserving fish with salt is considerably faster than air drying and is easy to do at home. Covering fish in a blanket of salt forces the protein molecules in the flesh to unravel, just as if they had been cooked. Salt slowly seeps in as moisture is drawn out, resulting in firm, flavorful fish. This method is known as dry curing. Including sugar in the curing mix adds sweetness and also helps preserve the fish. You can also wet-cure fish by immersing them in a densely salted solution, which retains more moisture. A wet cure is often used with smaller fish or with fish that are going to be smoked.

TEXTURE
CURED FISH HAS A FIRM, DRY TEXTURE; HOME-CURED SALMON HAS A TEXTURE REMINISCENT OF SMOKED SALMON.

IN PRACTICE

HOW TO DRY-CURE SALMON
Choose the freshest fish for curing—buy sushi-grade fish, or purchase your fillet from a reputable source and freeze it for 24 hours before defrosting to kill any parasites that are present. To add extra flavor to the outside of the fish, include citrus zest, peppercorns, herbs, or toasted spices in the curing mix and put in a food processor to combine.

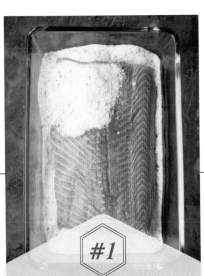

#1

PREPARE THE CURING MIX
Combine 1lb 2oz (500g) fine salt and 1lb 2oz (500g) extra-fine sugar to make a curing mix. Cover the base of a flat shallow dish with half the curing mix. Place one clean, dry, 1lb 9oz (700g) skinned salmon fillet in the dish, and cover it with the remaining curing mix.

#2

MAXIMIZE CONTACT WITH SALT
Cover the dish with plastic wrap and place a heavy object on top of the fish to flatten it. This presses the fish down into the curing mix and helps create a firm texture. Leave to cure in the fridge—allow 24 hours of curing for each 1in (2.5cm) thickness of fish.

#3

CHECK THE CURE
Uncover the fish and check its texture—it should feel firm. If it is still mushy, recover the fish with the curing mix and plastic wrap and weight it before returning to the fridge for 24 hours. Once ready, rinse the fish and pat it dry. Refrigerate and eat within 3 days.

What happens when you
SALT-BAKE FISH?

This ancient cooking technique is simpler than it looks.

Of all the ways to cook fish, covering it in salt before baking seems one of the most extravagant. A whole fish, such as a sea bass, sea bream, or snapper, is seasoned before being encased in salt moistened with egg white, then baked. The salty, golden-brown shell is cracked open to reveal a perfectly cooked fish.

How it works

The salt covering acts very much like pastry, parchment, or foil covering, preventing water from escaping. The fish steams in its own moisture, rather than being cooked by the hot, dry oven air. Egg white proteins solidify as they cook, which helps hold the salt shell around the fish during baking. As salt diffuses into fish very slowly, very little penetrates the flesh in the time it takes to cook—this means that it tastes similar to other forms of baked fish.

400°F
(200°C) is the **optimum temperature** for **salt baking** fish.

SALT BAKING ORIGINS

THE EARLIEST RECORDS OF SALT BAKING ARE FOUND IN TUNISIA IN THE 4TH CENTURY BCE.

Serving cured fish
Acids released during the curing process give fish an intense tangy taste, so it is best served in thin slices. You may want to discard the saltier outer layer.

Is it better to buy fresh or FROZEN FISH?

Freezing fish halts the growth of bacteria and microbes, and muscle-digesting enzymes in fish are stalled.

Fragile fish oils quickly turn rancid and natural bacteria that coat them breed well in the fridge (see p68).

Fish can be frozen with more success than other meats as their flexible muscle membranes suffer less damage from sharp ice crystals. If "flash frozen" (see below), ice crystal damage is negligible, and texture and taste are almost identical to a fresh fish. But low-powered home freezing will damage delicate fish proteins.

So, if fish has been caught very recently and kept on ice, fresh is best, otherwise buy it prefrozen.

KNOW THE DIFFERENCE

Flash-freezing fish
Industrial blast freezers freeze fish rapidly to limit ice crystal formation.

⚡ **Freezing often starts** on board ships to halt spoilage, with fish cooled to around −22°F (−30°C). Once on shore, industrial freezer chambers blast fish with −40°F (−40°C) air to finish freezing rapidly.

Home freezing fish
Low-powered home freezers freeze slowly, allowing ice crystals to form.

❄ **The liquid in fish** is a salty mix of proteins and minerals. The salt lowers the freezing point, which slows home freezing even further, increasing damage to muscle proteins from slowly expanding ice crystals.

Can I cook fish FROM FROZEN?

Cooking from frozen increases cooking time, but has benefits, too.

Cooking smaller fish from frozen works perfectly well. Large cuts of fish, and whole fish, run the risk of being uncooked in the center and burnt on the outside, so should be thawed before cooking.

Thin- to medium-thickness fillets cooked from frozen can rival fresh fish in taste and texture, and may even surpass them if a crispy skin is called for.

Ice crystals melt slowly in fish, increasing cooking time, but this delay can help to achieve crisp skin without the center overcooking.

If you do thaw fish, do this either on a rack in the fridge with a drip tray beneath, or put fish in a sealed bag in a bowl of icy water. Water speeds thawing, and keeping it very cold helps prevent bacteria from breeding.

FLAVOR TRANSFER

FLAVOR MOLECULES FROM PARCHMENT-BAKED FISH SEEP OUT INTO THE LIQUID BROTH AND CAN BE KEPT FOR A SAUCE BASE.

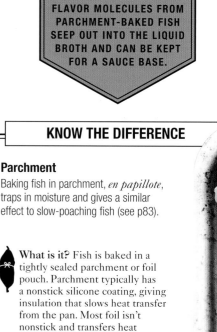

KNOW THE DIFFERENCE

Parchment
Baking fish in parchment, *en papillote*, traps in moisture and gives a similar effect to slow-poaching fish (see p83).

🎀 **What is it?** Fish is baked in a tightly sealed parchment or foil pouch. Parchment typically has a nonstick silicone coating, giving insulation that slows heat transfer from the pan. Most foil isn't nonstick and transfers heat more rapidly.

🎀 **Best for:** Ideal for cooking fillets. Herbs, spices, and vegetables can be added to suffuse the outer layers.

Uncovered
As with oven roasting meats, the outer layers of fish baked without a covering can dry, but this can be a good method for whole fish.

■ **How the fish cooks:** Fish is baked in the oven without a covering, with added oils and flavorings. Cooking is slow and the outer layers dry as heat moves into the center.

■ **Best for:** This is ideal for whole fish. Although the outer layers of the fish dry, as the surface temperature soars, the skin is crisped and browned while the center cooks gently.

Should I bake fish
IN PARCHMENT OR UNCOVERED?

Different methods for baking fish can have very different results.

The two main ways to bake fish have different results, so deciding on a method (see below) depends on your desired result. Fish cooked in parchment paper, known as *"en papillote,"* is an impressive dish to serve: a paper package is brought to the table and cut open, revealing a feast of seafood amidst a burst of aromatic steam. It's a showy dish, yet remarkably simple: fish is baked in parchment paper so that it cooks in its own juices. Foil can be substituted for parchment with a similar result; but, unlike parchment, foil isn't usually nonstick and heat travels through the metal quickly, so any part of the fish that isn't oiled may stick to the foil. Cooking fish in parchment produces succulent flesh and is an effective way to infuse fish with flavors.

Whole fish can also be baked uncovered to excellent effect as the high heat crisps the fish skin at 284ºF (140ºC) while the center of the fish cooks gently, retaining moisture.

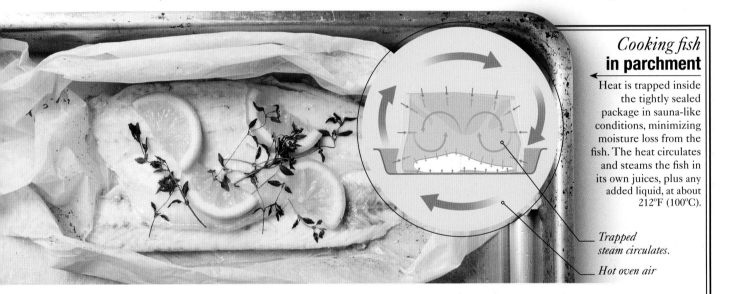

Cooking fish **in parchment**

Heat is trapped inside the tightly sealed package in sauna-like conditions, minimizing moisture loss from the fish. The heat circulates and steams the fish in its own juices, plus any added liquid, at about 212ºF (100ºC).

Trapped steam circulates.

Hot oven air

Cooking fish **uncovered**

The hot oven air doesn't transfer heat efficiently throughout the fish. The surface layers gradually dry out as moisture leaves the top layers and heat inches slowly toward the center of the fish.

Moisture escapes.

Heat slowly travels into the fish.

How can I keep fish moist
WITH DIFFERENT COOKING METHODS?

The makeup of fish is geared toward survival in cool waters; with delicate muscles and internal chemistry suited to colder climes, care needs to be taken not to overcook fish.

Many cooks find fish unforgiving because they don't realize how quickly its muscle proteins unravel and coagulate during cooking. In fish, this happens at 104–122°F (40–50°C), compared to 122–140°F (50–60°C) in red meat. Above this heat, muscle cells and connective tissue shrink, expelling fluid and turning the flesh dry and fibrous.

Achieving an "even" cook

The surface of fish cooks before the inside, the difference in temperature being termed a "temperature gradient," which is greater when cooking at high heats. When removed from the heat, residual heat in the fish goes on moving inwards, cooking the fish as it goes. This is known as carryover cooking and is more dramatic in high-heat gradients, for example, with pan-frying, so it's best to take fish out of a hot pan just before you think it's done. Slower cooking methods, such as poaching and sous vide, achieve more evenly cooked fish. The chart, right, uses three different cooking methods: sous vide, pan-fried, and poaching, to show how fish cooks with different heat gradients.

There are several ways to check if fish is done: flesh will be firm and not shiny, a bone can be pulled out without tugging, or a digital thermometer reads 140°F (60°C) in the centre.

A USEFUL CUT
TO HELP A TAPERING PIECE OF FISH COOK EVENLY, SCORE IT EVERY .4–.8IN IN THE THICKER PARTS.

"Naturally *delicate*, fish need to be *cooked* with care."

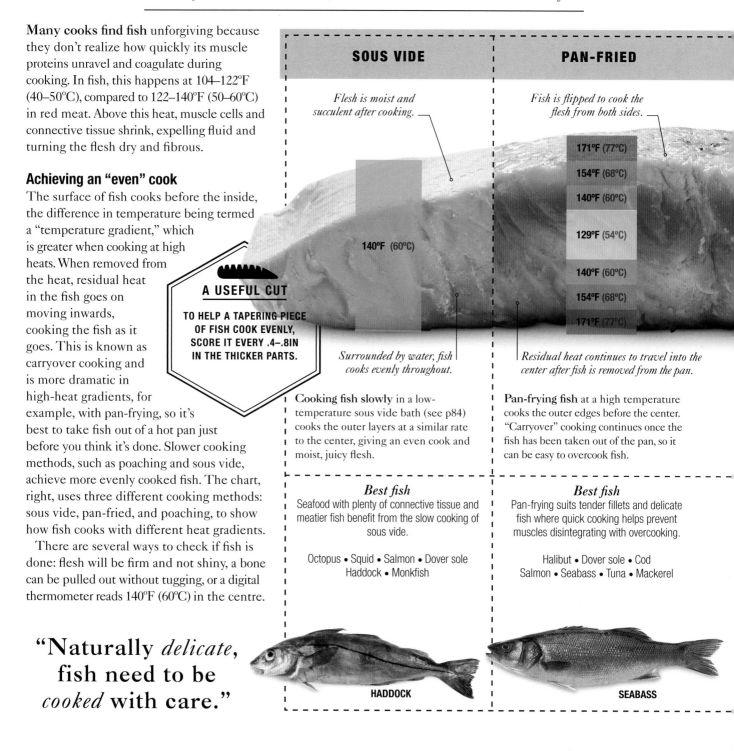

SOUS VIDE

Flesh is moist and succulent after cooking.

140°F (60°C)

Surrounded by water, fish cooks evenly throughout.

Cooking fish slowly in a low-temperature sous vide bath (see p84) cooks the outer layers at a similar rate to the center, giving an even cook and moist, juicy flesh.

Best fish
Seafood with plenty of connective tissue and meatier fish benefit from the slow cooking of sous vide.

Octopus • Squid • Salmon • Dover sole
Haddock • Monkfish

HADDOCK

PAN-FRIED

Fish is flipped to cook the flesh from both sides.

171°F (77°C)
154°F (68°C)
140°F (60°C)
129°F (54°C)
140°F (60°C)
154°F (68°C)
171°F (77°C)

Residual heat continues to travel into the center after fish is removed from the pan.

Pan-frying fish at a high temperature cooks the outer edges before the center. "Carryover" cooking continues once the fish has been taken out of the pan, so it can be easy to overcook fish.

Best fish
Pan-frying suits tender fillets and delicate fish where quick cooking helps prevent muscles disintegrating with overcooking.

Halibut • Dover sole • Cod
Salmon • Seabass • Tuna • Mackerel

SEABASS

Can fish turn soggy if
POACHED SLOWLY?

Poached fish can be a delicate, flavorful dish; you should understand the anatomy of fish muscle in order to improve your poaching technique.

A delicate meat, fish requires careful cooking (see left). Poaching offers the cook an easy, fuss-free way to cook fish slowly and steadily. However, a common worry with poaching is that fish will become mushy and waterlogged if left sitting in water for a long period of time. In fact, fish muscle is unable to absorb much liquid at all because its cells are already saturated with water and so have little space to absorb more liquid from the poaching water. Poaching does help to keep fish moist because water cannot evaporate from the surface of the fish. A common mistake when poaching is to bring the water to a boil. At a rolling boil, timing becomes difficult and the outside layers of the fish can overcook and flake off in the turbulent water.

70%
of the weight of **fish muscle** cells is water, so cells are unable to absorb more.

Flavor infusion
Ingredients such as vegetables, lemon, and herbs can be added to the poaching water to infuse extra flavor into the fish. However, these flavorings don't carry especially well in water and won't penetrate far into the fish, so the results can be disappointing. Poaching in fish stock, vegetable stock, or wine rather than plain water is a slightly more effective way to to flavor the surface.

POACHED

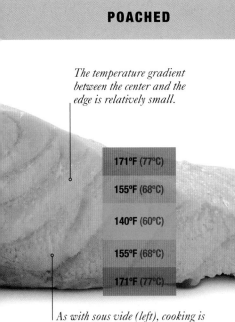

The temperature gradient between the center and the edge is relatively small.

171°F (77°C)

155°F (68°C)

140°F (60°C)

155°F (68°C)

171°F (77°C)

As with sous vide (left), cooking is fairly even and flesh is tender.

Poaching fish in water is best done at a gentle simmer (see right). Poaching has a lower temperature gradient than frying, so fish is cooked more evenly throughout.

Best fish
This is a versatile method that works for many types of fish, but is particularly effective for meatier varieities.

Salmon • Halibut • Trout • Dover sole
Turbot • Tuna

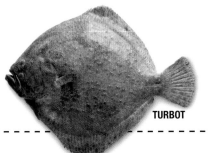

TURBOT

KNOW THE DIFFERENCE

Deep poaching
With deep poaching, a pan of liquid is brought to a gentle simmer of 160–185°F (71–85°C) and the fish is completely submerged in the liquid.

 Deep poaching is a very gentle way to cook fish, helping to ensure that it remains tender. With sufficient liquid, all of the ingredients are fully submerged and can infuse some of their flavors into the liquid and outermost layers of the fish.

 Completely covered in the poaching liquid, fish is evenly cooked throughout, and the cooking time is a reliable 10–15 minutes.

Shallow poaching
For shallow poaching, a wide pan of liquid is brought to a gentle simmer of 185–199°F (85–93°C). The fish is partially submerged in liquid—to just one-third of the way up.

 The smaller amount of liquid used in shallow poaching can be flavored and reserved and used to make a concentrated, intense sauce after cooking that is infused with flavor molecules from the fish.

 Timing is less reliable with shallow poaching because some of the fish is out of the water. Lightly covering the surface with a sheet of parchment paper traps steam to help cook the top of the fish.

The Process of
SOUS VIDE

Done correctly, the texture and freshness of food cooked sous vide—meaning "under vacuum"—is unparalleled.

The French-created practice of sous vide cooking is increasingly popular. The equipment needed for sous vide may appear high tech, but the principles are simple—food is cooked at low temperature for a fairly long time inside a sealed, airless bag. Two pieces of equipment are needed to cook sous vide: a vacuum sealer that extracts air from, and seals, the cooking bag, and a water bath to cook at a precise temperature. A thermometer-controlled heater keeps the water a steady temperature that matches the desired final temperature of the food. The results are incredibly consistent and food is cooked evenly throughout.

How it works
Food is placed in an airless bag and heated in water at a controlled low temperature.

Best for
Fish fillets, chicken breasts, pork chops, steaks, lobster, eggs, carrots.

What to consider
As with other low-temperature cooking techniques, food isn't browned, so if you want a seared edge or crispy skin, you will need to sear food before or after sous vide cooking.

105°F
(41°C) is the heat setting for rare salmon; 140°F (60°C), for well-done salmon.

LOW AND SLOW
MEAT AND FISH CAN BE LEFT AT A DESIGNATED TEMPERATURE FOR THREE HOURS WITHOUT FEAR OF OVERCOOKING.

FRESH ONLY
SOUS VIDE CAN INTENSIFY GOOD AND BAD AROMAS, SO USE FISH AND MEAT THAT ARE VERY FRESH, WITHOUT A HINT OF SPOILAGE.

See inside
Heat from the water bath penetrates the food's surface from all directions. The airless bag stops moisture entering or leaving and the core of the food gradually reaches the same temperature as the edges, so there's no temperature gradient (see p82). Food is cooked evenly, with no dried edges or undercooked centres.

Flesh is cooked through evenly.

Food is heated from all directions.

Key
◁····· Heat from water travels into food
◀—— Water temperature held at 60°C (140°F)

KNOW THE DIFFERENCE

Sous vide
Sealed and held at a constant temperature, it's almost impossible to overcook food.

Cooking time: Food is cooked slowly in water only and flavoring is added to the sealed bag.

Flavor: Vacuum-sealed bags hold in flavor and moisture. The Low pressure in the bag helps to draw the aromas and flavors of the juices into the meat.

Poaching
Food is immersed in liquid and simmered at a higher temperature than sous vide.

Cooking time: Food cooks faster and can be easily overcooked. It can be poached in a variety of liquids, including water, stock, milk, or wine.

Flavor: While flavors from the liquid can suffuse the fish during cooking, flavor can also be lost from the food into the cooking liquid.

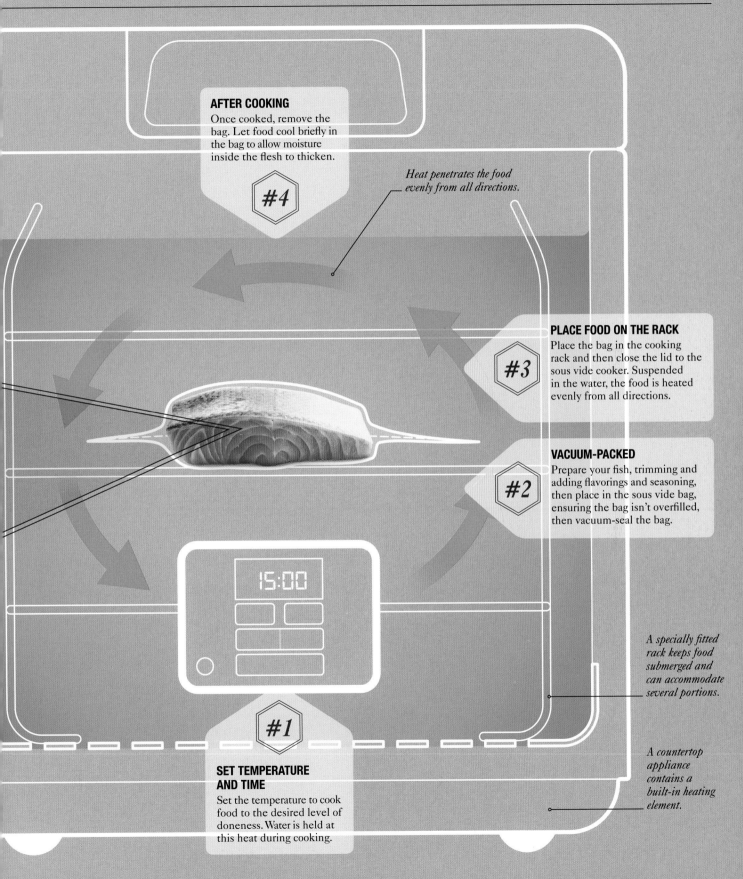

AFTER COOKING
Once cooked, remove the bag. Let food cool briefly in the bag to allow moisture inside the flesh to thicken.

#4

Heat penetrates the food evenly from all directions.

PLACE FOOD ON THE RACK
Place the bag in the cooking rack and then close the lid to the sous vide cooker. Suspended in the water, the food is heated evenly from all directions.

#3

VACUUM-PACKED
Prepare your fish, trimming and adding flavorings and seasoning, then place in the sous vide bag, ensuring the bag isn't overfilled, then vacuum-seal the bag.

#2

15:00

A specially fitted rack keeps food submerged and can accommodate several portions.

#1

SET TEMPERATURE AND TIME
Set the temperature to cook food to the desired level of doneness. Water is held at this heat during cooking.

A countertop appliance contains a built-in heating element.

How do I cook fish to have CRISPY, GOLDEN SKIN?

The crisp crunch of perfectly browned skin is the ideal counterbalance to soft, flaky fish meat.

CHOOSING FISH

AVOID RUBBERY- OR THIN-SKINNED FISH. SEA BASS, SNAPPER, SALMON, FLOUNDER, AND COD ALL CRISP WELL.

Achieving a crisp, golden-brown skin is all about cooking over a very high heat. This causes moisture to sizzle away, allowing the skin to reach 284°F (140°C), the minimum temperature needed to trigger the Maillard reaction (see pp16–17)—a chemical reaction between amino acids and sugars that crisps the skin and creates a delicious flavor and brown color. If the skin is not dry enough, heat energy will be expended driving off excess moisture instead of kick-starting the Maillard reaction, and the flesh may overcook before the skin is dry enough to brown. If the pan is not hot enough and there is no sizzling, a chemical reaction occurs between proteins in the skin and metal atoms in the pan, causing them to fuse together and the fish to stick. Thoroughly drying the fish skin and using an oil with a high smoke point on a high heat will help fish skin crisp beautifully.

(see pp16–17)

IN PRACTICE

PAN-FRYING FISH

Pan-frying a skin-on fillet is a quick and delicious way to yield fish with crispy skin and moist, flaky flesh. Use a heavy-bottomed frying pan or skillet; this will hold heat better than a thin-based frying pan. For larger cuts of fish that are too thick to cook through on the stove, transfer the browned fish into a preheated oven to finish cooking.

#1

#2

#3

DEHYDRATE FISH SKIN WITH SALT
Rub fine sea salt across the surface of a piece of descaled, medium-sized fish fillet with the skin on. Cover both sides with salt. Place it in a dish, cover with plastic wrap, and refrigerate 2–3 hours to allow the salt to draw out moisture. Dry it thoroughly by dabbing it with a paper towel.

HEAT OIL TO BELOW SMOKE POINT
Heat a heavy-bottomed frying pan over high heat. Add 1 tbsp sunflower oil (or other oil with a high smoke point—see pp192–3), and heat to just below smoke point. Place the fish in the pan; the skin should start sizzling immediately. Use a fish spatula to apply even pressure to make sure that heat passes evenly across the skin.

PRESS, FLIP, AND COOK THROUGH
As it cooks, collagen fibers shrink, causing the fish to buckle, so keep on pressing down to make sure the fillet remains flat. Fry the fish until the flesh is opaque two-thirds of the way through. Carefully flip over to finish cooking. Once the fish is cooked through, serve immediately, with the skin side up to preserve the crispiness of the skin.

RED SNAPPER

Mucus layer produced by glands will crisp during cooking.

Scale

Collagen fibers shrink when cooked.

Layer of subcutaneous fat prevents the flesh from cooking too quickly.

Muscle tissue

The anatomy of fish skin

Fish skin is very different from the flesh: rich in fat (up to a tenth of its weight), toughened by the hardy protein collagen, and heavy with moisture. Fish skin also produces a layer of slimy mucus, designed to insulate the living creature, in addition to a layer of inedible bony scales.

Why don't you NEED TO REST FISH?

Fish muscle has a different structure than meat muscle, so it must be treated differently.

Some cooks suggest that fish should be rested in the same way you would rest meat after cooking. There is no harm in doing this, but unless it is a large whole fish (see box below), it is unlikely to make very much difference in your finished dish.

Muscle moisture and temperature

Resting red and white meat helps increase its juiciness slightly by giving time for the liquid inside the muscle to cool and thicken up (see p59). During resting, fragmented proteins in meat mix with moisture to form an unctuous jus within the meat. Fish contain fewer of these proteins, so resting does not have the same effect. Furthermore, having little connective tissue and no stringy sinews, fish has a more delicate texture than meat from land-dwelling animals. This means that any increase in juiciness caused by resting would be very difficult to discern.

Resting fish, like resting meat, also helps to even temperature throughout the flesh. However, because most fish are thin, this effect is negligible. When serving fish, the priority is to serve it while still warm, rather than to achieve an even temperature.

<table>
<tr><td>**DID YOU KNOW?**</td><td>

Whole fish can benefit from resting
Although for most fish, resting is unnecessary, some large whole fish will benefit from a few minutes' resting.

Reduces flaking
Allowing a whole, dense fish—such as tuna or monkfish—to rest for 5 minutes or so before serving allows proteins in the fish flesh to firm up, reducing flaking and making slicing cleaner.

Conserves heat
Whole fish hold heat better than fillets, as the flesh is still enclosed by skin—this means that there's less danger of the fish cooling too much during resting.

</td></tr>
</table>

Tuna used in sashimi has a low infection risk.

Highest-quality fish
Only well-sourced, top-quality fish, properly stored and prepared with the utmost care, is used in authentic sashimi dishes.

Can I eat SASHIMI SAFELY?

Knowing how sashimi is prepared can ease worries about safety.

Sashimi, as with any uncooked food, is never risk-free, but stringent controls mean properly prepared sashimi poses a low risk of infection.

"Sashimi-grade" fish

Fish used for sashimi are line caught individually, quickly killed (to reduce lactic acid buildup, which degrades fish), then placed on ice to prevent bacteria from growing. To help grade fish, fish farmers, traders, and producers use a chemical test to measure how much the energy stores have been depleted, then value each fish based on freshness.

A bigger risk than bacteria comes from worms: these invade the living animal's flesh and, if ingested, can burrow into our intestines, causing persistent diarrhea and pain. Freezing kills these pathogens and "sashimi- or sushi-grade fish" is a term used to indicate that fish has been frozen to at least –4°F(–20°C) before sale. Reassuringly, the types of tuna served as sashimi (bluefin, yellowfin, albacore, and bigeye) dwell in very deep, cold waters, away from worms.

Eating sashimi in a reputable sushi restaurant that prides itself on selecting only the finest-quality fish, storing it at very cold temperatures, and being fastidious about hygiene is extremely safe. To enjoy sashimi at home without anxiety, it is important to do the same.

How does CITRUS JUICE "COOK" RAW FISH?

"Ceviche"—cooking raw fish with lemon juice—can be a useful addition to a cook's repertoire.

The ceviche technique, which originated in South America, requires nothing more than mixing raw fish with citrus juice and leaving this to sit, ideally in the fridge, to "cook." The science behind this mysterious alchemy is actually quite easy to understand.

The acid effect

The acid in citrus juice works on fish proteins in a similar way to heat, disturbing the structure of the proteins within the delicate fish muscle and causing them to unravel, or "denature," in much the same way that they do when cooked.

For acid to cook fish, it needs to have a pH of less than 4.8 for proteins to denature—lemon and lime juice have a pH of about 2.5. The citrus penetrates the surface, "cooking" it, gradually turning the shiny, uncooked flesh into firm, white meat. The acidity gives the fish a tartness and tang. For extra sweetness, add fruit juice or tomatoes, or chili can be added to the mix to provide some heat.

Getting the timing right
The length of time fish needs to "cook" ceviche-style depends on the texture you wish to achieve.

Ceviche cooking guidelines
Cut a skinless fillet of fish into cubes or thin slices of around 1in (2cm), then follow these timing guidelines. Leaving fish for longer than 25 minutes will create a chalky, completely cooked consistency.

- **Rare–medium:** 10–15 mins
- **Medium:** 15–25 mins
- **Medium–well done:** 25 mins

"Most fresh fish should be **edible uncooked**, but industrial-scale fish production means that contamination is common in many fish, where **quality control** is less stringent than it is for sashimi-grade fish."

Why do shellfish
CHANGE COLOR WHEN COOKED?

Heat reveals a previously hidden color.

Crustaceans are one of the most successful classes of animal; they have existed in our seas for more than 200 million years. One reason for their longevity is their ability to blend into their surroundings—the grayish-blue color of a shrimp, for example, is hard to spot in the murky depths of the ocean. Yet cook them, and a wonderful color transformation takes place as their natural camouflage blooms orange-pink.

Where does the orange-pink color come from?

Lobster, crab, shrimp, prawns, and other crustaceans are orange-pink when cooked for the same reason that flamingos are pink and salmon are orange (see p70). A red pigment, called astaxanthin, is produced in the plankton and algae on which crustaceans feed, which accumulates in their shell and flesh. No one is sure exactly why crustaceans store this pigment, although it may protect them against UV damage from the sun if they are in shallow waters. Crustaceans hide this orange-pink color when they are alive to keep them concealed from predators.

Cooking reveals the orange color, but should not be a guide for doneness. Larger shellfish, such as lobster and crab, will change color before they are fully cooked. Always make sure the cooked meat is white, firm, and opaque.

HIDDEN TALENTS

THE DRAMATIC COLOR CHANGE OF SHELLFISH OCCURS AS THEIR NATURAL CAMOUFLAGE COOKS AWAY.

Blue crustacyanin

This is a protein that crustaceans' bodies produce when they are alive. The blue crustacyanin attaches to the pigment astaxanthin (see right) and holds it in check, hiding it. This conceals the animal from predators because it takes on the muted hue of crustacyanin instead.

Crustacyanin proteins clamp around each end of an astaxanthin molecule to hide it.

Astaxanthin molecules are revealed when crustacyanin proteins unravel on cooking.

↑ Red
astaxanthin

This strongly colored pigment comes from the crustaceans' diet and is hidden in its body by the protein crustacyanin (see left). The heat of cooking causes the protein molecules to unwind and lose their original shape, which forces crustacyanin to release astaxanthin and let its true color shine through.

MYTH BUSTER

———— *Myth* ————
LOBSTERS CRY OUT WHEN PLUNGED INTO BOILING WATER.

———— *Truth* ————
Lobsters can't cry out because they have no vocal cords, but you may hear the sound of trapped air escaping from the shell. To cook a lobster kindly, freeze it for 2 hours to render it unconscious first.

What are the rules
WHEN COOKING
MUSSELS?

With a little know-how, you'll find that mussels are one of the easiest seafoods to prepare, and one of the quickest to cook.

Mussels should be cooked alive because they spoil quickly after they die. If you don't intend to cook your live mussels immediately, store them on ice or in a bowl covered with a damp cloth in the coldest part of the fridge (storing them in water will kill them). Before cooking, be wary of any open mussels: those that are already open and do not close when tapped are dead and should be thrown away. While cooking, don't pluck out mussels as soon as they open—research shows that early openers are usually not fully cooked. If ever in any doubt, always let your senses guide you. Infected or dead mussels will smell bad and may have a tacky surface.

MYTH BUSTER

———— *Myth* ————
NEVER EAT MUSSELS THAT REMAIN CLOSED AFTER COOKING.

———— *Truth* ————
The meaty morsel inside a mollusc shell cooks as it sits in simmering water, regardless of whether the shells open. The two shells are held shut by two *adductor* muscles, which are some of the strongest muscles in the animal kingdom. When heated, these muscles slowly weaken as the proteins cook, but within any batch of mussels, some specimens will have stronger adductor muscles than others—their shells may not pop open, but if you pry them open they will be cooked.

PREPARING MUSSELS

Follow a few simple rules to make sure you have only the cleanest, freshest mussels in your cooking pot.

Mussels use their "beards," or byssus threads, to attach themselves to a surface.

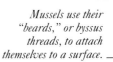

1

CHECK FOR FRESHNESS
Discard mussels that are broken or cracked, or that are open and do not close when tapped (see above).

2

CLEAN AND RINSE IN COLD WATER
Scrape off any barnacles with a knife, then scrub with a brush under cold running water.

3

REMOVE THE BEARD LAST
Pinch the stringy beard and pull it away from the top of the shell to the hinge at the bottom.

EGGS & DAIRY

In focus
EGGS

The egg is a nutritional and culinary wonder, and a near-essential ingredient in any cook's larder.

Eggs are one of the most versatile ingredients in the kitchen—able to bind, coat, clarify, thicken, and aerate food. They owe their incredible powers to their combination of proteins, fats, and emulsifiers.

Yolks are rich in fat, and these fats are suspended inside microscopically sized globules coated in an emulsifier called lecithin. Lecithin helps fats and water to mix, making egg yolks the vital binding ingredient for oil and vinegar in mayonnaise. Egg whites are mainly made of water, with some protein—when vigorously beaten, egg white proteins unravel to form an airy structure that can be combined with sugar to make meringue or folded into cakes to add volume. Added whole, eggs provide structure, moisture, and flavor. And because eggs are designed to provide for a growing chick, they are a nutrient-rich ingredient unto themselves, and happen to contain amino acids in near-perfect proportions for human health.

KNOW YOUR EGGS

The basic structure of bird's eggs remains consistent across different species—fatty yolk suspended in a watery white, encased in a hard shell. However, the ratio of fats to proteins varies, having an impact on the eggs' flavor. The size of the egg and porousness of the shell also varies. For this reason, different eggs are best suited for different culinary purposes. Here is a summary of some of the key varieties.

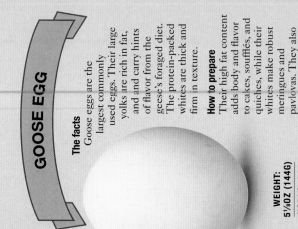

GOOSE EGG

The facts
Goose eggs are the largest commonly used eggs. Their large yolks are rich in fat, and and carry hints of flavor from the geese's foraged diet. The protein-packed whites are thick and firm in texture.

How to prepare
Their high fat content adds body and flavor to cakes, soufflés, and quiches, while their whites make robust meringues and pavlovas. They also make rich omelets.

WEIGHT:
5⅛OZ (144G)
KCALS: 266

Air cell
Air seeps into the egg through the porous shell, forming a bubble at one end of the egg—a small air cell indicates freshness.

Shell
Hard and brittle, the shell protects its contents from damage. It is perforated with tiny pores to allow gases to pass in and out of the egg.

Thin albumen
Making up about 40 percent of the egg white, the white closest to the shell is thin-textured, and cooks slowly. A small amount of thin albumen also surrounds the yolk.

DUCK EGG

The facts
Very porous shells mean duck eggs should be stored away from strong aromas. They have a higher yolk-to-white ratio than chicken eggs, making them richer tasting.

How to prepare
Pickling, brining, salting, and curing all work well with duck eggs. Their high fat content lends succulence to cakes and bakes.

WEIGHT:
2¼OZ (70G)
KCALS: 130

CHICKEN EGG

The facts
By far the most commonly used egg, chicken eggs have a good balance of yolk and white that suits many different culinary uses. Their yolks are relatively small compared to other types of egg, with a higher proportion of white.

How to prepare
Use as a binding agent in baking or an emulsifier in mayonnaise, or cook as it is.

WEIGHT:
1¾OZ (50G)
KCALS: 71

QUAIL EGG

The facts
Tiny and attractively speckled, quail eggs have a subtle, earthy flavor. The firm whites and hard shells can be tricky to peel.

How to prepare
Fry, hard-boil, or pickle quail eggs for use in snacks, hors d'oeuvres, or bento boxes.

WEIGHT:
¼OZ (9G)
KCALS: 14

Thick albumen
About 60 percent of the albumen—the thick part of the white—is made of water and protein. As the egg ages, the thick albumen shrinks.

Yolk
The yolk comprises fat globules wrapped in lecithin. It is made of minutely thin, concentric rings, separated by thin membranes.

Germinal disc
This just-visible spot is where the egg cell develops into a chick in a fertilized egg.

Chalazae
These twisting columns of thick albumen secure the yolk. They are most visible in very fresh eggs.

LAYING DOZENS

IN A YEAR, A LAYING HEN PRODUCES EGGS EQUAL TO EIGHT TIMES HER OWN BODY WEIGHT.

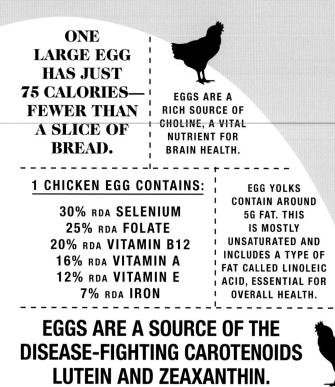

ONE LARGE EGG HAS JUST 75 CALORIES— FEWER THAN A SLICE OF BREAD.

EGGS ARE A RICH SOURCE OF CHOLINE, A VITAL NUTRIENT FOR BRAIN HEALTH.

1 CHICKEN EGG CONTAINS:

30% RDA SELENIUM
25% RDA FOLATE
20% RDA VITAMIN B12
16% RDA VITAMIN A
12% RDA VITAMIN E
7% RDA IRON

EGG YOLKS CONTAIN AROUND 5G FAT. THIS IS MOSTLY UNSATURATED AND INCLUDES A TYPE OF FAT CALLED LINOLEIC ACID, ESSENTIAL FOR OVERALL HEALTH.

EGGS ARE A SOURCE OF THE DISEASE-FIGHTING CAROTENOIDS LUTEIN AND ZEAXANTHIN.

EGG YOLKS CONTAIN THE SUBSTANCE LECITHIN, WHICH PREVENTS CHOLESTEROL FROM BEING ABSORBED.

EGG WHITES ARE LOW IN CALORIES AND ARE FAT-FREE.

AN EGG CONTAINS 7g HIGH-QUALITY PROTEIN, WITH MORE PROTEIN FOUND IN THE WHITE THAN THE YOLK.

SOME CHICKENS HAVE DIETS SUPPLEMENTED WITH FLAXSEED AND SOMETIMES FISH OILS TO ADD EXTRA OMEGA-3 TO THEIR EGGS.

DUCK, GOOSE, AND QUAIL EGGS ARE MORE CONCENTRATED IN VITAMIN B12 AND IRON THAN CHICKEN EGGS.

EGG WHITES CONTAIN 60% OF THE EGG'S PROTEIN, WHILE MANY OF AN EGG'S FAT-SOLUBLE VITAMINS ARE LOCATED IN THE CHOLESTEROL AND FAT IN ITS YOLK.

Should I limit how many EGGS I EAT?

Forming a compact source of nutrients, eggs are often referred to as a "complete" food.

Tightly packed with protein, energy, fats, vitamins, and minerals, eggs are seen as providing a complete source of nutrition in one neat package. However, in the 1950s, concerns about cholesterol in eggs affecting heart health, closely followed by egg-borne salmonella scares, fractured our trust in the benefits and safety of eggs.

What we know today

Today, we know that many of the fears about the dangers of eggs aren't true and their safety has improved greatly in the past 20 years. Salmonella food poisoning from eggs is now far less of a problem than it was 30 years ago, and in some countries it has been virtually eradicated. Worries about cholesterol levels in eggs have also receded as research has shown that dietary sources of cholesterol are far less of a problem for the majority of people than was once thought (see Myth Buster, below).

In terms of nutrition, eggs are hard to beat, providing a host of nutrients and antioxidants, as shown, left. Today, nearly all international healthy eating guidelines have removed restrictions on the number of eggs that should be eaten each week, and studies suggest that children and healthy adults can happily eat an egg a day.

MYTH BUSTER

—— *Myth* ——
EGGS RAISE CHOLESTEROL LEVELS

—— *Truth* ——
Eggs are high in cholesterol, but eating cholesterol-rich foods isn't as risky as was once thought. High levels of "bad" LDL cholesterol in the blood can clog arteries, increasing the risk of serious health issues. But it's foods high in saturated fats, such as fatty meats, creams, butter, and cheese, that cause the body to overproduce cholesterol, while dietary cholesterol has limited impact. Egg yolks also contain a substance that prevents the cholesterol it contains from being absorbed. Generally, only those with genetically inherited high cholesterol levels should limit their egg intake.

Are there more nutrients in FREE-RANGE EGGS?

Eggs are produced on a scale never before seen, and can offer us a safe, cheap, and highly nutritious food.

Chickens have fared badly from industrial-scale farming. Birds are often housed in cramped wire cages in barns or sheds where temperature and lighting conditions force them to lay eggs all year round. Fed a supplemented grain mix designed for optimal egg producing, an indoor-farmed hen can convert 4½lb (2kg) of feed into an incredible 2¼lb (1kg) of eggs.

The life of an animal affects the quality of the food it provides (see p40), so it's no surprise that while indoor-farmed hens lay more eggs, each egg is nutritionally inferior to eggs from free-roaming chickens (see right). Flavor differences are subtle, but for the cook, eggs from a reputable local outlet where chickens lead a pastured life are best for nutrition.

ORGANIC	FREE-RANGE	INDOOR-FARMED

Conditions Chickens have free and easy access to outdoors and are able to feed on pasture.	**Conditions** The amount of outdoor access free-range chickens have varies, with some spending much time in a barn.	**Conditions** Chickens kept inside and fed on grain.
Nutrients Amounts vary, but eggs can have up to double the amount of omega-3 and vitamin E, 25 percent less saturated fat, and more minerals.	**Nutrients** There is wide variation, but eggs have similar nutrient values to those from organic chickens.	**Nutrients** Forced to lay eggs at high rates in stressful conditions, these chickens' eggs have fewer vitamins and omega-3 fats and more saturated fats than eggs from free-roaming chickens.

Is it safe to eat RAW EGGS?

Uncooked eggs are a key ingredient for many classic dishes, such as mayonnaise, aioli, and mousse.

The biggest worry with recipes that use raw eggs or runny yolks is ingesting *Salmonella* bacteria along with the egg, which causes food poisoning.

The control of *Salmonella*

Eggs pick up *Salmonella* when they come into contact with infected feces. The shell has a protective coating (see right), so provided it doesn't crack, its contents should be safe. Strict regulations now mean that infected eggs are rare. In the US, eggs are sometimes given a protective mineral oil coating, and in Europe chickens are vaccinated. Many countries grade eggs to indicate that they've met safety regulations. Cooking kills bacteria, and in most countries raw eggs are often safe, but food safety guidelines vary between nations. Pasteurized eggs—heated briefly to destroy bacteria—are sold where raw eggs are off the menu, though these are slightly less flavorful.

Protective cuticle layer

Salmonella bacteria

The tiniest crack can let Salmonella access the egg.

Porous egg shell

Infection-fighting proteins in the white offer some protection.

The egg's protective outer case →

Salmonella is usually present on the shell of an egg that has come into contact with infected feces. The harmful bacteria may penetrate the core, but the shell has a bug-proof coating (the cuticle) so provided that the shell doesn't crack, its contents are fairly safe. Any egg with the tiniest crack should be discarded.

Where is the best place to STORE MY EGGS?

The storage of eggs, while seeming like a trivial issue, can be a surprising source of disagreement.

Where you store your eggs can depend on where you live. In the US, chickens aren't routinely vaccinated against *Salmonella*, so refrigerating is advised to slow the growth of bacteria. European advice is to keep eggs in a cool pantry because it is thought that condensation in a fridge can encourage bacteria to proliferate. This difference may be partly due to rates of *Salmonella*, which historically are slightly lower in Europe, while in the US, eggs are washed and sprayed with a chemical sanitizer to remove bugs, although this can also strip off the protective antibacterial cuticle layer (see p97), making them more vulnerable. Aside from official guidelines, how you want to use your eggs can influence storage. The table, right, shows how keeping eggs in the fridge or at room temperature can affect their efficiency for different cooking methods and uses.

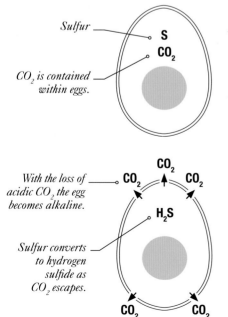

Storing eggs in the fridge
If you chill eggs, avoid using the egg holders in a refrigerator door. Opening and shutting the door shakes the eggs, speeding the thinning of the white. Keep them toward the back in an airtight container to slow moisture loss.

USE	WHERE	WHY
Separated	Fridge	Chilled is best if separating yolks for mayonnaise because the yolks stay firmer.
Boiled	Fridge or room	A boiled egg will take slightly longer to cook if chilled, although the end result is identical.
Scrambled	Fridge or room	Whether eggs are room temperature or chilled makes little difference for scrambling.
Fried	Room	A cold egg lowers the temperature of the pan and the oil, so frying can take a little longer.
Poached	Room	For poaching, a cold egg reduces the water temperature, slowing cooking a little and making the white more likely to spread.
Cakes	Room	For foaming yolks for a cake or whisking whites for meringue, room temperature lets proteins unwind and mesh together more easily. Cakes have a slightly finer, more even consistency.

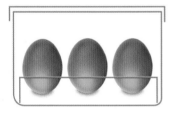

Sulfur

S
CO_2

CO_2 is contained within eggs.

Proteins in fresh eggs
Each protein type has a unique shape, and many of the egg white proteins keep their form with the help of powerful sulfur atoms. While contained in the egg white, the sulfur atoms don't give off an aroma.

CO_2

CO_2 ↑ CO_2

With the loss of acidic CO_2 the egg becomes alkaline.

H_2S

Sulfur converts to hydrogen sulfide as CO_2 escapes.

CO_2 CO_2

The aging egg
As eggs age, carbon dioxide (CO_2) escapes through tiny pores in the shell. The eggs become more alkaline, and this change in acidity forces proteins to unravel and let go of sulfur atoms, which turn into a foul-smelling hydrogen sulfide gas.

Why do rotten eggs SMELL BAD?

Proteins in egg white break down as eggs age.

The strong smell of rotten eggs comes mostly from the whites and is due to hydrogen sulfide, a gas so noxious that it was used as a chemical weapon in World War I. The gas is created when certain sulfur-containing proteins in the egg white unravel. When cooked to above 140°F (60°C), sulfur starts to break free, which creates the eggy smell of hydrogen sulfide. The sulfurous-smelling sulfide vapor is also released when an egg ages. The illustration, left, shows how changing levels of carbon dioxide degrade the egg white proteins, causing the release of the repulsive-smelling hydrogen sulfide gas.

How can I tell if an
EGG IS FRESH?

Gases pass into and out of an eggshell's microscopic pores, affecting how long the egg will last.

As soon as an egg is laid, moisture starts to evaporate from the white through the pores of the shell. The shrinking interior of the egg pulls in 4ml of air each day, forming a slowly expanding air bubble called the "air cell."

How to gauge freshness

The expanding air bubble serves as a guide to the age of an egg. If you hold an egg close to your ear and shake it, a sloshing noise suggests that the air bubble has grown sufficiently for the egg contents to splash around inside it and the

MEASURING UP

EGG INSPECTORS MEASURE THE HEIGHT OF THE EGG WHITE, SCORED AS "HAUGH UNITS," TO ASSESS FRESHNESS.

egg should be discarded. The water test, below, can also help you assess the freshness of an egg before using it.

Once it's cracked, check the white and yolk. Egg whites have two layers: a thick, gloopy layer surrounded by a thin, watery layer. In an old egg, the thin white loses its stickiness and forms a pool, the thick white reduces, and the yolk gets weaker. The yolk soaks up moisture from the egg white as it ages, stretching it and making it waterlogged. The yolk looks flabbier, is more likely to break, and will have a diluted flavor.

TYPE OF TEST	FRESH EGG	1 WEEK OLD	2 WEEKS OLD	3 WEEKS OLD	5+ WEEKS OLD
The water test Carefully place an egg in a bowl of water. If the egg floats, as shown far right, so much moisture has evaporated from the egg and the air bubble has grown to such an extent that it is no longer dense enough to sink and should be thrown away. Eggs that sink to the bottom but tilt or stand upward are past their best, but usually perfectly safe to eat. Eggs that lie flat at the bottom of the bowl are the freshest.	A small air bubble means this fresh egg is dense enough to sink. *Air bubble less than ¹⁄₈in (3mm)*	As the egg loses moisture, it becomes less dense and starts to tilt.	The growing air bubble means the egg gradually loses density and is almost upright.	An egg that stands upright is past its peak of freshness.	Extensive moisture loss causes old eggs to float.
The cracking test When cracked, a fresh egg has a thick, slightly cloudy white and a high, round yolk. As eggs age, the white becomes thinner and more transparent and the yolk flatter.	A fresh egg has a high yolk and thick white. *White holds shape*	*Egg white thins*	Egg whites spread more on older eggs.	Over time, the yolk flattens out and the white loses color.	*Watery white spreads out more.*
Using eggs as they age The freshest eggs are the best. However, although the success of some cooking methods depends on freshness, older eggs can still produce good results for certain uses.	Fresh eggs with firm whites are ideal for most uses, especially poaching and boiling (see p100).	At around one week, eggs are still relatively fresh, although not ideal for poaching.	Older egg whites can be easier to whip into peaks for meringues.	Keep older eggs in the fridge and use for making cookies or boiling and pickling as they're easier to peel.	Once an egg has reached this stage, it should be discarded.

Is it true that only
FRESH EGGS POACH WELL?

Poaching an egg so that it is a tidy, compact sphere with a runny center takes some care.

It is easy to make a mess of a poached egg, but fresh eggs give the best results because they have a strong membrane surrounding the yolk. Once outside of its shell and plunged in hot water, the membrane holds together remarkably well.

In addition, fresh eggs have more of the thick egg white and less of the thinner, watery egg white (see p99) that causes the straggly white mess that disfigures so many poached egg attempts. The older an egg is, the runnier the thin white becomes as it is progressively diluted by water spreading from the thick egg white. And while older eggs can make a well-shaped poached egg, the lack of a strong membrane and a spreading white makes it harder to achieve.

Apart from the appearance of the egg, another reason to use the freshest eggs for poaching is that they have a better taste, with no off flavors. The step by step below guides you through the best practice for poaching.

IN PRACTICE

MAKING THE PERFECT POACHED EGG

Along with freshness, there are several methods that will help you keep the white together in the pan, such as adding salt and vinegar to the cooking water. The steps below will help you perfect your egg-poaching technique.

#1

#2

#3

REMOVE THE THIN EGG WHITE

Crack the egg and put it into a sieve or slotted spoon to get rid of any thin egg white. Removing the thin white at this stage will prevent it from separating during cooking and reduce the amount of straggly, detached strands of egg white appearing in the cooking water. If poaching multiple eggs, place each strained egg into an individual ramekin.

AID EGG-WHITE COAGULATION

Half-fill a saucepan with water, taking note of the amount of water that has been used. For around each liter of water, add ¼oz (8g) of vinegar and ½oz (15g) of salt. These two substances disturb the proteins in the egg when it is added, helping the white solidify more quickly. This reduces the amount of time it has to spread out while still in its runny, uncooked form.

TURN UP THE HEAT

Heat the water to just below a light simmer—about 180–190°F (82–88°C). You could use a digital thermometer to measure the temperature of the water. Avoid using rapidly boiling water, because the turbulence will break the egg white apart. The bubbles will also disturb the water's surface, making it more difficult to see whether the egg is cooked, and the higher temperature will make it easier to overcook.

POACH IN ADVANCE

POACHED EGGS KEEP IN
THE REFRIGERATOR FOR UP
TO TWO DAYS. REHEATED
IN WATER, THEY TASTE
FRESHLY COOKED.

#4

SWIRL THE WATER

If poaching only one or two eggs,
create a mini-whirlpool in the center
of the heated cooking water by
swirling it in the pan. The circular
motion will keep the egg together
when it first enters the water.

#5

LOWER THE EGG

Gently drop the egg into the water
from as close as possible using the
ramekin or a slotted spoon. It should
sink to the bottom of the pot. At this
stage, you can continue to stir the
water gently around the egg to keep
it intact. If you are poaching multiple
eggs at the same time, gently stir the
individual eggs around so that they
remain separate.

#6

WATCH IT RISE

Cook the egg for 3—4 minutes.
Vinegar reacts with the egg white to
release carbon dioxide during cooking.
As the proteins coagulate, tiny gas
bubbles are caught in the solidifying
white, reducing its density. Conversely,
the salt increases the density of the
water slightly, so that, when cooked,
the egg rises to the surface. Remove
it with a slotted spoon and blot with
a paper towel.

How can I cook soft-boiled eggs with RUNNY YOLKS?

A flowing, golden yolk in a solid white can be tricky to achieve.

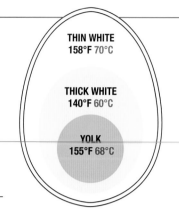

THIN WHITE
158°F 70°C

THICK WHITE
140°F 60°C

YOLK
155°F 68°C

Setting times
As shown above, the yolk sets
after the thick egg white, but
before the thin egg white.

Part of the trick to cooking an egg as you want it is to understand that it has three layers (not two): the thin egg white, thick egg white, and egg yolk. Each layer has different types and amounts of protein, which cook at different temperatures (see right) and at different rates.

The thick egg white cooks first, followed by the yolk, and lastly the thin, watery egg white—this contains the least protein. In truth, there is no perfect formula for runny yolks because every egg is a little different. The methods below assume a large egg at room temperature.

COOKING METHOD	COOKING TEMPERATURE	HOW IT WORKS	HOW EFFECTIVE IS IT?	WHAT TO LOOK OUT FOR
BOILING	**212°F** **100°C**	**The egg** is plunged into boiling water and cooked for 3–5 minutes.	**A high temperature** and short cooking time make the margin of error for under- or overcooking the yolk small.	**Chilled eggs** cook better at the longer end of the time range, while old and medium-sized eggs cook slightly quicker. Water temperature drops with each egg added, so allow longer for multiple eggs.
STEAMING	**196°F** **91°C**	**The egg** is placed in a lidded pan with a thin layer of boiling water and steamed for 5 minutes 50 seconds.	**Cooked at a lower** temperature, this gives more control; both the thick and thin egg white will cook. Very effective.	**Increase cooking time** by 40 seconds for chilled eggs; reduce by 30 seconds for medium-sized eggs. Minimize carryover cooking by dousing eggs in cold water for 20–30 seconds after cooking.
SOUS VIDE	**145°F** **63°C**	**The egg** is placed in a hot water bath and cooked for 45 minutes.	**A low temperature** gives more control but the thin egg white remains watery.	**Crack the cooked egg** instead of peeling it, because the thin white will be runny. Use instead of poached eggs.

What's the best method for PEELING HARD-BOILED EGGS?

You can sidestep the problem of the egg white crumbling as you peel the shell.

Two thin membranes separate the egg white from the shell—an inner membrane encloses the egg white, and an outer membrane coats the inside of the shell. Between the two membranes is an air-filled bubble (which causes an old egg to float in water; see p99). The proteins within the membranes unravel during cooking, then stick to one another when they cool, effectively gluing the shell to the egg white. "Shocking" the egg in ice-cold water (cool water is not cold enough) immediately after cooking for a couple of minutes firms up the membrane proteins and causes the egg white to shrink back from the shell—the shell and outer membrane then peel away easily.

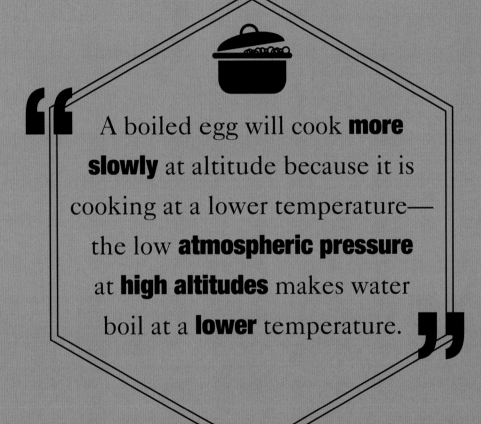

"A boiled egg will cook **more slowly** at altitude because it is cooking at a lower temperature—the low **atmospheric pressure** at **high altitudes** makes water boil at a **lower** temperature."

How do I make the perfect SCRAMBLED EGGS?

One of the simplest dishes any cook can attempt, perfect scrambled eggs are easy to achieve with a little understanding of chemistry.

When a beaten egg is cooked, it miraculously thickens into a custard-like mass as the proteins change shape and interlink (see below). Eggs contain dozens of different protein types, each with a different unraveling, or "denaturing," temperature, so they gradually form clumps and solidify, making scambled eggs a forgiving dish to cook. These proteins provide the cooked egg with texture, but can also cause sticking by chemically fusing to the metal of the pan. Continuous stirring and scraping is essential, and adding a teaspoon of oil or butter helps prevent sticking.

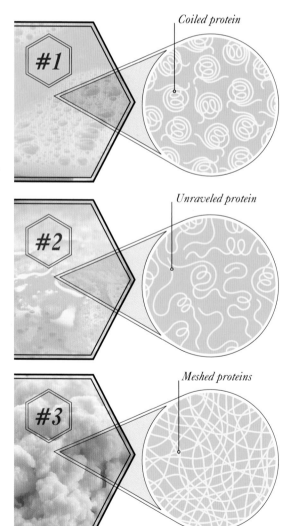

#1

Coiled protein

Proteins in raw egg

Long, tightly coiled protein molecules float freely in the watery egg yolk and white, resembling nests of uncooked noodles. Beat the egg with a fork or whisk until yolk and white are combined—this disperses protein and fat.

#2

Unraveled protein

Proteins in partially cooked egg

Heat gives protein molecules energy, making them vibrate and move quickly and strike one another. The proteins unravel and start to stick to one another, so stir the mixture constantly to prevent large protein clumps forming.

#3

Meshed proteins

Proteins in scrambled egg

Around 140°F (60°C), the molecules begin to mat, forming a messy tangle. These quickly create solid masses. Keep stirring until the egg reaches your desired texture, add pepper, then serve immediately.

IN PRACTICE

#1

INFUSE MILK WITH FLAVOR

Pour 1 pint (600ml) whole milk into a heavy-bottomed pan. Add the seeds of 1 vanilla bean to the pan, along with the empty bean. Place the pan over medium heat and bring to just below boiling point. Heating helps to infuse the milk with the vanilla's flavor molecules. As soon as the milk bubbles, remove it from the heat. Leave for 15 minutes to infuse flavor further.

What is the secret of
CREAMY, SMOOTH CUSTARD?

Custard forms the basis of many luscious desserts, and making it is simple to master.

A custard is a sweetened milk or cream sauce thickened with egg. Understanding a few key principles will help you combine these ingredients into a silky-smooth custard (see below). Eggs thicken milks and creams into custard because of their special blend of proteins. Rather than clumping into scrambled egg, they can be coaxed into a threadlike mesh or scaffolding throughout the liquid. Left to their own devices in a heated pan, egg proteins huddle together and set into tough lumps, "curdling" the custard.

Continuously stirring the mixture forces the proteins to stretch out into a loose, three-dimensional mesh, and helps prevent lumps. Molecules in milk and cream, as well as sugar, obstruct the proteins, increasing their fusing temperature from 140°F (60°C) to 174–81°F (79–83°C). Heating gradually over a gentle heat is essential so that you can stop when the mixture thickens (at 173°F/78°C), but before clumping.

USES FOR CUSTARD

AS WELL AS BEING A SAUCE FOR DESSERTS, CUSTARD IS USED TO MAKE ICE CREAM, CRÈME CARAMEL, AND CRÈME BRÛLÉE.

MAKING CUSTARD

This method produces a pouring custard, also known as a crème anglaise, ideal for drizzling over desserts or as a base for making ice cream (see pp116–117). For a thicker custard, use 10fl oz (300ml) heavy cream and 10fl oz (300ml) whole milk. You can also add one or more extra egg yolks, but be careful not to add too many, as this can create an eggy flavor.

#2

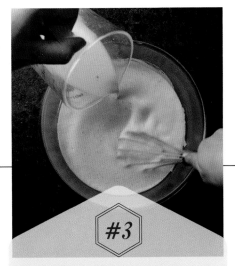

#3

#4

COMBINE EGG PROTEINS AND SUGAR
Place 4 large egg yolks and 1¾oz (50g) fine sugar in a large, heatproof bowl. The egg proteins and fat in the yolk will thicken the custard, as well as add a rich flavor. Whisk together until smooth and pale in color to ensure that the sugar is fully dissolved. The sugar will increase the temperature that the egg proteins will denature at (see opposite), making it hard for them to bind into uneven lumps.

ADD HOT INGREDIENTS TO COLD
Transfer the milk into a heatproof cup, remove the vanilla bean, and rinse the pan to remove any residue. Gradually pour the still-warm milk mixture onto the egg mixture in a thin stream, whisking all the time. Adding the warm milk slowly, while whisking, ensures that the temperature of the egg mixture rises gradually. This prevents the egg proteins from getting too hot and clumping together.

HEAT TO FORM A PROTEIN MESH
Pour the mixture back into the pan. Place over medium heat and stir constantly. Check the texture regularly—at around 172°F (78°C), egg proteins start to form a mesh that thickens the mixture so that it coats the back of a wooden spoon, which is the correct texture. As soon as this happens, remove the pan from the heat. Use immediately, or allow to cool before storing in the refrigerator.

Does it matter if yolk gets into my
WHIPPED EGG WHITES?

Whipped correctly, egg whites will inflate eight-fold into a snow-like foam.

Egg whites are mostly water and protein—and no fat. Whipping unravels the tightly wound proteins into strands that trap air bubbles puff it up into a pillowy foam (see below). Some recipes add acids, such as cream of tartar, lemon juice, or vinegar, to help unravel the proteins; copper atoms have a similar effect, which is why copper bowls are traditionally used for whisking. Fat and grease spell disaster for an egg white foam because oil molecules will displace proteins as they try to mesh around pockets of air (see below). Egg yolk is particularly potent: just one drop in two egg whites will make it impossible to form an egg white foam, but you may be able to rescue it if there is only a trace of yolk (see What you can do, below). Sugar interferes with foam creation too, but it helps stiffen the egg whites later; so add it in the middle stage of whipping.

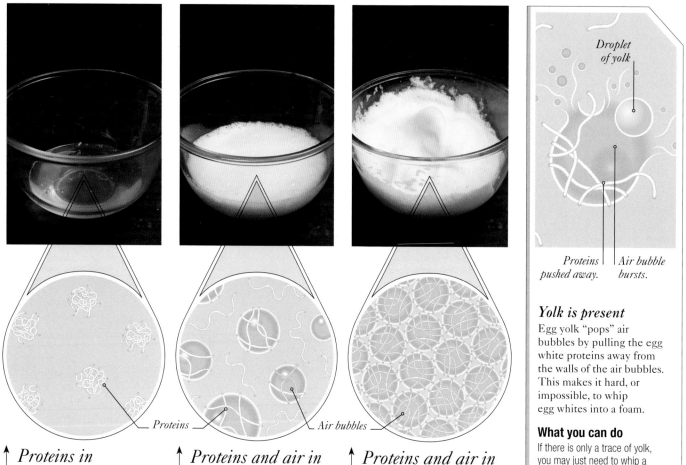

Droplet of yolk

Proteins pushed away.   *Air bubble bursts.*

Yolk is present
Egg yolk "pops" air bubbles by pulling the egg white proteins away from the walls of the air bubbles. This makes it hard, or impossible, to whip egg whites into a foam.

What you can do
If there is only a trace of yolk, you may just need to whip a little more. If that fails, add cream of tartar (which as an acid speeds protein unraveling) and whip again—this may rescue the foam, but there is no guarantee.

Proteins *Air bubbles*

↑ *Proteins in*
raw egg white

Tightly wound proteins must be unraveled, or denatured, to create foam. Whip egg whites in a clean, grease-free bowl to eliminate fat.

↑ *Proteins and air in*
whipped egg whites

The friction of whipping tears and denatures the proteins, the proteins, and also introduces air bubbles. Keep whipping the egg whites vigorously.

↑ *Proteins and air in*
completed foam

Protein strands cluster around the bubbles, trapping air. Further whipping meshes the proteins together, creating a firmer texture.

How can I prevent
BROKEN MAYONNAISE?

Blending egg yolk with oil and flavorings creates a creamy sauce.

Mayonnaise is actually a gel of microscopic oil droplets suspended in a watery liquid. This combination is possible because egg yolk contains an emulsifier—a substance that binds oil and water—called lecithin. To make mayonnaise you must blend approximately four parts oil into one part water—each teaspoon of oil must be broken up into 10 billion droplets to mix properly. Start with minimal liquid—just egg yolk (which is 50 percent water).

Add the oil slowly, a little at a time, and blend thoroughly, as shown below. The concentrated lecithin in the thick yolk will coat each microscopic oil droplet. Use ingredients at room temperature—lecithin takes longer to emulsify water with oil when chilled. Adding the oil too quickly may cause breaking, but your mayonnaise can be rescued (see What you can do, below).

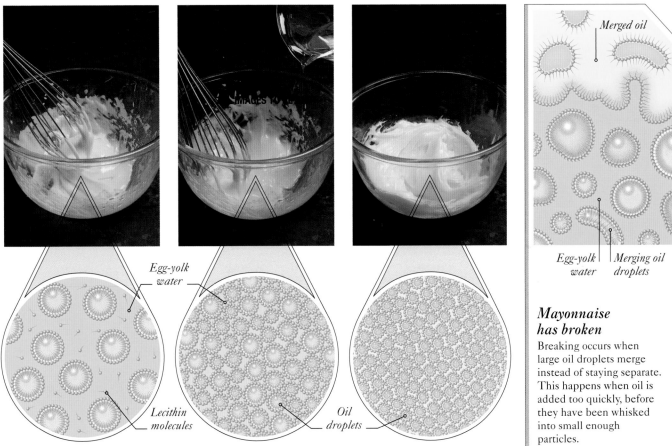

Egg-yolk water

Lecithin molecules

Egg-yolk water

Oil droplets

Merged oil

Egg-yolk water | *Merging oil droplets*

Oil droplets in
raw egg yolk

Oil will naturally aggregate into large drops. Beat the yolk well, and then add oil little by little, blending fully before adding more oil.

Oil droplets in
thickened mixture

The mixture thickens as the oil breaks into smaller drops. Drizzle in the remaining oil very slowly, whisking vigorously the entire time.

Oil droplets in
finished mayonnaise

Individual microscopic oil drops float in the base liquid, held in place by lecithin. Once all the oil is incorporated, add other watery ingredients and seasoning.

Mayonnaise has broken

Breaking occurs when large oil droplets merge instead of staying separate. This happens when oil is added too quickly, before they have been whisked into small enough particles.

What you can do

Add 1–2 tsp water and whisk again. If that fails, slowly re-add the separated mix into a fresh egg yolk.

In focus

MILK

A nutrient-dense beverage in itself, milk transforms into a host of key ingredients including butter, cream, yogurt, cheese in all its varieties, crème fraîche, and more.

The cornerstone to dairy milk's versatility is the role of its proteins and fats. Fats in milk are wrapped into microscopic globules with a water-soluble skin. Less dense than water, these float to the surface and knit together to form a thick, fatty layer. In the processing of most milks, fat is separated to produce cream and skim milk. For 1%, 2%, and whole milk, fat is then added

back in the correct ratio. Today, nearly all commercially produced dairy milk is homogenized to stop further separation: it is sprayed through nozzles at high pressure to break large fat globules into smaller fragments that find it hard to bind together and cannot float to the top, giving a smooth mouthfeel. Non-dairy milks (see right) offer a nutritious alternative.

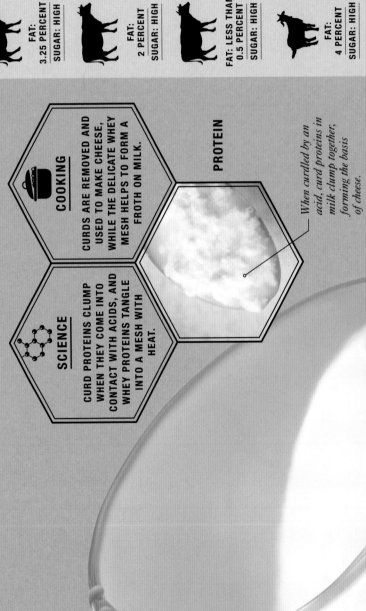

SCIENCE

CURD PROTEINS CLUMP WHEN THEY COME INTO CONTACT WITH ACIDS, AND WHEY PROTEINS TANGLE INTO A MESH WITH HEAT.

COOKING

CURDS ARE REMOVED AND USED TO MAKE CHEESE, WHILE THE DELICATE WHEY MESH HELPS TO FORM A FROTH ON MILK.

PROTEIN

When curdled by an acid, curd proteins in milk clump together, forming the basis of cheese.

KNOW YOUR MILK

Different types of milk have varying levels of fat and sugar, which can affect how they are used. Sugar levels vary only a little in dairy milks, although non-dairy milks tend to contain less sugar. Milk is also a high-quality source of protein.

DAIRY

Whole cow's milk
Rich in natural fats, whole milk is the milk of choice for baking, helping to keep baked goods moist, with a good "crumb" for a light, moist texture.

FAT: 3.25 PERCENT
SUGAR: HIGH

2% cow's milk
Lower in fat, this has slightly more protein than whole milk. It tastes less rich, but still works well for both drinking and cooking.

FAT: 2 PERCENT
SUGAR: HIGH

Skim cow's milk
This low-fat milk is is perfect for frothing coffee drinks as there are fewer fat globules to prevent the whey proteins from thickening and foaming.

FAT: LESS THAN 0.5 PERCENT
SUGAR: HIGH

Goat's milk
This strong-flavored milk is good for making cheese, butter, and ice cream. Small fat globules and little protein mean it is slow to separate.

FAT: 4 PERCENT
SUGAR: HIGH

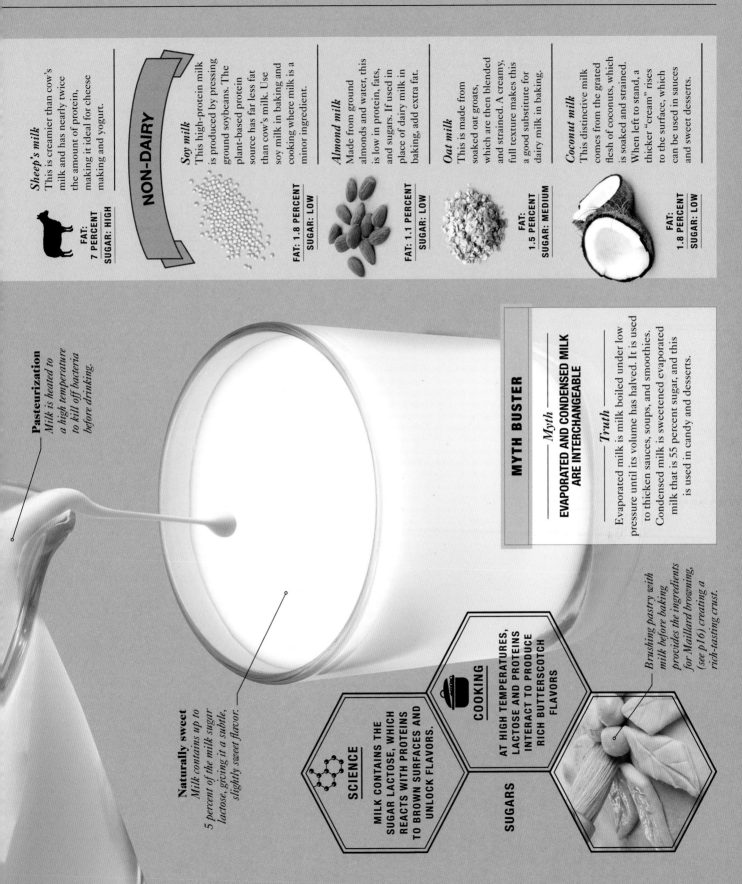

Sheep's milk
This is creamier than cow's milk and has nearly twice the amount of protein, making it ideal for cheese making and yogurt.

FAT: 7 PERCENT
SUGAR: HIGH

NON-DAIRY

Soy milk
This high-protein milk is produced by pressing ground soybeans. The plant-based protein source has far less fat than cow's milk. Use soy milk in baking and cooking where milk is a minor ingredient.

FAT: 1.8 PERCENT
SUGAR: LOW

Almond milk
Made from ground almonds and water, this is low in protein, fats, and sugars. If used in place of dairy milk in baking, add extra fat.

FAT: 1.1 PERCENT
SUGAR: LOW

Oat milk
This is made from soaked oat groats, which are then blended and strained. A creamy, full texture makes this a good substitute for dairy milk in baking.

FAT: 1.5 PERCENT
SUGAR: MEDIUM

Coconut milk
This distinctive milk comes from the grated flesh of coconuts, which is soaked and strained. When left to stand, a thicker "cream" rises to the surface, which can be used in sauces and sweet desserts.

FAT: 1.8 PERCENT
SUGAR: LOW

Pasteurization
Milk is heated to a high temperature to kill off bacteria before drinking.

Naturally sweet
Milk contains up to 5 percent of the milk sugar lactose, giving it a subtle, slightly sweet flavor.

MYTH BUSTER

— *Myth* —
EVAPORATED AND CONDENSED MILK ARE INTERCHANGEABLE

— *Truth* —
Evaporated milk is milk boiled under low pressure until its volume has halved. It is used to thicken sauces, soups, and smoothies. Condensed milk is sweetened evaporated milk that is 55 percent sugar, and this is used in candy and desserts.

SCIENCE
MILK CONTAINS THE SUGAR LACTOSE, WHICH REACTS WITH PROTEINS TO BROWN SURFACES AND UNLOCK FLAVORS.

COOKING
AT HIGH TEMPERATURES, LACTOSE AND PROTEINS INTERACT TO PRODUCE RICH BUTTERSCOTCH FLAVORS

SUGARS

Brushing pastry with milk before baking provides the ingredients for Maillard browning (see p16) creating a rich-tasting crust.

Why do we PASTEURIZE MILK?

Every cook wants to use the best ingredients, but while raw milk tastes better, it's not without its risks.

Like any raw animal product, milk is prone to contamination—a cow's udders don't swing far from its rear. Industrialization multiplied this risk—with large quantities of milk collected in huge vats, one bad batch could contaminate an entire load. Pasteurization, heating milk to high temperatures, is a method of killing these microbes, making milk safe for the masses. Today,

unpasteurized "raw" milk tends to come from small farms with high levels of hygiene where infections are uncommon. However, raw milk still carries risk, with 60 percent of food poisoning outbreaks in the US arising from unpasteurized milk. Raw milk cheese is generally safe, as harmful microbes are killed by the salt and acidity. Nearly every major health body advises us to avoid drinking unpasteurized milk.

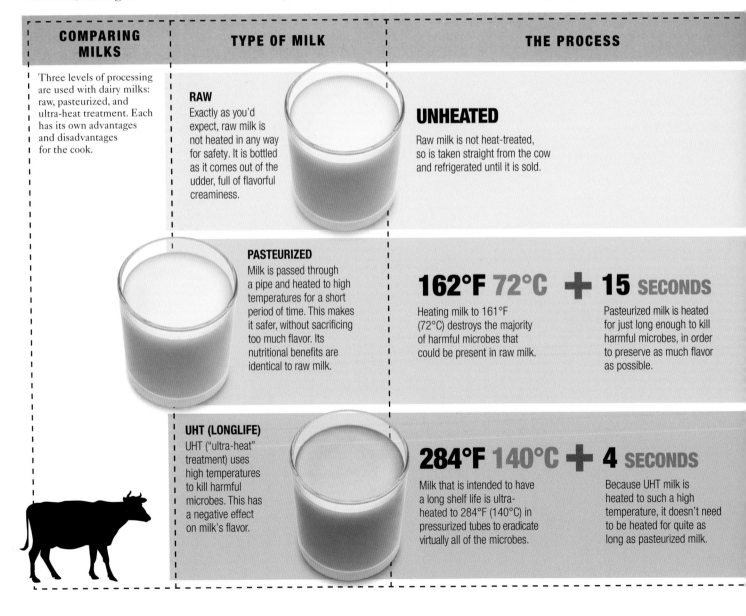

COMPARING MILKS	TYPE OF MILK	THE PROCESS	
Three levels of processing are used with dairy milks: raw, pasteurized, and ultra-heat treatment. Each has its own advantages and disadvantages for the cook.	**RAW** Exactly as you'd expect, raw milk is not heated in any way for safety. It is bottled as it comes out of the udder, full of flavorful creaminess.	**UNHEATED** Raw milk is not heat-treated, so is taken straight from the cow and refrigerated until it is sold.	
	PASTEURIZED Milk is passed through a pipe and heated to high temperatures for a short period of time. This makes it safer, without sacrificing too much flavor. Its nutritional benefits are identical to raw milk.	**162°F 72°C** Heating milk to 161°F (72°C) destroys the majority of harmful microbes that could be present in raw milk.	**＋ 15 SECONDS** Pasteurized milk is heated for just long enough to kill harmful microbes, in order to preserve as much flavor as possible.
	UHT (LONGLIFE) UHT ("ultra-heat" treatment) uses high temperatures to kill harmful microbes. This has a negative effect on milk's flavor.	**284°F 140°C** Milk that is intended to have a long shelf life is ultra-heated to 284°F (140°C) in pressurized tubes to eradicate virtually all of the microbes.	**＋ 4 SECONDS** Because UHT milk is heated to such a high temperature, it doesn't need to be heated for quite as long as pasteurized milk.

Milk consistency

In times gone by, the cream in milk used to rise to the top of the bottle. Nowadays, this doesn't happen in industrially produced milk—including UHT and most pasteurized milk (see below)—because of a process called homogenization. In order to prevent separation and improve the creaminess, milk is forced through nozzles at high pressure. This breaks fat globules into smaller pieces that cannot reconnect to one another and so are unable to float to the top.

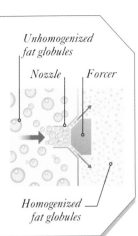

Unhomogenized fat globules

Nozzle   *Forcer*

Homogenized fat globules

THE RESULT

HOW TO USE	LONGEVITY	SAFETY
Undeniably richer and more creamy, raw milk retains all of its flavor molecules and protein, so it is ideal for making cheeses.	Raw milk begins to lose its flavor after only a day. It starts to go bad 7–10 days after production.	Because raw milk contains lots of microbes, drinking it has its risks. Health bodies advise against doing so.
HOW TO USE Ideal for drinking and for use in sauces and custards, pasteurized milk retains flavor molecules while homogenization (see box, above) adds creaminess.	**LONGEVITY** Pasteurized milk stays flavorful for several days before it starts to lose its flavor. It lasts up to 2 weeks after pasteurization.	**SAFETY** Consuming pasteurized milk in any form is low-risk, as long as it is used before its given expiration date.
HOW TO USE Ultra-heat treatment destroys proteins and sugar, reducing creaminess and giving a "burnt" taste. Best used only if access to a fridge is limited.	**LONGEVITY** Because almost all microbes are destroyed and UHT is sealed in sterile packaging, it can last for as long as 6 months after it is treated.	**SAFETY** Even safer than pasteurized; there are almost no risks associated with consuming UHT milk, as long as it's within its "use by" date.

Can I cook successfully with
LOW-FAT DAIRY PRODUCTS?

Low-fat foods just need a little more care when cooking.

Fat is vital for flavor perception, mouthfeel, and texture. Cooking with lower quantities of it can be a challenge. Fat globules capture flavor-containing molecules and spread them through a cooked dish; fats then coat the tongue so flavors linger for longer on the palate. Low-fat sauces curdle when heated, and, in desserts, cheesecakes are more difficult to set with low-fat cream cheese. In savory dishes, extra spices and seasoning can help make a delicious dish when using low-fat dairy. Add extra garlic, onions, herbs, or spices to the dish, and aim to stimulate as many taste sensations as possible by using salty, bitter, sour, and sweet ingredients.

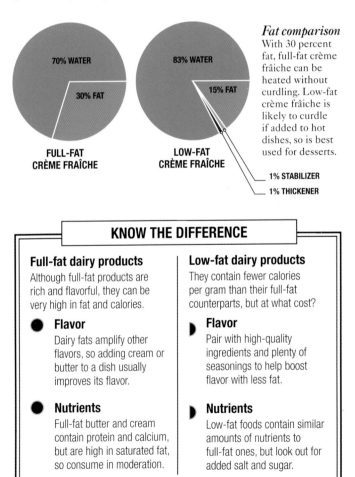

70% WATER

30% FAT

FULL-FAT CRÈME FRAÎCHE

83% WATER

15% FAT

LOW-FAT CRÈME FRAÎCHE

1% STABILIZER

1% THICKENER

Fat comparison
With 30 percent fat, full-fat crème fraîche can be heated without curdling. Low-fat crème fraîche is likely to curdle if added to hot dishes, so is best used for desserts.

KNOW THE DIFFERENCE

Full-fat dairy products
Although full-fat products are rich and flavorful, they can be very high in fat and calories.

● **Flavor**
Dairy fats amplify other flavors, so adding cream or butter to a dish usually improves its flavor.

● **Nutrients**
Full-fat butter and cream contain protein and calcium, but are high in saturated fat, so consume in moderation.

Low-fat dairy products
They contain fewer calories per gram than their full-fat counterparts, but at what cost?

▶ **Flavor**
Pair with high-quality ingredients and plenty of seasonings to help boost flavor with less fat.

▶ **Nutrients**
Low-fat foods contain similar amounts of nutrients to full-fat ones, but look out for added salt and sugar.

Which type of
CREAM
SHOULD I USE?

For such a straightforward product, shopping for cream can be surprisingly confusing.

Cream is the cornerstone on which much classical French and European cooking has been built. Cream is made up of the microscopic spheres of "milk fat," or "butterfat," separated from milk (see right), which glide over the tongue and give a silky mouthfeel unlike any other oil or fat. Added to other foods, cream carries flavor molecules and amplifies flavor in sweet and savory dishes, while also carrying its own buttery notes. Although delicate in consistency, cream is more robust than milk, and heavy creams can easily bubble on high heat without curdling.

The large selection of creams to choose from can be bewildering, but the key difference in most creams is simply the amount of milk fat they contain. The chart opposite shows the quantity of fat in the different types of cream and how this affects how each type of cream can be used.

HOW MUCH FAT?

THE TERMS "BUTTERFAT" AND "MILK FAT" CAN USUALLY BE USED INTERCHANGEABLY—BOTH REFER TO THE FATS IN DAIRY PRODUCTS.

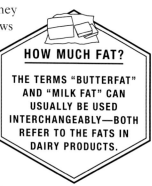

Fat globules in milk

Fat globules in milk are less dense than the liquid in which they float. Protein molecules attach to fat globules, causing them to latch onto each other when close together, and then rise. Being buoyant, fat globules were traditionally skimmed off the surface for cream. Today, cream is extracted in a centrifuge and homogenized before being sold (see p110).

TYPES OF CREAM

How cream is made
Large processing plants separate fat globules from milk in high-speed centrifuges, creating "0 percent fat" skim milk and thick, or heavy, cream that is about 50:50 fat to liquid.

RAW MILK

0% FAT
SKIM MILK

45–50% FAT
THICK CREAM

Cream is diluted with different amounts of skim milk to create the various cream types.

Less dense than water, fat globules rise to the surface.

Fat globules cluster, creating a dense fluid.

Fat globules have a water-soluble skin.

PROCESS

Spinning and diluting
Milk has around 3.7–6 percent fat when it leaves the udder, depending on the breed of cow. When processed in a spinning centrifuge, the fat-free skim milk is thrown off, leaving a high-fat cream. The faster the spinning, the more liquid is flung out and the denser the cream will be. A centrifuge spun at 150 revolutions a second collects cream that has 45–50 percent fat and skim milk that is almost devoid of fat. Light cream, whipping cream, and heavy cream are then made by adding some separated cream back into the skim milk.

Heating
Cream was traditionally heated to make a denser, richer product, and this technique is still used today for clotted cream.

Fermenting
Before centrifuges were used, it would take hours for thick cream to separate from milk. It would often ferment due to microbes in the milk. After cream has been diluted (see above), this method is used today in carefully controlled conditions to make sour cream and crème frâiche.

PRODUCT	FAT CONTENT	HEAT IT?	WHIP IT?	POUR IT?	BEST USED FOR
LIGHT CREAM	18% FAT	X	X	✓	Light cream isn't suitable for cooking because its lower fat content means it is likely to curdle when heated, especially if is mixed with an acid. Use light cream for pouring over fruit, drizzling onto soups before serving, or adding to desserts for a finishing flourish and creamy flavor contrast.
WHIPPING CREAM	35% FAT	✓	✓	X	Cream with over 35 percent fat can be whisked into a sturdy, pillowy foam. The whisk smashes fat globules apart, which then coagulate around air bubbles.
HEAVY CREAM	48% FAT	✓	✓	X	All creams with over 25 percent fat are safe for cooking on high heat as they do not curdle. The large number of fat globules in the cream means that the curdling casein proteins floating in the liquid are unable to join together to form lumps.
CLOTTED CREAM	55% FAT	X	X	X	The heating process that makes clotted cream produces complex burned and buttery notes as the sugars and proteins react and interact with the fats. This dense, rich cream is traditionally eaten in the UK as an accompaniment to scones and desserts or made into ice cream.
SOUR CREAM	20% FAT	X	X	X	This fermented cream has a fresh tang, adding richness and tartness to both savory and sweet dishes. However, the fat content is not high enough to stop casein proteins from clumping together and separating a sauce with acid ingredients. It's used in goulash, soups, and spicy South American dishes.
CRÈME FRÂICHE	30% FAT	✓	X	X	This is fermented in the same way as sour cream, but a higher fat content makes this thicker cream suitable for cooking because it won't curdle when heated with acid ingredients such as tomatoes. Use crème frâiche to enrich a pasta dish, or add to soups and other sauces.

How can I heat milk
WITHOUT A SKIN FORMING?

Though often discarded, the skin that can form on heated milk is actually full of highly nutritious whey proteins.

Milk is a versatile ingredient, providing delicate flavors while able to withstand prolonged heating. Unlike the proteins in other foods, milk curd proteins do not unravel when heated to a boil, and can survive at temperatures of up to 338°F (170°C). It can be simmered happily for a long time, gradually developing hints of vanilla, almond, and butter as new flavor molecules evolve. As the milk boils, the milk sugars (lactose) and proteins are brought together, triggering the Maillard reaction (see pp16–17), to create intense butterscotch flavors. However, the less abundant whey proteins in milk (see p108) aren't completely heat-resistant, and these start to unravel at around 158°F (70°C). If milk is heated for long enough, sticky, cooked whey proteins will float to the surface and settle as a tacky layer. With time and continued cooking, this layer will thicken and dry out, eventually forming a "skin" on the surface. If the skin is left in place and the milk is unstirred, the temperature of the milk beneath the skin will soar—as it would if it was in a sealed pan—and will boil over the side of the pan in an explosive fashion. Once a skin has thickened and congealed, stirring won't break it up and it will need to be picked off. To avoid burned milk and a skin from forming in the first place, try one or more of the suggestions below.

FULL OF GOODNESS

SKIN THAT FORMS ON SOY MILK CAN BE DRIED AND COOKED AS "YUBA," A HIGHLY NUTRITIOUS MEAT ALTERNATIVE.

Seal in steam with a lid
Once the milk has been heated and is cooling, placing a lid on the pan will keep the steam trapped inside, making it harder for a skin to dry out and set firmly.

Seal in steam with parchment
As an alternative to a lid, place a sheet of parchment paper—known as a "cartouche"—directly on top of the milk to stop steam from escaping. A cartouche can also be used if heating milk in a microwave.

Break up whey proteins
Regular stirring stops whey proteins from clumping. Whisking the surface during heating also makes it hard for whey to form a skin. As the milk cools and settles, whey will readily rise, so continue to stir.

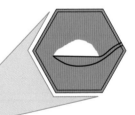

Add sugar granules
For sweet custards and sauces, sprinkle sugar on the surface as it is cooling. The jagged granules will prevent the whey proteins from easily forming a skin.

When the temperature reaches 158°F (70°C), coiled-up whey proteins start to unravel and stick to one another.

Unraveled, whey proteins coagulate together and rise to the surface of the milk to form a solid skin.

HOW TO PREVENT A SKIN FORMING

In East-Asian cuisine, the **milk skin** is considered the essential element in a **"double skin milk pudding,"** a panna cotta–type dessert that has been heated and cooled twice.

Can I make ice cream at home without an ICE-CREAM MAKER?

Without an ice-cream maker, time needs to be given to stirring and churning.

An ice-cream maker is convenient, but it's perfectly possible to make ice cream without one (see step by step below). Coaxing a sugar-cream mix into the silky-smooth dessert we all know and love needs time and care, and it's helpful to have an appreciation of the molecular structure of your ingredients. Milk fat globules that capture the churned air have water-soluble coats (see pp108–9) that need to be stripped away to make ice cream. When combined with an emulsifier, such as lecithin from egg yolks, this coat is peeled off, allowing fat molecules to coalesce into larger, creamy blobs. Whisking the mixture causes these fats to gather around air bubbles, strengthening their structure. It is these suspended air bubbles that help give a light, soft mouthfeel. Ice crystals are the enemy of smooth ice cream, and so sugar, along with a little salt, should be added to disrupt the formation of ice crystals. Even the tiniest of ice crystals feel unpleasant,y gritty on your tongue, so it's vital to keep them as small as possible. When freezing, speed is of the essence—the faster the ice cream is frozen, the smaller the ice crystals will be.

Bearing these principles in mind, it's possible to make delicious ice cream at home.

SMOOTH ICE CREAM

COMMERCIAL ICE CREAM IS PUMPED THROUGH PIPES COOLED TO AROUND −40°F (−40°C) TO REDUCE CRYSTAL FORMATION.

IN PRACTICE

MAKING ICE CREAM

When making ice cream at home, it's best to start with a custard as your base, as it contains a natural emulsifier in the form of egg yolks and sufficient sugar and fat to create a creamy texture. The cooked egg and milk proteins help stabilize the mixture. You can use ready-made, high-fat fresh custard, or make your own using the method on pp104–05.

#1

#2

#3

PREPARE AND COOL THE CUSTARD
Place a shallow, freezerproof metal or plastic container in the freezer. Keeping equipment cold speeds freezing, which helps achieve a silky-smooth ice cream. Prepare a double quantity of custard (see pp104–105) and pour it into a heatproof bowl. Place the bowl of custard inside a larger bowl filled with ice cubes, then leave to cool, stirring occasionally.

MINIMIZE ICE-CRYSTAL FORMATION
Pour the cooled custard into the pre-chilled container. Shallow containers are best because they have a larger surface area, which speeds freezing to give a smoother finished texture. Place the container in the freezer. After 45 minutes, remove the mixture from the freezer and whisk it vigorously to break up the ice crystals. Return it to the freezer.

WHISK REGULARLY
Continue to check the mixture every 30 minutes, whisking vigorously each time. Whisking not only breaks up ice crystals, but also incorporates air, improving the texture. Make sure that you close the freezer door quickly after opening, to help maintain sub-freezing temperatures. Continue for about 3 hours, until the ice cream has begun to set and solidify.

Do ice-cream makers make creamier
ICE CREAM THAN WHISKING BY HAND?

For ice-cream enthusiasts, a maker is a worthwhile investment.

In the same way that bread makers have taken all the wrist work out of making a fresh loaf of bread, so ice-cream makers have done away with the tiresome churning needed to make ice cream. It is possible to make delicious ice cream without an ice-cream maker (see facing page), but if you're serious about ice-cream making, it's a good idea to invest. Continuous churning smashes large ice crystals before they have a chance to gain a foothold, making light, fluffy ice cream that would be difficult to make by hand. Churning also gradually adds air bubbles to the mix, turning milky-sweet slush into a frozen aerated foam.

Microscopic ice crystals

Tiny air cavities

Sugar solution

Fat globules clump together around air bubbles.

#4

FINAL FREEZE TO SOLIDIFY

Once the ice cream is well set and you can no longer whisk it, return to the freezer and chill for a final hour. This final freeze solidifies the ice cream completely before serving. As it's only possible to beat a certain amount of air into the mixture by hand (see right), this ice cream can deteriorate if left in the freezer, so serve within 2–3 days.

STRAWBERRY ICE CREAM

Molecular anatomy of ice cream

The smooth surface of ice cream is in fact a landscape of microscopic airy caves. Each hollow is contained by a mushy wall made of fat and supported by ice crystals. Continuous churning with an ice-cream maker and rapid freezing shrink the gritty-textured ice crystals.

Is it worth MAKING MY OWN YOGURT?

Preparing yogurt at home is relatively simple and can produce interesting flavor variations.

Yogurt was first discovered five millennia ago when our ancestors realized that letting whole milk "go bad" produced a long-lasting sour, thickened milk. Traditionally, various bacteria species and types would "chew" milk sugars, gradually producing acid, which slowly destabilized casein proteins, causing them to mat into a gel-forming lattice, rather than into clumps. Today, yogurt bacteria have been sanitized and standardized, and, apart from probiotic yogurts, only two yogurt bacteria are commonly used. As with cheese, what we have gained in reliability and safety, we have lost in diversity and variety.

ORIGINS OF YOGURT

THE WORD *YOGURT* DERIVED FROM THE TURKS, WHO NAMED THE DENSE MILK "YOGURMAK," MEANING "TO THICKEN."

The two bacteria we use today, *Streptococcus thermophilus* and *Lactobacillus delbrueckii*, work together as a pair, feeding on each other.

Bacteria for yogurt making can be bought as a dried culture, although it is easier to use a spoonful of an existing yogurt as a "starter" for new yogurt, as shown below, since most yogurts contain live bacteria. Yogurt starters can be propagated for years and handed down, potentially nurturing rare, alternative flavor-generating bacteria. However, research shows that many heirloom cultures actually originated from a yogurt that contained the two most common commercial strains.

MAKING YOUR OWN YOGURT

The yogurt-making step-by-step process shown here uses existing live yogurt to create a new batch of homemade yogurt. Once you have completed your batch of yogurt, you can start a new batch using a few spoonfuls of the yogurt you have made, within seven days, while the acid-making microbe numbers are still high.

#1 UNWIND CURD PROTEINS

Heat 3½ pints (2 liters) whole milk over low heat until it reaches 185°F (85°C), stirring occasionally. Heating removes unwanted bacteria, unsettles the curd proteins so they will unwind more easily, and cooks some whey proteins to help thicken the yogurt. Remove the pan from the heat and allow the milk to cool to 104–113°F (40–45°C), a temperature ideal for bacterial growth.

#2 ADD THE CULTURE

Transfer the cooled milk to two 1¾-pint (1-liter) sterilized preserving jars (or a thermos), leaving a little space at the top of each jar. Add 1–2 tablespoons of live yogurt to each jar and stir well to combine.

#3 DEVELOP LACTIC ACID

Screw or clip the lids tightly onto the jars and wrap the jars in clean tea towels, leave in a warm place for 6–8 hours to ferment. This gives time for the bacteria to create lactic acid, which destabilizes the proteins and creates a lattice-like gel.

Why does yogurt separate
IN SPICY DISHES?

Yogurt is a key ingredient in many Indian and Pakistani dishes.

The trick to using yogurt while retaining a glossy curry sauce is knowing when to add it. Yogurt contains the same milk proteins that can curdle milk and light cream, and, having a similar fat content to milk, it will separate into curds and whey when cooked at high heat alongside acids. It isn't the spices that make yogurt separate, but acidic ingredients such as tomatoes, vinegar, lemon juice, or fruits. The higher the temperature, the faster the curdling, so to avoid yogurt separating, add it toward the end of cooking, when a dish is cooling, not simmering. Alternatively, use crème frâiche, which has a similar refreshing fermented flavor, but a fat content of 30 percent, so it can be simmered without separating.

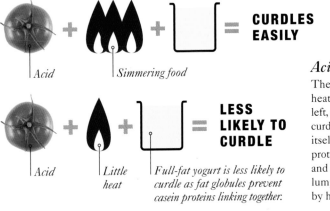

Acid + *Simmering food* + = **CURDLES EASILY**

Acid + *Little heat* + = **LESS LIKELY TO CURDLE**

Full-fat yogurt is less likely to curdle as fat globules prevent casein proteins linking together.

Acid and heat
The combination of heat and acid, shown left, causes yogurt to curdle. Although acidic itself, yogurt's curd protein lattice is flimsy and crumples into lumps if overstressed by heat and strong acid.

Is it worth taking
PROBIOTIC YOGURT?

Bugs in our intestines boost our immunity and provide nutrients.

Each person's mix of intestinal microbes is unique and affected by overall health, stress levels, and, most critically, diet. Science shows us that an unbalanced population of gut microbes (the "intestinal flora") is linked to many medical maladies. Probiotic yogurts contain large amounts of "good bacteria," which can help push out bugs that can take a toll on our health, helping restore digestive health and well-being. Often, though, claims are overhyped. We do know that probiotics are good for preventing diarrhea when traveling, and for treating antibiotic-related diarrhea by nurturing good gut bacteria eradicated by antibiotics. However, products vary and those prescribed by doctors can contain more bacteria.

#4

ENJOY OR REFRIGERATE
Once fermented, the yogurt is ready to eat, or can be stored in the fridge for up to two weeks, where bacteria growth will slow. For thicker, Greek-style yogurt, strain the yogurt at this point through a very fine cheesecloth or coffee-filter paper for several hours until thickened.

In focus
CHEESE

There are over 1,700 types of cheese in the world, and this huge variety stems from simply fermenting the curds found in animal milks.

On its most basic level, cheese is a congealed lump of curdled milk that has been fermented (partially digested) by microbes. Cheese-making starts with a choice of milk, which can be from a cow, buffalo, goat, sheep, and even camel milk. Many cheese makers choose to use raw, rather than pasteurized, milk (see p110–111), as this retains the subtle flavor molecules that are lost in high heats. "Starter" bacteria are added, and the milk is then heated to the ideal temperature for the new microbes to flourish. Then, acid or rennet (see p125) is added to the milk, which causes proteins in the milk to clump together, ensnaring milk's creamy fat globules, and float to the surface. These clumps of fat and protein are "curds," and the remaining liquid is "whey." Buoyant curds are cut into pieces—walnut-sized pieces for soft

cheeses, and tiny grains for hard cheeses. The curds are drained of excess whey and scooped into molds. Fresh, soft cheeses may be left for a few hours or days to solidify, but aged cheeses will undergo a series of further processes before being ready to eat. Some cheeses are weighted or pressed to remove moisture and create a harder-textured cheese, and some are "washed" in brine, wine, or cider to create a soft rind patinated with flavorful molds. Cheeses are left to mature in temperature- and humidity-controlled rooms for months at a time, to allow microbes to develop complex flavors.

Molds spread on the surface of aged cheese grow into a living rind that stops the cheese from drying out.

SCIENCE

BACTERIA, FUNGI, AND YEASTS FERMENT MILK CURDS, ADDING COMPLEX FLAVORS TO DIFFERENT TYPES OF CHEESE.

COOKING

USE STRONG-FLAVORED CHEESES SPARINGLY. PAIR CHEESES WITH INGREDIENTS THAT COMPLEMENT THEIR FLAVOR PROFILE.

COLOR

Blue molds from the penicillin family grow inside blue cheeses.

KNOW YOUR CHEESE

The many processing decisions made by the cheese maker—including which milk to use, how small to cut the curds, and how long to age the cheese—impact the flavor and properties of the finished cheese.

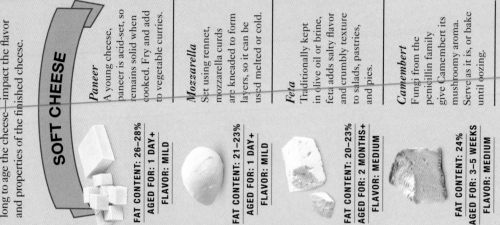

SOFT CHEESE

Paneer
A young cheese, paneer is acid-set, so remains solid when cooked. Fry and add to vegetable curries.

FAT CONTENT: 26–28%
AGED FOR: 1 DAY+
FLAVOR: MILD

Mozzarella
Set using rennet, mozzarella curds are kneaded to form layers, so it can be used melted or cold.

FAT CONTENT: 21–23%
AGED FOR: 1 DAY+
FLAVOR: MILD

Feta
Traditionally kept in olive oil or brine, feta adds salty flavor and crumbly texture to salads, pastries, and pies.

FAT CONTENT: 20–23%
AGED FOR: 2 MONTHS+
FLAVOR: MEDIUM

Camembert
Fungi from the penicillin family give Camembert its mushroomy aroma. Serve as it is, or bake until oozing.

FAT CONTENT: 24%
AGED FOR: 3–5 WEEKS
FLAVOR: MEDIUM

Bavaria Blu

Made from a mixture of milk and cream, Bavaria Blu is a mild blue cheese with high fat content. Its rich flavor complements rye and nut breads.

FAT CONTENT: 43–44%

AGED FOR: 4–6 WEEKS

FLAVOR: MILD

HARD CHEESE

Monterey Jack

Based on a Spanish-Mexican cheese, Monterey Jack is sweet and tart in flavor. Grill it or grate it atop beans or chili.

FAT CONTENT: 28–30%

AGED FOR: 1–12 MONTHS

FLAVOR: MEDIUM

Emmentaler

This herbaceous, fragrant cheese is made with milk from cows that graze in Alpine meadows. Grate into fondues, grill on bread, or eat cold.

FAT CONTENT: 28–32%

AGED FOR: 4–18 MONTHS

FLAVOR: MILD

Manchego

Dry in texture with a nutty flavor that matures to peppery when aged, Manchego is best served raw. Slice it finely, or cut it into thin wedges.

FAT CONTENT: 39–40%

AGED FOR: 6–18 MONTHS

FLAVOR: MEDIUM

Parmigiano-Reggiano

Aged for years at a time, Parmigiano Reggiano, or Parmesan, is packed with flavor. It adds umami notes to pastas, sauces, soups, and salads.

FAT CONTENT: 28%

AGED FOR: 18–36 MONTHS

FLAVOR: STRONG

CAMEMBERT

The type of milk helps to determine the color of the cheese.

Surface microbes release protein-digesting enzymes, which create an oozy texture.

Very ripe soft cheeses often have a soft, collapsing interior.

COOKING

A MOIST, WELL-AGED CHEESE BLENDS BEST IN A SAUCE. MILD, SOFT CHEESES ADD TEXTURE AND FRESH FLAVORS.

SCIENCE

TEXTURE DEPENDS ON HOW MUCH WHEY IS LEFT IN THE CURDS, WHICH BACTERIA ARE USED, AND HOW LONG THE CHEESE IS LEFT TO RIPEN.

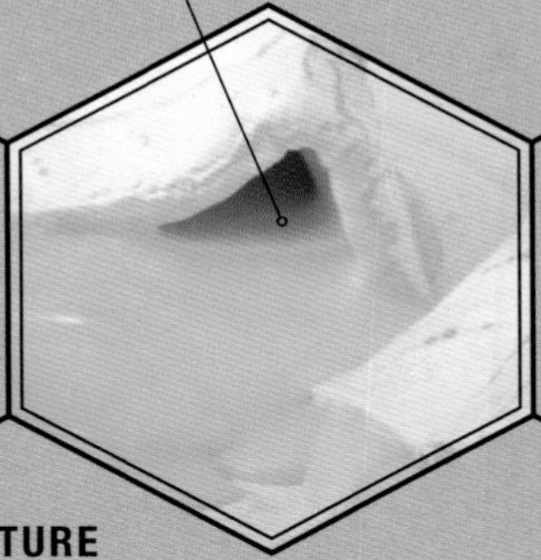

TEXTURE

If the veins in blue cheese are mold, WHY IS IT EDIBLE?

We have evolved to live in harmony with bacteria.

The reputation of bacteria as being harmful is undeserved; in fact, many are beneficial. Traditionally, microbes that gave cheese its character reflected the microbiology of the area. Today, cheese is made with pasteurized milk, eradicating naturally occurring microbes. Of the molds that have survived, *Penicillium fungi* are most widely used; they cause the blue veins in strong-tasting cheeses and are quite safe. One of the oldest blue cheeses, Roquefort, owes its greenish-blue veins to *Penicillium roqueforti*, the same mold used in Stilton and Danish blue. Gorgonzola and some other French cheeses rely on *Penicillium glaucum*, which gives a slightly different flavor.

"Roquefort *owes its greenish-blue* veins *to Penicillium roqueforti.*"

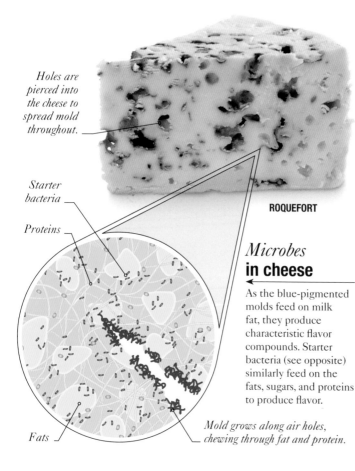

Holes are pierced into the cheese to spread mold throughout.

ROQUEFORT

Starter bacteria

Proteins

Fats

Mold grows along air holes, chewing through fat and protein.

Microbes in cheese

As the blue-pigmented molds feed on milk fat, they produce characteristic flavor compounds. Starter bacteria (see opposite) similarly feed on the fats, sugars, and proteins to produce flavor.

Why are some cheeses SO STRONG AND SMELLY?

With more than 17,000 varieties of cheese worldwide, there is an incredible diversity of taste and aroma.

Creamy brie, buttery Gouda, crumbly Parmesan, brothy Cheddar, and mild-tasting paneer are just some of the numerous varieties of cheese. Within this family of cheeses are the super-smelly ones, such as Muenster, Limburger, Roquefort, and Stilton. The universe of cheese is testimony to the creativity of cheese makers throughout the ages, but it is the microbes, or bacteria, that are the real stars of the show. The several-hundred-strong ensemble cast of bacteria, fungi, and yeasts brings life to a bland, salty lump of white curd. By digesting (fermenting), fat, proteins, and milk sugar, they excrete a complex selection of flavorful (and sometimes very smelly) molecules, as shown in the flowchart, opposite. Certain bacteria have especially strong smells. For example, Muenster and Limburger owe their "old socks" smell to *Brevibacterium*, which also flourishes in the moisture between toes!

Stand-out smelly cheeses
The smelliest cheeses tend to be those that have "smear cultures" of bacteria or white molds deliberately spread over their surface as they ripen.

CAMEMBERT

PONT L'EVEQUE

MUENSTER

EPOISSES

BRIE DE MEAUX

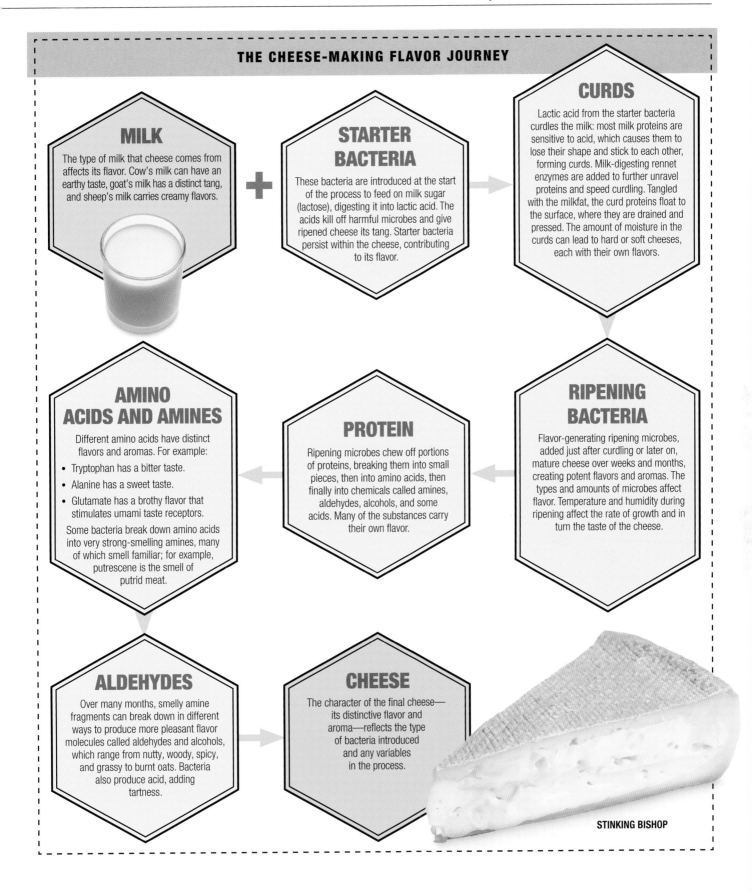

THE CHEESE-MAKING FLAVOR JOURNEY

MILK

The type of milk that cheese comes from affects its flavor. Cow's milk can have an earthy taste, goat's milk has a distinct tang, and sheep's milk carries creamy flavors.

STARTER BACTERIA

These bacteria are introduced at the start of the process to feed on milk sugar (lactose), digesting it into lactic acid. The acids kill off harmful microbes and give ripened cheese its tang. Starter bacteria persist within the cheese, contributing to its flavor.

CURDS

Lactic acid from the starter bacteria curdles the milk: most milk proteins are sensitive to acid, which causes them to lose their shape and stick to each other, forming curds. Milk-digesting rennet enzymes are added to further unravel proteins and speed curdling. Tangled with the milkfat, the curd proteins float to the surface, where they are drained and pressed. The amount of moisture in the curds can lead to hard or soft cheeses, each with their own flavors.

AMINO ACIDS AND AMINES

Different amino acids have distinct flavors and aromas. For example:

- Tryptophan has a bitter taste.
- Alanine has a sweet taste.
- Glutamate has a brothy flavor that stimulates umami taste receptors.

Some bacteria break down amino acids into very strong-smelling amines, many of which smell familiar; for example, putrescene is the smell of putrid meat.

PROTEIN

Ripening microbes chew off portions of proteins, breaking them into small pieces, then into amino acids, then finally into chemicals called amines, aldehydes, alcohols, and some acids. Many of the substances carry their own flavor.

RIPENING BACTERIA

Flavor-generating ripening microbes, added just after curdling or later on, mature cheese over weeks and months, creating potent flavors and aromas. The types and amounts of microbes affect flavor. Temperature and humidity during ripening affect the rate of growth and in turn the taste of the cheese.

ALDEHYDES

Over many months, smelly amine fragments can break down in different ways to produce more pleasant flavor molecules called aldehydes and alcohols, which range from nutty, woody, spicy, and grassy to burnt oats. Bacteria also produce acid, adding tartness.

CHEESE

The character of the final cheese— its distinctive flavor and aroma—reflects the type of bacteria introduced and any variables in the process.

STINKING BISHOP

Why does some cheese GET STRINGY?

Not all cheese forms warm strands between pizza slices.

Stilton and Cheddar offer a flavor punch, but separate into greasy lumps if heated. In hard or mature cheeses, the casein (curd) proteins are bound so tightly that they don't soften until they are at about 180°F (80°C)—long after the fats have liquefied and drained away at 86–104°F (30–40°C). But some soft cheeses, such as ricotta, don't melt because they're made by curdling milk with acid, rather than rennet (see opposite); the acid causes curd proteins to knot irreversibly.

How stringy cheeses are formed

What makes cheese such as mozzarella so stringy is how the milk was curdled, how long it ripened, and the balance of fat and moisture, which makes casein proteins bind loosely (see left). Mozzarella is made by adding bacteria to milk before rennet, heating, then kneading curds like bread (a technique called "pasta filata") to encourage the protein to align into fibers.

Casein proteins in **young cheese** ➤

In cheeses such as mozzarella, protein networks bind together, but not tightly enough to clump, and are separated sufficiently by fat molecules, which allows them to bridge one another in long, stretchy strands.

Fats bridge the protein strands when they melt.

Aligned loosely in one direction, these proteins turn stringy as fats melt.

Should I avoid PROCESSED CHEESE?

Processed cheese is made from similar raw materials as unprocessed, but is far removed from the original food.

In the mid-1800s, the first American cheese factory was founded in New York, producing large volumes of fairly bland Cheddar. In 1916, entrepreneur James L. Kraft went on to pioneer processed cheese from shredded offcuts. The offcuts had been pasteurized, melted, and mixed with citric acid and substances called phosphates, which tear calcium away from the casein (curd) proteins, allowing the curds to mold together evenly.

Today's processed cheese is an amalgam of different cheeses, milk whey proteins, salt, and flavorings, bound with emulsifiers (substances that allow fats and water to mix). If you prefer "natural" foods you may want to avoid processed cheese, but it's nearly impossible to get a glossy magma-like cheese topping on a burger with non-factory-made cheese.

KNOW THE DIFFERENCE

Processed cheese
Processed cheese is usually pressed and shaped into slices before packaging in plastic. It can also be sold in a block or can.

■ **This** is made from a variety of cheeses and contains whey proteins and salt, with artificial colorings and preservatives added to give uniformity of taste and appearance and prolong shelf life.

■ **Processed cheeses** have less calcium (to weaken the proteins and make the cheese moldable), and contain thickeners and emulsifiers, which hold fats and water together when they are heated.

Unprocessed cheese
Natural cheese is sold in a variety of shapes and sizes and can then be grated, sliced, or cut up and used as required.

◣ **To make unprocessed cheese**, the whey is drained off and the cheese is made from the milk curds, rennet enzymes or acid, and salt, then ripened over a period of time.

◣ **With fewer additives**, this may contain colorings and enzymes to speed ripening. Cheese that isn't processed develops its flavors from the milk and rennet during ripening.

Can I make perfect
SOFT CHEESE AT HOME?

Like brewing beer at home, cheese making can be a simple or involved process.

Cheese-making kits are available, which include recipes and "cultures" (pre-prepared and carefully measured packets of microbe spores). Unfermented cheese, however, can be made at home without any special equipment, culture samples, or even rennet, the enzyme commonly used in cheese making (see right).

The first stage in making cheese is to curdle milk. Microbes in milk, specifically bacteria called *lactobacilli*, digest milk to create lactic acid, which achieve this. Most milk proteins, casein proteins, are sensitive to acid; they lose their shape and stick together. Acids can also be added directly without the help of bugs. This is done with mascarpone and paneer, when vinegar or lemon juice is added to warm milk. Curdling milk is made easier by adding the protein-breaking enzyme rennet, found in calf's offal. This curdles milk rapidly, causing casein proteins to clump in a structured way. Ripening bacteria, fungi, and yeasts can then be added to develop flavors. Harder cheese is pressed and left to ripen for weeks or months.

The step by step below is a simple recipe for making soft cheese using an acid to help the curdling process.

FOR VEGETARIANS

VEGETARIAN RENNET IS MADE BY GROWING MOLDS THAT PRODUCE ENZYMES SIMILAR TO THOSE IN CALF RENNET.

MAKING SOFT CHEESE

This quick recipe for ricotta-style soft cheese produces a cheese that is far fresher than its store-bought equivalent. Cheeses are best stored loosely wrapped (and in an airtight container if refrigerated), if at all, and ideally should be eaten at their ripening temperature because flavor molecules in chilled cheese are not released as readily.

IN PRACTICE

#1

#2

#3

CURDLE AND SEPARATE THE CURDS
Pour 1¾ pints (1 liter) whole milk into a saucepan over low heat. Heat gently to 165–194°F (74–90°C). Remove from the heat. Add 1½ tsp salt and 2 tbsp white wine vinegar or the juice of 1 lemon to unravel the proteins. Stir and allow to cool for 10–15 minutes until the mix has curdled and the curds have separated.

DRAIN OUT THE REMAINING WHEY
Remove the more solid curds from the liquid whey using a slotted spoon. Place the curds in a muslin bag. Tie the bag with string and hang the curds over a bowl or sink to allow the excess whey to drip out. For very soft ricotta, drain for 20–30 minutes, or leave overnight for a crumbly, dry texture.

SERVE IMMEDIATELY OR CHILL
Unwrap the bag to reveal the set curds, and then serve the soft cheese right away, or place in an airtight container and store in the fridge for up to three days.

RICE, GRAINS & PASTA

In focus
RICE

It may be small, but rice is a dense, nutritional storehouse. No wonder it is the staple food of nearly half of the world's population.

As a seed, rice is designed to nourish the next generation of rice plant—much like an egg nourishes a developing chick. Removing each grain's shell-like, inedible husk reveals an edible kernel coated in a nutritious, colored bran—this is "brown" rice. The delicate oils in the bran oxidize and turn rancid in months, so rice is "polished," or milled, to improve its shelf life. This abrasion leaves behind only the starch-filled core, or endosperm—this is "white" rice. The densely packed starch crystals in

the endosperm are chalky and barely edible uncooked. Cooking in water at least 150°F (65°C) breaks open the hard starch and binds it with water in a softening process called gelatinization. Rice contains two types of starch: amylopectin and amylose. Knowing how these starches respond to heat and water helps you pick the most suitable rice variety (see below and panel).

SCIENCE
STICKY RICE IS HIGH IN SOFT, LOOSELY PACKED AMYLOPECTIN STARCH AND LOW IN HARD AMYLOSE STARCH.

COOKING
AMYLOPECTIN STARCH SEEPS READILY FROM RICE GRAINS INTO THE COOKING WATER, COATING THEM IN A STICKY GEL.

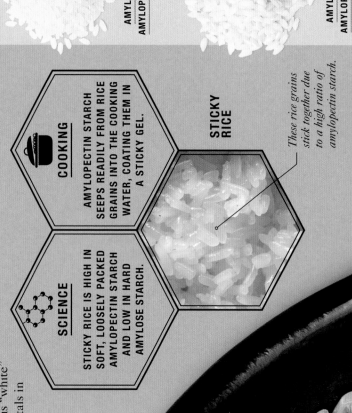

STICKY RICE

These rice grains stick together due to a high ratio of amylopectin starch.

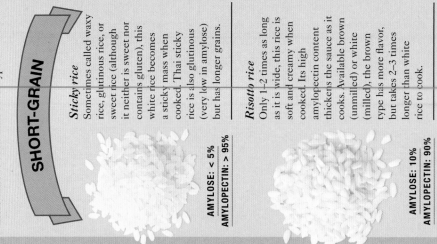

KNOW YOUR RICE

Rice varieties vary in their ratio of amylose to amylopectin starch, but as a general rule the longer the grain, the more amylose it contains. Small amylose starch crystals are tightly packed, hence long-grain rices need more time to cook than other types.

SHORT-GRAIN

Sticky rice
Sometimes called waxy rice, glutinous rice, or sweet rice (although it neither is sweet nor contains gluten), this white rice becomes a sticky mass when cooked. Thai sticky rice is also glutinous (very low in amylose) but has longer grains.

AMYLOSE: < 5%
AMYLOPECTIN: > 95%

Risotto rice
Only 1–2 times as long as it is wide, this rice is soft and creamy when cooked. Its high amylopectin content thickens the sauce as it cooks. Available brown (unmilled) or white (milled), the brown type has more flavor, but takes 2–3 times longer than white rice to cook.

AMYLOSE: 10%
AMYLOPECTIN: 90%

MEDIUM-GRAIN

Paella rice

About 2–3 times as long as it is wide, this white rice is moist and slightly sticky when cooked, but retains some "bite." Varieties include calrose, valencia, and bomba. Some risotto rice is also medium-grain.

AMYLOSE: 15–17%
AMYLOPECTIN: 83–85%

LONG-GRAIN

White rice

Mild-flavored and versatile, long-grain white rice is one of the most commonly used rice varieties. It's about 4 times as long as it is wide, and cooks to a fluffy texture due to higher amylose levels. Basmati is a popular long-grain rice from South Asia that is firm, aromatic, and nutty.

AMYLOSE: 22%
AMYLOPECTIN: 78%

Wild rice

Although it is called "rice," this comes from a different plant. The bran is left intact, giving it a firm, chewy consistency. It requires a lot longer to cook (up to an hour) than other "true" rice varieties.

AMYLOSE: 2%
AMYLOPECTIN: 98%

Bran coating
The bran coating imbues cooked brown rice with a nutty taste and chewy texture.

Nutrient-dense
Brown rice contains the living "germ" of the seed as well as fiber- and protein-rich bran.

Cooking time
Brown rice takes two to three times longer than white rice to cook because hot water needs to penetrate the tough bran layer.

These rice grains stay separate, firm, and springy due to a higher ratio of amylose starch.

SCIENCE

FLUFFY RICE CONTAINS A HIGHER PROPORTION OF HARD, TIGHTLY PACKED AMYLOSE STARCH THAN STICKY RICE.

COOKING

AMYLOSE STARCH IS DIFFICULT TO SOFTEN, WHICH HELPS RICE GRAINS HOLD THEIR SHAPE WHEN COOKED.

FLUFFY RICE

BROWN LONG-GRAIN RICE

How much water SHOULD I ADD TO MY RICE?

Package instructions shouldn't be taken as gospel.

Each type of rice, whether short-grain, basmati, brown, or wild, absorbs almost the same amount of water. The real reason we use more water for long-grain, brown, and wild rices is that these grains take longer to cook, so more of the cooking water evaporates away during this time. However, although most rice varieties can absorb as much as three times their weight in water, too much fluid makes the cooked grains mushy and slimy. To cook any variety of rice to perfection (slightly firm and not too sticky), use equal amounts of water and rice—a ratio of 1:1 water:rice—plus extra water for evaporation. For a reasonable approximation of the "evaporation water" for white rice fill the pan with water to about 1in (2.5cm) above the level of the rice. But be aware that water evaporates faster from wide pans, so these may need extra water.

EVAPORATION

THE SHAPE AND SIZE OF YOUR PAN, NOT RICE QUANTITY, DETERMINE HOW MUCH WATER EVAPORATES.

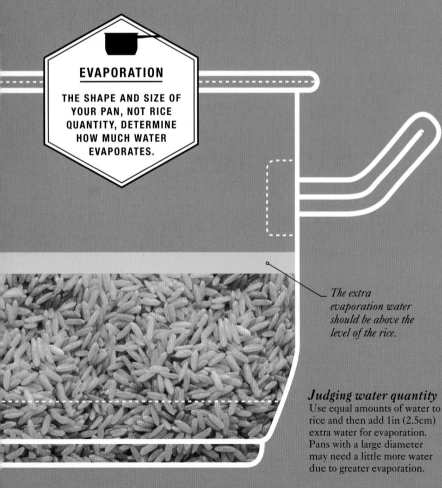

The extra evaporation water should be above the level of the rice.

Judging water quantity
Use equal amounts of water to rice and then add 1in (2.5cm) extra water for evaporation. Pans with a large diameter may need a little more water due to greater evaporation.

IN PRACTICE

#1

REMOVE EXCESS STARCH
Rinse the rice before cooking to wash off surface starch and reduce stickiness. Place 1lb (450g) long-grain rice in a sieve, and rinse under cold water until the water runs clear. Washing also removes dust and microscopic debris, but avoid repeated drenching, because this may also wash off aromatic flavor molecules.

How can I cook
FLUFFY RICE EVERY TIME?

Avoid mushy rice by following some simple principles.

PROTECTIVE BRAN

WHITE RICE LEACHES MORE STICKY STARCH THAN BROWN RICE BECAUSE ITS BRAN HAS BEEN REMOVED.

Rice must be heated in water at 150°F (65°C) before water can force its way into the dense, inedible starch granules inside each grain, transforming them into a soft, edible gel, a process called gelatinization. However, in the process, white rice can leach a lot of starch into the cooking water, turning the water cloudy. As the starch-filled liquid cools on the cooked rice, it dries to a sticky layer. To cook rice that is fluffy, rinse off excess starch before you heat the rice, and don't soak all-purpose long-grain rice overnight because this will cause the water-engorged grains to turn mushy and clump together during cooking. Also make sure you are using the right quantity of water (see left).

COOKING RICE

All you need to cook tender, fluffy, nonsticky long-grain rice is a pan with a tight-fitting lid. The rice is first boiled at high heat to allow the starches to start gelatinizing, and then steamed so that all the remaining cooking water is absorbed, leaving no starch-filled water behind to form a sticky coating on the rice.

#2

GELATINIZE THE STARCH

Put the rinsed rice in a pan with water. The water should reach approximately 1in (2.5cm) above the level of the rice in the pan to allow for evaporation (see left). Bring to a rolling boil with the pan uncovered. When rice reaches 150°F (65°C), the starches begin to swell with water and soften, or gelatinize.

#3

ABSORB MOISTURE

Once the pan has nearly boiled dry and the grains softened, allow the rice to absorb the cooking water by lightly steaming it. Cover with a tight-fitting lid, reduce the heat to very low, and simmer gently for a further 15 minutes, until the water is absorbed. Do not lift the lid and let the steam escape or stir the rice while cooking.

#4

SEPARATE THE GRAINS

When the rice has absorbed the cooking water, remove the pan from the heat to prevent the rice from overcooking. With the lid still on, leave to stand for 10 minutes or more. As the rice slowly cools, the softened starch crystals will firm up (a process called retrogradation), causing the grains to separate. Use a fork to gently fluff up the rice just before serving.

Is it okay to
REHEAT COOKED RICE?

Reheating rice requires extra care.

An unpleasant soil bacteria called *Bacillus cereus* lives on the surface of moist rice. Cooking kills the original bacteria, but not all their hardy spores—these chrysalis-like seeds may sprout into life on cooked rice and release toxins that can cause abdominal pain, vomiting, and diarrhea if eaten.

Danger of cooling slowly

Bacillus cereus starts to multiply and release its toxins on cooked rice between 39–131°F (4–55°C). Cooked rice becomes unsafe once the bacteria and toxins reach a critical level, but the smell and appearance of the rice is unchanged. Always cool promptly and store cooked rice at less than 41°F (5°C) to slow growth—the quicker you do this, the safer leftover rice will be to use.

COOKED-RICE TIMELINE

TIME	WHAT HAPPENS	WHAT TO DO
WITHIN 10–60 MINS	Cooked spores may have hatched into living bacteria. They multiply on cooked rice at room temperature and release toxins.	• Serve as soon as possible. • Cool leftovers—transfer to shallow dishes, or rinse and drain in cold water, and then refrigerate.
DAY 1	Bacteria grows slowly in the refrigerator. Levels may be low enough for reheating if cooked rice was cooled within an hour the previous day.	• Use today if you want to reheat. • Make sure rice is piping hot. • Do not reheat more than once.
DAY 2	Bacteria level is dangerous for reheating, which will trigger a surge in toxin production (see below).	• Use for cold dishes only. • Do not reheat.
DAY 3	Bacteria level is dangerous for reheating, which will accelerate growth and produce more toxins.	• Use for cold dishes only. • Do not reheat. • Discard if not used.

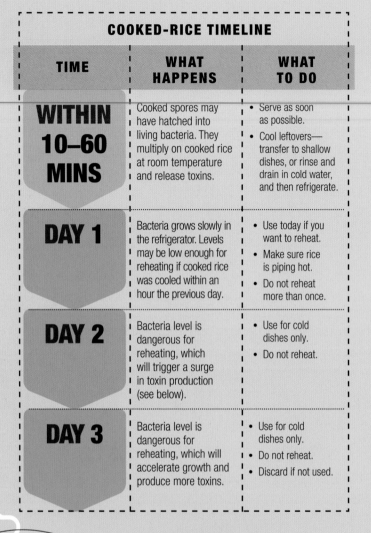

Bacteria spores in cooked rice

On cooked rice, heat-resistant *Bacillus cereus* spores reawaken into active bacteria. They can multiply quickly at room temperature and early in cooking to release toxins that cause food poisoning. Reheating cooked rice may kill the new bacteria, but will not destroy the toxins.

Spores develop into bacteria.

Bacteria release toxins.

Emetic toxins (causing vomiting) produced at 53–99°F (12–37°C).

Diarrheal toxins produced at 50–109°F (10–43°C).

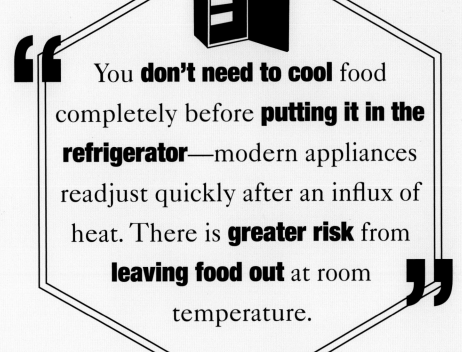

"You **don't need to cool** food completely before **putting it in the refrigerator**—modern appliances readjust quickly after an influx of heat. There is **greater risk** from **leaving food out** at room temperature."

The Process of PRESSURE COOKING

Trapped inside a tightly sealed pan, superheated steam inside the pressure cooker cooks food rapidly.

Pressure cookers often languish at the back of the cabinet, unused, but they are an incredible tool for time-pressed cooks. An extremely tight-fitting lid stops steam from escaping so the air pressure in the pan rises. This in turn raises the boiling point of water, creating a very hot, steamy cooking environment. As a result, the cooking times for stews, soups, stocks, and grains are cut drastically.

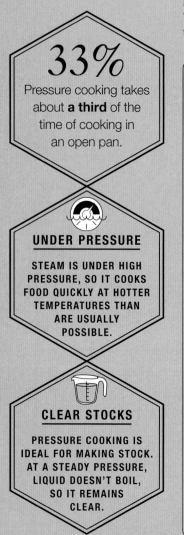

33%
Pressure cooking takes about **a third** of the time of cooking in an open pan.

UNDER PRESSURE
STEAM IS UNDER HIGH PRESSURE, SO IT COOKS FOOD QUICKLY AT HOTTER TEMPERATURES THAN ARE USUALLY POSSIBLE.

CLEAR STOCKS
PRESSURE COOKING IS IDEAL FOR MAKING STOCK. AT A STEADY PRESSURE, LIQUID DOESN'T BOIL, SO IT REMAINS CLEAR.

RELEASE PRESSURE
Once the food is cooked through, follow the manufacturer's instructions to release pressure. Drain off excess liquid and serve the food immediately.

#6

Water molecules penetrate grains.

Individual grains swell sideways as water bonds with starch to form a soft gel.

Superheated water cooks grains rapidly.

See inside
Because the chamber inside the cooker is under high pressure—around 15psi (pounds per square inch)—water molecules need more energy to emerge as steam, meaning that water reaches the boiling point at 248°F (120°C), rather than 212°F (100°C). These superheated water molecules cook food much faster than boiling or steaming.

Key
- - - - ► Movement of water molecules
- - - - ► Heat traveling from water

TURN ON THE HEAT
After securing the lid, place the pan on the stovetop over medium-high heat.

#4

VENT STEAM

#5 Once the cooker reaches pressure, steam is emitted from a vent in the lid. At this point, reduce the heat to medium-low, to prevent further pressure increase and loss of water. Continue to cook for the specified cooking time.

Highly energized water molecules fill the pan at twice the density of a normal pan, cooking the food from all angles.

The handle has two parts that lock together to seal in steam—it may also have a pressure gauge.

CLOSE AND LOCK THE LID

Lock the lid and pan together using the handle. This ensures that no steam can escape, so increases air pressure inside the cooker.

#3

An airtight sealing ring helps retain pressure inside the cooker.

Steam circulates inside the pressure cooker.

PLACE FOOD IN THE COOKER

#2 Foods such as chicken can be cooked in a steam basket or trivet above the water. Softer, faster-cooking foods, including vegetables, are best cooked in a steamer basket.

ADD LIQUID

#1 The quantity of water, broth, or stock you need to use depends on the model of pressure cooker you have, so always check the manufacturer's instructions. For grains and vegetables, use around 1 cup of water for every 15 minutes of cooking time. For soups and stews, liquid should reach between half and two-thirds of the way up the pan.

Stovetop pressure cookers often have a thick base made of three layers of metal, in order to spread heat evenly.

Why is WHOLE GRAIN BETTER THAN PROCESSED?

Whole grains contain bran—rich in key nutrients.

Whole-grain foods, also called whole wheat or whole meal, are made from grains and cereals that contain all of the bran and germ (see below). Flours labeled "brown" contain less bran, while the labels "multigrain," "stone-ground," or "100 percent wheat" indicate that they contain the nutrient-dense germ, but not all of the bran.

Bran carries both nutty flavor notes and many nutrients. The fiber of bran is not digested, but bulks up food, triggering feelings of fullness. A fifth of the fiber is "soluble," which turns into a gloopy gel in the gut, helping to slow sugar and cholesterol absorption from food.

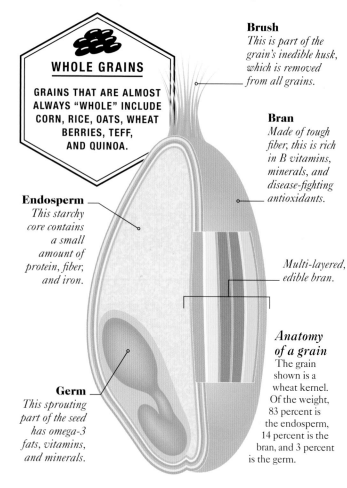

WHOLE GRAINS

GRAINS THAT ARE ALMOST ALWAYS "WHOLE" INCLUDE CORN, RICE, OATS, WHEAT BERRIES, TEFF, AND QUINOA.

Brush
This is part of the grain's inedible husk, which is removed from all grains.

Bran
Made of tough fiber, this is rich in B vitamins, minerals, and disease-fighting antioxidants.

Endosperm
This starchy core contains a small amount of protein, fiber, and iron.

Multi-layered, edible bran.

Germ
This sprouting part of the seed has omega-3 fats, vitamins, and minerals.

Anatomy of a grain
The grain shown is a wheat kernel. Of the weight, 83 percent is the endosperm, 14 percent is the bran, and 3 percent is the germ.

Do I really need to SOAK PULSES BEFORE I COOK THEM?

Soaking reduces cooking time, but at a cost.

Beans and lentils, known as "pulses" when dried, are rich in protein, carbohydrates, fiber, and many nutrients, such as the essential B vitamins. Many recipes say that pulses need to be soaked before cooking, but this is not quite the case.

For pulses to be edible, the moisture lost in the drying process must be restored. This can be done by simply cooking them for a long time (up to 2 hours for large beans). Soaking restores some water into the dried beans before cooking, reducing cooking time, but usually affects texture, turning beans mushy and making them blander. Use the chart, opposite, as a guide on whether or not to soak.

> *"Many recipes say that pulses need to be soaked before cooking, but this is only a half-truth."*

Should I salt the water?

The notion that it is bad to add salt to beans before or during cooking is wrong. Adding salt to the water (about 3 tsp/15g per quart/liter) enhances flavor and stops pulses from becoming too waterlogged and mushy because salt "pulls" a little of the water away from the less-salty bean, slowing the speed at which water penetrates the skin. Salt will eventually penetrate the bean, where it destabilizes the tough pectin glue that holds the cells together, ultimately cooking them quicker and more evenly.

Soaking in salty water increases size by 80%

Soaking in plain water increases size by 120%

CANNELLINI BEAN

TYPE OF PULSE		THE EFFECTS OF SOAKING		
The size of the pulse you are using affects how much cooking time it needs and how much it benefits from soaking.		*Overnight soak* Leave pulses in cold water overnight (or for a period of around 8 hours before cooking).	*Rehydration boost* Soak for 30–60 minutes in cold water just before cooking to kick-start rehydration.	*Integrated quick soak* Boil pulses 1–2 minutes, remove from heat, cover, and soak in the hot water for 30 minutes; then cook.
Split peas and beans These small pulses have been cracked down the middle after harvesting, so they have an exposed core. **SPLIT PEAS**		Unless very old, a long soak isn't needed as the exposed core means they hydrate rapidly.	Split pulses rehydrate quickly when cooked, so there's little to gain from a short presoak.	The shorter cooking time for split pulses means an integrated soak is unnecessary.
Small pulses Includes pinto beans, adzuki beans, and any pulse the size of a black bean and smaller. **BLACK BEANS**		Small pulses can become waterlogged from a long soak and lose bite and subtle flavor.	Short soakings speed cooking slightly without causing loss of texture.	Saves just 5 minutes overall cooking time, but allows more flavor-generating reactions.
Large beans and chickpeas Includes beans that are cannellini size and larger. Dried chickpeas are dense so slow to rehydrate. **KIDNEY BEAN** **CHICKPEA**		Soaking overnight can reduce cooking time by up to 40 percent, but can affect flavor.	Gives just a small reduction in cooking time, but preserves flavor and texture.	Large pulses rehydrate and preserve flavor. Shaves off around 30 minutes cooking time.

BEAN SIZE COMPARISON
Use this chart to figure out whether (or how) to soak each type of pulse.

OLD AND DRY
REGARDLESS OF SIZE, THE OLDER A PULSE IS, THE MORE IT WILL HAVE DRIED OUT, SO SOAKING IS BENEFICIAL.

SPLIT PULSE	SMALL PULSES				CHICKPEA AND LARGE PULSES			
SPLIT PEA	PUY LENTIL	SOYBEAN	BLACK BEAN	PINTO BEAN	CHICKPEA	CANNELLINI BEAN	KIDNEY BEAN	BUTTER BEAN

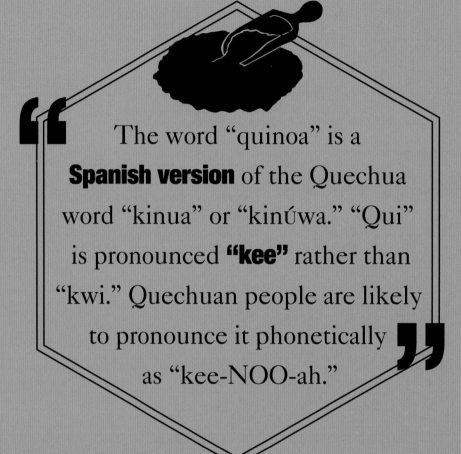

The word "quinoa" is a **Spanish version** of the Quechua word "kinua" or "kinúwa." "Qui" is pronounced **"kee"** rather than "kwi." Quechuan people are likely to pronounce it phonetically as "kee-NOO-ah."

Why exactly is
QUINOA SO SPECIAL?

The Incas cultivated and ate quinoa as a staple food and gave it a sacred status, calling it the "mother grain."

Marketed as a "whole food," quinoa is increasingly popular, with all the hallmarks of a "superfood": it is gluten-free, is nutritious, and, originating from South America, has a long, fascinating history. Sidelined by wheat and other crops, quinoa is, however, a "superfood" that might live up to the hype, being extremely high in protein and full of nutrients (see box, right).

About the same size as mustard seeds, the most popular variety, "white" quinoa, looks like couscous and can be cooked in the same way as rice (see pp130–131), producing a fluffy grain. It can also be popped like popcorn if you dry roast it, turning it into a crunchy topping for soups and breakfast cereals.

NUTRIENT FEAST

HIGH IN PROTEIN, QUINOA BOASTS ALL NINE ESSENTIAL AMINO ACIDS, OMEGA FATS, B VITAMINS, AND MINERALS.

While nutritionally quinoa is considered a whole grain, it isn't a true grain because it is not the seed of a grass plant; rather, quinoa is related to beets and spinach, so it is called a "pseudograin." Quinoa also looks different from other grains, sporting wormlike strings when cooked (see below).

"Similar in *appearance to couscous*, quinoa *is cooked in the same way as rice.*"

UNCOOKED	COOKED

Other grains
In most grains, such as pearl barley and millet, the germ, which contains many of the nutrients, is buried inside the starchy core. Whole-grain foods preserve the germ, but in refined grains this is often removed through milling (see p136).

The germ, the part that sprouts into a new plant, is housed inside the grain.

The germ may split open after cooking but the germ remains inside.

A BITTER BITE

QUINOA IS RINSED OF ITS NATURAL COAT OF PARASITE-REPELLING BITTER SAPONINS.

Quinoa
This differs in appearance from other grains because the protein- and mineral- rich embryo part of the seed (the germ) is coiled around the outside rather than buried in the core.

The quinoa germ is on the edge of the grain.

When cooked, the germ separates, indicating that the grain is cooked through.

A QUICK DISH

QUINOA IS A FAST-COOKING STAPLE TO RUSTLE UP, COOKING IN JUST 15–20 MINUTES.

How can I keep beans from GIVING ME GAS?

Don't be put off by beans—in fact, eat more.

Rich in fiber, protein, and essential nutrients, beans are thoroughly good for health. However, for people who do not normally eat this high-fiber food, a meal of beans gives the gas-producing bacteria in the gut a sudden excess of fuel to feast on, thus proliferating. These bacteria digest the food that we can't, namely fiber, and produce gas as a by-product. Soaking dried beans and peas before cooking and draining away the water is thought to help remove some soluble fibers, such as the oligosaccharides, which are usually the culprit for producing gas. Soaking cannot remove insoluble fiber, however, so this is often ineffective. A better strategy is to eat beans and other pulses regularly in small quantities, so that gas-producing bacteria do not suddenly overrun their non-gas-producing counterparts.

Is it true that uncooked KIDNEY BEANS ARE POISONOUS?

Like many plants, kidney beans contain toxic substances.

Kidney bean plants are poisonous, producing a toxic substance to keep animals from eating them. In kidney beans the poison is called phytohemagglutinin, which, if swallowed, damages the gut lining, leading to severe vomiting and diarrhea. As few as four raw kidney beans are enough to send the intestines into a painful rage. Phytohemagglutinin is destroyed only at high temperatures; it actually becomes more potent when warmed, so undercooked beans are even nastier than raw ones and have been known to cause outbreaks of poisoning after being stewed at a low temperature for many hours. When fully softened, kidney beans must be boiled hard for at least 10 minutes to destroy the phytohemagglutinin and make them safe; this can be done toward the beginning or at the end of cooking. Canned beans are already cooked so they are always safe. Cannellini beans and broad beans contain phytohemagglutinin in smaller amounts, so while less dangerous, these also should be cooked well.

The pressure that builds to a bang

Cooking popcorn causes its core to heat up, turning the water inside to steam. Entombed within the popcorn's tough hull, the steam cannot escape, so as the kernel gets hotter, the pressure rises. At 356°F (180°C), the pressure inside has soared to nine times normal air pressure, and the hull explodes with a bang.

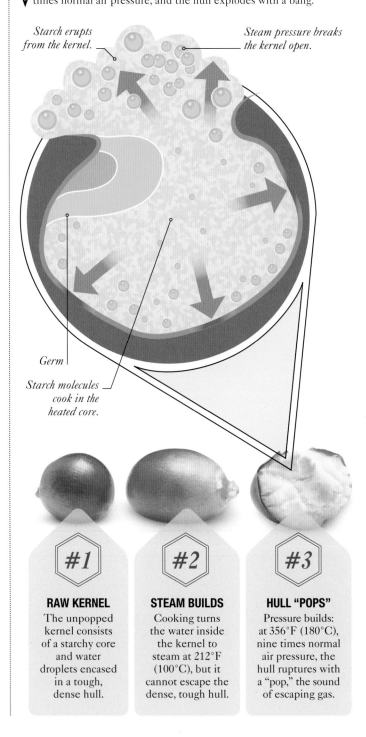

Starch erupts from the kernel.

Steam pressure breaks the kernel open.

Germ

Starch molecules cook in the heated core.

#1
RAW KERNEL
The unpopped kernel consists of a starchy core and water droplets encased in a tough, dense hull.

#2
STEAM BUILDS
Cooking turns the water inside the kernel to steam at 212°F (100°C), but it cannot escape the dense, tough hull.

#3
HULL "POPS"
Pressure builds: at 356°F (180°C), nine times normal air pressure, the hull ruptures with a "pop," the sound of escaping gas.

Why does
POPCORN POP?

Cooking triggers an incredible explosion that turns hard-shelled seeds into fluffy white popcorn.

Popcorn is special among corn varieties. The kernels of all types of dried corn will pop, but most do it with a whimper—popcorn seeds have a remarkably dense and tough outer hull formed from very tightly knit cellulose fibers, which gives them their explosive popping potential.

The popcorn plant looks almost identical to a regular corn plant, except that the tassels on the stalks droop on popcorn plants rather than stand upright as they do on sweet corn. The kernels, which are mostly starch and water, are left to dry on the cob until they can easily be rubbed off. At harvest, they contain about 14 percent moisture in the core, and this water will turn to steam when heated and cause a violent eruption. For this reason, popcorn should be stored in an airtight container to preserve the residues of moisture that power its explosion when cooked. Old, very dry popcorn will not pop, and will instead be left as burned, acrid-tasting unpopped kernels at the bottom of the pan, called "old maids."

As a whole grain, popcorn is high in fiber and low in calories, especially when air-popped (blasted with hot air) rather than cooked in oil. Weight for weight, popcorn contains more antioxidants per serving than most fruit and vegetables and more iron than beef.

Starch spurts from the core in all directions due to the spinning motion, cooling rapidly as it expands.

The whole bloom takes only one-fifteenth of a second to form after the hull cracks.

The dense hull is finally overcome by steam pressure.

#4

PROPULSION
Heat has cooked the starchy core, and as it emerges from the cracked hull, it sends the kernel spinning.

#5

STARCH BLOOMS
The force of the steam causes the cooked starchy innards to gush from the kernel as it spins in the air.

#6

FLUFFY CORN
In milliseconds, the innards cool and set into a bloom of crisp, white starch that is up to 40–50 times its original size.

How can I make my own FRESH PASTA?

Making your own pasta is surprisingly simple, but the type of flour you use can make all the difference.

Pasta-making recipes often suggest using "00" flour, which is the Italian grade for the most finely milled, powdery flour. These tiny particles mix easily and help make a silky-smooth pasta; however, 00 flour is not essential. White all-purpose or cake flours also give excellent results and have an equivalent protein content—00 flour is typically low in protein at 7–9 percent. A low-protein flour is important when making fresh egg pasta because the eggs provide the protein needed to bind the pasta together, so using a high-protein flour would result in a dense,

rubbery pasta. Durum wheat flour, used in pasta, has a high protein (gluten) content, so it isn't suitable for fresh pasta recipes that contain eggs.

The step by step below shows you how to make pasta dough by hand. A food processor is useful for making pasta in larger batches, but care is needed to avoid overmixing, which can cause too much gluten to form and make a stiff dough. Pulse for 30–60 seconds, stopping when the mix has a coarse, couscous-like texture that presses together into a dough; then turn out and knead the dough on the work surface.

A STRONG DOUGH

IF YOUR FLOUR DOESN'T CONTAIN HARD LUMPS, THERE'S NO NEED TO SIFT AS YOU WANT TO AVOID AN AIRY MIX.

MAKING FRESH PASTA

Using a pasta machine, as shown here, is by far the easiest way to roll out and thin pasta dough. If you are using a rolling pin, divide the dough into pieces and roll out each piece individually until around 2mm thick. The flour used in this recipe is 00 flour, but an all-purpose flour, or a cake flour/all-purpose flour mix (2:1), can be used instead.

#1

#2

COMBINE THE EGGS AND FLOUR
Pour 6oz (165g) 00 flour onto a clean, dry work surface and make a well in the center so liquid doesn't escape. Crack 2 eggs into the well and add ½ tsp salt. Drizzle with olive oil for a smooth, easy-to-handle dough. Beat the eggs in the well lightly with a fork, and then gradually draw flour into the center and bind with the eggs.

KNEAD AND REST DOUGH
Push the remaining flour into the center. Knead the dough firmly by hand for 10 minutes to build gluten networks and create a strong, elastic dough. If too dry, add a little water or olive oil for moisture; add flour to absorb moisture if too wet. Wrap in plastic wrap to keep it moist, and rest it in the refrigerator for an hour for the starch granules to absorb moisture and the gluten fibers to spring back.

ROLL AND FLATTEN DOUGH
Unwrap the dough. On a floured surface, roll the dough out into a circle and then pass it through a pasta machine three times on the thickest setting to further develop the gluten. Fold the dough into thirds, flatten it, and pass through the machine again. Repeat six times.

> "A *low-protein flour* is needed in egg pasta to keep the pasta from becoming too *dense and rubbery*."

#4

ROLL TO FINAL THICKNESS

Continue to roll the dough through the machine on decreasing settings until you reach one notch before the finest setting—this is the ideal thickness for cut pastas. Dough intended for stuffed pastas should be rolled all the way to the finest setting.

#5

CUT TO SIZE

Fold the dough into thirds with the folds at the top and bottom, and then cut it into strips: ½in (1cm) wide is the standard size for pappardelle, ¼in (6mm) for tagliatelle. Cook until al dente in boiling water (see pp144–145).

Pairing pasta and sauces

Pasta comes in a multitude of shapes and sizes, many devised for a specific type of dish. Pasta geometry should be paired with the thickness and viscosity (or stickiness) of the sauce.

- **Traditional spaghetti noodles** tangle easily, so they naturally entwine with and hold sauces containing coarsely cut vegetables, seafood, or meat pieces.

- **Flat strips,** such as tagliatelle, capture thick sauces, such as bolognese or ragù, well, but the long, flat surface sticks and clumps together with sticky cheese sauces.

- **Tube-shaped pasta noodles,** such as penne, with a smaller surface area, slide past each other in gloppy sauces, so they work well with thick, oily, and thin sauces.

- **Ridged pasta** Thin, oily, or tomato-based sauces pair with ridged, spiraled, or textured shapes, such as penne rigate, because the contours and bumps help the low-surface-tension sauce cling to the pasta.

- **Shell-shaped pasta** is ideally proportioned to capture a medium-thickness sauce.

- **Round gnocchi potato dumplings** are well suited for thick cheese sauces because these larger dumplings are less likely to gravitate toward each other and clump together.

Is fresh pasta better
THAN DRIED?

Many of us think of dry pasta as a cheap alternative to fresh, but in Italy these are treated as separate ingredients.

Dry pasta is usually cheaper than fresh, but not necessarily inferior; indeed its production in Italy is highly regulated. Conversely, mass-produced fresh pasta can have a gluey texture that is a poor imitation of truly freshly made pasta.

Dried and fresh pasta have different uses in Italy. Fresh pasta, made with eggs, has a tender consistency and more luxurious buttery flavor than dried and pairs well with creamy or cheese-based sauces. Dried pasta has a firmer bite so is easier to cook al dente, and is robust, so best paired with oily, meaty sauces (the exception being bolognese, traditionally served with fresh tagliatelle). Choosing which pasta to use really comes down to ingredients rather than pasta type.

KNOW THE DIFFERENCE

Dried pasta
Available in a range of shapes and varieties, dried pasta is a convenient pantry basic.

- Dried pasta is made with strong durum wheat flour and water. The kneaded dough is rested so the gluten networks strengthen. It is then rolled repeatedly before being cut into shapes. The high gluten levels give the pasta enough strength to withstand being cooked in boiling water.

- Dried pasta takes longer to cook (9–11 minutes) because the starch granules need to rehydrate fully first.

Fresh pasta
This has a relatively short shelf life and needs to be kept refrigerated before use.

- Fresh pasta substitutes water for either whole eggs or egg yolks. The fat lends tenderness while the egg protein substitutes for the gluten in durum flour, strengthening the pasta so it can withstand boiling water. The durum wheat flour is thus not needed.

- Fully hydrated, it cooks in boiling water very quickly (in 2–3 minutes).

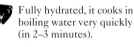

Stir pasta in the early stages of cooking to prevent it sticking together.

How does adding salt
TO MY PASTA WATER HELP?

The traditional way to cook pasta is to throw the pasta into a large pot of water and add a sprinkle of salt, but the benefit of the salt is often misunderstood.

Adding salt to pasta water improves the taste of pasta, makes it easier to cook it al dente, and removes some of the sticky starch. Some also believe that adding salt speeds cooking, but in fact the opposite is true.

The speed of boiling
Adding salt to almost simmering water makes the water bubble up to give the illusion that the salt is bringing on a boil, but the particles of salt simply stimulate bubbles,

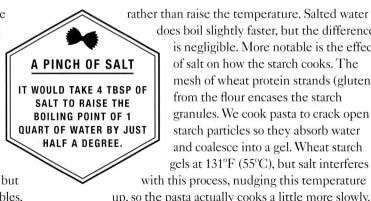

A PINCH OF SALT

IT WOULD TAKE 4 TBSP OF SALT TO RAISE THE BOILING POINT OF 1 QUART OF WATER BY JUST HALF A DEGREE.

rather than raise the temperature. Salted water does boil slightly faster, but the difference is negligible. More notable is the effect of salt on how the starch cooks. The mesh of wheat protein strands (gluten) from the flour encases the starch granules. We cook pasta to crack open starch particles so they absorb water and coalesce into a gel. Wheat starch gels at 131°F (55°C), but salt interferes with this process, nudging this temperature up, so the pasta actually cooks a little more slowly.

Does adding oil to cooking water
KEEP PASTA FROM STICKING?

Dribbling a dash of olive oil into the cooking water is common practice, believed to give pasta a smooth coating and to keep it separated.

Clumps of bland, sticky pasta aren't appetizing. Advice on how to stop pasta sticking ranges from adding olive oil to stirring the water. Knowing how and when to apply the advice will help you perfect your pasta cooking.

Adding a dash of lubricating oil before serving helps pasta to separate.

The role of stirring

Observant cooks will be skeptical of the merits of adding oil to the cooking water as oil simply blobs on the surface, away from the pasta. It is more effective to stir pasta in the early stages of cooking, when starch on the pasta surface turns into a sticky gel. As pasta firms, the pieces will separate and you can stop stirring.

When to add oil

The next sticking point is at the end of cooking, as pasta cools and starch from the water becomes gluey. Unless using a sauce, a drizzle of olive oil now coats the pasta to stop it sticking. Rinsing cooked pasta in fresh hot water also removes this starchy glue.

SAUCE THAT STICKS

KEEP SOME OF THE STARCHY PASTA WATER TO USE AS A THICKENING AND BINDING AGENT IN YOUR SAUCE.

How starch acts on pasta

Dried pasta takes about 8 minutes to cook. Knowing the right moment to stir or add oil will ensure it doesn't stick.

Starch seeps from the pasta surface into the cooking water.

BEFORE COOKING
Dry pasta contains starch granules that are held in place by a protein mesh. Cooking breaks open the granules.

1–2 MINUTES
Pasta swells as it takes in water, and gets sticky as starch turns gel-like. Stir continuously now to help stop sticking.

3–6 MINUTES
Starch continues to soften on the surface of the pasta. Stir occasionally to keep the pasta separated.

7–8 MINUTES
Once outer starch layers have firmed, they stop sticking together and you can stop stirring the pasta.

AFTER COOKING
Add a drizzle of olive oil (if not using a sauce) or rinse the pasta in just-boiled water to stop it sticking.

VEGETABLES, FRUITS, NUTS & SEEDS

Are organic fruits and vegetables
BETTER THAN NON-ORGANIC?

Many believe that organic produce, grown without artificial pesticides or fertilizers, has better flavor and more nutrients.

Taste isn't just about a food's aroma and flavor molecules. Research shows that our beliefs about the food we eat tangibly affect its flavor, and that the moral satisfaction we get when we eat ethically produced organic produce enhances our enjoyment of the food. The nutritional and flavor claims made by organic food producers, however, are not always borne out by science. Testing shows mixed results for nutrient levels, the consensus being that organic has only a slight edge. The flavor molecules in organic and nonorganic produce are similar and trained tasters rarely spot differences. Farming methods can impact quality (see right). Organic produce is most likely to come from small, local farms.

SOIL DEEP

MORE NUTRITIONALLY IMPORTANT THAN ORGANIC STATUS IS THE QUALITY OF THE SOIL AND THE MINERALS IT PROVIDES.

KNOW THE DIFFERENCE

Small-scale production
Produce from small farms can have the edge in terms of flavor.

- **Harvest from small** farms distributed locally has less time to degrade and is less likely to be bruised, which helps preserve flavor.

- **Small farms** are more likely to grow intense-tasting heirloom varieties (see below) and sweet-tasting vine-grown produce than industrial-scale farms.

Large-scale production
Mass-producing fruits and vegetables can impact flavor.

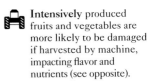

- **Intensively** produced fruits and vegetables are more likely to be damaged if harvested by machine, impacting flavor and nutrients (see opposite).

- **Mass-produced** varieties can taste bland, but some have been bred to be sweeter and more palatable than bitter heirloom varieties (see below).

HEIRLOOM FRUITS AND VEGETABLES

Dozens of traditional fruit and vegetable varieties exist, compared to the handful of highly productive commercial varieties we are used to buying.

HEIRLOOMS CAN HAVE INTENSE FLAVOR.

THE BITTER-TASTING CRAB APPLE HAS 15 TIMES MORE ANTIOXIDANTS THAN THE SWEET, MORE WATERY GOLDEN DELICIOUS.

93%
of vegetable crop varieties are estimated to have become extinct in the past century.

MANY VARIETIES CAN HAVE A SOUR TASTE.

Are heirloom varieties
TASTIER?

Keeping rare varieties of fruits and vegetables alive helps us to continue diversity in the plant kingdom.

Heirloom breeds are traditional varieties that have not been cross-pollinated in the past 50 years for intensive farming. They promise us a flavor of the past, with a stronger tasting, more nutritious product. Heirloom varieties can offer more vitamins and antioxidants, although the total mineral content is dictated by soil quality, rather than the actual breed.

It is no secret that many fruit and vegetable breeds of old were smaller, tougher, and more bitter tasting than the produce of today, which has been specifically bred to be larger, softer, and generally sweeter. Whether heirlooms are tastier really comes down to personal preference, but for the cook in search of an intensity of flavor that modern vegetables don't deliver, an heirloom variety can be a worthwhile investment.

Do fruits and vegetables lose
NUTRIENTS AS THEY AGE?

Fresh fruits and vegetables are incredible sources of a wide range of vitamins and minerals.

From the moment a crop is picked, plucked, or dug up, the clock starts to tick. A fruit or vegetable doesn't die when it's harvested, but continues to take in oxygen and live for days or weeks. However, cut off from the mother plant, vitamins and nutrients in the fruit or vegetable are used up from its stores, leaving fewer nutrients for us when we finally eat the produce.

Several factors affect how quickly nutrients are lost. Heat and light take a toll on many vitamins, especially sunlight-sensitive B vitamins

HEAT DAMAGE

SPINACH LOSES OVER TWO-THIRDS OF ITS FOLATE IF LEFT AT ROOM TEMPERATURE FOR JUST FOUR DAYS.

and vitamin C, which are abundant in citrus fruits, bell peppers, tomatoes, broccoli, and leafy greens. Vitamins A and E are less fragile, and fiber and minerals also survive well for long periods. The amount of nutrients lost depends on the type of vegetable, harvesting, distribution, storage, and soil conditions—poor soil means produce has fewer nutrients to start with. The chart below shows the journey of produce from harvesting to consumption and how nutrient stores are depleted along the way.

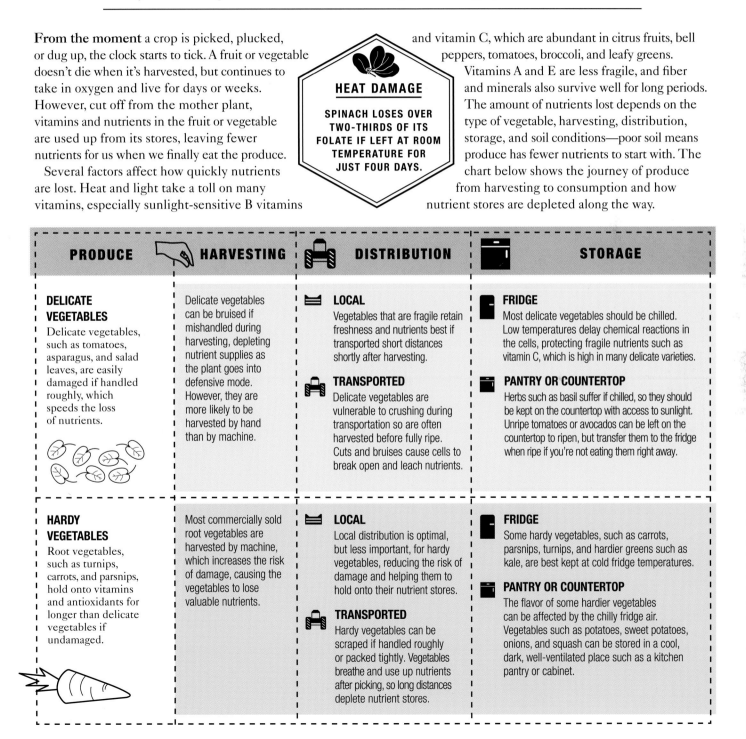

PRODUCE	HARVESTING	DISTRIBUTION	STORAGE
DELICATE VEGETABLES Delicate vegetables, such as tomatoes, asparagus, and salad leaves, are easily damaged if handled roughly, which speeds the loss of nutrients.	Delicate vegetables can be bruised if mishandled during harvesting, depleting nutrient supplies as the plant goes into defensive mode. However, they are more likely to be harvested by hand than by machine.	**LOCAL** Vegetables that are fragile retain freshness and nutrients best if transported short distances shortly after harvesting. **TRANSPORTED** Delicate vegetables are vulnerable to crushing during transportation so are often harvested before fully ripe. Cuts and bruises cause cells to break open and leach nutrients.	**FRIDGE** Most delicate vegetables should be chilled. Low temperatures delay chemical reactions in the cells, protecting fragile nutrients such as vitamin C, which is high in many delicate varieties. **PANTRY OR COUNTERTOP** Herbs such as basil suffer if chilled, so they should be kept on the countertop with access to sunlight. Unripe tomatoes or avocados can be left on the countertop to ripen, but transfer them to the fridge when ripe if you're not eating them right away.
HARDY VEGETABLES Root vegetables, such as turnips, carrots, and parsnips, hold onto vitamins and antioxidants for longer than delicate vegetables if undamaged.	Most commercially sold root vegetables are harvested by machine, which increases the risk of damage, causing the vegetables to lose valuable nutrients.	**LOCAL** Local distribution is optimal, but less important, for hardy vegetables, reducing the risk of damage and helping them to hold onto their nutrient stores. **TRANSPORTED** Hardy vegetables can be scraped if handled roughly or packed tightly. Vegetables breathe and use up nutrients after picking, so long distances deplete nutrient stores.	**FRIDGE** Some hardy vegetables, such as carrots, parsnips, turnips, and hardier greens such as kale, are best kept at cold fridge temperatures. **PANTRY OR COUNTERTOP** The flavor of some hardier vegetables can be affected by the chilly fridge air. Vegetables such as potatoes, sweet potatoes, onions, and squash can be stored in a cool, dark, well-ventilated place such as a kitchen pantry or cabinet.

Is it better to eat VEGETABLES RAW?

Cooking vegetables is neither inherently bad nor good.

Cooking has a mixed effect on nutrients, destroying vitamins and antioxidants in some foods, while increasing them in others. For example, tomatoes release more of the relatively rare antioxidant lycopene and carrots release more beta-carotene when cooked, but vitamin C (also in tomatoes), several B vitamins, and certain enzymes are destroyed by heating. To optimize health, it's important to eat a variety of cooked and raw vegetables. The chart below shows how some vegetables retain important nutrients if eaten raw and others release valuable nutrients when cooked.

BETTER RAW	BETTER COOKED
Broccoli Heat damages the enzyme myrosinase that makes anti-cancer compounds.	**Carrots** Cooked carrots supply a greater number of heart-protecting carotenoids.
Watercress As with broccoli, heat damages the important enzyme myrosinase.	**Spinach** Gentle cooking makes the beta-carotene and iron in spinach more absorbable.
Garlic Heat reduces the amount of the health-boosting enzyme allicin.	**Cabbage** Steamed or gently boiled cabbage releases more carotenoids.
Onions These retain more antioxidant flavonoids and cancer-fighting sulfur compounds.	 **Tomatoes** These release more of the antioxidant lycopene after cooking.
Red pepper These are high in vitamin C, an unstable vitamin that is damaged in heat.	**Asparagus** Cooking makes cancer-fighting ferulic acid in asparagus more absorbable.

Making the most of veggies
The green tops of vegetables such as carrots, which we usually discard (see below), are perfectly edible and add a peppery tang to side dishes and salads.

How to use green vegetable tops
Use the green tops of the vegetables below as a flavorful addition to a salad, sautéed alongside other greens, or mixed in a soup or broth for extra bite.

Carrot • Radish • Turnip • Beet

Alkaloids in carrot greens have a peppery taste.

Carrot tops contain more vitamin C than the root.

CARROT TOPS

Should I throw away THE GREEN TOPS?

Uncertainty about safety puts many off eating green tops.

The green, spindly leaves that adorn the top of vegetables such as carrots have long been thrown into soups and broths, but many of us are uncertain about how edible they are. Recent scares over "poisonous" alkaloid chemicals in carrot leaves have put many people off using these, and a resemblance to poisonous hemlock adds to the reluctance to eat the green tops. Alkaloids in carrot greens do lend a slightly bitter taste and, in high enough doses, can be poisonous, but the amounts consumed in carrot tops are of little concern. In fact, many of the bitter-tasting herbs and salad plants, such as arugula, owe their pleasant, cutting flavors to the bitter alkaloids they contain. Treat carrot tops and other green tops as you would any herb; although, as with other strong-tasting leaves, avoid overpowering dishes with them.

Is it better to peel
OR SCRUB?

*Many of us have been taught to peel vegetables
to remove dirt and bitter-tasting skin.*

Traditional advice was to peel tough, dirt-ingrained, bitter vegetable skins. Today, however, many vegetables have been bred to be fleshier and thinner-skinned, making the skins far more palatable.

Research shows that the skin contains a host of beneficial nutrients, including antioxidant plant chemicals called phytochemicals. The pigments that give vegetable peel its color are an indicator of the antioxidants it contains. Vegetables, such as carrots, whose skins are the same color as the flesh, have antioxidants spread throughout the flesh, so lose fewer vitamins if peeled. But in most vegetables, nutrients are concentrated just beneath the skin.

Peeling vegetables has the benefit of removing more pesticide residues than scrubbing, but the amount of pesticides on vegetables is usually tiny and many of them are destroyed with cooking. Overall, washing or gently scrubbing is the best way to retain a vegetable's goodness.

If peeled, damaged cells go into defensive mode and quickly use up nutrient stores.

Sweet potato nutrient store
Vegetable skins contain vitamin C and other valuable antioxidants. Peeling the skin of a sweet potato removes up to 35 percent of its vitamin C content.

In sweet potatoes, iron, potassium, and calcium lie just beneath the skin.

Can leaving mushrooms in the sun really
INCREASE THEIR VITAMIN D CONTENT?

Fungi have a unique nutritional profile, more akin to that of animals, and can supply important nutrients.

Mushrooms are fungi, and have a unique flavor and a meat-like texture. They are higher in protein than most fruits and vegetables, and contain amino acids that give them an umami, savory flavor. Fungi also contain vitamins D and B12, normally only found in animal products. However, mushrooms need UV light to make vitamin D, and because they are typically grown indoors, they contain little of the "sunshine" vitamin. However, because mushrooms live after harvesting, putting them out in strong sunlight for at least 30 minutes will allow their skin to create abundant vitamin D (see right).

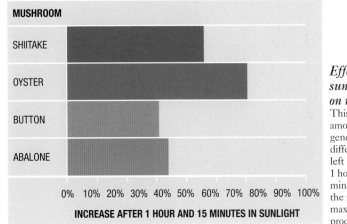

MUSHROOM

SHIITAKE

OYSTER

BUTTON

ABALONE

0% 10% 20% 30% 40% 50% 60% 70% 80% 90% 100%
INCREASE AFTER 1 HOUR AND 15 MINUTES IN SUNLIGHT

Effect of sunlight on mushrooms
This table shows the amount of vitamin D generated by different mushrooms left in sunlight for 1 hour and 15 minutes. Chopping the mushrooms first maximizes vitamin D production.

The Process of
STEAMING

During steaming water is boiled continuously, causing it to vaporize into steam, which then rises in the pan and transfers heat to the food above.

Steaming is one of the healthiest cooking methods. As food is not immersed in water, nutrients that can leach into water are preserved and food cooks without the need for fats. This energy-efficient method uses only a small amount of water. Water expands enormously when it turns to steam, and contains energy called "latent heat", released when it strikes the cool food. The diagram opposite demonstrates the steaming process, showing how food is cooked by the circulating steam.

Cut the vegetables into similar-sized pieces to ensure even cooking.

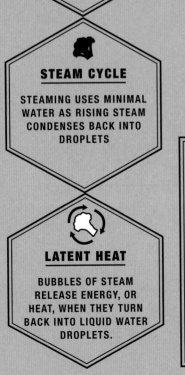

14%
of broccoli's **vitamin C** is lost with steaming, compared to 54 percent with boiling.

STEAM CYCLE

STEAMING USES MINIMAL WATER AS RISING STEAM CONDENSES BACK INTO DROPLETS

LATENT HEAT

BUBBLES OF STEAM RELEASE ENERGY, OR HEAT, WHEN THEY TURN BACK INTO LIQUID WATER DROPLETS.

Bring the water to a boil. This will ensure that enough steam is produced for even heat distribution. When the water boils, the molecules have enough energy to break free as bubbles of steam.

#2

#1

Heat a small amount of water—about 1in (2.5cm)—in the bottom pan of a steamer. When heated, the movement of water molecules quickens, energy increases, and the water temperature rises to 212°F (100°C).

KNOW THE DIFFERENCE

Steamed
Food cooked via steam convection.

- **Cooking time:** Slightly longer than with boiling.
- **Flavor and texture:** Preserves sweetness and texture of food.
- **Nutrients:** Holds vitamins and minerals well.

Boiled
Cooks directly in boiling water.

- **Cooking time:** Direct contact with water transfers heat quickly, speeding cooking times.
- **Flavor and texture:** May be lost on delicate foods. Suits robust foods such as potatoes.
- **Nutrients:** Nutrients can seep into water.

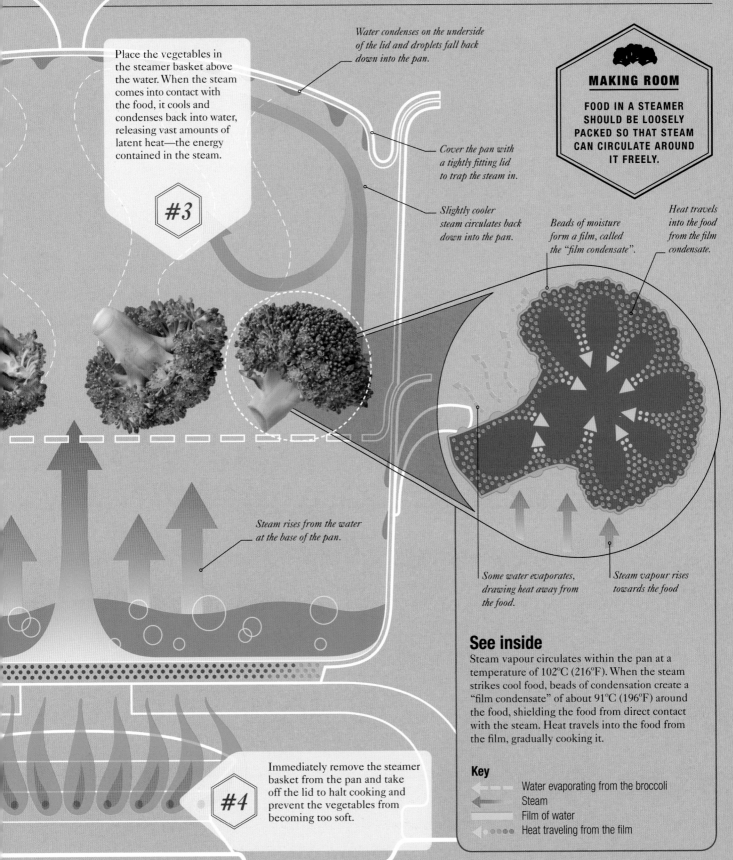

Place the vegetables in the steamer basket above the water. When the steam comes into contact with the food, it cools and condenses back into water, releasing vast amounts of latent heat—the energy contained in the steam.

#3

Water condenses on the underside of the lid and droplets fall back down into the pan.

Cover the pan with a tightly fitting lid to trap the steam in.

Slightly cooler steam circulates back down into the pan.

MAKING ROOM

FOOD IN A STEAMER SHOULD BE LOOSELY PACKED SO THAT STEAM CAN CIRCULATE AROUND IT FREELY.

Beads of moisture form a film, called the "film condensate".

Heat travels into the food from the film condensate.

Steam rises from the water at the base of the pan.

Some water evaporates, drawing heat away from the food.

Steam vapour rises towards the food

See inside

Steam vapour circulates within the pan at a temperature of 102°C (216°F). When the steam strikes cool food, beads of condensation create a "film condensate" of about 91°C (196°F) around the food, shielding the food from direct contact with the steam. Heat travels into the food from the film, gradually cooking it.

Immediately remove the steamer basket from the pan and take off the lid to halt cooking and prevent the vegetables from becoming too soft.

#4

Key

Water evaporating from the broccoli
Steam
Film of water
Heat traveling from the film

How do I chop an onion WITHOUT CRYING?

Learn how to combat an onion's self-defense mechanism.

Like many vegetables, onions don't like being eaten. Damage to onion cells results in their releasing an irritating gas called the lachrymatory factor (see Cell anatomy, below), intended to ward off animals and insects. Once this gas reaches the surface of your eyes, it reacts with water on your eyeballs and turns into sulfuric acid, among other irritating chemicals. Your eyes then release tears in an effort to wash away the painful acid. There are a variety of ways to reduce how much of the irritating gas reaches your eyes (see below), but whichever strategy you use, always use a sharp knife and try to make as few incisions as possible to cause the least damage to cells and so minimize the release of irritants.

Chilling
Keep onions in the fridge or put them in the freezer for 30 mins before use to slow down the release of enzymes.

Precooking
Blanch whole onions briefly before use to deactivate irritant-releasing enzymes.

Face protection
Wear tightly fitting goggles and a nose plug to help prevent irritants from reaching your tear ducts.

Immersion
Chop onions in a bowl of water or under a running tap to keep the irritating mist from reaching your face.

Irritating sulfur-containing gas.

Sulfur-containing amino acid.

Enzymes freed from damaged cells react with amino acids to make irritating gas.

Cell anatomy of a raw onion cell

Slicing or chopping onions damages onion cells, activating defensive enzymes. These enzymes cause sulfur molecules in the cell to split and release an irritating gas called the lachrymatory factor.

Why do different-colored PEPPERS TASTE DIFFERENT?

There's more to pepper flavor than meets the eye.

Of all the many colors of pepper, green ones are the odd ones out. They are under-ripe peppers, rather than a variety in their own right. This means that they contain plenty of chlorophyll, a green pigment that harnesses the power of sunlight to create energy. As the pepper reaches maturity, chlorophyll is no longer needed to supply the plant with fuel, so it breaks down, and, as in an autumn leaf, other pigments reveal themselves. The colors and flavors that develop depend on the variety of pepper (see right). The texture softens as the pectin that holds the fruit together weakens, carbohydrates break down into sugars, and new flavors and aromas develop.

YELLOW

Flavor
Light and fruity-tasting, yellow peppers take their color from lutein.

How to use
Their natural sweetness suits eating raw, grilled, or broiled.

ORANGE

Flavor
Rich in brightly colored beta-carotene, orange peppers are mild and sweet.

How to use
Finely slice them and add raw to salads, chop finely and add to dips, or use as a sweet note in stir-fries.

200%
Red peppers contain **twice as much sugar** as green peppers.

MAKING PAPRIKA
SWEET OR SLIGHTLY FIERY RED PEPPERS ARE FIRST DRIED AND THEN GROUND TO CREATE PAPRIKA.

> **"Green peppers *are actually* under-ripe peppers, *rather than* a variety *in their own right.*"**

GREEN

Flavor
Packed with green-tinted chlorophyll, green peppers are firm and the most aromatic, with a fresh "green" smell.

How to use
Chop into small pieces and use sparingly in stews or curries to bring added freshness and vibrancy.

RED

Flavor
Red peppers are sweet and juicy, with a deep color due to pigments called capsanthin and capsorubin.

How to use
Use to add body and flavor to sauces and stews, or stuff with grains, ground beef, or feta.

PURPLE

Flavor
Semisweet and firm, flavor can vary depending on the variety.

How to use
Purple peppers often have a contrasting green interior so they make visually stunning salads or crudités.

BROWN

Flavor
A variant of red pepper varieties, brown peppers ripen to a rich mahogany brown and have a sweet flavor.

How to use
As heat causes their color to fade, brown peppers are best served raw.

How do I roast vegetables
WITHOUT THEM GETTING SOGGY?

The holy grail of oven-cooked vegetables is a flavorful, crispy coat and firm, tender flesh.

Roasted vegetables should be the crowning glory of a dinner, but all too often are limp and greasy. But with a little scientific know-how, it's possible to produce a pan of perfectly crisp and firm vegetables each time.

Keeping moisture in

Vegetables have a very high water content. Losing too much water, which happens easily in an arid oven, makes vegetables wrinkle. Partly cooking vegetables by lightly steaming or gently simmering before crisping them in the oven helps them to stay firmer, cook faster, and dry out less. Between 110°F (45°C) and 150°F (65°C), a protective plant enzyme, pectin methylesterase, is permanently switched on. This strengthens pectin "glue" to bind the vegetable cells, which helps keep vegetables from losing moisture and wilting when they are roasted. Very gentle cooking is key. Alternatively, cover the roasting pan with foil in the early stages of cooking as shown below so that the vegetables cook first in their own steam before crisping in the hot oven air.

90%

of a **carrot** is water. Potatoes are around 80 percent water.

ROASTING FIRM, CRISPY VEGETABLES

When roasting root vegetables, such as carrots, parsnips, and potatoes, cut the vegetables into similarly sized pieces and avoid layering them. This technique can be used for roasting one type of root vegetable or for a mixture of different vegetables—just make sure that your pan is big enough to fit them all in without overcrowding.

IN PRACTICE

#1
CUT VEGETABLES EVENLY
Preheat the oven to 400°F (200°C). Cut 2¼lb (1kg) mixed root vegetables and 1 large red onion into evenly sized pieces—this will ensure that they cook evenly. Drizzle with 2 tbsp olive oil, season with salt and freshly ground black pepper, and toss to coat.

#2
ARRANGE VEGETABLES LOOSELY
Arrange the vegetables in a large, shallow roasting pan in a single layer. Sprinkle with aromatic woody herbs, such as rosemary or thyme. Avoiding overcrowding helps steam escape evenly during the later stages of cooking, allowing the vegetables to crisp and brown.

#3
COVER BRIEFLY TO TRAP STEAM
Cover the roasting pan tightly with a piece of aluminum foil or lid to seal in moisture, and place in the preheated oven. Cook for 10–15 minutes, covered, so they cook first gently in their own steam to activate firming enzymes. Then remove the foil and return the vegetables to the oven.

#4

UNCOVER TO CRISP
Roast the vegetables, uncovered, for a further 35–40 minutes, or until the vegetables are tender and beginning to char around the edges. Remove from the oven and serve warm.

How do I cook vegetables to OPTIMIZE NUTRIENTS?

Cooking has mixed effects on the nutritional value of vegetables.

Of all the ways to cook vegetables, frying and boiling tend to lose most nutrients. Water transfers heat rapidly to food, but nutrients seep out into the water. Steaming retains nutrients well, though research also shows that vegetables benefit from different cooking techniques. For example, lightly griddling is slightly worse than steaming for most vegetables, but effective for broccoli, asparagus, and zucchini, and carrots gain more carotenoids when boiled rather than steamed. Research is also starting to show that sous vide (see pp84–85) retains most nutrients: the heat is carefully controlled and nutrients are sealed in the airtight bag.

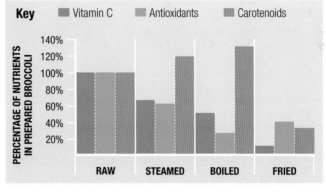

Cooking for nutrients
This chart shows nutrient levels for cooked versus raw broccoli. Heating reduces levels of most nutrients, so cooler methods are preferable. However, some methods can increase levels of carotenoids.

Does adding salt to the water cook VEGETABLES FASTER?

A common belief is that salt raises the temperature of boiling water.

While salt raises the temperature of boiling water a tiny amount (less than 34°F/1°C; see p144), this is not why vegetables cook better in salted water.

Salt and other minerals in cooking water have other important effects. Plant cells have rigid walls made from tough lignin and cellulose fibers, in order to keep plants upright. Cooking softens these woody fibers to make vegetables tender, but before heat from the stove can do this, chemical "glues" that fasten the plant cells together—pectin and hemicellulose—need to dissolve. The acidity, salt level, and amount of minerals in cooking water can either strengthen or weaken the molecular bonds that keep these glues strong. Salt drives apart the pectin strands that give the glue its integrity. The sodium in salt disrupts the connections between pectin molecules, so salted vegetables really will cook faster than unsalted ones.

What is the secret of the
PERFECT VEGETABLE STIR-FRY?

Making a stir-fry may seem like an easy dinner option, but doing it well requires skill and a lot of heat.

In a professional kitchen, a wok-wielding chef manipulates food at a ferocious speed. This is because stir-frying success is all about cooking food quickly, which requires high temperatures and fast-moving ingredients.

Feeling the heat

To make a perfect stir-fry, you need the wok to be as hot as possible and the oil smoking. When food strikes a very hot pan, water on its surface evaporates almost instantly and Maillard browning (see pp16–17) starts. Cooking oil molecules break apart in the searing heat of the pan, which turn into more tasty molecules that combine with those created by the Maillard process to create smoky stir-fry flavors. Pieces of food should be thinly sliced and evenly cut so that the outside doesn't burn before the center cooks and softens.

With such high temperatures, it is important to keep the food moving by constantly tossing or stirring it so it cooks evenly. Keep the burner turned up high and add fresh ingredients one at a time so the pan's surface stays hot. Even when airborne, the food continues to cook in the rising steam.

IN PRACTICE

MAKING A VEGETABLE STIR-FRY

For an authentic smoky stir-fry flavor, your stove needs to be on the highest heat setting, and the oil should be smoking before any food is added. A spatula and a high-sided wok are important for keeping everything in the pan. Don't let food linger at the sides of the wok as they are much cooler than the center, and will cook food too slowly.

#1

#2

#3

CHOP INTO SMALL PIECES
Chop 1lb 5oz (600g) of mixed vegetables (such as peppers, carrots, mushrooms, broccoli, and baby corn) into thin strips or pieces. Grate a thumb-size piece of ginger, and thinly slice a piece of lemongrass and two garlic cloves. Whisk 6 tbsp of soy sauce with 1 tbsp of sugar and 2 tsp of sesame oil.

BRING TO THE SMOKE POINT
Heat a large wok over high heat until a sprinkling of water evaporates within 2 seconds of contact with the wok. Add 1 tbsp peanut oil, and swirl the pan to coat its surface. When the oil starts to smoke, add the garlic, ginger, and lemongrass, and stir-fry them for 1–2 minutes to allow flavors to develop and infuse the oil.

DEVELOP AND SPREAD FLAVORS
Add the vegetables to the wok in small batches, in the order of how long they take to cook—harder vegetables first. Once all the vegetables are just cooked (they should still have a little bite), add the prepared sauce to the sides of the pan and stir-fry for another minute. Serve immediately over cooked rice or noodles.

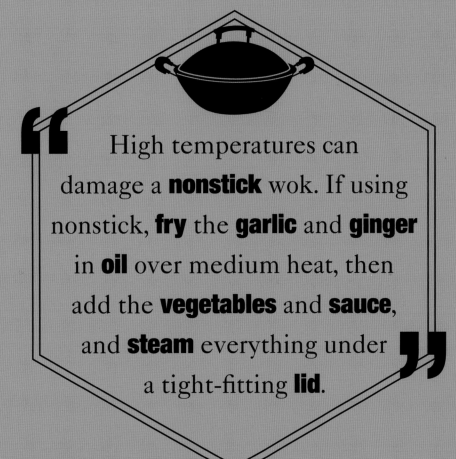

"High temperatures can damage a **nonstick** wok. If using nonstick, **fry** the **garlic** and **ginger** in **oil** over medium heat, then add the **vegetables** and **sauce**, and **steam** everything under a tight-fitting **lid**."

In focus
POTATOES

The most popular vegetable globally, more potatoes are grown than onions, tomatoes, zucchini, and beans combined.

The humble potato is a surprisingly versatile and nutritious ingredient. The vegetable itself is the plant's underground energy stockpile (the tuber) that provides fuel during the winter months. Rich in starch, potatoes have fewer calories than pasta and rice, and are a good source of fiber, minerals, and vitamins— especially potassium, vitamin C, and B vitamins. Colored potatoes, such as purple and blue varieties, also contain additional pigments

(called anthocyanins), which may help to lower the risk of cancer and heart disease. The number of potato varieties is bewildering, but from a cook's perspective, they group into "mealy" (floury) or "waxy" (see right), based on texture and consistency when cooked, and it is important to choose the right type for a dish. New potatoes are not a specific type of potato, but rather immature potatoes that are picked earlier in the season.

Potato skin
Fiber-rich, this comprises a layer called the periderm, which replenishes itself and protects the potato.

SCIENCE
PACKED WITH STARCH GRANULES, THE CELLS OF MEALY POTATOES RUPTURE WHEN THEY SWELL DURING COOKING.

Fluffy mashed potato

COOKING
EASY TO CRUSH, THESE ARE IDEAL FOR MASHING, ADDING TO SOUPS, AND CAN BE ROASTED AND FRIED.

MEALY

KNOW YOUR POTATOES

Some potatoes are more starchy compared to others. Mealy potatoes have cells densely packed with starch granules that burst open during cooking, creating a softer texture. Waxy potatoes contain less starch and stronger cells that give a firmer texture.

MEALY/FLOURY

Maris Piper
A high-starch mealy potato, it is ideal for roasting and fries. The starch cells rupture easily, forming a furry coat that can be browned into a tasty crust.

STARCH: HIGH
FIBER:
2.4G PER 100G

King Edward
This creamy potato with a characteristic red "blush" has a high starch content and a floury texture when cooked, ideal for mashing. When fried in oil, it has a malty aroma and a crispy edge.

STARCH: HIGH
FIBER:
1.3G PER 100G

Yukon Gold
With a fluffy texture and a medium starch content, these buttery-yellow potatoes work well mashed or baked. They retain their color even after cooking.

STARCH: MEDIUM
FIBER:
2.7G PER 100G

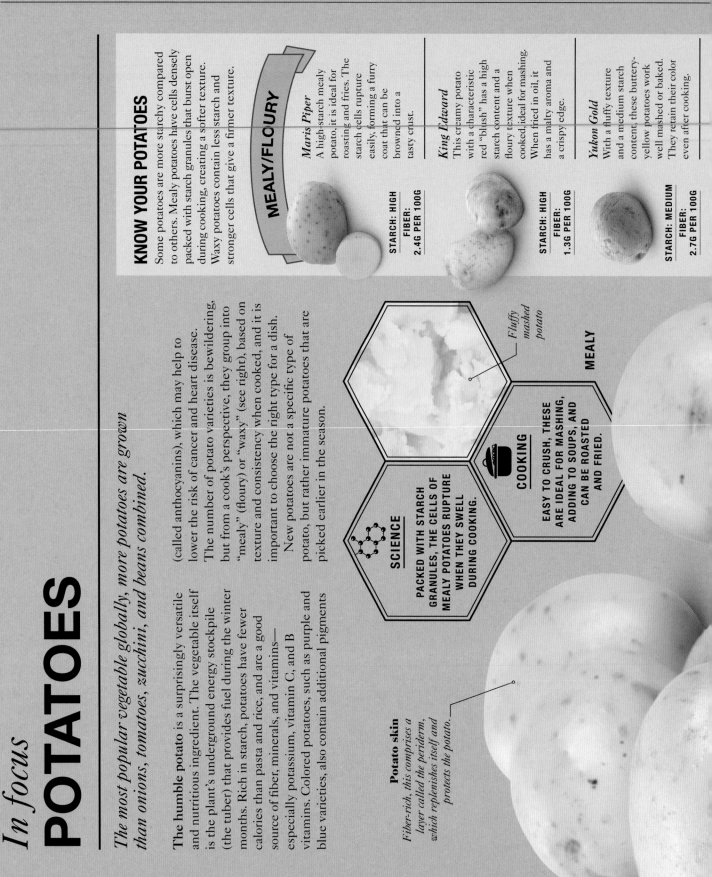

Rooster

Combining high starch with smooth, yellow flesh, this is a versatile potato that works well baked, roasted, mashed, and boiled.

STARCH: HIGH

FIBER: 1.6G PER 100G

WAXY

Charlotte

This smooth-fleshed, waxy potato has a relatively low number of starch granules and holds its shape during cooking, making the potatoes ideal for salads and gratins.

STARCH: LOW

FIBER: 1.0G PER 100G

Desirée

This popular red variety has creamy flesh and a firm, waxy texture that holds its shape well for boiling or wedges. Unlike very hard waxy potatoes, it can also be used for mashing.

STARCH: MEDIUM

FIBER: 1.3G PER 100G

Purple Majesty

Delicate and nutty in flavor, these waxy potatoes have succulent, firm, purple flesh that is especially suited for boiling and steaming.

STARCH: MEDIUM

FIBER: 1.17G PER 100G

Anya

These are firm in texture and have a slightly nutty flavor, making them ideal for salads or roasting with a pan of vegetables.

STARCH: LOW

FIBER: 1.2G PER 100G

Color variations
The starchy flesh of potatoes is commonly a yellow hue. Potatoes with red and purple-colored pigments have a higher antioxidant quota.

Blemishes and spots
Small, dark spots are known as lenticels, tiny orifices that enable the tuber to breathe. Moisture can make these swell, so potatoes should be kept in a dry place.

Firm texture.

COOKING
THEIR ABILITY TO HOLD THEIR SHAPE MEANS WAXY POTATOES ARE IDEAL FOR SALADS, ROASTS, BOILING, AND STEAMING.

SCIENCE
WAXY POTATOES HAVE A SMALLER AMOUNT OF FIRM AMYLOSE STARCH, LESS LIKELY TO BURST OPEN CELLS WITH COOKING.

WAXY

SWEET POTATOES
SWEET POTATOES ARE FROM AN ENTIRELY DIFFERENT PLANT FAMILY FROM MOST POTATOES, AND ARE ONLY A DISTANT RELATION.

"For dense, **creamy pomme purée–style** mashed potatoes, use waxy potatoes such as red potatoes. A purée needs a lot of blending, and starchy potatoes will release too much starch and become gluey."

How do I make
FLUFFY MASHED POTATOES?

Unlike purées that can be whipped into an ever-smoother blend, potatoes require more careful handling.

When mashed, potatoes are at risk of turning gluey and rubbery if overworked, so they should be treated with the same care that you would give a meringue or pastry dough.

For fluffy mashed potatoes, use mealy, or starchy, potatoes, such as Idaho or Russet, which are full of water-absorbent starch granules. When cooked, the starches swell and soften, meaning that the potatoes' cells easily separate under the force of a fork or masher (see below). Taken too far, however, the starch becomes an elastic-like amalgam, and what was a light and airy mash transforms into a sticky paste. When mashed potatoes start to cool, the starches lock together more tightly, known as retrogradation, firming them up further and making them hard, so mashed potatoes are best served right after cooking.

Adding water can cause potato starches to overgelatinize. Instead add fats, such as cream, butter, or oil, to lubricate starchy cells gently. When cooling, fat hampers retrogradation, so the potatoes can be chilled and reheated another day.

IN PRACTICE

MAKING SMOOTH MASHED POTATOES

The technique below uses a potato masher for a smooth mash. You can also use a potato ricer, which removes lumps without overworking the mixture. Chop the potatoes as indicated. If you slice them too thinly, this damages a lot of cells, causing them to leak calcium, which strengthens the pectin glue binding the cells, making mashing more difficult.

#1

#2

#3

CHOP INTO EVEN SIZES
Cut the potatoes into similarly sized pieces to ensure even cooking. Put the cut potatoes into a pan of cold, rather than boiling, water. This helps even out cooking and prevents the edges from softening excessively and disintegrating. Cook until soft-boiled, and then rinse to remove excess starch.

MASH TO RELEASE STARCH
Start to mash the potatoes to separate and rupture the cells so they release the gelatinized starch, forming a smooth, sticky gel that binds the mash. Do an initial mash without adding fat because the lubrication from the fat will make mashing difficult.

ENHANCE TEXTURE WITH FAT
After the initial mash, you can add fat such as butter, cream, or oil. This helps to thin out the increasingly starchy potato to keep the mash from becoming too gluey. Mash just until the potatoes are smooth and fluffy; overmashing will cause the swollen starch granules to knit together too tightly and create a rubbery texture.

The Process of
MICROWAVING

UNEVEN THAW
WATER MOLECULES IN ICE ARE LESS MOBILE THAN IN LIQUID, SO IT IS DIFFICULT TO DEFROST FOOD EVENLY IN A MICROWAVE.

BROWNING
MICROWAVES DON'T BROWN FOOD WELL: ONCE THE SURFACE HAS DRIED, THE MICROWAVE HEATING SLOWS DUE TO LACK OF MOISTURE.

ELECTROMAGNETIC
MICROWAVES AREN'T RADIOACTIVE; THEY ARE A TYPE OF ELECTROMAGNETIC RADIATION, LIKE LIGHT AND RADIO WAVES.

By heating water and fat molecules within food, rather than heating the surrounding air, microwaving is a quick and efficient cooking method.

Microwaves have a strange effect on water and fat molecules: they cause them to line up, like a sergeant calling them to attention. Changing the direction of the microwaves spins and agitates water and (to a lesser extent) fat molecules enough to heat them up (called dielectric heating) and so cook the food. Microwave cooking retains nutrients extremely well because of the quick cooking time and little extra water for the nutrients to leak into.

MYTH BUSTER

Myth
MICROWAVE OVENS COOK FOOD FROM THE INSIDE OUT.

Truth
This is only a half-truth. Microwaves penetrate food farther than direct heat—about 1in (2cm)—and heat up water as they go, but will not reach the core of the food (unless it is a very small piece).

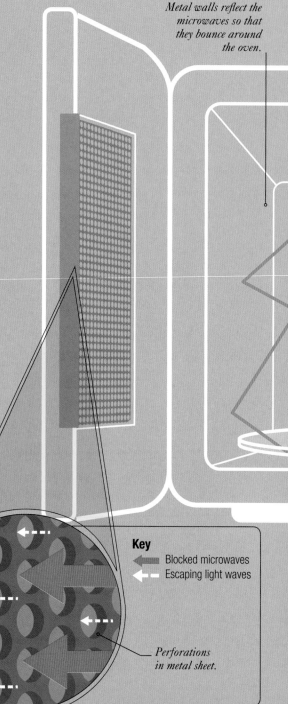

Metal walls reflect the microwaves so that they bounce around the oven.

See inside
The metal sheet inside the glass door has perforated holes about 1mm (¹⁄₂₅in) in diameter. The wavelength of microwaves is typically about 12cm (5in), so they cannot escape through the gaps, whereas visible light, which is 400–700 nanometres in wavelength, can escape, which allows you to see inside the oven.

Key
← Blocked microwaves
← Escaping light waves

Perforations in metal sheet.

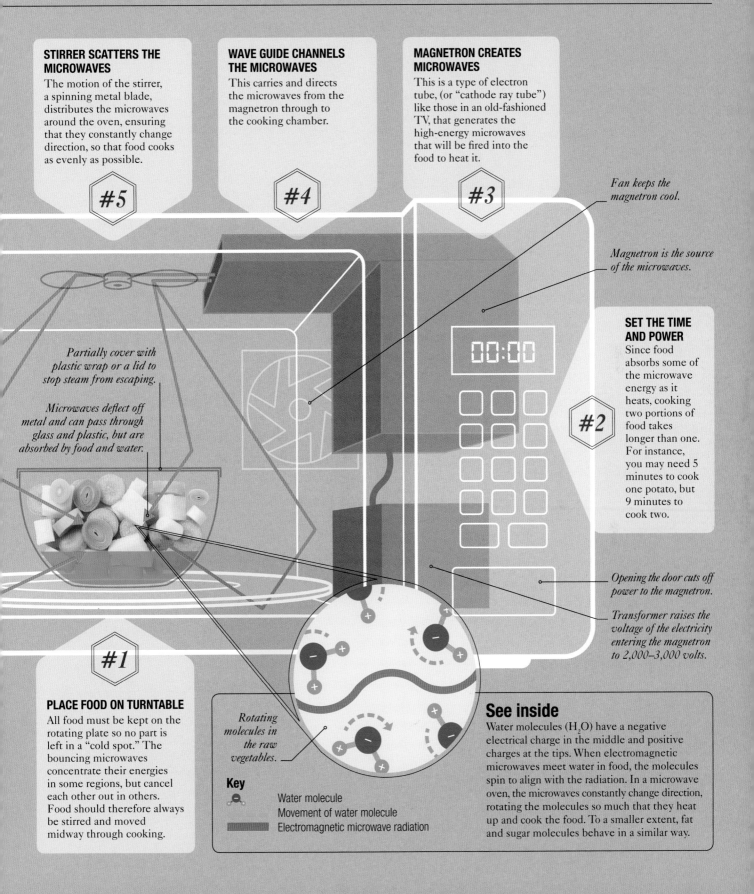

STIRRER SCATTERS THE MICROWAVES

The motion of the stirrer, a spinning metal blade, distributes the microwaves around the oven, ensuring that they constantly change direction, so that food cooks as evenly as possible.

#5

WAVE GUIDE CHANNELS THE MICROWAVES

This carries and directs the microwaves from the magnetron through to the cooking chamber.

#4

MAGNETRON CREATES MICROWAVES

This is a type of electron tube, (or "cathode ray tube") like those in an old-fashioned TV, that generates the high-energy microwaves that will be fired into the food to heat it.

#3

Fan keeps the magnetron cool.

Magnetron is the source of the microwaves.

SET THE TIME AND POWER

Since food absorbs some of the microwave energy as it heats, cooking two portions of food takes longer than one. For instance, you may need 5 minutes to cook one potato, but 9 minutes to cook two.

#2

Opening the door cuts off power to the magnetron.

Transformer raises the voltage of the electricity entering the magnetron to 2,000–3,000 volts.

Partially cover with plastic wrap or a lid to stop steam from escaping.

Microwaves deflect off metal and can pass through glass and plastic, but are absorbed by food and water.

#1

PLACE FOOD ON TURNTABLE

All food must be kept on the rotating plate so no part is left in a "cold spot." The bouncing microwaves concentrate their energies in some regions, but cancel each other out in others. Food should therefore always be stirred and moved midway through cooking.

Rotating molecules in the raw vegetables.

Key

- Water molecule
- Movement of water molecule
- Electromagnetic microwave radiation

See inside

Water molecules (H_2O) have a negative electrical charge in the middle and positive charges at the tips. When electromagnetic microwaves meet water in food, the molecules spin to align with the radiation. In a microwave oven, the microwaves constantly change direction, rotating the molecules so much that they heat up and cook the food. To a smaller extent, fat and sugar molecules behave in a similar way.

How does lemon juice keep SLICED FRUIT FROM TURNING BROWN?

Most fruit has a protective browning reaction.

Fruit has a host of enzymes and chemicals designed to deter pests, parasites, and bacterial invaders by turning its exposed flesh a mushy brown (see below). This enzymatic browning can be slowed, but is hard to stop completely without cooking the food (heating to 194°F/90°C or above permanently deactivates the browning enzyme). Otherwise, the most effective way to halt browning is to drizzle lemon juice over sliced fruit or vegetables because acids also disable the browning enzyme. Other, less effective methods include keeping cut fruit or vegetables under water or in syrup to keep oxygen out, and chilling or freezing to slow down the cascade of defensive chemical reactions.

How enzymes discolor fruit

Inside a fruit cell is a storage chamber called a vacuole. This contains substances called phenols, which spill out when a cell bursts. An enzyme, also released from the damaged cell, turns colorless phenols into rusty-brown pigments.

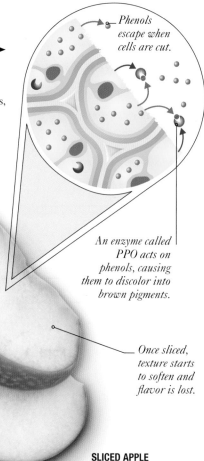

Phenols escape when cells are cut.

An enzyme called PPO acts on phenols, causing them to discolor into brown pigments.

Once sliced, texture starts to soften and flavor is lost.

SLICED APPLE

Is juicing a good substitute for WHOLE FRUITS AND VEGETABLES?

One juice holds much of our daily fruit-and-veggie quota.

Fruits and vegetables owe their firm structure to the rigid scaffolding that surrounds each of the trillions of cells within them. These tough cell walls are strengthened by indigestible cellulose and lignin. Advocates of juicing, or blending, produce suggest that breaking down fruits and vegetables helps the released nutrients to reach the bloodstream more quickly. However, conventional juicers lose precious fiber and nutrients in the discarded pulp. Blenders retain all of the pulp, but nutrients quickly degrade because protective enzymes start to brown produce as soon as it is damaged (see opposite). While juicers may not be an ideal replacement for whole fruits and vegetables, they are a highly nutritious accompaniment to a balanced diet.

THE PROCESS

WHOLE FRUITS AND VEGETABLES

Eating whole fruits and vegetables ensures that fiber is retained and, if produce is eaten right away, few nutrients are lost. Vegetables and fruits can leach nutrients during cooking, although some methods enhance nutrients (see p157).

BLENDER

High-powered blenders rapidly pulverize and purée fruits, vegetables, and seeds, which exposes the pulp to air. Added blades can also break up nuts. The pulp is puréed into the juice, so retaining the fiber.

JUICER

The sharp blades of a juicer spin at up to 15,000 times a second, breaking down woody fiber and shredding cells. The fibrous pulp is caught in a mesh, and the liquid contents drain out.

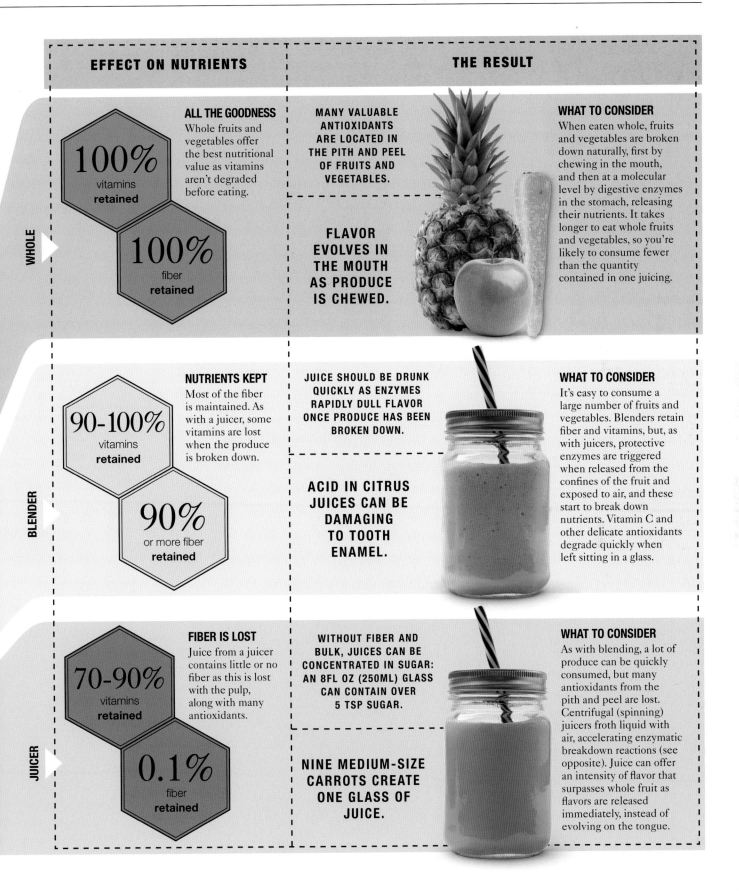

EFFECT ON NUTRIENTS

THE RESULT

WHOLE

100% vitamins retained

100% fiber retained

ALL THE GOODNESS
Whole fruits and vegetables offer the best nutritional value as vitamins aren't degraded before eating.

MANY VALUABLE ANTIOXIDANTS ARE LOCATED IN THE PITH AND PEEL OF FRUITS AND VEGETABLES.

FLAVOR EVOLVES IN THE MOUTH AS PRODUCE IS CHEWED.

WHAT TO CONSIDER
When eaten whole, fruits and vegetables are broken down naturally, first by chewing in the mouth, and then at a molecular level by digestive enzymes in the stomach, releasing their nutrients. It takes longer to eat whole fruits and vegetables, so you're likely to consume fewer than the quantity contained in one juicing.

BLENDER

90-100% vitamins retained

90% or more fiber retained

NUTRIENTS KEPT
Most of the fiber is maintained. As with a juicer, some vitamins are lost when the produce is broken down.

JUICE SHOULD BE DRUNK QUICKLY AS ENZYMES RAPIDLY DULL FLAVOR ONCE PRODUCE HAS BEEN BROKEN DOWN.

ACID IN CITRUS JUICES CAN BE DAMAGING TO TOOTH ENAMEL.

WHAT TO CONSIDER
It's easy to consume a large number of fruits and vegetables. Blenders retain fiber and vitamins, but, as with juicers, protective enzymes are triggered when released from the confines of the fruit and exposed to air, and these start to break down nutrients. Vitamin C and other delicate antioxidants degrade quickly when left sitting in a glass.

JUICER

70-90% vitamins retained

0.1% fiber retained

FIBER IS LOST
Juice from a juicer contains little or no fiber as this is lost with the pulp, along with many antioxidants.

WITHOUT FIBER AND BULK, JUICES CAN BE CONCENTRATED IN SUGAR: AN 8FL OZ (250ML) GLASS CAN CONTAIN OVER 5 TSP SUGAR.

NINE MEDIUM-SIZE CARROTS CREATE ONE GLASS OF JUICE.

WHAT TO CONSIDER
As with blending, a lot of produce can be quickly consumed, but many antioxidants from the pith and peel are lost. Centrifugal (spinning) juicers froth liquid with air, accelerating enzymatic breakdown reactions (see opposite). Juice can offer an intensity of flavor that surpasses whole fruit as flavors are released immediately, instead of evolving on the tongue.

How do bananas help RIPEN OTHER FRUIT?

Bananas hasten the ripening of other fruits in your fruit bowl; understanding the plant's survival tactics helps explain bananas' ripening powers.

Many plants develop their fruit in synchrony, maximizing their chances of attracting animals, which disperse plant seeds over a wide area. Ripening is coordinated by a chemical signal: ethylene gas, which plants release when the climate is right or if the fruit is damaged. Ripening softens fruit, releasing flavor molecules and increasing sugar levels (see opposite). As bananas produce large quantities of ethylene, they can be used to ripen climacteric fruits (fruits that ripen off the plant) at home.

> **"Ripening *is* triggered by a chemical signal—a gas called ethylene."**

CLIMACTERIC FRUITS

These fruits are ripened by ethylene, so you can hasten ripening by placing them near a ripe banana (see right).

Bananas • Melons • Guavas • Mangoes • Papayas • Passion fruits • Durians • Kiwis • Figs • Apricots • Peaches • Plums • Apples • Pears • Avocados • Tomatoes

NON-CLIMACTERIC FRUITS

Fruits that ripen only when they are on the plant and so cannot be ripened at home.

Oranges • Grapefruit • Lemons • Limes • Pineapples • Dragon fruits • Lychees • Peppers • Grapes • Cherries • Pomegranates • Strawberries • Raspberries • Blackberries • Blueberries

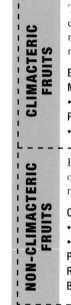

Green chlorophyll in unripe bananas is destroyed as the fruit ripens, revealing other colorful pigments.

Unripe, green bananas are packed with nutritious fiber.

UNDERRIPE

Underripe bananas are green or green and yellow, with thick skin and firm flesh. The starches have not yet begun to break down into sugars, and the cell walls are still tough and fibrous.

Best for
Slicing over oatmeal, making green banana fries, thickening smoothies, or using as an alternative to plantain.

36%

of the **carbohydrates** in a green banana are **sugar**; 83% in a yellow banana.

GOING BANANAS

OVER 110 MILLION TONS OF BANANAS ARE GROWN AND SOLD EVERY YEAR. INDIA IS THE WORLD'S LARGEST PRODUCER.

How do you use bananas at different stages OF RIPENESS?

Hard green bananas quickly become speckled and soft, but you can still use them in cooking.

You may be tempted to buy already-ripe bananas for a quick snack fix, but if you opt for green bananas instead, you're providing yourself with a whole host of culinary options. As bananas ripen from green to yellow to brown, they become softer, more flavorful, and sweeter. Underripe bananas are packed with fiber and pectin-strengthened cells, and add structure and mild flavor to dishes. Soft, sweet, ripe bananas lend themselves to eating raw or using in baking (see right). Bananas ripen quickly, so whichever level of ripeness you prefer, use them swiftly or freeze them to halt the ripening process.

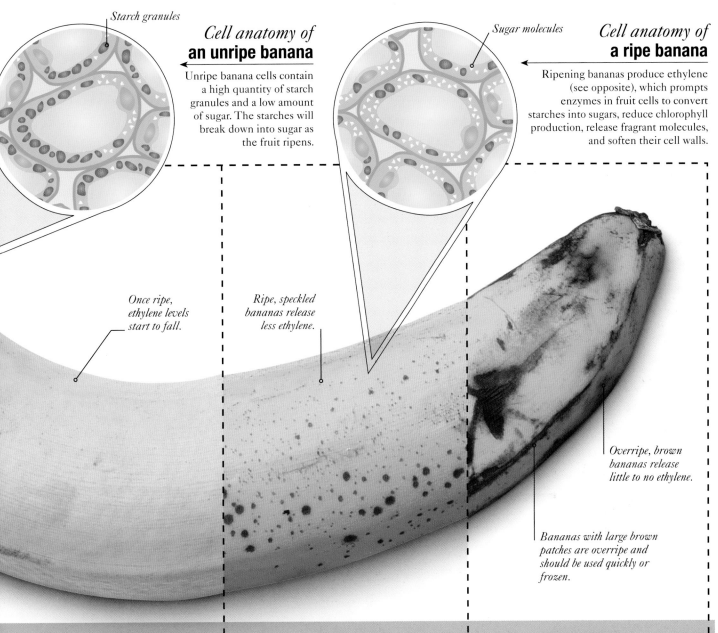

Starch granules

Cell anatomy of an unripe banana

Unripe banana cells contain a high quantity of starch granules and a low amount of sugar. The starches will break down into sugar as the fruit ripens.

Sugar molecules

Cell anatomy of a ripe banana

Ripening bananas produce ethylene (see opposite), which prompts enzymes in fruit cells to convert starches into sugars, reduce chlorophyll production, release fragrant molecules, and soften their cell walls.

Once ripe, ethylene levels start to fall.

Ripe, speckled bananas release less ethylene.

Overripe, brown bananas release little to no ethylene.

Bananas with large brown patches are overripe and should be used quickly or frozen.

RIPE	VERY RIPE	OVERRIPE

Ripe bananas are slightly firm, with creamy flesh and yellow, sometimes speckled skin. Flavor molecules and sugars have developed sweet, fruity notes, and they can still withstand cooking. Bruising hastens ripening.

Best for
Eating raw, blending into smoothies, baking in tarts or pies, or slicing into custard or caramel sauce.

Very ripe bananas are soft-textured with heavily speckled, bright yellow skin. Ethylene production is now past its peak, so the banana will ripen other fruits slowly. They are flavorful and packed with sugar.

Best for
Baking in cakes and muffins, caramelizing, adding flavor and sweetness to smoothies, or freezing and blending into a simple "ice cream."

Overripe bananas are mushy-textured with brown-mottled, deep yellow skin. Rich with natural sugars, they have a very strong flavor. They won't ripen other fruits, but use quickly or freeze for later use.

Best for
Baking in cakes and muffins, mashing into pancake batter, sweetening smoothies or oatmeal, or flavoring milkshakes.

Can I cook soft fruit from
FROZEN?

Frozen fruit is convenient, but some care is needed when cooking with it.

Prefrozen soft fruits open the oven door to the possibility of year-round blueberry muffins, and are a great alternative to fresh fruit in desserts, as long as you understand how subzero temperatures change soft fruit. Like most frozen foods, fruits suffer damage when frozen because spiky ice crystals form inside them (see right). Commercially frozen fruits are rapidly "flash frozen" to at least –4°F (–20°C) to limit how large these ice crystals grow, but because fruits contain so much water—typically over 80 percent—they lose much of their natural bite.

Because of this damage, thawed soft fruit will have a softer, more mushy consistency than fresh and will leak an unsightly puddle of fruit juice. This colored fluid isn't added liquid but the natural fruit juice escaping. For making smoothies, juices, and flavored milks, this is not a problem, but for baking, the liquid can cause ugly splotches. Follow the tips below right to cook successfully with frozen soft fruit.

> ## "Commercially *frozen fruit is* 'flash frozen' *to limit ice crystal damage.*"

FRESH ONLY

FROZEN FRUIT ISN'T SUITABLE FOR OPEN TARTS, FOR WHICH IT IS IMPORTANT FOR FRUIT SLICES TO RETAIN THEIR SHAPE AND BITE.

FRESH

FROZEN

DEFROSTED

▲ *Cell structure in a* **fresh blueberry**

Cell walls are undamaged in fresh fruit, and the fruit's firm scaffolding is fully intact.

▲ *Ice crystals in a* **frozen blueberry**

Spiky ice crystals form inside the fruit as it sets in the freezer, damaging the fruit's internal structure.

Cooking tips

- To avoid having too much fruit juice leak out during cooking, don't thaw fruit before cooking with it—it will weigh the same as when fresh, so it can be used in the same amounts.
- Cook frozen fruit for slightly longer to allow for the extra energy needed to thaw the fruit.
- If frozen berries have started to thaw before they are put in a baking mix, dust them with sugar or flour to soak up the juices.
- The chilling process can cause the fruit to turn brown. Sugar and ascorbic acid can help slow the fruit's browning enzymes, so it can be worth buying frozen fruit with these ingredients, bearing in mind that they give the dish a slightly sweeter and tarter flavor.

▲ *Cell damage in a* **thawed blueberry**

As the ice melts, the microscopic puncture holes in the cell walls are unplugged, causing the juice inside the cells to leak out.

How can I cook fruit without it
TURNING MUSHY?

Fruit is all too often neglected by cooks, but this naturally sweet ingredient can deliver a host of fresh flavors and dimensions to sweet and savory dishes.

To cook fruit successfully, pick the right variety (see below) and use when appropriately ripe.

What happens during ripening

As fruit ripens, natural enzymes go to work, breaking down starches into sweet sugars, releasing fruity aromas, destroying green pigments, and weakening the strong pectin chemical "glue" that holds the cell walls together. Cooking breaks down pectin further, so if you want fruit to hold its shape and texture, cook with it when it is ripe enough to taste sweet but is still firm. Pectin is strengthened by cooking with

PECTIN BOOST

IF YOU ARE COOKING IN A HARD-WATER AREA, THE ADDED CALCIUM IN THE WATER WILL STRENGTHEN PECTIN, KEEPING FRUIT FIRM.

acid (see below) and sugar. Sugar pulls water away from pectin, so it dissolves more slowly.

Poaching fruit with acids, such as lemon juice or wine, and a sweet syrup will also keep them firm. For purées and sauces, cook first without sugar to quickly soften fruit, then sweeten later. If baking at lower temperatures, blanch fruit first on high heat for a couple of minutes to disable a pectin-strengthening enzyme, pectin methylesterase: it can stop fruit from softening because it's permanently active at less than 149°F (65°C), and only deactivated at 180°F (82°C).

CHOOSING APPLES

Some apple varieties hold up to cooking better than others. Pectin glue is bound with calcium and strengthened by acid. Low-acidity eating apples are less tart, but don't withstand cooking well.

COOKERS	EATERS

Pectin bonds

Cell walls are tightly joined.

Air spaces between cells are larger.

There are fewer pectin bonds along cell walls.

Pectin in cooking apples

Acidic, tart-tasting varieties, such as Granny Smith, have cells bound together by more pectin than eating apples, which helps to strengthen the cell walls.

COOKING APPLE

EATING APPLE

Pectin in eating apples

Eating-apple cells have less pectin than cooking apples and are bound together more loosely. Their low acidity further weakens the pectin so the cell walls are less stable.

Why are olives BRINED?

When fresh, all but the ripest olives are hard to bite and even harder on the taste buds.

Fresh olives are extremely bitter and barely edible thanks to a bitter substance called oleuropein. To soften them and remove oleuropein, they need to be soaked, cured, and/or fermented. Repeated dousing with plain water will wash away enough oleuropein to make olives edible, although traditionally olives are left in salt to shrivel or ferment for at least six weeks (see right).

Food producers can now make olives edible within one to two hours (see right) using a technique based on one used during Roman times, which involved adding wood ash to water to break apart oleuropein.

MAKING OLIVES EDIBLE

METHOD	TIME	RESULT
INDUSTRIAL-SCALE SOAKING Unripe olives are soaked in huge tanks in "lye," or caustic soda. This breaks the stringent oleuropein molecules apart; the tough, waxy skin softens, the cell walls fracture, and the "pectin" glue that binds cells dissolves.	**1–2 HOURS**	This produces a firm, easily sliced olive, but the taste can be bland, with a slight chemical aftertaste. Often canned and used as pizza toppings.
TRADITIONAL SOAKING **Washing** Olives are washed repeatedly over a couple of weeks in fresh plain water to remove as much oleuropein as possible.	**1–2 WEEKS**	This removes some, but not all, of the bitterness, so washed olives may be subsequently brined.
Salting Olives are fermented in brine or cured in salt for at least six weeks. In this form of pickling, taste and aroma evolve as salt-resistant microbes acidify to form new flavor molecules.	**6 PLUS WEEKS**	Olives may be wrinkled (if just cured in salt), and have a concentrated flavor, enhanced by oils, herbs, and spices.

> **"A substance** *called oleuropein* **accounts** *for the* **bitter taste** *of fresh olives."*

Are black olives really DYED?

Olives start life a cheery green and slowly ripen into a dark purplish black.

As a fresh olive fully ripens, it becomes wrinkled and develops a strong, earthy flavor. Something of an acquired taste, the mass-produced "black olives" sold in cans or jars are often not the potent fruit that have been given time to ripen, but are the less flavorful green olives masquerading as their more mature counterparts.

California "ripe black olives" take the lye-washing process described above a step further by repeatedly washing green olives until

95% of olives grown in the United States are California olives, grown over 27,000 acres.

they have been soaked to the core. The olives are then "manipulated" into turning black: air is bubbled through the soaking water to oxidize and darken surface pigments called phenols, and then an iron salt, called ferrous gluconate, is added to fix the color change to an inky black. These olives have the appearance of a ripe black olive, but the firm and smooth consistency of a green one. A favorite topping for pizzas, they are easily sliced and are not bitter.

"Cooks in **Roman** times realized that mixing **wood ash** into the water that olives were soaking in quickly **de-bittered** the olives. The ash turned the water **alkaline**, breaking apart the astringent oleuropein molecules."

In focus
NUTS

Densely packed with essential nutrients, nuts add crunch and creaminess to a wide variety of dishes.

Nuts have evocative aromas, enhancing the taste of other ingredients and lifting both sweet and savory dishes.

These little nuggets of nutrition and flavor are loaded with oils and protein—a plant pours its resources into its nuts and seeds to give the next generation the best chance of survival—and have sustained our species for at least 12,000 years. Weight for weight they have more calories than most other ingredients (except cooking oil and butter), averaging about 800 calories per 4¾oz (135g). This means they are best consumed in moderation. Many people consider nuts a "superfood" because, as well as protein, they contain a spectrum of important minerals and vitamins. They also have high omega-3 and unsaturated fat levels.

Most nuts can be eaten raw, but toasting or roasting them adds an extra level of flavor and texture. Watch them carefully while they cook, as, due to their size, it is easy to overcook them.

KNOW YOUR NUTS

Nuts can be shelled, unshelled, and blanched to remove the skin. Pale flesh indicates freshness—areas of darkness suggest that oils have started to oxidize. All nuts contain fat and are a source of protein, but some have higher levels than others.

NUTS

Cashews
Cashews have a smooth, buttery texture. An unusually high starch content makes them useful for thickening sauces and soups.

FAT: LOW
PROTEIN: HIGH

Pistachios
Sweet and meaty, this member of the cashew family is high in protein and fiber, so it bulks out sweet and savory dishes. Chop them and sprinkle them over food to add color.

FAT: LOW
PROTEIN: HIGH

Almonds
Sweet almond's skin is nutrient dense, notably containing flavonoids, which are good for heart health. With a malleable texture, they can be eaten whole, sliced, or ground into flour.

FAT: LOW
PROTEIN: HIGH

SCIENCE
CRUSHING SOFT-TEXTURED NUTS BREAKS OPEN THE TINY PACKETS OF OIL THAT ARE LOADED IN THE CELLS.

COOKING
CRUSH CASHEWS AND BRAZIL NUTS IN A MORTAR AND PESTLE TO FORM NUT BUTTERS AND PASTES.

BUTTERS

Almond butter

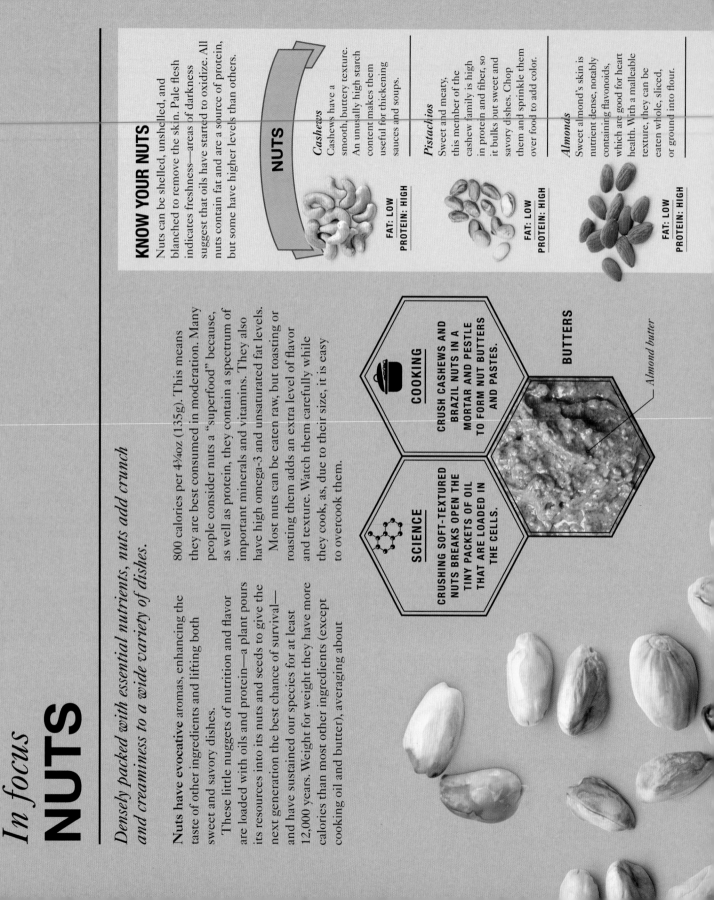

Hazelnuts
Sweet, crunchy, and full of healthy oils, hazelnuts provide texture and body to dishes—try them as a topping on salads.

FAT: MEDIUM
PROTEIN: MEDIUM

Walnuts
These large, meaty nuts, high in bitter-tasting tannins, balance flavor well with sweeter ingredients. They have been described as the healthiest nut due to their antioxidant levels.

FAT: MEDIUM
PROTEIN: MEDIUM

Brazil nuts
These large nuts have a chewy, soft texture, making them ideal for creating nut butters or milks. This is because the oil within the cells form globules like the fats in milk.

FAT: MEDIUM
PROTEIN: MEDIUM

Pecans
With a sweet, rich flavor, pecans add crunch to desserts and baked goods. They contain the same healthy fats found in olives and avocados, and vitamin B3.

FAT: HIGH
PROTEIN: LOW

Macadamia
Macadamias have a soft texture and a creamy flavor, so they are ideal for sweet dishes or baked goods. Although high in fat, much of this is monounsaturated fat, which can help to lower cholesterol.

FAT: HIGH
PROTEIN: LOW

Bitter skins
The papery skin on many nuts is packed with antioxidants, but often has a bitter, off-putting taste. When lightly roasted, the skin usually peels off easily.

Pistachios

Structure of nuts
Nuts are essentially hard, single-seeded fruits that grow and ripen encased within a hard shell.

Roasted cashew nuts

TOASTING OR ROASTING

SCIENCE
HEAT CONVERTS SUGARS AND PROTEINS INTO MORE FLAVORFUL MOLECULES THROUGH MAILLARD BROWNING (P16).

COOKING
TOAST OR ROAST NUTS TO RELEASE COMPLEX, BUTTERY FLAVORS AND GIVE THEM A MORE CRISPY TEXTURE.

NOT A REAL NUT
ACTUALLY FROM A PLANT IN THE PEA FAMILY, PEANUTS AREN'T TRUE NUTS, BUT LEGUMES.

How can I enjoy the FRESHEST NUTS?

Nuts owe much of their unique character to the oils they contain, which also affect their longevity.

The healthful, aromatic oils concealed within nuts are unsaturated, making them good for our arteries but bad for storing. These delicate fat molecules are easily broken apart by light, heat, and moisture, and react readily with oxygen, fragmenting and degrading into acidic and offensive-tasting molecules.

What should I look for?

You should aim to buy and use nuts that are no more than six months old—use the tips below to ensure you enjoy the very freshest nuts. If you buy nuts from a market, ask the seller to break a nut open so you can check its quality. The flesh should look pale—any darkening or shininess suggests that the nut has been damaged, meaning that oil has started seeping from the cells and the nut will have already begun to turn stale. In the same way, high temperatures also cause the sealed oil packages within the cells to break open, hastening rancidity. When the shell and skin are intact, these protective casings preserve the nut for months after it has fallen from the plant.

Finally, ensure you store nuts carefully to maintain freshness (see box, below).

DRY NUTS

THE SHELL AND SKIN OF NUTS ARE DESIGNED TO KEEP WATER OUT, HELPING TO PRESERVE NUTS AFTER THEY HAVE BEEN HARVESTED.

Protective outer casings or shells protect nuts from the damaging effects of light and heat.

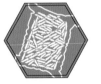

Buy vacuum-packed

If fresh nuts aren't available, look for vacuum-packed ones. Without air, nuts can last for up to two years.

Buy in season

Typical harvest time is late summer to early autumn; avoid buying nuts in early summer.

Buy whole and unprocessed

These taste the freshest as the shell and skin protect the nut and keep out moisture.

Roast your own

Avoid buying ready-roasted nuts; instead, roast your own at home (see opposite).

How should I store nuts?

To maintain freshness, keep nuts in an airtight container in a dark, cool place. Light directly damages the delicate fat molecules, while heat and air speed the breakdown reactions. Better still, store nuts in the freezer in small batches. Nuts have a low moisture content, so they don't suffer the ice-crystal damage that other frozen foods do.

Do nuts and seeds
TASTE BETTER COOKED?

Bound by oils and with fragile cell walls, nuts and seeds have a pleasant mouthfeel and subtle flavor.

Heating nuts and seeds to above 284°F (140°C) triggers the same Maillard flavor reaction (see pp16–17) that gives other foods an aromatic crust and irresistible browned coating with complex nutty, roasted, and buttery flavors. Nuts can lose moisture during roasting, but rather than dry out they become creamier. Inside individual nut cells, microscopic packets of oil (called oleosomes) burst open, seeping their contents throughout the nut. A roasted nut is softest when warm and the oil most runny, so it is best sliced just after cooking.

Add nuts early to stir-fries so that they brown, but if they reach 356°F (180°C), they char, a reaction called pyrolysis, and will tarnish the dish with bitter, acrid flavors.

A SOFT NUT

UNLIKE OTHER NUTS, CHESTNUTS ARE HIGH IN MOISTURE AND STARCH, SO THEY HAVE A SPONGY TEXTURE WHEN COOKED.

ROASTING NUTS AND SEEDS

Roasting nuts and seeds is simple, but since they are small, they quickly burn. Shaking, stirring, and tossing helps to cook them evenly. Let the flavors and aromas released from the Maillard reactions be a guide to doneness, and remove them from the heat just as they reach a golden brown because they continue to cook away from heat, known as "carryover cooking."

IN A FRYING PAN	IN THE OVEN	IN THE MICROWAVE

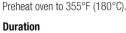

The most straightforward way to toast nuts and seeds is in a dry or lightly oiled pan. Oil isn't essential but makes cooking easier because it helps heat from the pan travel into the nuts and seeds more evenly.

Equipment
Heavy-based frying pan or skillet.

Temperature
Medium-high heat (355°F/180°C).

Duration
1–2 minutes.

✓ **Pros**
A speedy method.

✗ **Cons**
Needs close attention to ensure all-over toasting; nuts and seeds can easily overcook.

To oven roast, spread lightly oiled nuts and seeds over a baking sheet and cook in a preheated oven. Shake and check every two to three minutes until golden brown.

Equipment
Baking sheet.

Temperature
Preheat oven to 355°F (180°C).

Duration
5–10 minutes.

✓ **Pros**
Requires less attention than pan-frying or microwave cooking.

✗ **Cons**
Uses a lot of energy, unless the oven is on for another reason; can easily overcook.

Toasting in a microwave is energy efficient. Research also indicates that microwaving is better than roasting for releasing a nut's aromas. Spread nuts and seeds on a plate and check and stir at one-minute intervals.

Equipment
Microwave-proof plate or dish.

Temperature
Medium-high power setting.

Duration
3–8 minutes (with checks each minute).

✓ **Pros**
Fast and effective (and requires minimal cleanup).

✗ **Cons**
Surface browning is less prominent; smearing with oil first encourages browning.

HERBS, SPICES, OILS & FLAVORINGS

In focus

HERBS

Herbs bring a dish to life with their fragrance. We perceive flavor mostly through smell, which herbs deliver via aromatic essential oils.

Herbs' fragrant, flavor-giving chemicals make up just 1 percent of an herb's weight and come from tiny oil droplets embedded within their leaves. These essential oils are meant to repel animals that would eat the plant and are toxic in large quantities, which is why we use herbs in small amounts. Most herbs' flavor-giving compounds dissolve and disperse well in oil but poorly in water. Cooking with some oil or fat (such as cream) allows herb flavors to infuse a dish far better than without. Herb flavors are more potent in alcohol than in water. The two main groups of herbs, hardy and tender, are used in different ways.

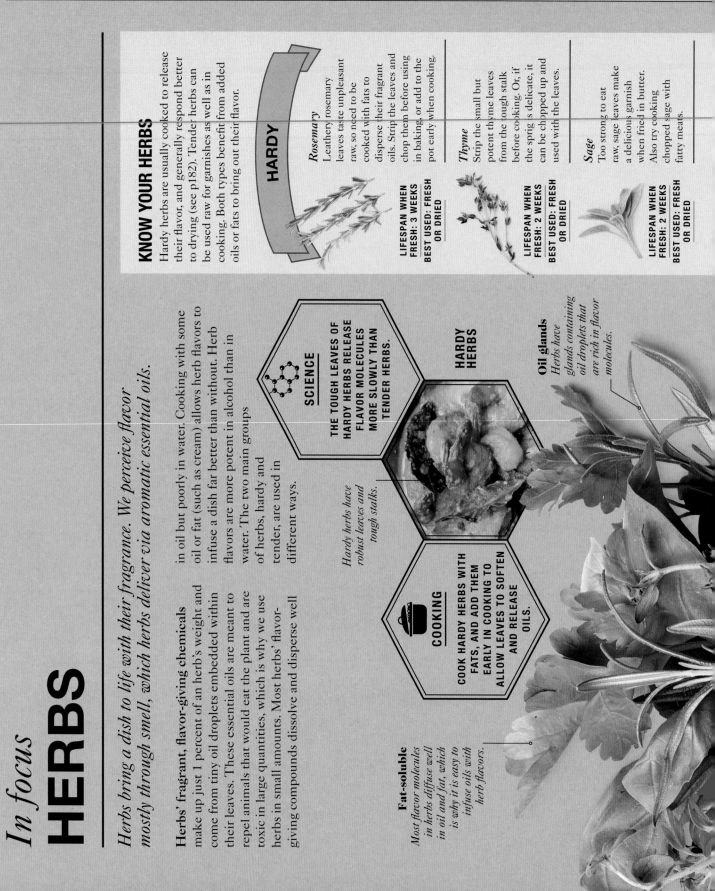

SCIENCE

THE TOUGH LEAVES OF HARDY HERBS RELEASE FLAVOR MOLECULES MORE SLOWLY THAN TENDER HERBS.

COOKING

COOK HARDY HERBS WITH FATS, AND ADD THEM EARLY IN COOKING TO ALLOW LEAVES TO SOFTEN AND RELEASE OILS.

Hardy herbs have robust leaves and tough stalks.

HARDY HERBS

Oil glands
Herbs have glands containing oil droplets that are rich in flavor molecules.

Fat-soluble
Most flavor molecules in herbs diffuse well in oil and fat, which is why it is easy to infuse oils with herb flavors.

KNOW YOUR HERBS

Hardy herbs are usually cooked to release their flavor, and generally respond better to drying (see p182). Tender herbs can be used raw for garnishes as well as in cooking. Both types benefit from added oils or fats to bring out their flavor.

HARDY

Rosemary
Leathery rosemary leaves taste unpleasant raw, so need to be cooked with fats to disperse their fragrant oils. Strip the leaves and chop them before using in baking, or add to the pot early when cooking.

LIFESPAN WHEN FRESH: 3 WEEKS
BEST USED: FRESH OR DRIED

Thyme
Strip the small but potent thyme leaves from the tough stalk before cooking. Or, if the sprig is delicate, it can be chopped up and used with the leaves.

LIFESPAN WHEN FRESH: 2 WEEKS
BEST USED: FRESH OR DRIED

Sage
Too strong to eat raw, sage leaves make a delicious garnish when fried in butter. Also try cooking chopped sage with fatty meats.

LIFESPAN WHEN FRESH: 2 WEEKS
BEST USED: FRESH OR DRIED

Bay

Tough bay leaves yield their woody flavor slowly. The fresh leaves taste slightly bitter, so they benefit from drying. Add dry leaves to oil at the start of cooking.

LIFESPAN WHEN FRESH: 2 WEEKS

BEST USED: DRIED

TENDER

Mint

Cutting or crushing the leaves releases the oils for a more potent flavor. The stalks are discarded in cooking.

LIFESPAN WHEN FRESH: 2 WEEKS

BEST USED: FRESH

Basil

Roll basil like a cigar and slice it cleanly to prevent browning. Unlike other herbs, basil wilts if chilled, so store it at room temperature.

LIFESPAN WHEN FRESH: 2 WEEKS

BEST USED: FRESH

Flat-leaf parsley

This versatile herb is excellent used raw as a garnish, but also works well in cooked dishes if added toward the end of cooking. Dried parsley lacks flavor; fresh is best.

LIFESPAN WHEN FRESH: 3 WEEKS

BEST USED: FRESH

Cilantro

High or prolonged heat will degrade the flavor molecules in cilantro, so add it at the end of cooking. Dry or yellow leaves have lost their flavor, so discard them.

LIFESPAN WHEN FRESH: 3 WEEKS

BEST USED: FRESH

Releasing flavor
Cutting or crushing herbs bursts the oil glands and releases flavor molecules.

Storing hardy herbs
Wrap hardy herbs in a paper towel to absorb excess moisture, and then keep in an airtight container in the refrigerator.

Storing tender herbs
Keep tender herbs upright with the stems in a small quantity of water, in the same way you would keep fresh flowers.

COOKING

CHOP TENDER HERBS FOR A GARNISH JUST BEFORE SERVING, OR ADD AT THE END OF COOKING TO KEEP FLAVORS INTACT.

SCIENCE

TENDER HERB LEAVES AND STALKS DISPERSE FLAVOR MOLECULES QUICKLY ONCE PICKED OR CHOPPED.

TENDER HERBS

Tender herbs have delicate leaves and soft stalks.

BUNCH OF HERBS

What's the best way to PREPARE FRESH HERBS?

The way in which fresh herbs are handled directly correlates to the intensity and speed of the flavor release.

Herbs' flavor molecules are found in oil glands in or on the surface of the leaf (see below). When damaged, the oil glands erupt, releasing the aromatic essential oils, which hold the herb's flavor.

There is no "one size fits all" rule when it comes to preparing herbs, but it is best to think of them as being "hardy" or "delicate." Hardy herbs, such as rosemary and bay, generally come from dry climates. Their tough leaves are good at holding

VARIETY MATTERS

SOME VARIETIES OF HERBS ARE LESS PRONE TO BROWNING, SUCH AS NAPOLETANO BASIL.

onto moisture and oils, and therefore flavor. Delicate herbs, such as basil and cilantro, have fragile leaves and a milder, more floral scent, and their flavor evaporates quickly. Many delicate herbs, in particular basil and mint, are prone to browning because they have high levels of a browning enzyme, polyphenol oxidase (PPO), which is activated when cells are damaged.

The table below looks at different ways to prepare hardy and delicate herbs to help preserve their flavors.

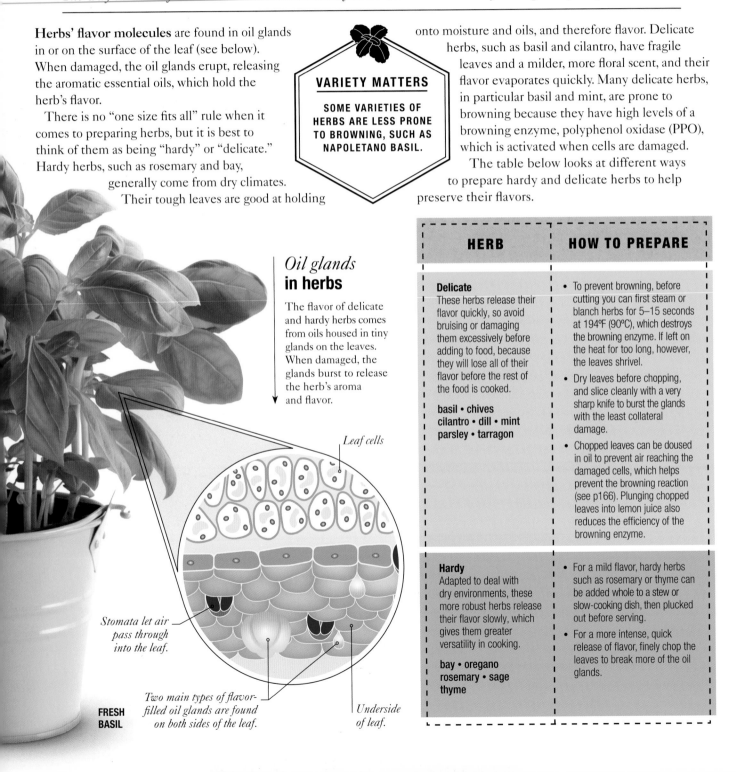

Oil glands in herbs

The flavor of delicate and hardy herbs comes from oils housed in tiny glands on the leaves. When damaged, the glands burst to release the herb's aroma and flavor.

Leaf cells

Stomata let air pass through into the leaf.

Two main types of flavor-filled oil glands are found on both sides of the leaf.

Underside of leaf.

FRESH BASIL

HERB	HOW TO PREPARE
Delicate These herbs release their flavor quickly, so avoid bruising or damaging them excessively before adding to food, because they will lose all of their flavor before the rest of the food is cooked. **basil • chives cilantro • dill • mint parsley • tarragon**	• To prevent browning, before cutting you can first steam or blanch herbs for 5–15 seconds at 194°F (90°C), which destroys the browning enzyme. If left on the heat for too long, however, the leaves shrivel. • Dry leaves before chopping, and slice cleanly with a very sharp knife to burst the glands with the least collateral damage. • Chopped leaves can be doused in oil to prevent air reaching the damaged cells, which helps prevent the browning reaction (see p166). Plunging chopped leaves into lemon juice also reduces the efficiency of the browning enzyme.
Hardy Adapted to deal with dry environments, these more robust herbs release their flavor slowly, which gives them greater versatility in cooking. **bay • oregano rosemary • sage thyme**	• For a mild flavor, hardy herbs such as rosemary or thyme can be added whole to a stew or slow-cooking dish, then plucked out before serving. • For a more intense, quick release of flavor, finely chop the leaves to break more of the oil glands.

How do I get THE BEST FROM DRIED HERBS?

Apart from bay leaves, herbs' aromatic substances readily evaporate when the leaf is dried.

When dried, many of herbs' aromatic molecules escape as as flavor-containing oils evaporate. Also, each herb has a unique combination of aromatic substances, which evaporate at different rates, so a dried herb can have quite a different taste.

Hardy herbs from warm climates stand up to drying better than delicate herbs, as their tough leaves and stems have evolved to lock in moisture when exposed to the harsh midday sun. Trapped in the leaf, their flavor molecules are better retained when dried. The dried herb is then able to deliver an intense, near complete, flavor profile.

Even the herbs most suited to drying suffer from flavor loss over time. As with fresh herbs, how you treat dried herbs can maximize flavor (see right).

Use the right amount
Use around one-third the volume of a dried herb as you would fresh.

Grind before using
Grinding dried herbs in a mortar and pestle before use helps release flavorful oils.

Cook in oil
Liberate dried herbs' fat-friendly flavor molecules by cooking them in oil.

Store carefully
Light and heat degrade flavor. Store in an airtight container in a cool, dark place.

Make your own
For the most flavorful dried herbs, dry fresh herbs at home in the oven.

DRIED ROSEMARY

When should I ADD HERBS DURING COOKING?

Adding delicate and hardy herbs at the right moment during cooking helps to bring out the most flavor.

As with the preparation of herbs, whether an herb is delicate or hardy determines how best to cook with it.

Hardy herbs tend to have powerful "meaty" and hearty flavors, compared to the fruitier, more delicate flavor of fresh herbs. The resilient structure of their leaves and the potent substances that make up their oils mean they are best added early on in cooking to give time for their flavor molecules to diffuse throughout the food. The flavors of delicate herbs evaporate quickly, so they are best added in the last couple of minutes of cooking, or sprinkled on as a garnish. If they are added too soon, the nuances of their flavor will be destroyed by the heat of the pan before they get anywhere near the plate.

START OF COOKING
bay • oregano • rosemary
sage • thyme

END OF COOKING
basil • chives • cilantro
dill • mint • parsley
tarragon

Can how I prepare garlic
AFFECT ITS STRENGTH?

Belonging to the same allium family as onions and leeks, garlic contains plenty of pungent sulfur.

As with onions and leeks, flavors are released when garlic cells are damaged. The plant's defense mechanisms convert sulfur-containing proteins into molecules that have a strong smell and a biting flavor. This fiery garlic-flavored material is called allicin, which, like capsaicin in chiles (see p190), triggers heat sensors on the tongue.

Garlic strength

The more a garlic clove is damaged or crushed, the more allicin is generated and the more pungent it becomes. Leaving crushed garlic a minute before using it amplifies its flavor as defensive enzymes continue to produce allicin. At room temperature, the amount of allicin in a damaged clove peaks at around 60 seconds, then mellows as allicin and other molecules break down into more complex flavors. At above 140°F (60°C), the allicin-generating enzymes are deactivated.

Garlic breath

When digested, allicin in garlic produces distinctive-smelling sulfuric substances that lead to "garlic breath." It's hard to mask this smell completely, because the molecules are absorbed into the bloodstream, but there are ways you can reduce its intensity.

What you can do:

- Some plant-based foods have enzymes that break apart allicin: try combining garlic with mushrooms, parsley, basil, mint, cardamom, spinach, or eggplant.
- Enzymes in apple and salad greens break down odorous molecules.
- Acid in fruit juice deactivates flavor-generating enzymes.
- Dairy fats in milk trap garlic's fragrant molecules.

MINT

GARLIC STANDBY

IF KEPT AIRTIGHT, COOL, AND DRY, ALLICIN IN DRIED GARLIC POWDER REMAINS STABLE FOR MONTHS.

PREPARATION AND PUNGENCY

Different preparations for garlic can have subtle or significant effects on its pungency when raw and cooked.

FINELY CHOPPED

Chopped coarsely with a knife, damage is minimal and little juice is produced.

- **Raw:** With a mellow flavor, this works well in dressings, provided there are no large pieces.
- **Cooked:** When heated, it remains mild and sweetens as starches break down sugars.

CRUSHED

A garlic press produces moist, noodle-like shreds, damaging many cells.

- **Raw:** Flavor is strong but sweet. When pressed to this consistency, it disperses easily in dishes.
- **Cooked:** Moderate pungency. The damp slivers can scorch, so cook lightly in oil before adding liquids.

GROUND

Mashing in a pestle and mortar breaks down even more cells than pressing.

- **Raw:** Flavor intensity is slightly stronger than crushed garlic. It disperses well in dishes.
- **Cooked:** When heated, this has mild heat and sweetness, and offers strong, complex aromas.

PURÉED

Puréeing garlic to a smooth paste maximizes cell damage.

- **Raw:** Cell damage is extensive, increasing allicin production to create intense flavor and heat.
- **Cooked:** Heating mellows the intensity dramatically, and sweetness is spread through food.

"The ancient tradition of **"curing"** garlic by hanging up chains of intact bulbs for two weeks allows sugars and **flavor-containing** compounds to pass from the stems into the cloves, and garlic to develop a more **intense** flavor."

How can I get the most
FLAVOR FROM SPICES?

Most spices are hardy ingredients that are laden with aromatic flavor-carrying substances.

Spices come from any part of the plant apart from the leaf, such as the root, bark, or seeds, and can be used either whole or ground. Most whole spices come predried, which is sometimes done at a very high temperature. However, unlike herbs, spices benefit from drying, developing a more intense flavor.

Being from a part of the plant that has deliberately tough defenses from the elements, spices are inherently tough, so their full flavor often needs to be coaxed out. Damaging whole spices releases defensive enzymes to trigger a chain reaction of flavors, just as it does with garlic.

Cooking whole spices for a long time also breaks apart the cells, and high heat triggers Maillard browning (see p16), creating exciting deep, nutty aromas.

In ground spices, the crushed cells have already started their flavor chain reactions, so these need to be treated with greater care. Follow the tips below to get the most out of both whole and ground spices.

A GOOD SOAK

DRIED MUSTARD SEEDS GIVE A STRONG SCENT ONLY ONCE HYDRATED, SO THEY BENEFIT FROM PRESOAKING FOR 3–4 HOURS.

WHOLE SPICES

Encased in fibrous plant tissue, flavor needs to be drawn out.

CRACKING, CRUSHING, OR GRINDING WHOLE SPICES KICK-STARTS THE FLAVOR-MAKING PROCESS.

WHOLE SPICES BENEFIT FROM LONG COOKING TIMES, SO THEY ARE BEST ADDED EARLY IN COOKING.

HIGH HEATS DEVELOP AND RELEASE FLAVOR.

CARDAMOM SEEDS ▶

GROUND SPICES

Flavor escapes more quickly from precrushed spices.

STORE GROUND SPICES IN AN AIRTIGHT CONTAINER.

KEEP IN A COOL, DARK PLACE TO PRESERVE FLAVOR MOLECULES.

FLAVOR REACTIONS FROM THE PRECRUSHED CELLS HAVE ALREADY STARTED, SO ADD LATER IN COOKING TO REDUCE THEIR COOKING TIME.

GROUND SPICES BURN EASILY, SO AVOID VERY HIGH HEATS.

◀ GROUND CARDAMOM

Why do recipes often say to add SPICES TO OIL AT THE START?

Cooking in oil helps to carry flavor through the dish.

Cooking whole or just-crushed spices in oil before other ingredients helps heat to pass into the spice evenly and avoids scorching. Most importantly, spices "bloom" in oil: flavor molecules are created in the heat and dissolve in the oil, enhancing the flavor of both oil and spice (see left).

A flavor carrier

As with herbs, for most spices, the majority of their characteristic flavor-carrying substances dissolve in oil better than water and the flavor molecules permeate out into the oil. For example, dried chili flakes, cooked in oil for 20 minutes at 200°F (93°C), release twice the amount of fiery-hot capsaicin as when cooked in water.

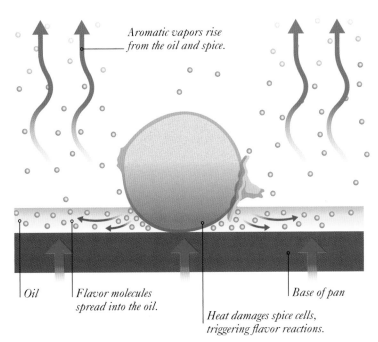

Aromatic vapors rise from the oil and spice.

Oil

Flavor molecules spread into the oil.

Heat damages spice cells, triggering flavor reactions.

Base of pan

WHEN A SPICE "BLOOMS"

Why is saffron SO EXPENSIVE?

Much imitated, authentic saffron has a lingering, penetrating hay-like aroma with notes of cinnamon and jasmine.

The thin, dark red saffron threads are the tiny "stigmas" that grow out of the *Crocus sativus* flower. Harvested individually by hand, each bloom makes only three stigmas: it takes an astonishing 100,000 to 250,000 plants and over 200 hours of labor to yield 1 pound (0.45kg) of spice.

This precious commodity has over 150 flavor-carrying substances. For everyday cooking, turmeric makes a good yellow-colored substitute but has a harsher flavor, so it can't be swapped for saffron in sweet dishes. Unusually for spices, saffron's flavor molecules dissolve better in water than oil. Steeping saffron for 20 minutes helps rehydrate the threads and improves flavor. Soaking isn't essential, but can help you get all of saffron's flavor.

> **"Saffron** *has over* **150** *different flavor-carrying substances that give the spice its* **uniqueness."**

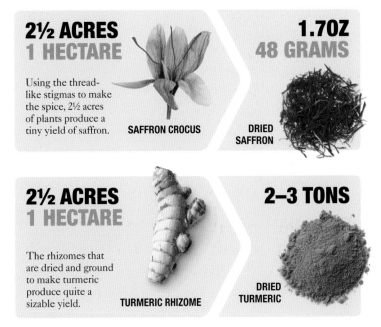

2½ ACRES
1 HECTARE

Using the thread-like stigmas to make the spice, 2½ acres of plants produce a tiny yield of saffron.

SAFFRON CROCUS

1.7OZ
48 GRAMS

DRIED SAFFRON

2½ ACRES
1 HECTARE

The rhizomes that are dried and ground to make turmeric produce quite a sizable yield.

TURMERIC RHIZOME

2–3 TONS

DRIED TURMERIC

In focus
CHILES

Chile peppers' active ingredient, capsaicin, is a toxic irritant that produces a burning sensation when we come into contact with it. However, in moderation, capsaicin creates an enjoyable spiciness.

Capsaicin evolved to protect peppers from being eaten, and does repulse nearly every mammal. We humans, however, have put chiles into our food for at least 6,000 years. Capsaicin doesn't actually have a flavor or smell—when it enters the mouth it simply causes pain by directly binding onto the nerves in the mouth and tongue that detect pain from heat sources. This tricks our brain into sensing burning heat (see p190). Despite this, chili heat is a popular flavoring.

Contrary to popular belief, the seeds of a chile pepper are not the hottest part, and, in fact, have little, if any, heat whatsoever. The flesh of the pepper isn't particularly hot either; most of the capsaicin is produced in tiny droplets on the soft, cream-colored placenta in the center of the fruit (see below). While most cooks believe that removing the seeds will reduce the heat of a chile pepper, it is really the action of scraping away the white placenta that creates this effect.

KNOW YOUR CHILES

The most well-known rating of a chile pepper's "hotness" is the Scoville scale, which is measured in units of SHU. The strength of a species of chile can vary greatly. Below is a selection of chiles from around the world that are popular in cooking.

SCOVILLE SCALE

Scotch bonnet
These very hot peppers are sweet in flavor. Add them whole to stews and curries, but take care not to burst them and add too much heat.

100,000–350,000 SHU
¾–1¼IN (2–3CM) IN DIAMETER

Thai chiles
Often called "bird's eye chiles," these tiny peppers are very hot. Their flavor complements citrus and coconut and they are often used in Thai curries.

100,000–350,000 SHU
1½–3IN (4–8CM) LONG

Piri piri
Although most piri piri plants are now found across Africa, the species is originally from South America. Piri piri sauce is originally from Portugal.

50,000–100,000 SHU
3–4IN (8–10CM) LONG

SCIENCE
CAPSAICIN, THE HEAT-CONTAINING ELEMENT OF CHILES, DISSOLVES WELL IN OIL, BUT VERY BADLY IN WATER.

COOKING
COOK CHILES IN OIL OR FAT-CONTAINING SAUCES SO THAT HEAT AND FLAVOR SUFFUSE THROUGH THE DISH.

BITTER TASTES
REMOVING SEEDS FROM A CHILE DOESN'T ACTUALLY REDUCE HEAT, BUT THE SEEDS DO CONTAIN BITTER-TASTING SUBSTANCES.

FRESH

Chili and onion flavoring

Stem

Skin
Mostly flavorless, the skin will brown and char when roasted.

Aji limon
Sometimes referred to as the "lemon drop" pepper, these Peruvian chiles have a citrus-like taste—hence their name. Use them to add spice to meat dishes and stews.

30,000–50,000 SHU
2–3IN (5–8CM) LONG

Serrano
Serrano peppers have a brighter, fresher flavor than many other varieties, so are often eaten raw or in cold dishes. Smoking or roasting will enhance their flavor. They are a key ingredient in Mexican cuisine.

10,000–25,000 SHU
1¼–2IN (3–5CM) LONG

Jalapeño
Jalapeño peppers can be quite variable in heat level. In Mexican cuisine, when they are smoke-dried, they are referred to as "chipotle" peppers.

3,500–10,000 SHU
2–3IN (5–8CM) LONG

Cascabel
This round chile has a nutty, sweet flavor and is small in size. It pairs well with meat, chicken, and fish, and is often toasted and used in sauces and stews.

1,500–2,500 SHU
¾–1¼IN (2–3CM) IN DIAMETER

Pimiento
Milder than most chiles, pimiento peppers originate from Spain. They are sweet, succulent, and aromatic, and are often used to stuff olives.

100–500 SHU
3–4IN (8–10CM) LONG

Flesh
This slightly watery part of the chile adds crunch and texture

Seeds
White and flavorless, the seeds carry almost no capsaicin.

Placenta
The fiery hot capsaicin is produced and stored as minute droplets in the white placenta.

Chipotles are smoke-dried jalapeño chiles

COOKING
REMOVE STEMS AND SEEDS AND TOAST DRIED CHILES UNTIL THEY BLISTER. THEN SOAK THEM, BLEND, AND ADD TO A SAUCE.

SCIENCE
DRYING CHILES INTENSIFIES FLAVORS, PRODUCING COMPLEX EARTHY AND NUTTY FLAVORS.

DRIED

THAI CHILE

How can I tame food that's TOO HOT?

As with oversalting, it can be hard to counteract chile heat while cooking, but there are a few tricks you can use.

Unfortunately, it is hard to eliminate the effect of the burning capsaicin molecules in chiles (see right).

Prevention is the best cure—when cooking with fresh or dried, whole or flaked chiles, try to add only a small quantity at a time, and then taste the dish and add a little more if necessary (spiciness will lessen as the dish cools). If you have already added too much chile while cooking, there are a number of different ingredients you can add to tone down, or distract from, the heat (see below). When seasoning spicy dishes, also bear in mind that chile heat takes longer to kick in than other tastes—there is a short delay before the capsicin triggers the heat receptors on the tongue (see right).

Water or vegetables
Adding water or more vegetables to the sauce will dilute capsaicin molecules over a wider area, dispersing their heat.

Cream or yogurt
Dairy fat globules, surrounded by emulsifying casein proteins, soak up some of the capsaicin molecules.

Limit salt
Salt increases the sensitivity of heat receptors on the tongue to capsaicin, increasing chile's fiery power.

Honey or sugar
Intensely sweet ingredients, such as honey or sugar, reduce the sensitivity of heat receptors on the tongue, balancing chile heat.

Avoid acid
Acidic foods, such as vinegar and citrus juice, trigger heat-sensitive nerves on the tongue. Add alkaline baking soda to reduce heat.

What's the best way to TAKE AWAY CHILE HEAT?

Learn science-based strategies for reducing chile burn.

The "heat" we feel from chiles is due to a substance called capsaicin, which has the devious capability to attach to heat-sensing receptors on pain nerves (see below). To your brain, physical burning and chile "heat" are identical sensations. Most of the accepted antidotes for chile burn—including alcohol and fizzy drinks—make it worse, but if you're in agony, there are a few quick fixes to lessen the pain (see right). Time is the best healer: the burning sensation created by most chiles will dull after three minutes, and after 15 minutes it should completely disappear.

WAYS TO EASE CHILE BURN

Ice
Placing an ice cube or two in your mouth can negate the burning sensation after you've eaten too much chile. The ice cubes' freezing temperature confuses your brain into ignoring some of the chile heat.

Milk and yogurt
Fats and casein proteins in milk and yogurt absorb capsaicin, preventing more of its fiery molecules from bonding with pain receptors. Their fridge-cold temperature also has a soothing effect on your tongue.

Mint
Just as capsaicin affects the heat-sensitive nerves in your mouth, so the menthol in mint stimulates your cold-perceiving nerves. Chew on a few fresh mint leaves, or add mint to a cooling yogurt sauce, to help counteract fiery chile sensations.

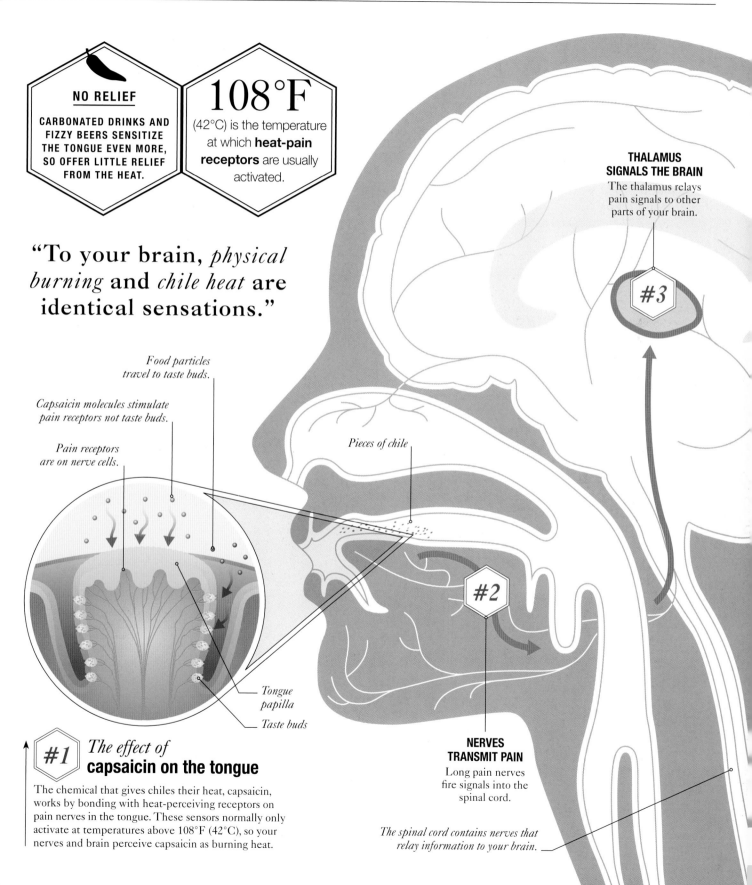

NO RELIEF

CARBONATED DRINKS AND FIZZY BEERS SENSITIZE THE TONGUE EVEN MORE, SO OFFER LITTLE RELIEF FROM THE HEAT.

108°F
(42°C) is the temperature at which **heat-pain receptors** are usually activated.

THALAMUS SIGNALS THE BRAIN
The thalamus relays pain signals to other parts of your brain.

#3

"To your brain, *physical burning* and *chile heat* are identical sensations."

Food particles travel to taste buds.

Capsaicin molecules stimulate pain receptors not taste buds.

Pain receptors are on nerve cells.

Pieces of chile

#2

Tongue papilla

Taste buds

NERVES TRANSMIT PAIN
Long pain nerves fire signals into the spinal cord.

#1 *The effect of* **capsaicin on the tongue**

The chemical that gives chiles their heat, capsaicin, works by bonding with heat-perceiving receptors on pain nerves in the tongue. These sensors normally only activate at temperatures above 108°F (42°C), so your nerves and brain perceive capsaicin as burning heat.

The spinal cord contains nerves that relay information to your brain.

In focus

OIL AND FAT

As well as suffusing flavor molecules from other foods, oils and fats carry their own flavors, too, making them an ingredient in their own right.

Oils are fats that are liquid at room temperature and are typically plant-based. Other cooking fats are usually solid and animal-based. Oils are generally rich in unsaturated fats, while animal fats are high in saturated fats, which can raise cholesterol. Both enhance the taste and mouthfeel of food. Flavor molecules from herbs and spices dissolve easily in oil, so flavors suffuse a dish fully. Oil is easy to infuse with ingredients

such as chili, lemon, rosemary, and basil. But more than this, oils and fats can cook food at very high temperatures, but they must be treated with care. When they are heated to their limit (see "smoking point," right), molecules are ripped apart and the oil or fat disintegrates and darkens, giving off acrid vapors and tasting foul. Faint blue smoke signals that a pan should be taken off the heat.

SCIENCE

OIL CARRIES FLAVOR MOLECULES AND CONDUCTS HEAT EFFICIENTLY TO THE SURFACE OF FOOD.

COOKING

OIL FORMS A LUBRICATING FILM BETWEEN FOOD AND METAL TO STOP FOOD FROM STICKING AND FALLING APART.

OIL

KNOW YOUR OIL AND FAT

Unrefined oils contain minerals, enzymes, and flavor-carrying impurities, which have a tendency to burn. All oils and fats burn at a different temperature, known as the "smoke point." These smoke points are listed below to help you choose the right oil or fat for your particular cooking method.

OILS

Extra virgin olive oil
This thick, highly flavorful oil has a low smoke point, making it unsuitable for frying. It is best used for drizzling and as a base for dressings.

SMOKE POINT:
320°F (160°C)
FAT: 91.5G PER 100G

Olive oil
More versatile than virgin olive oils, cooking olive oil (a mix of unrefined and refined oils) has a higher smoke point, so it can be used to impart a mild olive flavor to fried foods.

SMOKE POINT:
390°F (200°C)
FAT: 91.5G PER 100G

Canola/rapeseed oil
This general-purpose oil has earthy, nutty flavors, but lacks taste when overrefined. It has a fairly high smoke point and can be used for frying and roasting.

SMOKE POINT:
400°F (205°C)
FAT: 91.7G PER 100G

Peanut oil
A high smoke point makes this ideal for stir-frying food at a high temperature. Unusual for nut oils, its mild, nutty flavor is retained even after cooking.

SMOKE POINT:
450°F (230°C)
FAT: 91.4G PER 100G

Coconut oil
Increasingly popular, this heavy oil melts from solid to liquid at just above room temperature. If unrefined, coconut oil can smoke excessively during frying.

SMOKE POINT:
350°F (175°C)
FAT: 97.3G PER 100G

SATURATED FATS

Butter
This has an unparalleled flavor in sauces, baked goods, and pastries. Up to 16 percent water, butter has a low smoke point that is unsuitable for frying at a high heat.

SMOKE POINT:
350°F (175°C)
FAT: 82.9G PER 100G

Ghee (clarified butter)
Nutty-flavored ghee is widely used in Indian cooking. Water is removed to create this "clarified" butter, leaving only fat. It has a high smoke point useful for frying.

SMOKE POINT:
445°F (230°C)
FAT: 100G PER 100G

Lard and tallow
Rendered from pork fat (lard) or beef fat (tallow), these fats are solid at room temperature. Highly stable, they can withstand repeated use in deep-fat frying.

SMOKE POINT:
365°F (185°C) LARD
400°F (205°C) TALLOW
FAT: 98.8G PER 100G

Flavor enhancer
Good-quality olive oils offer complex fruity, peppery, green, and floral flavor sensations.

Best storage
Olive oils are best kept in bottles with green or dark glass to prevent UV light from reaching the oil and accelerating the breakdown of flavor molecules.

SCIENCE
PROTEIN TRACES AND OTHER SOLIDS IN FATS REACT WITH HEAT TO SPEED BROWNING AND FORM NEW AROMAS.

Adding butter
Butter enhances flavor and texture, giving pastry added flakiness.

COOKING
SATURATED FATS ARE BEST USED TO ENRICH AND ADD TEXTURE TO SAUCES, PASTRIES, AND BAKES.

BUTTER

EXTRA VIRGIN OLIVE OIL

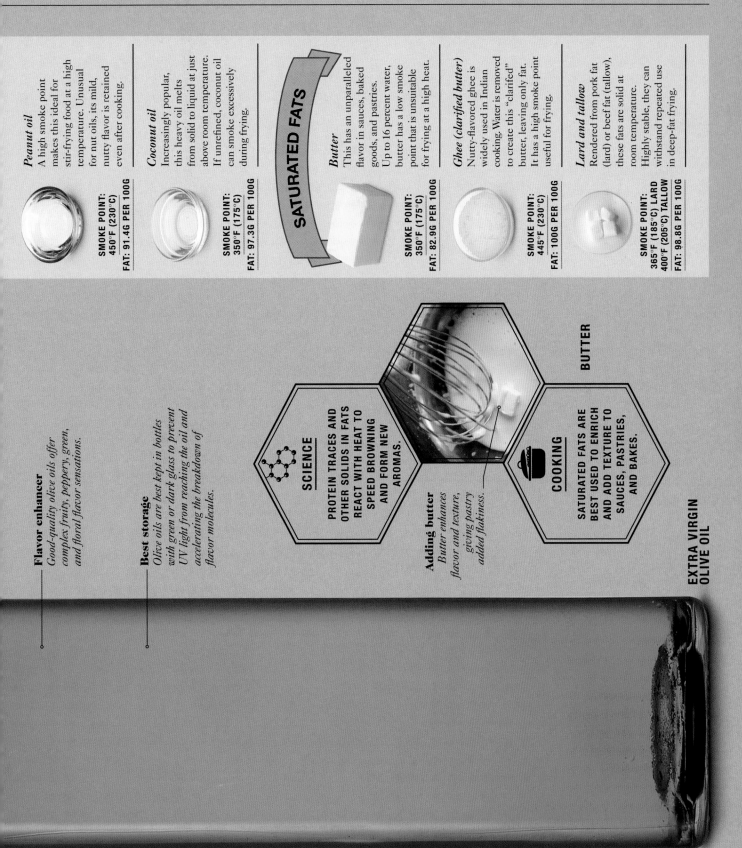

Why are some OLIVE OILS BETTER QUALITY THAN OTHERS?

"Extra virgin" denotes quality, but we are often confused by terms such as "cold pressed" and "first pressed."

When olives are harvested for oil making, they are ground into a yellowish-brown sludge called a paste. Traditionally, hemp mats were soaked in this paste and squeezed with a press to force out the oil. Today, most olive oil is extracted by spinning the paste in a centrifuge. This faster method with less air exposure yields better quality. Warming the paste makes it easier to draw oil out, but this can be at the expense of flavor because heat causes fragrances to evaporate and speeds the rate at which oil turns rancid. "Cold pressed" or "cold extracted," a label that attracts a high markup, means an oil has not been warmed above 81°F (27°C). For quality guarantee, choose oils labeled "virgin": olives are fresh pressed or spun only once to extract the best-quality oil. Acid levels indicate that fat molecules have broken into fatty acids due to damage or poor processing. The top virgin oil grades are low acidity (see below).

EXTRA VIRGIN OLIVE OIL
Reserved for oil rated as having excellent flavor. To be awarded "extra," it needs an acidity of less than 0.8 percent.

VIRGIN OLIVE OIL
This must meet international taste standards, and it has acidity levels below 1.5 percent to indicate overall quality.

OLIVE OIL
Below "virgin" standards, these are often refined to remove impurities. Lacking flavor, refined oils withstand high cooking heats.

> **"Virgin olive oils** *are pressed or* **spun only once** *to extract the best-quality oil. No virgin oil can be* **pressed** *more than once—the words 'first pressed' are marketing* **spin."**

How do I pick the most flavorful virgin oils?

Picking the best, most flavorful, fresh, and fruity oil is not straightforward. A dark green color does not mean it is good—some of the finest oils are light colored. Look for a harvest date within the past 12 months for the freshest oil or, failing that, a best-before date two years in the future. Unfiltered olive oil may have sediment in the bottle, but this doesn't mean it has a better flavor and it may turn rancid faster. Taste first to judge the quality.

What's the best way to
STORE OLIVE OIL?

Like wine, delicately flavored unrefined oils will turn rancid and musty tasting if carelessly stored.

Heat, light, and air all destroy flavors in oils. Although few in overall number, oil aroma molecules have a strong effect on the nose, and come from the squeezed fruit, seed, or nut. The flavors in oil are best when fresh and do not evolve or improve with age, so storing oils is about preserving the aromas for as long as possible.

Oxygen is disastrous for oil flavors, so always keep oils stored in an airtight container. Heat speeds up the flavor-tainting

A LITTLE HELP

BOTTLES SEALED WITH A BUBBLE OF INERT GAS, SUCH AS NITROGEN OR ARGON, AT THE TOP HAVE A LONGER SHELF LIFE.

reactions, and light wreaks havoc on the fragile molecules in unrefined oils. Attractive-looking green olive oils contain plenty of the leafy green plant pigment chlorophyll, which absorbs even more of the sun's energy, making green oils prone to turning rancid more quickly. Even when the bottle is cool and completely airtight, the energy from the sun's rays, especially the most powerful UV rays, is enough to trigger oxidation (see below).

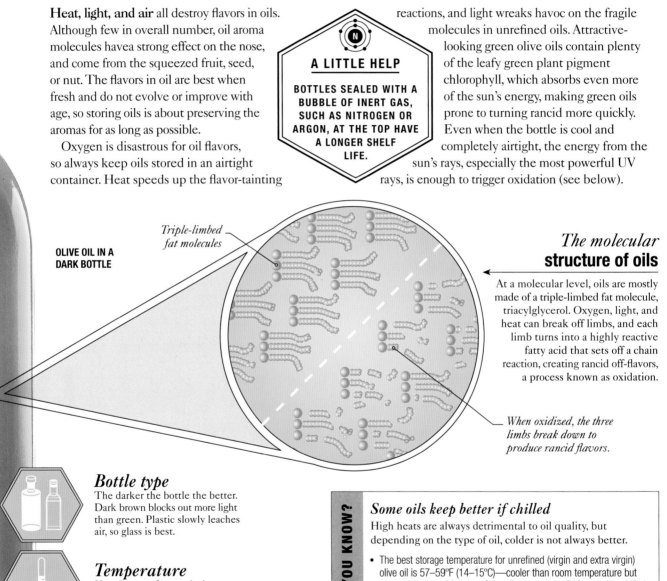

OLIVE OIL IN A DARK BOTTLE

Triple-limbed fat molecules

The molecular **structure of oils**

At a molecular level, oils are mostly made of a triple-limbed fat molecule, triacylglycerol. Oxygen, light, and heat can break off limbs, and each limb turns into a highly reactive fatty acid that sets off a chain reaction, creating rancid off-flavors, a process known as oxidation.

When oxidized, the three limbs break down to produce rancid flavors.

Bottle type
The darker the bottle the better. Dark brown blocks out more light than green. Plastic slowly leaches air, so glass is best.

Temperature
Heat hastens flavor-tainting reactions, so keep oils away from heat sources and sunlight.

Exposure to air
Oxygen destroys oils' flavors. Always store oil in an airtight container.

DID YOU KNOW?

Some oils keep better if chilled
High heats are always detrimental to oil quality, but depending on the type of oil, colder is not always better.

- The best storage temperature for unrefined (virgin and extra virgin) olive oil is 57–59°F (14–15°C)—cooler than room temperature but warmer than a refrigerator. Olive oils do not benefit from being chilled because when the temperature drops, the most stable and light-resistant fats in olive oil turn solid first, leaving the more delicate and vulnerable triacylglycerol molecules behind as a liquid.

- Refined cooking oils have had most of their flavors removed along with any impurities when they were filtered or cleaned, giving them a longer shelf life. Unlike other oils, nut and seed oils tend to last longer in a refrigerator, although they may turn cloudy or solidify.

Why does food cook
FASTER WHEN IT'S FRIED?

Frying is the favored technique of time-pressed cooks—the chemistry of oils explains the speedy nature of cooking in a frying pan or deep-fat fryer.

Frying is one of the fastest ways to cook food. It's quicker than water-based techniques because oil reaches temperatures far greater than water: frying typically operates around 348–445°F (175–230°C), compared to a maximum of 212°F (100°C) for boiling in water. Oil also heats up faster than water and transfers its heat into food far more effectively than even the hottest oven.

Frying for flavor

Cooking in oil is not just about speed and heat, however. When the surface of a frying piece of food—bare or battered—hits 284°F (140°C), Maillard browning begins (see pp16–17) and the food starts to form a flavorful, crunchy surface. At 329°F (165°C), sugars in the food caramelize, adding extra complexity of flavor to the food. Butter is one of the most flavorful fats, but it's best to choose a high-smoke-point oil for frying (see pp192–193), because this will allow the oil to heat to the high temperatures necessary for browning and caramelization without the butterfat burning. Oils can be reused several times and get better with use. As some fat molecules react in heat, they develop pleasant flavors and penetrate further into food, giving a denser crust.

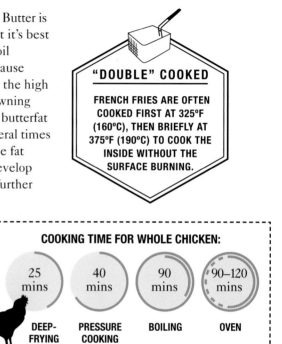

"DOUBLE" COOKED

FRENCH FRIES ARE OFTEN COOKED FIRST AT 325°F (160°C), THEN BRIEFLY AT 375°F (190°C) TO COOK THE INSIDE WITHOUT THE SURFACE BURNING.

Comparing cooking rates
The table compares the rate at which different cooking methods will cook a whole chicken. Moisture must steam away from the surface of the food before it can exceed 212°F (100°C), when it will start browning.

COOKING TIME FOR WHOLE CHICKEN:

25 mins	40 mins	90 mins	90–120 mins
DEEP-FRYING	PRESSURE COOKING	BOILING	OVEN

Why is fried food
BAD FOR YOUR HEALTH?

Frying is a notoriously unhealthy cooking method—but there are ways to reduce the health risks.

Without a doubt, fried food contains more energy (calories) than food cooked by any other means. This is because oil is absorbed into the food during cooking. Fat isn't evil, but too much of it certainly isn't good for the waistline— gram for gram, fat contains more than twice as many calories as protein or carbohydrates. Super-heated steam bursts out of frying food as it cooks in the hot oil (see pp76–77), limiting how much oil penetrates into the food during cooking—around 80 percent of the oil that soaks into food does so in the first few seconds *after* it is taken out of the frying pan or deep-fat fryer. This means that promptly blotting away excess oil (using paper towels) is a good way to reduce the fat content of fried food.

Calories aside, frying can also be bad for your health if the oil gets too hot. If hot oil is giving off a blue haze or smoke, it is reaching its smoke point (see pp192–193) and harmful, acrid-tasting chemicals are starting to form. When frying, choose oil with a high smoke point (see pp192–93), opt for healthier fats, and heat oil carefully.

COUNTING CALORIES

JUST ONE TABLESPOON OF FAT CONTAINS 120KCAL (500KJ), SO USE AS LITTLE OIL AS POSSIBLE AND FRY IN MODERATION.

"Reusing oil gives fried food an **even better taste** because partly oxidized oils add extra flavor. When too many fats have oxidized, the oil becomes rancid and should be discarded. **"**

How does
ALCOHOL ENHANCE FOOD?

Its inebriating effects aside, alcohol has an important place in the kitchen thanks to the flavors it gives to food.

Wines, beers, and ciders enhance stews, sauces, and desserts not only from the actual alcohol they contain, but by imparting sweetness from a drink's sugars, sharpness from its acids, and savory notes from its amino acids, which develop as they interact with the food.

Careful cooking

Alcoholic drinks need gentle simmering because many subtle aromatic flavor molecules evaporate quickly, potentially concentrating less-pleasant tastes, and turning the remaining liquid excessively acidic. Wine that is reduced for too long can develop an astringency from tannins, the substances fruit produce to deter parasites, so avoid cooking with vintage wine because its nuanced flavors will vaporize in the other ingredients. Use the chart, right, as a guide to flavor pairings between alcohol and food.

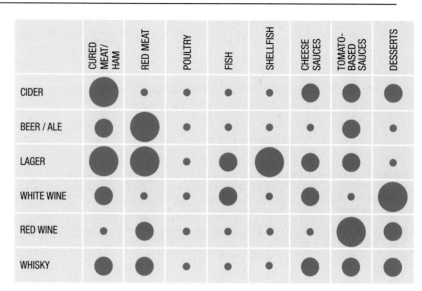

Cooking with alcohol
The chart, above, shows how drinks pair with different foods during cooking. The bigger the circle, the better the pairing.

30%
is the minimum alcohol strength needed to flambé food.

NO FLAME

WINE AND BEER WON'T FLAMBÉ BECAUSE THEY GIVE OFF INSUFFICIENT FLAMMABLE VAPORS TO CATCH FIRE.

What happens
WHEN I FLAMBÉ FOOD?

Flambéing is a showy way to liven up a dish.

While flambéing is an impressive spectacle, the technique is straightforward. High-strength warm or room-temperature liquor is poured into a nonsimmering pan and ignited by tilting the pan into a flame or by igniting with a long-handled lighter. It is not the liquid that burns, however, but the alcohol vapors as they evaporate: bluish tongues of fire hover slightly above the dish, consuming the fumes.

It is best to pour off most of any existing sauce that is in the pan before adding the alcohol because the concentration of alcohol in the sauce needs to be sufficiently high for the dish to ignite—if there is less than 30 percent alcohol in the sauce, it will be hard to light. Alcohol fumes rise quickly, so keep hair and sleeves out of the way and keep a large metal lid on hand in case of flare-ups.

A better taste?

Flavor-wise, flambéing does little. The flames can reach 500°F (260°C), which is more than enough to char the surface of the food and give a scorched taste, but in practice most of the heat hovers above the food. "Blind" taste tests show that flames don't improve taste in any way, and many chefs consider flambéing more showmanship than cooking, done purely to build anticipation and impress the diners.

Does alcohol really evaporate
WHEN I COOK WITH IT?

The more you cook alcohol, the more it evaporates, but some alcohol always remains.

Alcohol readily dissolves and releases aroma molecules, enhancing flavor. However, some cooking, simmering, or diluting is important because if alcohol is too strong—above about 1 percent concentration of the finished dish—it dampens other flavors, overwhelming the palate with bitter heat. Alcohol also triggers pain receptors, so add alcoholic drinks with care.

How much alcohol is left?

Cooking does encourage alcohol to evaporate, but even after a prolonged period of cooking, some alcohol will be left in the dish.

Eliminating alcohol from a dish is a matter of patience—even after two hours on a hot stove, as much as 10 percent of the intoxicating alcohol will remain in the sauce, worth bearing in mind when adding alcohol to your dish.

> **"Cooking** *does encourage* alcohol to **evaporate,** *but even after prolonged cooking some* **alcohol** *is left in the dish."*

MYTH BUSTER

———— *Myth* ————
FLAMBÉING BURNS OFF ALL THE ALCOHOL

———— *Truth* ————
Contrary to conventional cookbook wisdom, flambéing does not burn off the alcohol. When the air concentration of alcohol just above the pan drops to below 3 percent, there is no longer enough fuel to keep the flame going and it goes out. At this point, more than two-thirds of the alcohol is still left in the pan.

ALCOHOL RETAINED DURING COOKING

The diagram below shows the percentage of alcohol retained after baking or simmering in a dish for different lengths of time. While after 15 minutes, 60 percent of alcohol has evaporated, after 1 hour, 25 percent remains, and even after 2½ hours some is still present.

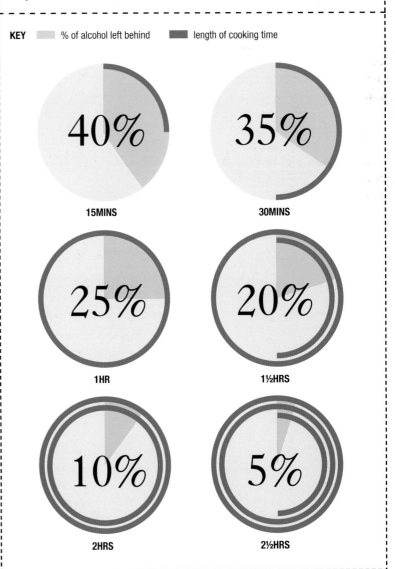

KEY ▓ % of alcohol left behind ▓ length of cooking time

40% — 15MINS
35% — 30MINS
25% — 1HR
20% — 1½HRS
10% — 2HRS
5% — 2½HRS

How can I keep my
SALAD DRESSING FROM SEPARATING?

The molecular makeup of oil and vinegar makes separation inevitable—another element is needed to bind the two.

Mixing olive oil and balsamic vinegar produces a cloudy foam of tiny oil droplets that hold for a few minutes before the oil separates on the surface. On a molecular level, water molecules are "polar" because they have an uneven electrical charge. Shaped like boomerangs, they have a small positive charge at each tip and a negative one in the bend. Water molecules cling to one another as the negative bends nestle against the positive tips of

ADDED BONUS

AN EMULSIFIED MIX KEEPS SALAD FRESHER AS IT STOPS OIL PENETRATING INTO AND DARKENING THE LEAVES.

nearby molecules. Nonpolar substances, such as oil, have no such attracting powers, so rise to the top of a dressing. Adding an "emulsifier," which binds fats and water, holds these two elements together. Mustard seeds contain a thick, gloppy emulsifier called mucilage. One tablespoon of mustard mixed into 8fl oz (240ml) of vinaigrette (3:1 oil to vinegar) provides suffiencient mucilage to bind the dressing together enough to coat salad leaves.

Is there much variation among different grades of
BALSAMIC VINEGAR?

With a thousand-year history, balsamic vinegar has been crafted to produce a dark, sweet, richly flavored condiment.

Made from grape juice, balsamic vinegar has a very special production method. Vinegars, such as white wine vinegar, are made by mixing an alcoholic drink with acid-producing bacteria that digest the alcohol, a process called acidification. Balsamic vinegar is made by simultaneously fermenting and acidifying grape juice, producing a condiment a world apart from other vinegars. Authentic balsamic vinegar should

originate from the Emilia-Romagna region in northern Italy, although, this is often not the case, and cheaper varieties fail to offer the complexity of flavor. A DOP (Denominazione di Origine Protetta) stamp indicates top-quality balsamic. Look, too, for an IGP (indicazione geographica protetta) label, and Consorzio di Balsamico Condimento, an accreditation from the Italian balsamic vinegar control organization.

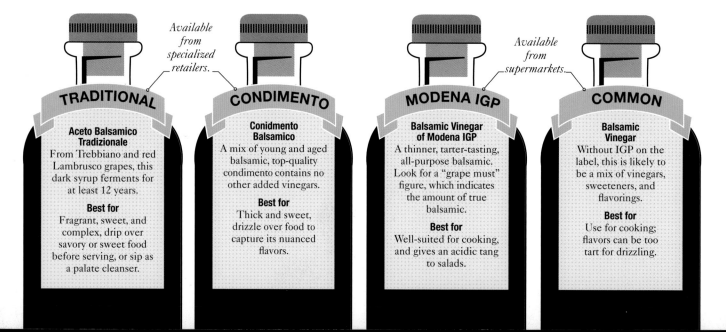

Available from specialized retailers.

TRADITIONAL

Aceto Balsamico Tradizionale
From Trebbiano and red Lambrusco grapes, this dark syrup ferments for at least 12 years.

Best for
Fragrant, sweet, and complex, drip over savory or sweet food before serving, or sip as a palate cleanser.

CONDIMENTO

Conidmento Balsamico
A mix of young and aged balsamic, top-quality condimento contains no other added vinegars.

Best for
Thick and sweet, drizzle over food to capture its nuanced flavors.

Available from supermarkets.

MODENA IGP

Balsamic Vinegar of Modena IGP
A thinner, tarter-tasting, all-purpose balsamic. Look for a "grape must" figure, which indicates the amount of true balsamic.

Best for
Well-suited for cooking, and gives an acidic tang to salads.

COMMON

Balsamic Vinegar
Without IGP on the label, this is likely to be a mix of vinegars, sweeteners, and flavorings.

Best for
Use for cooking; flavors can be too tart for drizzling.

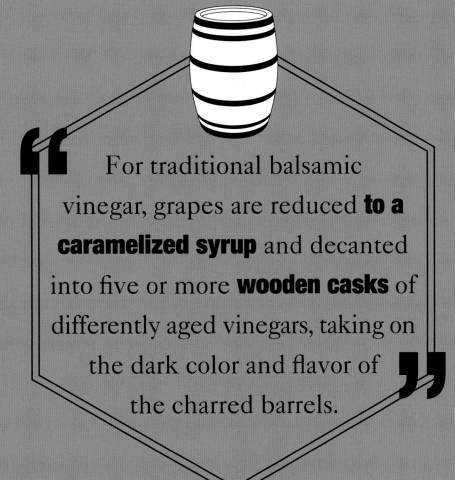

" For traditional balsamic vinegar, grapes are reduced **to a caramelized syrup** and decanted into five or more **wooden casks** of differently aged vinegars, taking on the dark color and flavor of the charred barrels. "

In focus
SALT

Of all the seasonings in the kitchen, none is more important than salt—a sprinkle of salt can intensify flavors and transform our food.

Our bodies are programmed to crave salt as it is essential for them to function. However, too much salt has been linked to high blood pressure, so it's important to control consumption. Salt has its own basic taste, but also affects how we experience other tastes, reducing bitterness and enhancing sweetness and umami—many desserts add salt just to amplify sweetness. As well as its flavor-enhancing powers, salt has specific culinary uses. It is added to dough to help gluten proteins form, making bread stronger and increasing its volume when baked; it dries out the surface of meat and fish to help it crisp; is used in brines to increase meat's succulence; and preserves all manner of foods. The difference in refined and unrefined salt (see right) is mostly due to texture.

Salt formation
Unrefined coarse salts have irregularly shaped crystals, unlike the regular cubic structure of refined salts.

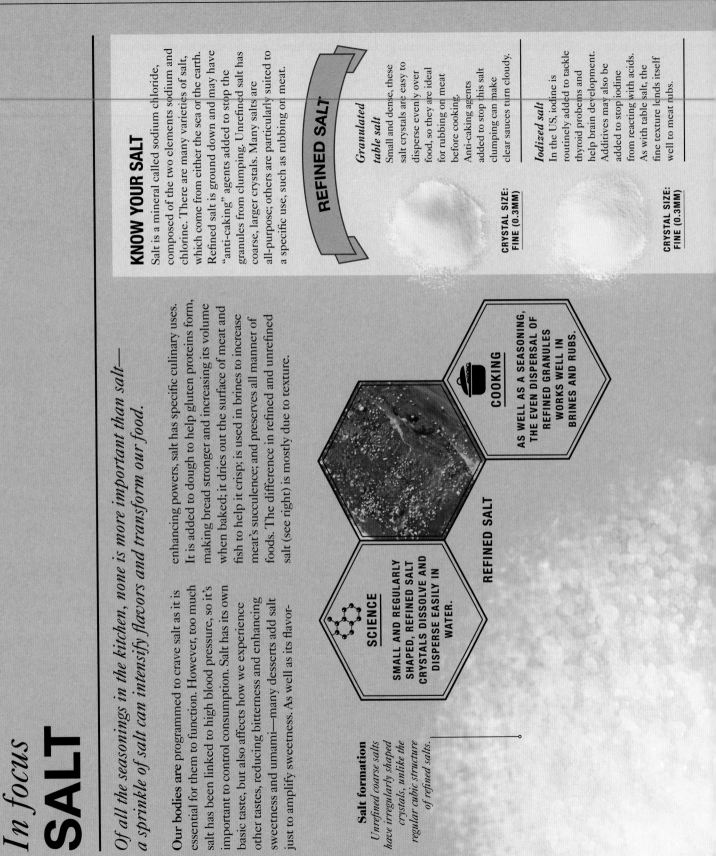

SCIENCE
SMALL AND REGULARLY SHAPED, REFINED SALT CRYSTALS DISSOLVE AND DISPERSE EASILY IN WATER.

COOKING
AS WELL AS A SEASONING, THE EVEN DISPERSAL OF REFINED GRANULES WORKS WELL IN BRINES AND RUBS.

REFINED SALT

KNOW YOUR SALT

Salt is a mineral called sodium chloride, composed of the two elements sodium and chlorine. There are many varieties of salt, which come from either the sea or the earth. Refined salt is ground down and may have "anti-caking" agents added to stop the granules from clumping. Unrefined salt has coarse, larger crystals. Many salts are all-purpose; others are particularly suited to a specific use, such as rubbing on meat.

REFINED SALT

Granulated table salt
Small and dense, these salt crystals are easy to disperse evenly over food, so they are ideal for rubbing on meat before cooking. Anti-caking agents added to stop this salt clumping can make clear sauces turn cloudy.

CRYSTAL SIZE: FINE (0.3MM)

Iodized salt
In the US, iodine is routinely added to tackle thyroid probems and help brain development. Additives may also be added to stop iodine from reacting with acids. As with table salt, the fine texture lends itself well to meat rubs.

CRYSTAL SIZE: FINE (0.3MM)

UNREFINED SALT

Curing salt
Used for food preservation, curing salts are a mixture of table salt with added sodium nitrite, which helps to inhibit the growth of bacteria that cause the serious condition of botulism food poisoning.

CRYSTAL SIZE: FINE (0.3MM)

Coarse salt
These larger, less ground crystals are known as rock salt, and have a jagged shape that adds texture to food. Use as seasoning during cooking, or for sprinkling before serving—the larger crystals make it easy to judge how much is being added.

CRYSTALS: LARGE AND NONUNIFORM

Sea salt
With little processing, this contains trace amounts of minerals such as magnesium chloride. Sea salt is a good general-purpose salt for use in cooking and tastes the same as coarse salt.

CRYSTALS: COARSE OR FLAKED; CAN BE FINE

Colored salts
A variety of gourmet salts are available, such as Himalayan pink salt, whose mild flavors are discernible if sprinkled before serving. These add a subtle, crunchy texture to dishes.

CRYSTALS: LARGE AND NONUNIFORM

Salt
Most salt crystals are a white color, often with a translucent quality. Trace minerals can lend some varieties a different hue.

SCIENCE
BITING INTO UNREFINED SALT ON THE SURFACE OF FOOD RELEASES A BURST OF FLAVOR.

COOKING
THE SUBTLE FLAVOR OF UNREFINED SALT HELPS REMOVE BITTERNESS WHEN ADDED AT THE END OF COOKING.

UNREFINED SALT

COARSE ROCK SALT

Can I SALVAGE OVER-SALTED DISHES?

Cooking with salt is something of a discipline.

Unfortunately, there is no way to remove salt once it has been added to food (see below). It may be possible to mask excess salt by distracting the taste buds with added sugar, fat, or a sour ingredient such as lemon juice, but our tongues are so highly attuned to salt that this rarely works. Some cooks suggest adding potatoes to soak up salt, then plucking them out before serving, but the science shows us that this doesn't work. As potatoes cook, they will absorb a little of the cooking liquid, but they won't pull out the salt. Remove the potatoes and the concentration of the sauce will be the same. The only reliable way to salvage an oversalted dish is to dilute it by adding more liquid. Adding extra bulk with more ingredients might also help a little by reducing how much sauce ends up in your mouth with each bite.

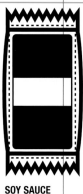

"Chemical" soy sauce

Soy sauce in a packet is usually a "chemical" yeast-free imitation. Solid leftovers from soybeans that have been used for making oil are mixed with strong hydrochloric acid. The acid breaks down starches and proteins into sugars and amino acids, and the throat-burning acidity is then reduced with sodium carbonate (washing soda). Flavored and colored with corn syrup, it's often so unpleasant that real soy sauce is mixed in.

SOY SAUCE PACKET

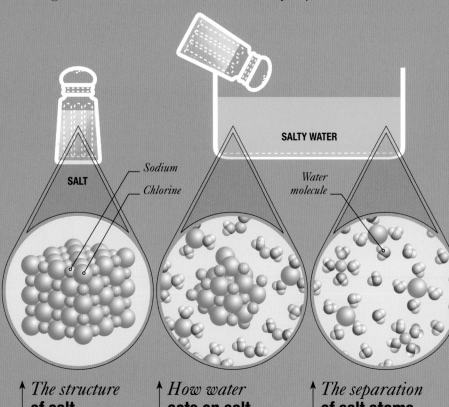

SALT

Sodium

Chlorine

SALTY WATER

Water molecule

The structure of salt

Salt is made up of sodium and chlorine atoms (see p202). When the two atoms meet, they lock together to form a lattice-like crystal.

How water acts on salt

When salt is put in a sauce, water molecules swarm around the salt crystals and start to pull the sodium and chlorine atoms apart.

The separation of salt atoms

The sodium and chlorine are hugged by water molecules and kept apart, so the salt can't be isolated and removed.

FLAVOR AND USES OF LIGHT SOY SAUCE

Light soy sauce has a thin consistency and saltier flavor.

USE AS AN EVERYDAY, ALL-PURPOSE SEASONING TO ADD SALTINESS AND EXTRA FLAVOR.

USE AS THE GO-TO SAUCE FOR SPLASHING IN STIR-FRIES.

USE AS A FLAVORING FOR LIGHT-COLORED MEATS SUCH AS CHICKEN TO AVOID DARKENING THE FLESH.

| USE TO ADD A DELICATE FLAVOR TO SUSHI. | SPLASH ON COLD APPETIZERS OR USE FOR DIPPING DUMPLINGS. |

Is it better to use
LIGHT OR DARK SOY SAUCE FOR COOKING?

Packed with rich umami flavor, tart, sweet, and pleasantly salty, soy sauce can bring life to a plate of bland rice.

Many people assume that light soy sauce is a thinned-down version of the real thing. It isn't, and also has nothing to do with "light" low-calorie foods. Light and dark soy sauces are different ingredients with distinct uses (see below).

Soy sauce starts life as a mix of cooked soybeans and roasted wheat. It is fermented twice—first for three days with a mold called *Aspergillus* that breaks down starches into sugars. Next, salt, yeast, and *Lactobacillus* bacteria are added, which, over about six months, chew up the sugars to make tangy lactic acid. Dark soy sauce is fermented longer, giving it a stronger taste. During fermentation, a variety of other microbes break down various components of the bland soybean into flavor molecules that carry the familiar soy sauce taste. Fermented soy sauce contains about 2 percent alcohol and, crucially, proteins are broken down into the amino acid glutamic acid, which gives soy sauce its savory umami flavor. Much of what we buy is Japanese soy sauce, which is sweeter and thicker than the (usually wheat-free) Chinese sauces.

LABEL ALERT

AVOID SOY SAUCE THAT CONTAINS HYDROLYZED VEGETABLE PROTEIN, WHICH INDICATES A CHEAP IMITATION SAUCE.

FLAVOR AND USES OF DARK SOY SAUCE

Fermented longer, dark soy sauce has a strong, robust flavor.

THIS CAN BE USED TO GIVE COLOR TO NOODLE DISHES. USE SPARINGLY TO AVOID OVERPOWERING FOOD.

OFTEN WITH ADDED SUGAR AND MOLASSES, IT HAS A SWEET FLAVOR.

HEADY, THICK, AND LESS SALTY, IT IS IDEAL FOR MARINADES, BRAISES, AND STEWS.

ITS SWEETER FLAVOR MAKES DARK SOY SAUCE AN IDEAL DIPPING SAUCE FOR HOT AND COLD APPETIZERS.

LIGHT SOY SAUCE ▲

▲ DARK SOY SAUCE

BAKING & SWEET THINGS

In focus FLOUR

Flour is indispensable in any kitchen. It is used to thicken and bind in both sweet and savory recipes, and forms the fabric of most modern baking.

Wheat-based flour is a core pantry ingredient. Flour is made by finely grinding down, or milling, the dried grain of the wheatgrass plant. After grinding, the different parts of the kernel—the starchy core (endosperm), the fibrous bran, and the nutrient-rich embryo (germ)—are sieved and separated. Much, if not all, of the flavorful bran and germ are typically discarded because their oils turn rancid easily. All grains are starchy, and when wheat flour is mixed with water and kneaded, for example, in

breadmaking, two proteins in flour form gluten, an incredibly strong, stretchy substance that captures bubbles of gas, helping bread to rise in the oven. Flours can be high or low in protein, reflecting how much gluten their dough will contain. It's important to pick a flour with the most suitable protein content for your particular culinary purpose (see right).

KNOW YOUR FLOUR

Flour comes in a range of types and colors, depending on how refined it is—white being the most refined—and its protein content, which reflects the amount of gluten in flour. For bread making, high-protein flours that form more elastic gluten are best. In cakes and pastries, starch is the key component and too much gluten creates a dense texture, so a low-protein flour is ideal. Pasta requires flour with sufficient gluten for flexibility, but not so much that the sheets are hard to roll.

HIGH PROTEIN

Strong flour
Also known as bread flour, this is made from hard-wheat varieties of flour with a high protein content that creates a dense, stretchy gluten mesh that traps air bubbles. In bread making, this elastic dough helps bread to rise well in the oven.

PROTEIN: 12–13%
STARCH: 66.8G PER 100G

Whole wheat flour
Whole wheat flours reserve the bran and the germ. "Brown" flours have some bran, and "multigrain" contains milled grains of various plants. These flours are used to make more flavorful, nutritious breads.

PROTEIN: 11–15%
STARCH: 61.8G PER 100G

SCIENCE
IN FRESHLY MILLED FLOUR THE GLUTEN IS WEAK. IT STRENGTHENS AS IT AGES IN RESPONSE TO AIR AS OXYGEN REACTS WITH PROTEINS.

COOKING
KNEADING AND RESTING ALLOW GLUTEN PROTEINS TO FORM AND STRENGTHEN. WHEN MIXED WITH YEAST, GLUTEN CAPTURES GAS BUBBLES.

GLUTEN

Gluten bubbles swell to create volume.

Nutrient-rich
Whole wheat flours contain the original proportions of bran and germ, the flavorful parts of the grain that are rich in fiber; protein, and nutrients such as iron and the family of B vitamins.

MEDIUM-LOW PROTEIN

00 flour
Also called pasta flour, 00 flour is the Italian grade for very finely ground flour. It has 7–11 percent protein, forming a medium-strength gluten that gives pasta bite. 00 flour can also be used for light pastry, cakes, and cookies.

PROTEIN: 7–11%
STARCH: 68.9G PER 100G

Plain white flour
Refined to remove the bran and germ, white flour is often enriched with nutrients lost from the bran and germ. This all-purpose flour gives a delicate texture to sweet bakes and helps thicken sauces.

PROTEIN: 7–10%
STARCH: 76.2G PER 100G

Self-rising flour
These flours have added baking powder. When mixed with water, the chemical sodium bicarbonate in baking powder reacts to release carbon dioxide, which helps cakes to rise.

PROTEIN: 7–8%
STARCH: 74.3G PER 100G

WHOLE WHEAT FLOUR

Sieving and separating
As whole wheat flour retains all parts of the grain kernel during the milling process, it has a darker, more heavily textured appearance than highly refined flours.

Careful storage
Whole wheat flours have a shorter shelf life than more refined flours, so they need to be stored in a cool area away from direct light.

Starch supports air bubbles in a cake mix.

STARCH

SCIENCE
ADDED TO CREAMED CAKE MIX, STARCH STRENGTHENS THE FOAM BUBBLE WALLS SO THEY KEEP THEIR SHAPE WHEN BAKING.

COOKING
LOW-PROTEIN FLOUR ALLOWS STARCH TO GIVE STRUCTURE AND TEXTURE WITHOUT THE TOUGHENING OF GLUTEN.

Why do I need to SIFT FLOUR?

Sifting flour was traditionally done to turn milled flour into a fine powder.

Today, flour particles have been milled and sifted to less than a quarter of a millimeter. However, sifting is still important for cake baking, not to break wheat starch down, but to aerate it by separating out the particles that have clumped together by settling or being squashed in a package. Sifting powdered ingredients into a cake mix disperses them and actually increases flour's volume. If unsifted, then the small clumps of powder will stick together in dense clusters when moistened and will be hard to break up with stirring and whisking. These clumps thicken the walls of the tiny bubbles that you are beating into the batter, weighing them down and resulting in a denser sponge.

HIGH-SPEED MIXING

A FOOD PROCESSOR HELPS TO DISPERSE FLOUR FOR CAKES, MAKING SIFTING LESS CRITICAL, THOUGH STILL IMPORTANT.

"Sifting aerates flour, *breaking up the clumps of flour particles* **that form when the flour is in the package."**

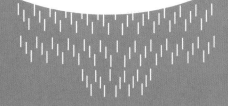

NO NEED TO SIFT

FOR BREAD MAKING, SIFTING MAKES NO DIFFERENCE AS FLOUR IS PRESSED TOGETHER DURING KNEADING.

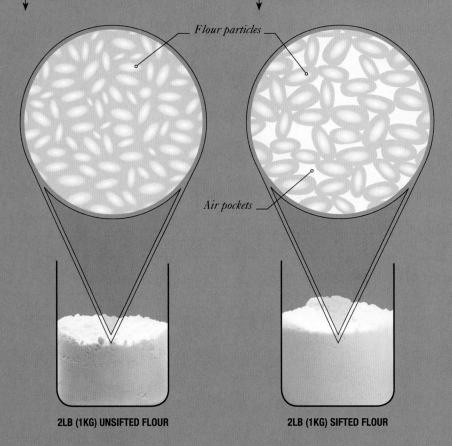

Flour added **without sifting**

When flour is poured from the package into a container without sifting, particles are packed together into a fairly dense, compact mass.

Flour added **after sifting**

The same amount of flour passed through a fine sieve almost doubles in volume, as particles that clumped together are separated and dispersed.

Flour particles

Air pockets

2LB (1KG) UNSIFTED FLOUR

2LB (1KG) SIFTED FLOUR

Why do baking recipes recommend ADDING SALT?

Such is the body's built-in desire for salt that everyone's taste buds are prepared to relish it.

Salt enhances the flavor of nearly all foods: umami, sweet, and sour taste receptors are made more sensitive by it, while bitterness is toned down. Too much salt can be overpowering, but just a tiny amount has a powerful effect on sweetness: adding a small pinch of salt to a cup of tea that has been sweetened with one teaspoon of sugar will make it taste as though it contains three teaspoons of sugar.

Too much sugar in a cake mix will produce a cake that is too soft because sugar holds on to moisture and interferes with the unwinding and reforming of proteins that form the cake's scaffolding mesh, making it less stable. (The same destabilizing effect is true for gluten proteins when sugar is added to bread.) Adding salt is an easy way to increase sweetness without compromising texture.

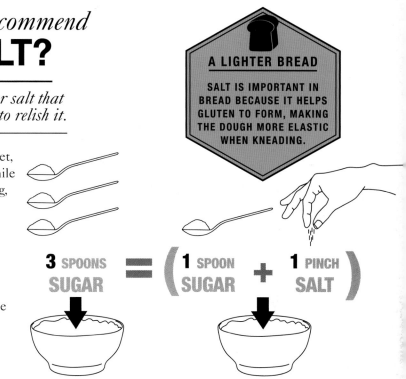

A LIGHTER BREAD

SALT IS IMPORTANT IN BREAD BECAUSE IT HELPS GLUTEN TO FORM, MAKING THE DOUGH MORE ELASTIC WHEN KNEADING.

3 SPOONS SUGAR **=** (**1** SPOON SUGAR **+** **1** PINCH SALT)

Can I use baking powder instead of BAKING SODA?

Though both are leavening agents, one crucial difference affects how these two ingredients are used.

Before leavening agents were created, air needed to be forced into a cake mix with brute force by beating.

Baking soda and baking powder add gas to a mix, but their compositions affect how they're used. Baking soda (bicarbonate of soda) needs an acid to be added to help a cake rise (see right), while baking powder already contains a powdered acid. If you wish to swap baking powder for soda, you need to substitute each teaspoon of baking powder with a quarter teaspoon of baking soda and half a teaspoon of an acid, such as cream of tartar. Conversely, swap each teaspoon of baking soda for 3–4 teaspoons of powder, and remove the cream of tartar. Be aware that some recipes use baking soda to balance acidity in other ingredients.

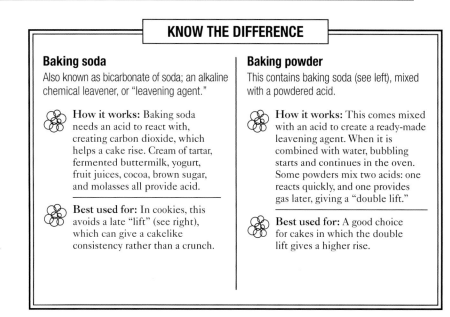

KNOW THE DIFFERENCE

Baking soda
Also known as bicarbonate of soda; an alkaline chemical leavener, or "leavening agent."

How it works: Baking soda needs an acid to react with, creating carbon dioxide, which helps a cake rise. Cream of tartar, fermented buttermilk, yogurt, fruit juices, cocoa, brown sugar, and molasses all provide acid.

Best used for: In cookies, this avoids a late "lift" (see right), which can give a cakelike consistency rather than a crunch.

Baking powder
This contains baking soda (see left), mixed with a powdered acid.

How it works: This comes mixed with an acid to create a ready-made leavening agent. When it is combined with water, bubbling starts and continues in the oven. Some powders mix two acids: one reacts quickly, and one provides gas later, giving a "double lift."

Best used for: A good choice for cakes in which the double lift gives a higher rise.

Which is the best
TYPE OF FAT
FOR BAKING?

Each type of fat has its virtues and inadequacies.

Fats have a tenderizing effect in baking, making cakes more crumbly and pastries flakier. They prevent water from mixing with the flour, slowing down the formation of gluten. Fat molecules also prevent gluten threads from bonding together as firmly, thus weakening the protein strands that can make a cake dense or a pastry tough. The water content of your chosen fat therefore affects the texture of your baked goods.

Texture is a consideration, but so are the ability to capture gas bubbles, its ease of use, flavor, and mouthfeel. Margarines and vegetable shortenings create very light cakes and are more forgiving than butter in making pastry, but butter wins when it comes to flavor in cakes and pastry. The table opposite explains the various virtues of, and suitable uses for, each type of fat in baking.

TEXTURE

WHEN YOU DON'T WHIP AIR INTO A CAKE, SUCH AS FRUIT-FILLED MUFFINS, A PURE FAT LIKE LIQUID OIL MAKES IT LIGHT.

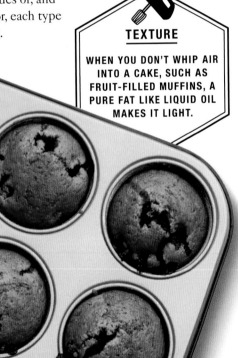

FRESHLY BAKED MUFFINS

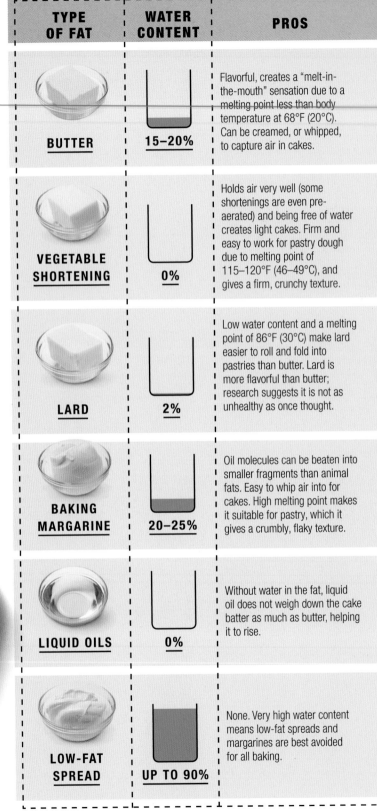

TYPE OF FAT	WATER CONTENT	PROS
BUTTER	**15–20%**	Flavorful, creates a "melt-in-the-mouth" sensation due to a melting point less than body temperature at 68°F (20°C). Can be creamed, or whipped, to capture air in cakes.
VEGETABLE SHORTENING	**0%**	Holds air very well (some shortenings are even pre-aerated) and being free of water creates light cakes. Firm and easy to work for pastry dough due to melting point of 115–120°F (46–49°C), and gives a firm, crunchy texture.
LARD	**2%**	Low water content and a melting point of 86°F (30°C) make lard easier to roll and fold into pastries than butter. Lard is more flavorful than butter; research suggests it is not as unhealthy as once thought.
BAKING MARGARINE	**20–25%**	Oil molecules can be beaten into smaller fragments than animal fats. Easy to whip air into for cakes. High melting point makes it suitable for pastry, which it gives a crumbly, flaky texture.
LIQUID OILS	**0%**	Without water in the fat, liquid oil does not weigh down the cake batter as much as butter, helping it to rise.
LOW-FAT SPREAD	**UP TO 90%**	None. Very high water content means low-fat spreads and margarines are best avoided for all baking.

CONS	BEST USED FOR
Challenging to use in pastry. It is hard to mix when chilled, but melts quickly at 68°F (20°C), leaking its water into the flour and stiffening pastry dough. Produces slightly denser sponge cakes.	Offers superior flavor and mouthfeel in pastry and cookies. Its flavor is less pronounced, and mouthfeel less important, in cakes.
Lack of flavor. Does not "melt in the mouth" because it is solid at body temperature and may make pastry taste greasy in the mouth. This synthetic product is unhealthy if made with hydrogenated fats (also known as trans fats).	Gives sponge cakes height, an airy texture, and a delicate crumb. Creates very flaky texture in pastry, but mouthfeel and flavor may be a drawback.
Less suitable for sweet baked goods, unlike butter, due to its mild, savory aroma. Some supermarket versions are hydrogenated to extend shelf life, adding harmful trans fats.	Complements savory baked goods and pastries.
Made in a similar way to vegetable shortenings, margarine also lacks flavor, and may create a greasy mouthfeel in pastry. Contains more moisture than shortenings.	Creates a light, high, crumbly cake. Tastes indiscernible from butter in light sponge cakes. Choose a margarine with a fat percentage of 80 percent or more for the lightest cakes.
Cannot be creamed to hold air, so is suitable only for cakes that rely solely on leavening agents to give them volume. Will not create flaky pastries because it can't separate gluten sheets into layers.	In cakes that are not creamed at all, such as carrot cake, liquid oil creates a very light, moist texture. Can also replace solid fat in pie crusts.
Not formulated to be creamed and capture air. High water content creates a dense, heavy texture in cakes and makes flaky pastries an impossibility.	None. In addition to low-fat spreads, spreadable margarines also contain too much water to be suitable for baking.

How important is it to PREHEAT THE OVEN?

It's worth allowing extra time for preheating.

A fully preheated oven is insurance against temperature drops, but it means allowing time for both the air and the metal walls inside the oven to reach the target temperature. The hot metal acts as a store of heat, known as a "heat sink," radiating its heat inward to keep the oven temperature steady. Whenever the oven door is opened, hot air rushes out; the small heating element must battle to reheat the air if the walls are cold, but hot oven walls will recover the correct air temperature rapidly.

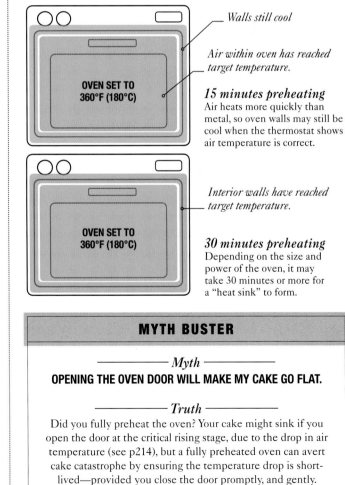

Walls still cool

Air within oven has reached target temperature.

OVEN SET TO
360°F (180°C)

15 minutes preheating
Air heats more quickly than metal, so oven walls may still be cool when the thermostat shows air temperature is correct.

Interior walls have reached target temperature.

OVEN SET TO
360°F (180°C)

30 minutes preheating
Depending on the size and power of the oven, it may take 30 minutes or more for a "heat sink" to form.

MYTH BUSTER

———— *Myth* ————
OPENING THE OVEN DOOR WILL MAKE MY CAKE GO FLAT.

———— *Truth* ————
Did you fully preheat the oven? Your cake might sink if you open the door at the critical rising stage, due to the drop in air temperature (see p214), but a fully preheated oven can avert cake catastrophe by ensuring the temperature drop is short-lived—provided you close the door promptly, and gently.

Why hasn't my CAKE RISEN?

Understanding the chemistry behind cake baking should help you identify what has gone wrong.

A cake goes through three stages of baking. The first stage is the rising phase, when the sweet batter inflates. In the second stage, the cake solidifies, fixing in place the hollows, or bubbles, that have formed in the batter. A bake ends with the third, "browning" stage.

How you mixed your batter, the quantities of ingredients used, and the oven temperature will all affect how well,

A FLUFFY MIX

IF USING A FOOD PROCESSOR, CREAM BUTTER AND SUGAR FOR AT LEAST TWO MINUTES FOR A LIGHT MIX.

or not, your cake rises. Normal baking temperatures are 350–375°F (175–190°C), but home oven thermostats are often unreliable and can be off by as much as 45°F (25°C). Preheating the oven ensures that the temperature recovers rapidly if the door is opened during baking (see p213). The table below charts the progress of a bake and explores the possible reasons for failure at each stage.

THE THREE STAGES OF CAKE BAKING

	STAGE 1: RISING			STAGE 2: SOLIDIFYING	
	32–176°F 0–80°C			**176–284°F 80–140°C**	
WHAT'S GOING ON?	**Bubbles expand** Baking powder starts to act. Bubbles of air captured inside the creamed mix expand and the rate of carbon dioxide–producing chemical reactions speeds up as the temperature climbs. *Air whisked into cake batter.*	**Double rise** If double-acting baking powder has been used to give a late rise (see p211), then at 122°F (50°C) the secondary acid goes to work, producing more gas to help rising. *New air bubbles form.*	**Bigger bubbles** From 158°F (70°C), water starts to steam off rapidly. The water vapor further expands the tiny voids inside the firming batter, and the bubbles continue to grow. *Steam inflates bubbles further.*	**Proteins unwind** At 176°F (80°C) egg proteins unwind and reform into a firm gel. In the absence of gluten, egg proteins provide the molecular supports that give cake its texture. It is crucial that there be enough egg within the cake. *Proteins reform around air bubbles.*	**Starch absorbs water** As the cake solidifies, starches in the flour soak up water and start the process of "gelatinizing" into what will become the cake's soft crumb. Sugar slows down the setting of starch, so very sweet cakes take longer to firm up. *Starch forms crumb.*
WHAT'S GONE WRONG?	**Undermixed** If butter and sugar haven't been creamed enough, they won't capture sufficient air. Creamed butter and sugar should be light, fluffy, and not sticking to the bowl.	**Wrong amounts** If there is too little leavening agent, there won't be enough gas for a rise; too much makes an excessively gassy batter that collapses in on itself.	**Heavy batter** If there is too much flour or liquid, or it was overstirred, making dense gluten fibers, the batter may be heavy. Sift flour to lighten it (see p210).	**Wrong temperature** If the oven is too hot, the outside of the batter will solidify before the gas has expanded enough to make the cake rise. The remaining trapped bubbles burst through the roof of the cake, splitting the top. If the oven is not hot enough, the cake will not set in time to capture the expanding bubbles, which then combine in large cavities and collapse the cake.	

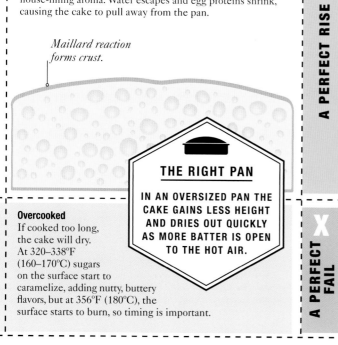

STAGE 3: BROWNING

>284°F >140°C ✓

Surface browns
The surface is dry, and at 284°F (140°C), sugars and proteins interact and trigger Maillard reactions (see p16), creating the golden-brown crust that gives a freshly baked cake its house-filling aroma. Water escapes and egg proteins shrink, causing the cake to pull away from the pan.

Maillard reaction forms crust.

A PERFECT RISE

THE RIGHT PAN

IN AN OVERSIZED PAN THE CAKE GAINS LESS HEIGHT AND DRIES OUT QUICKLY AS MORE BATTER IS OPEN TO THE HOT AIR.

Overcooked
If cooked too long, the cake will dry. At 320–338°F (160–170°C) sugars on the surface start to caramelize, adding nutty, buttery flavors, but at 356°F (180°C), the surface starts to burn, so timing is important.

X A PERFECT FAIL

Why do cakes get hard and
COOKIES GET SOFT?

Thinking about the concentration of ingredients in these sweet treats helps to explain how they age.

Cakes become dry and firm over time because moisture evaporates from the sponge and starch sets into hard "crystals," a process known as "retrogradation" (see below). This process speeds up at cold temperatures, so always keep cake in a tin at room temperature and never put bread in the fridge. Cookies, on the other hand, have a greater concentration of an ingredient that keeps them moist—sugar. Sugar molecules attract water, a quality called "hygroscopy" (see below), and over time this makes cookies increasingly damp. Honey and brown sugar (which contains molasses) are more hygroscopic than table sugar, so use these in place of white sugar if you want to produce a gooier cookie or brownie.

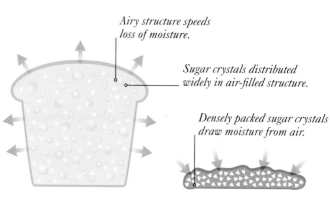

Airy structure speeds loss of moisture.

Sugar crystals distributed widely in air-filled structure.

Densely packed sugar crystals draw moisture from air.

CAKE

Retrogradation
Water evaporates from the starchy, honeycombed sponge, causing gel-like starches to lose moisture and cluster into dry crystals, known as retrogradation.

COOKIE

Hygroscopy
Sugar is hygroscopic, which means that over time, sugar in a baked cookie soaks up water from the circulating air, making the cookie increasingly damp.

"Honey and brown sugar *are particularly hygroscopic, meaning they attract water, so are ideal for* **soft cookies.**

What is a sourdough
STARTER?

*For millennia, bakers would set aside a wet,
frothy dough for making their next batch of bread.*

In the age of purified, dried yeast granules, bakers no longer
need to preserve yeast by setting aside a batch of fermenting
dough as a "starter" for their next bake. However, this practice
has been revived by the rising popularity of traditional,
artisanal food. Sourdough, bread made with a starter containing
cultivated wild yeast, often has a more complex flavor than
bread made with pure yeast. This is because starters contain a
combination of yeasts, as well as any bacteria growing on the
wheat when it was milled. Because the wild bacteria present
vary, different starters produce breads with a slightly different
taste. *Lactobacillus* (like those that make milk sour) and other
acid-producing bacteria living in the starter produce lactic and
acetic acid, giving the bread its characteristic sourness.

Online retailers sell granule "starters" that contain dried
yeast (and other microbes) extracted from an old sourdough
starter, but it isn't difficult to make your own (see right).

MAKING A SOURDOUGH STARTER

TIME	WHAT TO DO
DAY 1	• Add 7oz (200g) of bread flour and 6¾fl oz (200ml) of tepid water to a large glass jar and stir them into a paste. Cover the top of the jar with a breathable fabric and secure with a rubber band. • Leave the jar in a warm (not hot) place. The yeast and bacteria present in the flour will start to multiply.
DAYS 3–6	• On day 3 or 4, once your starter is bubbling, throw away half of it—about 7oz (200g). Then add 1oz (100g) of bread flour and 1fl oz (100ml) of water, stirring them into the mix. The yeast need a continuous supply of fresh food to continue to multiply at a fast rate, or their numbers will stagnate and they will start to die. Repeat daily. • A beery froth may appear on the top—simply pour it away or mix it in.
DAYS 7–10	• Your starter should now be frothing and have an acidic, beer-like smell. • At this stage you can use it to make bread. Take half of your starter to use in your dough, and feed your remaining starter with flour and water. For the bread, use a ratio of 2:1 flour to starter. • If there is no froth after 10 days, you may need to start again.

Carbon
dioxide bubbles

Lactobacillus

Other acid-
producing
bacteria

Yeast

Other wild
bacteria

Sourdough
under the microscope

Sourdough starter culture contains a variety
of microbes that contribute to the bread's taste
and texture. Fertilizers and pesticides can have
a significant effect on the amount of bacteria
and yeast present in flour, so try to use organic
or (if you can find it) wild wheat flour.

"If you **don't bake** bread **often**, you can **keep** your **starter** in the **fridge** unfed for up to **two weeks**. Just **remember** to take it **out**, **feed** it, and leave it in a **warm** place **24 hours before** you want to **bake**."

What are the basics of a
GOOD BREAD DOUGH?

A simple bread dough is easy to master, with a little understanding of gluten formation.

There has never been any one way to make bread—ask a dozen bakers how they make their loaves, and you will get 12 different answers. The simplest doughs comprise only flour and water.

Forming a dough

Mixing flour with water forms a dough of bonded proteins, starches, and water molecules. Two proteins present in flour—glutenin and gliadin—fuse together to form long, stretchy proteins called gluten. Mixing and kneading is important, as it helps proteins to coalesce into a strong

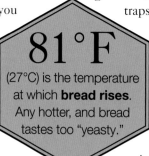

81°F
(27°C) is the temperature at which **bread rises**. Any hotter, and bread tastes too "yeasty."

gluten mesh (see below). When heated, this gluten mesh traps gas bubbles and then solidifies, giving baked bread its texture and structure (see pp220–221).

Rising loaves

Yeast, baking powder, and baking soda transform densely textured flatbread into an airy, risen loaf. All three ingredients release gas when cooked, expanding within the dough to make bread rise. Yeast—a tiny living organism— is the most popular leavening agent, as it lends both flavor and airiness to cooked loaves (see below).

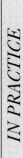

IN PRACTICE

PREPARING BREAD DOUGH

The early stages of bread making are crucial for ensuring a good bake. Yeast must be hydrated and strong gluten structures formed in order to create a springy, soft, flavorful loaf. This recipe is for a yeast-risen white loaf, but you can adapt it to use a sourdough starter (see p216) or whole-wheat flour (see pp208–209).

#1

#2

#3

AERATE THE FLOUR

Place 1lb 10oz (750g) strong white flour in a large bowl. Thoroughly mix in ½oz (15g) instant dried yeast and 2 tsp salt. Yeast will convert starches in the flour into sugars, which it feeds on to create carbon dioxide and ethanol, making bread rise. Salt adds flavor to the dough, strengthens gluten networks, and prevents yeast from growing too fast and producing "yeasty" flavors.

HYDRATE YEAST WITH TEPID WATER

Make a well in the center of the dry ingredients and pour in 15fl oz (450ml) tepid water. Starches in the flour absorb water molecules, swelling in size and helping to form a thick dough. Glutenin and gliadin proteins in the flour fuse together when moist, forming gluten. Tepid water hydrates and warms the dried yeast, causing it to start multiplying.

MIX TO FORM GLUTEN

Gradually draw the flour into the liquid, mixing with a wooden spoon until all the flour is incorporated. Stirring encourages more proteins to form and starts to fuse gluten strands into a mesh, which will give bread its structure and texture. Continue mixing with the spoon until the soft, sticky dough comes away from the sides of the bowl.

#4

KNEAD TO STRENGTHEN GLUTEN

Turn the dough onto a lightly floured work surface and knead: fold it over toward you, and then push it down and away with the heel of your hand. Turn the dough, fold it, and push it away again. If the dough is too sticky to work with, leave it for 1–2 minutes to allow starches in the flour to absorb moisture.

#5

KNEAD UNTIL SMOOTH AND ELASTIC

Continue kneading for 5–10 minutes. Kneading for this long helps proteins in the dough mesh together to form a stretchy gluten mesh. When baked, this mesh captures gas bubbles released by the yeast and then solidifies, creating a well-textured loaf. Continue to knead until the dough is smooth and stretchy, with no visible lumps.

#6

LEAVE TO RISE

Shape the kneaded dough into a ball and place it in a large, lightly greased bowl. Cover with oiled plastic wrap and leave to rise at room temperature for 1–2 hours (see p220). Over time, enzymes break down carbohydrates in the flour to produce sugar. Yeast feeds on this sugar and releases ethanol and carbon dioxide, which causes the dough to balloon.

Why do you need to proof dough
BEFORE BAKING IT?

Allowing time for proofing pays dividends for flavor and texture.

Yeast—the single-cell fungus that causes bread to rise—benefits from a long fermentation time. In addition to creating bubbles of carbon dioxide gas, lending height and volume to dough, yeast also releases chemicals that contribute complex flavors.

The second rise

After the initial, time-consuming rise (see pp218–219), it's important to knock the air out of the swollen loaf and leave it for a second rise, or "proof." Knocking out the yeast-created bubbles forces

BREAD AHEAD

YOU CAN PROOF DOUGH OVERNIGHT IN THE REFRIGERATOR TO SLOW THE ACTION OF YEAST AND DEVELOP FLAVOR.

them to reform into a smoother-textured dough. As the tiny yeast cells break down starches to digest sugars in the flour, they grow and release ethanol and other chemicals, which work together to create bread's flavor.

Baking in a hot oven

Commercial ovens bake bread at 500°F (260°C) and upward, in order to achieve a well-risen loaf with a crispy crust. When baking at home, maximize your chances of a successful loaf by preheating your oven (see below).

IN PRACTICE

PROOFING AND BAKING BREAD

Using a simple recipe for yeast-risen white dough (see pp218–219), this method allows time for yeast to ferment and create a flavorful, open-textured loaf. After step one, you can divide the dough into smaller loaves or rolls, rather than a single large loaf. You can also proof overnight in the refrigerator, to allow more time for flavor development.

PUNCH DOWN THE RISEN DOUGH

After 1–2 hours at room temperature, kneaded dough will have doubled in size, because yeast produces bubbles of carbon dioxide gas. Turn the dough out onto a lightly floured surface, punch to deflate it, and knead for 1–2 minutes. This pops air bubbles in the dough, allowing smaller bubbles to reform, creating a smooth dough.

PROOF IN THE PAN

Shape the dough into an oval. Place in a greased 2¼lb (1kg) loaf pan. Cover the pan with a clean, damp kitchen towel, to help retain moisture in the dough. Leave to rise again in a warm place for 1½–2 hours, or until the dough has doubled in size. This second rise, or "proof," allows chemicals released by fermenting yeast to develop flavors in the dough.

BAKE TO SET STARCH AND GLUTEN

Meanwhile, preheat the oven to 450°F (230°C). Remove the cloth from the loaf, sprinkle it with flour, and place in the hot oven. When the loaf enters the oven, yeast in the dough warms, producing more gas before it gives out its last gasp at about 140°F (60°C), when it dies in the heat. The dough softens, while ethanol and water rapidly evaporate—this steam further expands bubbles in the loaf.

RISE AND SHINE

THE FINAL RISE, OR "OVEN-SPRING," HAPPENS IN THE FIRST 10 MINUTES OF BAKING, BEFORE THE CRUST SOLIDIFIES.

#4

ALLOW MOISTURE TO EVEN OUT

Bake for 30–40 minutes, or until the loaf is well risen. The crust should be firm and golden, as sugars and proteins in the dough react in the Maillard reaction (see p16). Turn the loaf out onto a wire rack, to allow heat to dissipate. Leave to cool before cutting, to allow moisture to even out throughout the loaf, and starches to firm up into an even crumb.

The Process of
OVEN BAKING

A relatively slow cooking method, the heated chamber of the oven primarily uses hot, dry air to transfer heat to food.

Hot, dry oven air is slow at cooking food, and an oven's heating element is typically small and low-powered. In a preheated oven, the walls warm the air and radiate heat directly into the food, the thickest parts of the walls radiating the most heat rays. Fan ovens cook food faster than conventional ones as they circulate air more efficiently and reduce the temperature difference between the top and the bottom of the oven. The chamber quickly empties of hot air when the oven door is open, so preheating is vital.

DATA

How it works
A small heating element heats the metal walls and oven air, which both transfer heat into the food.

Best for
Bread, cakes and cookies, biscuits, potatoes; large cuts of meat and fish.

What to consider
For successful baking, preheat the oven long enough that the metal walls have reached the desired temperature.

EXTRA HEAT
EMULATE A REAL STONE OVEN BY PLACING A PIZZA STONE ON A LOWER RACK. IT WILL RETAIN AND RADIATE LARGE AMOUNTS OF HEAT UPWARD.

HUMIDITY CONTROL
SPRAYING WATER IN THE OVEN OR PLACING ICE CUBES INSIDE INCREASES HUMIDITY, REDUCING COOKING TIME.

SPRING-CLEAN
ACCUMULATED GRIME ON THE OVEN WALLS AND DOOR REDUCES THE AMOUNT OF HEAT RADIATED.

See inside
When baking bread, water in the dough and alcohol in the yeast evaporate, and the steam expands as gas bubbles in the loaf. This puffing up is called the "oven spring". Gluten stiffens, starch absorbs the remaining moisture, and the internal starch–gluten scaffold sets.

Key
Liquid surrounding gas bubble
Starch–gluten matrix

A liquid film forms around gas bubbles then dries as bread bakes.

Bubbles grow as steam and carbon dioxide from the yeast expand in the hot temperatures.

KNOW THE DIFFERENCE

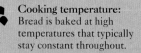

Baking
Nonsolid mixtures are baked until solid. Foods such as potatoes are baked dry.

Cooking temperature: Bread is baked at high temperatures that typically stay constant throughout.

Flavor and texture: Texture changes: gas bubbles form in cakes, breads, and soufflés to give an airy texture. Foods are not cooked in oil or covered in liquid. Breads and cakes may be glazed.

Roasting
Roasting refers to heating solid foods such as meat until browned and cooked through.

Cooking temperature: Meat is typically cooked at lower temperatures for longer so the dense tissue cooks throughout. Heat is increased at the start or end to brown the surface.

Flavor and texture: Dry oven air dehyrates meat and vegetables, but foods usually have a coating of oil or fat to enhance browning.

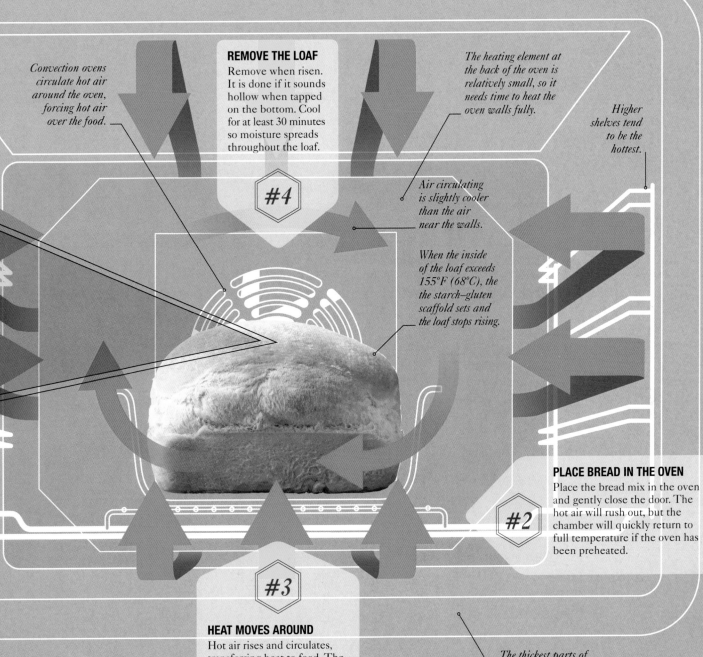

SET THE TEMPERATURE

#1 Preheat the oven to the desired temperature. Convection ovens cook faster than conventional ovens, so the temperature may be set slightly lower.

Convection ovens circulate hot air around the oven, forcing hot air over the food.

REMOVE THE LOAF

Remove when risen. It is done if it sounds hollow when tapped on the bottom. Cool for at least 30 minutes so moisture spreads throughout the loaf.

#4

The heating element at the back of the oven is relatively small, so it needs time to heat the oven walls fully.

Higher shelves tend to be the hottest.

Air circulating is slightly cooler than the air near the walls.

When the inside of the loaf exceeds 155°F (68°C), the the starch–gluten scaffold sets and the loaf stops rising.

PLACE BREAD IN THE OVEN

#2 Place the bread mix in the oven and gently close the door. The hot air will rush out, but the chamber will quickly return to full temperature if the oven has been preheated.

#3

HEAT MOVES AROUND

Hot air rises and circulates, transferring heat to food. The hot metal walls both heat the air and radiate heat into the food.

The thickest parts of the oven wall radiate the most heat.

Why doesn't GLUTEN-FREE BREAD RISE VERY WELL?

In addition to helping bread rise, gluten keeps starchy foods bound together, keeping bread from becoming too crumbly.

Wheat is so useful because when it is mixed with water, two wheat proteins join together to form gluten (see right) which is strong and elastic enough to trap gas bubbles and allow bread to rise. Non-wheat flours don't produce gluten so their bread tends to be flat. To remedy this, a sticky thickener, such as xanthan gum, is often added. Mixed with water, xanthan gum turns into a thick and slimy gel that is strong enough to hold gas bubbles. Emulsifiers, substances that mix with fats and water, may also be used because of their tendency to cluster around gas bubbles. Because no starch is quite like wheat nutritionally or texturally, gluten-free flours are usually a blend of starches, to give a range of nutrients and a consistency similar to that of wheat flour.

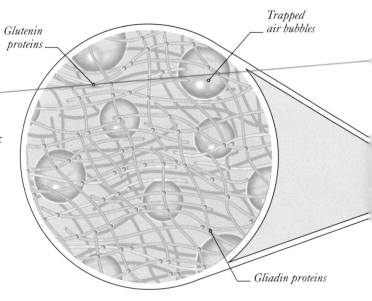

Glutenin proteins

Trapped air bubbles

Gliadin proteins

How gluten forms and helps bread rise

Well-kneaded wheat dough has threads of gluten, which are made when the proteins glutenin and gliadin bind together. The gluten captures yeast's gas bubbles, helping bread to rise.

Why isn't homemade bread as light AS STORE-BOUGHT?

The modern loaf is the product of an industrial process that has been progressively refined to produce a near-weightless bread.

As with so many of our foods that were once laboriously crafted by hand, the drive to feed a growing population at an ever-cheaper cost led to the discovery that machinery could do away with lengthy kneading and proving to create bread at hitherto unprecedented speed. With industrial mixers and a few extra ingredients, bread could be made on a huge scale from start to finish in under four hours (see right). Powerful mixers churn dough to form gluten so quickly that, with some chemical help, it doesn't need to rest or prove to become established, and can even be made with low-protein flour. Undoubtedly convenient, it's worth knowing how store-bought bread is made.

SOME EXTRA HELP

PRESERVATIVES SUCH AS ACETIC ACID HELP STORE-BOUGHT BREAD LAST A WEEK OR MORE WITHOUT TURNING MOLDY.

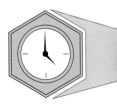

Time
Making the dough, kneading it, leaving it to proof, and then baking it can take six hours or more.

Color and texture
The color of homemade bread reflects the type of flour used; white loaves tend to have a yellow, rather than pure white, hue. More flour is used and gluten has longer to strengthen, giving a greater density and bite.

Taste
With more time to ferment, homemade bread has a stronger, "yeasty" flavor. It is denser than store-bought, so the flavor of the wheat flour is more pronounced.

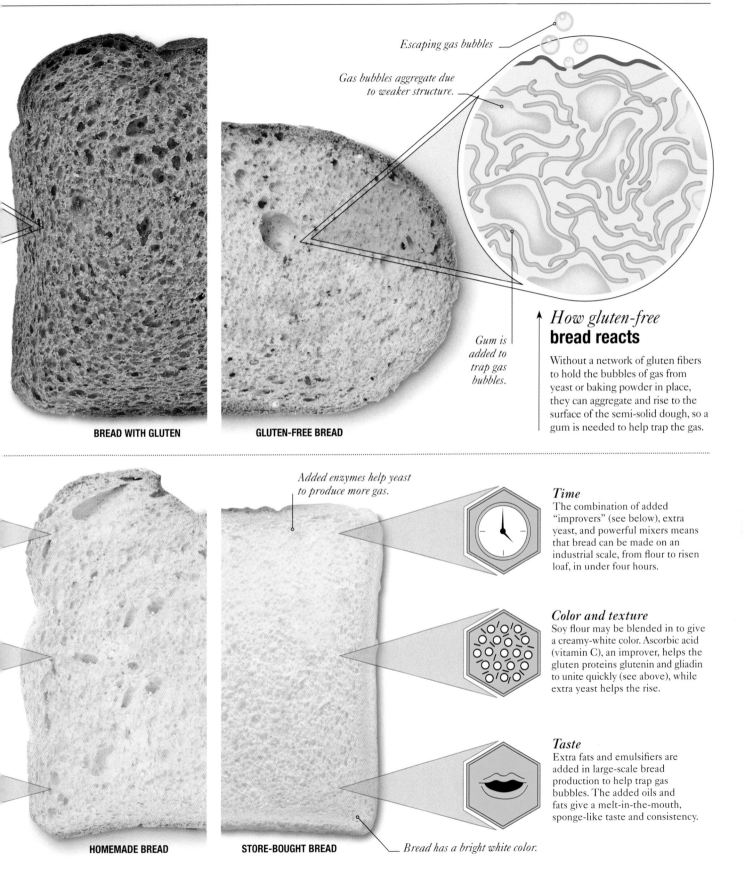

Escaping gas bubbles

Gas bubbles aggregate due to weaker structure.

Gum is added to trap gas bubbles.

BREAD WITH GLUTEN

GLUTEN-FREE BREAD

How gluten-free **bread reacts**

Without a network of gluten fibers to hold the bubbles of gas from yeast or baking powder in place, they can aggregate and rise to the surface of the semi-solid dough, so a gum is needed to help trap the gas.

Added enzymes help yeast to produce more gas.

HOMEMADE BREAD

STORE-BOUGHT BREAD

Bread has a bright white color.

Time
The combination of added "improvers" (see below), extra yeast, and powerful mixers means that bread can be made on an industrial scale, from flour to risen loaf, in under four hours.

Color and texture
Soy flour may be blended in to give a creamy-white color. Ascorbic acid (vitamin C), an improver, helps the gluten proteins glutenin and gliadin to unite quickly (see above), while extra yeast helps the rise.

Taste
Extra fats and emulsifiers are added in large-scale bread production to help trap gas bubbles. The added oils and fats give a melt-in-the-mouth, sponge-like taste and consistency.

Why shouldn't I "OVERWORK" PASTRY?

How pastry dough is handled and rolled is an important part of the pastry-making process.

Gluten only forms when flour is wet, so pastry needs enough water to make a pliable dough, but not so much that excess gluten makes a tough, rubbery pastry. Once chilled butter and flour have been worked into fine portions of dough, cold water is added—3–4 tablespoons per ¾ cup (100g) flour. It's vital that once water has been added, the dough is handled and rolled as little as possible to avoid too much gluten forming. Dough that springs back when rolled may be overworked. Adding extra flour and fat to disperse the gluten fibers may help.

KNOW THE DIFFERENCE

Pastry dough
Pastry dough needs careful handling with cool hands to minimize gluten production.

Texture: For a crisp, light pastry, too much strong, bouncy gluten is detrimental and can create a tough pastry.

Bread dough
In bread making, the aim of kneading is to create an abundance of gluten.

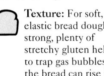

Texture: For soft, elastic bread dough, strong, plenty of stretchy gluten helps to trap gas bubbles so the bread can rise in the oven.

Butter in puff pastry

Chilled fat separates thin sheets of dough. When the dough is placed in a hot oven and the fat is still solid, moisture within it turns to steam, forcing the gluten-rich layers apart, puffing up the height fourfold.

Butter in flaky pastry

In this "quick" version of puff pastry, butter is spread in lumps throughout the dough. The resulting flaky pastry lacks tiering and crumbles haphazardly.

Butter in pie crust

In pie crust, fat surrounds dough particles, separating them. These small packets of fat are coated with flour to create a crumbly pastry.

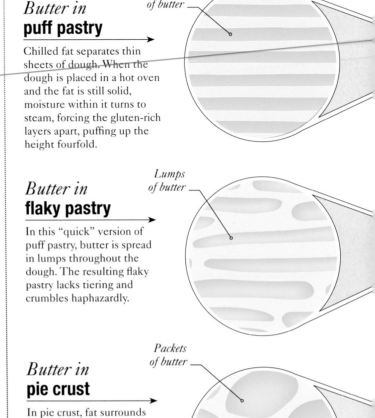

Layers of butter

Lumps of butter

Packets of butter

Do I always need to chill pastry before ROLLING IT OUT?

"Resting" pastry in the fridge allows stretched gluten to return to its normal shape.

You should always chill pastry for at least 15 minutes before rolling it (and between each round of folding and rolling when making puff pastry) by wrapping it in plastic wrap or parchment paper and placing it in the fridge. There are several reasons for doing this. Lowering the temperature slows gluten-forming reactions and stops solid fat from melting and leaking its moisture into the flour (butter is up to 20 percent water). This resting time also allows any water within the dough to spread evenly throughout, and less stretched gluten fibers spring back to their natural length, making shaping easier. It's worth resting dough again for 10–20 minutes once rolled so that it doesn't shrink back from the pan edges during baking.

A wooden rolling pin holds flour well and doesn't conduct heat from your hands.

A tapered, handle-less rolling pin allows pivoting and tilting.

PUFF PASTRY

FLAKY PASTRY

PIE CRUST

What's the secret to light
PUFF PASTRY?

The numerous wafer-thin layers in puff pastry gently splinter in the mouth.

Making puff pastry by hand is extremely time-consuming and seen as one of the most fiendishly difficult pastry types to master. A basic pastry dough is rolled flat and chilled, then a thick layer of chilled butter is spread on top and the pastry is folded with the ends meeting in the middle and re-rolled (see below). Six "turns" are called for in classic puff pastry, the number of layers growing exponentially as each gets thinner and thinner. Chilling is essential because if the butter melts when being rolled, the starches will swell, the pastry becomes floppy, and the butter layers will merge together. For best results, chill the pastry in a refrigerator for one hour before baking.

Pastry layer

Chilled rolled-out butter, roughly equivalent to the weight of the pastry.

STEP 1

One-quarter of the pastry is folded in on each side.

STEP 2

Rolled out and ready to fold again.

STEP 3

Making puff pastry
Butter is spread on the middle of the pastry layer. The pastry sides are folded over the butter and sealed. The process is repeated 6 times, creating 729 layers.

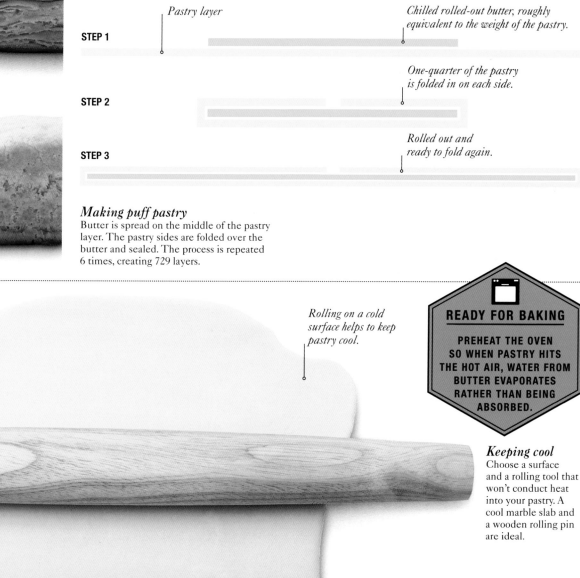

Rolling on a cold surface helps to keep pastry cool.

READY FOR BAKING

PREHEAT THE OVEN SO WHEN PASTRY HITS THE HOT AIR, WATER FROM BUTTER EVAPORATES RATHER THAN BEING ABSORBED.

Keeping cool
Choose a surface and a rolling tool that won't conduct heat into your pastry. A cool marble slab and a wooden rolling pin are ideal.

How do I prevent my pie from getting a "SOGGY BOTTOM" ?

Pastry is at its finest when it forms a firm, crisp, and buttery casing for the food it is showcasing.

Pastry dough is made up of at least 50 percent water-absorbing starchy flour, making it all too easy for a delicious, crispy-topped pie to end up with a soggy base.

During baking, microscopic starch crystals soak up water, "gelatinizing" into a smooth, soft gel; meanwhile elastic gluten dries; water from fat evaporates as steam; and, when fully dried, the surface browns and produces caramel-like aromas via the Maillard reaction (see pp.16–17). However, when a filling is added it can be hard for moisture to evaporate and the pastry is likely to absorb liquid from the filling.

Dense pastry with lots of fat may firm up without absorbing too much liquid because the fat will shield the flour from the filling. However, even with fat-rich bases, the base may still be undercooked when the filling is done. Follow the tips below to avoid a soggy base and produce deliciously crisp pastry.

A GOLDEN TOP

BRUSHING AIR-EXPOSED PASTRY WITH EGG GIVES EXTRA PROTEIN, WHICH ENHANCES BROWNING AND FLAVOR.

PREBAKING ("BLIND BAKING") THE BASE BEFORE ADDING A FILLING HELPS TO FIRM THE BASE AND KEEP LIQUID FROM BEING ABSORBED INTO IT. PRICK THE BASE WITH A FORK TO HELP STEAM ESCAPE, COVER WITH FOIL OR PARCHMENT, AND WEIGH IT DOWN (SEE BELOW); THEN BAKE AT 425°F (220°C) FOR 15 MINUTES.

BRUSHING THE BASE WITH BEATEN EGG OR EGG WHITE BEFORE BLIND BAKING HELPS PROTEINS TO FORM A WATER-RESISTANT LAYER.

FOR BLIND BAKING USE CERAMIC BAKING WEIGHTS, UNCOOKED RICE OR BEANS, OR EVEN WHITE SUGAR TO WEIGH DOWN THE BASE.

AVOID THICK CERAMIC DISHES FOR BAKING. THESE CONDUCT HEAT SLOWLY, LEADING TO A LIMP PASTRY WITH A GREASY COAT FROM THE SLOWLY MELTED BUTTER.

THE FILLING INSULATES THE BASE FROM THE HOT AIR SO THE DISH MATERIAL IS IMPORTANT. A DARK METAL DISH ABSORBS HEAT WELL, OR AN OVENPROOF GLASS DISH LETS HEAT RAYS PASS DIRECTLY INTO THE BASE. BOTH HEAT SWIFTLY SO THAT MOISTURE STEAMS AWAY.

IF THE OVEN'S ELEMENT IS AT THE BOTTOM, PUT THE PIE ON THE LOWER RACK TO HEAT THE BASE QUICKLY AND EVENLY.

BUTTER IS 10–20% WATER, SO COOKING PASTRY QUICKLY AT HIGH HEAT HELPS MOISTURE EVAPORATE RATHER THAN SOAK INTO THE FLOUR.

"Choosing the **right fat** is important to enhance flavor and provide a flaky, delicate texture. **Butter** melts into a thin liquid just below body temperature, at 90–95°F (32–35°C), to result in a **melt-in-your-mouth** sensation."

In focus
SUGAR

Few ingredients give us as much pleasure as sugar—but there's more to the sweet stuff than cakes and candy.

Nearly all of the sugar we sweeten our food with today has been extracted from either sugarcane or the turnip-like sugar beet. But sugar isn't just a sweetener; it has a range of other uses. Added to doughs and dairy, it prevents proteins from meshing tightly, so it helps make soft bread and smooth custards. In ice cream, it prevents grittiness by lowering the water's freezing point and keeping large ice crystals from developing. And sugar also controls the texture of baked goods by drawing moisture out of the air, keeping the goods softer for longer. If you heat sugar, it breaks down—or caramelizes—to transform into a rich-tasting syrup that can be cooled and set into shapes.

> "Each person
> on the planet
> *consumes
> an average of*
> **50lb (23kg)**
> *of sugar
> every year.*"

KNOW YOUR SUGAR

For much of modern humans' 200,000-year history, sugar was found in honey and dried fruits. Now, large-scale sugar production means we think of sugar as a simple white powder, but there is still much variety, with a range of white and brown sugars and syrups.

WHITE SUGARS

White sugar
This is sucrose, typically extracted from either sugar beet or cane. Common in home recipes, it is a versatile, all-purpose sugar.

GRAIN: FINE
REFINED

Fine sugar
Fine sugar dissolves more quickly than regular white sugar because it has finer granules. Ideal for whipping into egg whites and for syrups.

GRAIN: FINE
REFINED

Powdered sugar
The finest form of sugar, powdered sugar dissolves very quickly. Use for whipping into cream for smooth icing, or for dusting on top of desserts.

GRAIN: VERY FINE
REFINED

SCIENCE

WHEN HOT ENOUGH, SUGAR MOLECULES SMASH INTO EACH OTHER, BREAK, AND REFORM INTO HUNDREDS OF NEW SHAPES.

COOKING

CARAMELIZATION ADDS COMPLEXITY TO SUGAR'S FLAVOR, FORMING BUTTERY, NUTTY, AND RUM-LIKE NOTES.

CARAMEL

The caramelization process breaks apart sugar molecules into flavorful fragments.

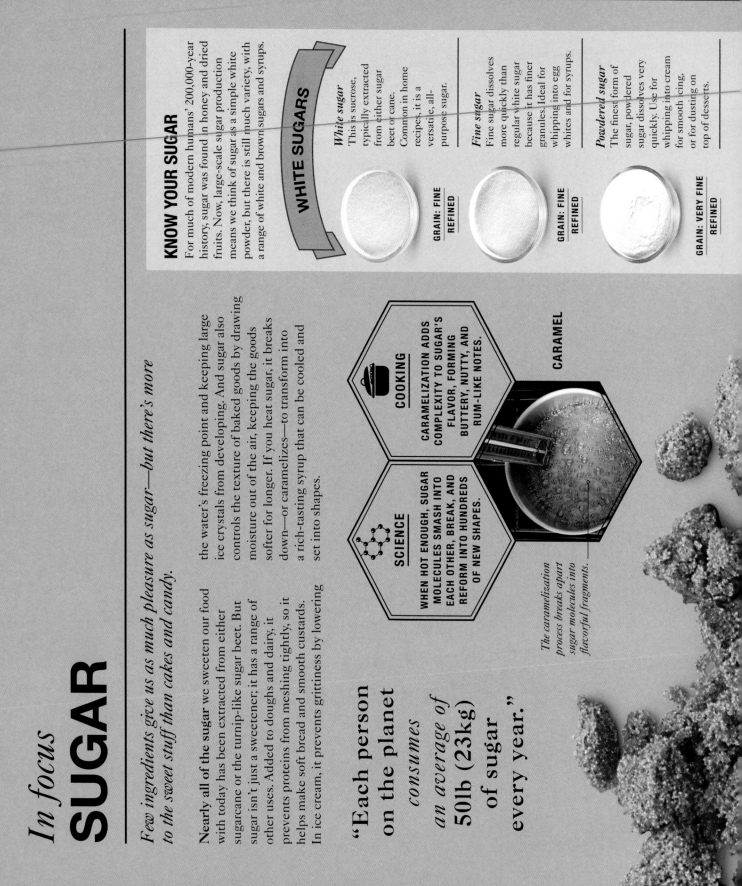

BROWN SUGARS

Brown sugar
Brown sugar is white sugar coated with molasses, giving it its brown color and a slightly bitter flavor. Ideal for flavoring and decorating.

GRAIN: FINE TO LARGE
REFINED & UNREFINED

Raw brown sugar
Raw sugars, such as muscovado, retain the liquid from sugarcane juice. With strong flavors, they're added to desserts and drinks.

GRAIN: LARGE
MINIMALLY REFINED

SYRUPS

Molasses
A thick, bittersweet syrup, this is extracted from boiled down sugar cane juice. Used in barbecue sauces, licorice, gingerbread, and in root beer.

GRAIN: LIQUID
UNREFINED

Corn syrup
When enzymes are added to cornstarch, this thick, sweet syrup is formed. This is a common sweetener in the food industry.

GRAIN: LIQUID
UNREFINED

Malt syrup
Used in baked goods and beer, this is made by cooking malted and unmalted barley grains. It's also available as a powder.

GRAIN: LIQUID
UNREFINED

Raw sugar's brown color comes from the molasses it retains from sugarcane juice.

When used in baking, invert sugar creates syrupy and soft textures.

COOKING
MOLASSES, BROWN SUGAR, AND HONEY CONTAIN INVERT SUGAR, SO THEY MAKE SOFT, GOOEY BAKED GOODS.

INVERT SUGAR

SCIENCE
INVERT SUGAR, A MIX OF GLUCOSE AND FRUCTOSE, IS SWEETER AND ABSORBS MORE MOISTURE THAN TABLE SUGAR.

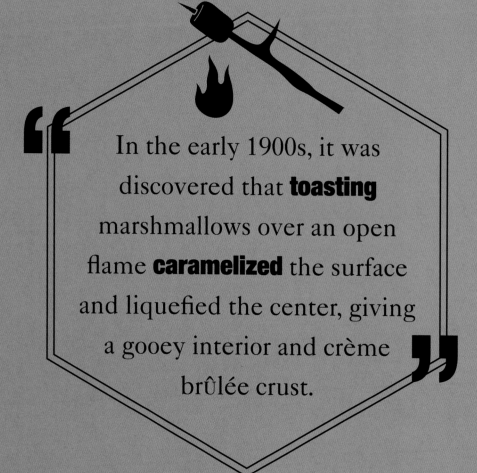

"In the early 1900s, it was discovered that **toasting** marshmallows over an open flame **caramelized** the surface and liquefied the center, giving a gooey interior and crème brûlée crust."

Can I make fluffy MARSHMALLOWS AT HOME?

These sweet white "pillows" have a long history.

The ancient Egyptians were the first to eat the gummy juice from the roots of the marshmallow plant. The glue-like sap found in the root, called mucilage, is made up of molecules of different sugars that intermingle to give a gummy consistency, perfect for a squishy confectionery.

In the 1800s, the French sweetened and whipped the gooey extract into an aerated foam, then developed the recipe further into marshmallow dough by adding egg whites, giving the gel added strength from the egg white proteins. Mucilage was eventually swapped for cheaper animal-based gelatin. Today, marshmallows are made by cooking down sugar into a thick syrup, adding gelatin powder and/or egg whites, then aerating into a semisolid foam. When cooled, they melt at body temperature into a soft, super-sweet goo in the mouth.

CORE INGREDIENTS

THIS CONFECTION IS A MIX OF COOKED SUGAR, GELATIN, AND WATER, WHIPPED UP INTO AN AERATED SPONGE.

ROLE OF SUGAR

THE THICK, SUGARY SYRUP LINES AND STRENGTHENS THE WALLS OF THE AIR BUBBLES IN THE MARSHMALLOW FOAM.

TIPS FOR MAKING MARSHMALLOWS AT HOME

Keep these tips in mind when following a marshmallow recipe.

DON'T UNDER- OR OVER-BEAT YOUR BATTER. LIKE MERINGUE, THE MIX SHOULD BE THICK AND FORM SOFT PEAKS, TO ENSURE A FEATHERLIGHT, FLUFFY CONSISTENCY.

THE KEY TO A MARSHMALLOW THAT SETS INTO A GOOEY CONSISTENCY IS HEATING THE SUGAR TO 250°F (121°C) TO CREATE A DENSE SYRUP.

USING A MIX OF SUGARS, SUCH AS HONEY AND GLUCOSE, MAKES SUGAR LESS LIKELY TO CRYSTALLIZE, AVOIDING A GRITTY TEXTURE.

THE MORE BUBBLES YOU BEAT IN, THE SWEETER THE MARSHMALLOW TASTES BECAUSE THE SUGAR MOLECULES COME INTO CONTACT WITH THE TONGUE FASTER.

LOWERING THE AMOUNT OF SUGAR AFFECTS CONSISTENCY, CREATING A MOUSSE-LIKE JELLY.

CORN SYRUP HAS MANY TYPES OF SUGAR AND GIVES A FIRM BITE.

What is the secret behind
CARAMELIZATION?

Heat shatters sugar molecules to form golden, buttery caramel.

Few culinary processes are more dramatic than caramelization, but transforming white sugar into a rich caramel is simply the work of heat alone.

How sugar responds to heat

Caramelization is not melting, but the "thermal decomposition" of sugar to create something entirely new. When hot enough, sugar molecules smash into one another with such violence that they shatter, before reforming into thousands of new types of fragrant molecules, ranging from pungent and bitter to subtle and buttery. There are two techniques for making caramel: wet and dry. The wet technique, shown below, opens up a world of culinary options (see table, right). The dry technique is less versatile, but is easy to do as it simply involves heating sugar in a heavy-bottomed pan. The sugar turns a molten amber, then brown, and its molecules break apart, losing their sweetness. When dark amber, the caramel is at its prime and can be poured over nuts for a brittle or used as the base of a sauce.

Caramel heated to 356–374°F (180–190°C) can be spread over nuts for a delicious nut "brittle".

THE "WET" CARAMEL TECHNIQUE

When water with dissolved sugar boils, it becomes more concentrated, gradually increasing the water's boiling point. As the temperature rises, the color darkens as sugar caramelizes. During cooling, crystals fuse into a solid that has a texture ranging from a soft gel to a hard brittle, depending on the concentration (see table, opposite).

DISSOLVE SUGAR IN WATER
Place 5fl oz (150ml) water, 12oz (330g) white sugar, and 4oz (120g) liquid glucose (if available) in a heavy-bottomed saucepan. Stir with a wooden spoon or rubber spatula. On medium heat, warm the syrup. Wipe the sides of the pan with a wet pastry brush to stop grains of sugar sticking to the sides, which could make syrup crystallize early, especially important for soft sweets and fudges.

SWIRL, DON'T STIR
Heat the mixture, monitoring the temperature carefully. As the sugar concentrates more, the boiling point rises. Stop at the desired stage (see table, above). For a caramelized result, continue until it is light golden. Gently swirl the mixture, but don't stir once the sugar has dissolved and is changing color as a solid spoon could encourage crystals to form and aggregate into clumps.

THE RIGHT TEMPERATURE
Watch carefully as the syrup gets more concentrated because the temperature will rise increasingly quickly as the sugar concentration rises. When at the deep brown stage, it sets into a hard brittle when cool. Heated syrup forms the basis of many sweets, toffees, and fudges. By adding milk, cream, or butter, the sugar and proteins brown to give butterscotch and toffee flavors.

TEMPERATURES FOR WET CARAMEL	
Boiling point and sugar concentration	**Behavior and appearance at room temperature**
234–240°F (112–115°C) Concentration: 85%	Forms a soft ball that can make fudge or pralines.
242–248°F (116–120°C) Concentration: 87%	Forms a firm but malleable ball that can be used to make caramels.
250–268°F (121–131°C) Concentration: 92%	Forms a hard ball that can be transformed into nougat or toffee.
270–290°F (132–143°C) Concentration: 95%	Forms a hard but pliable texture for hard toffees.
330°F (165°C) and above Concentration: 99%	Table sugar caramelizes, turning amber to brown. Stop before 410°F (205°C).

#4

HALT COOKING

Once the desired temperature is reached, stop cooking immediately. Plunging the bottom of the pan into a shallow bowl of iced water helps to halt heating if the mix is becoming too dark. For smooth caramel without grittiness, it's important not to disturb the pan. Using a variety of sugar types (such as sucrose and glucose) also gives a smooth texture by helping to prevent large crystals forming.

How do I get my JAM TO SET CORRECTLY?

Understanding how culinary gumming agents work can help you to hone your jam-making skills.

On the simplest level, jams are made of nothing more than fruit and sugar, boiled in water. It is the pectin in fruit (see below) that is the magical setting, or gumming, agent—a "hydrocolloid" that causes the fruit syrup to set firm as it cools.

We extract the chemical glue, pectin, from fruits by boiling them. Because there is just a small amount of pectin in most fruits, it needs to be concentrated then coaxed into a gel. A wide pan, no more than half full, has a big enough area for water to evaporate and the pectin to concentrate. When boiled gently in water for a few minutes until soft, the fruit cells start to rupture and much of the pectin escapes and dissolves into the water. Adding sugar to a ratio of 1:1 with the fruit sweetens and thickens the mix, drawing water away from the pectin molecules and forcing pectin strands to knit. Turning the heat up (for 5–20 minutes) causes the mix boil and froth vigorously. During this time the syrup thickens and pectin reforms into a gel-like configuration, woven enough to set the jam.

Glue-like strands of pectin bind the cellulose in the cell walls.

Tough cellulose fibers in cell wall

Air space

Vacuole inside cell

CHERRY SKIN FRUIT CELL

Sticky layer between cells (middle lamella)

Close up Pectin in fruit cells

Accounting for less than 1 percent of the fruit, pectin is concentrated in the core, seeds, and skin. It degrades as fruits age, so overly ripe fruit makes poor-quality jam. Fruits such as blackberries are high in pectin. Some, such as cherries and pears, have lower levels, so extra needs to be added during the jam-making process.

In focus CHOCOLATE

The most craved of all foods, chocolate has always been greatly treasured—the Aztecs even used cocoa beans as a currency and believed the cocoa tree was a bridge between heaven and earth.

With the range of chocolate products out there, you might think making chocolate is easy. Nothing is further from the truth.

Cocoa beans start out life looking white and slimy, encased in a hard, woody pod and tasting nothing like chocolate. Pried out of their pods, they are piled up and fermented to develop flavor, before being dried and shipped to chocolate factories.

At the factory, cocoa beans are roasted, adding an array of earthy, nutty flavors. They are then cracked and the waste shells removed, leaving only cocoa nibs, which are ground into a pulp of cocoa butter and solid cocoa fragments. At this stage, sugar and flavorings are added, before the chocolate is heated, tempered (see below), and shaped to form the shiny bars we see in stores.

Well-made chocolate has a smooth, shiny surface, showing it has been well tempered and stored in good conditions.

When chocolate is broken, hearing a loud snap is a sign that the bar has a good crystal structure, and will melt evenly in the mouth when eaten.

KNOW YOUR CHOCOLATE

Different types of chocolate contain varying levels of ground cocoa solids, cocoa fat (called "butter"), sugar, and milk powder to give them their individual properties. The ingredients are combined at the pulp stage of the production process, before the chocolate is tempered.

COCOA SOLIDS

100% cocoa chocolate

Made only from cocoa beans, with no sugar and sometimes with a little added cocoa butter, 100 percent chocolate is intensely flavored and bitter. Use sparingly in rich stews or with roasted meats.

COCOA MASS: 100%
SUGAR: 0%
MILK POWDER: 0%

Dark chocolate

Dark chocolate has added sugar to round out the cocoa's more bitter and astringent notes. The higher the cocoa solids, the more intense the flavor is. Use in brownies, cakes, and mousses, or combine with cream for smooth ganaches, or chocolates.

COCOA MASS: 35–99%
SUGAR: 1–65%
MILK POWDER: UP TO 12%

Dark milk chocolate

The milk solids lower the melting point of the chocolate, so it has a creamier mouthfeel and releases intense dark chocolate flavors faster, creating a nuanced, balanced flavor. Good for eating whole or grating over dishes.

COCOA MASS: 35–60%
SUGAR: 20–45%
MILK POWDER: 20–25%

Milk chocolate

This most widely eaten chocolate often has flavorings, such as dried fruit, nuts, or spices, and emulsifiers. Low-quality milk chocolate has vegetable oil rather than cocoa butter. Milk chocolate chips are used in baking as they have a lower melting point than darker chocolate.

COCOA MASS: 20–35%
SUGAR: 25–55%
MILK POWDER: 25–35%

NO-COCOA SOLIDS

White chocolate

The only cocoa white chocolate contains is cocoa butter, so it lacks the brown color and chocolaty flavor of cocoa solids. Cocoa butter has a very mild flavor, so the taste primarily comes from added sugar, milk powder, and vanilla flavoring.

COCOA MASS: 30% [BUTTER]
SUGAR: 40%
MILK POWDER: 30%

Using chocolate with a high percentage of cocoa in recipes brings a bitter edge to both sweet and savory dishes.

The cocoa bean variety and how it has been roasted gives dark chocolate a unique flavor.

Tempering involves heating chocolate until it reaches 113°F (45°C), then carefully cooling and rewarming it.

SCIENCE

TEMPERING BREAKS DOWN DIFFERENT-SIZED CRYSTALS, REFORMING THEM IN A UNIFORM STRUCTURE.

COOKING

USE TEMPERED CHOCOLATE TO COVER CONFECTIONERY SO IT HAS A GOOD SHINE, SNAP, AND MELTS EVENLY IN THE MOUTH.

TEMPERING

Why does chocolate from different countries TASTE SO DIFFERENT?

Chocolate lovers are quick to spot flavor variations in chocolate from different regions.

Chocolate eaten abroad never tastes quite like it does back home. One of the key reasons for this is varying legal requirements for chocolate labeling. Different countries have very different rules about how much cocoa a product needs to contain in order to be labeled as "chocolate." Confectionery companies take advantage of this to maximize profit margins, so a particular brand may taste completely different in different countries.

Cocoa percentage can vary hugely from bar to bar, so always check the ingredients list rather than relying on classifications such as "dark" or "milk." Avoid chocolate that substitutes cheap, greasy vegetable oils for smooth cocoa butter. The type and origin of the cocoa beans can also have a big impact on taste (see right and below).

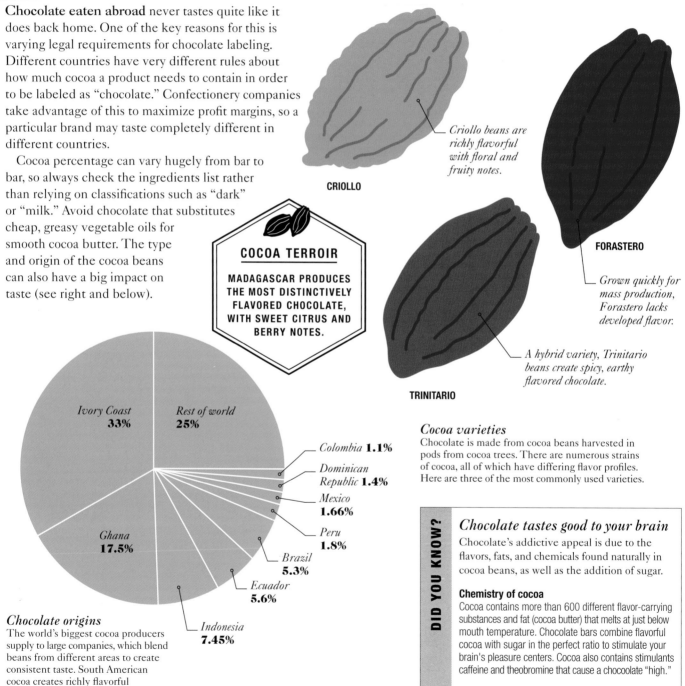

CRIOLLO

Criollo beans are richly flavorful with floral and fruity notes.

FORASTERO

Grown quickly for mass production, Forastero lacks developed flavor.

TRINITARIO

A hybrid variety, Trinitario beans create spicy, earthy flavored chocolate.

COCOA TERROIR

MADAGASCAR PRODUCES THE MOST DISTINCTIVELY FLAVORED CHOCOLATE, WITH SWEET CITRUS AND BERRY NOTES.

Ivory Coast **33%**

Rest of world **25%**

Ghana **17.5%**

Indonesia **7.45%**

Ecuador **5.6%**

Brazil **5.3%**

Peru **1.8%**

Mexico **1.66%**

Dominican Republic **1.4%**

Colombia **1.1%**

Cocoa varieties

Chocolate is made from cocoa beans harvested in pods from cocoa trees. There are numerous strains of cocoa, all of which have differing flavor profiles. Here are three of the most commonly used varieties.

Chocolate origins

The world's biggest cocoa producers supply to large companies, which blend beans from different areas to create consistent taste. South American cocoa creates richly flavorful chocolate with fruity and floral notes.

DID YOU KNOW?

Chocolate tastes good to your brain

Chocolate's addictive appeal is due to the flavors, fats, and chemicals found naturally in cocoa beans, as well as the addition of sugar.

Chemistry of cocoa

Cocoa contains more than 600 different flavor-carrying substances and fat (cocoa butter) that melts at just below mouth temperature. Chocolate bars combine flavorful cocoa with sugar in the perfect ratio to stimulate your brain's pleasure centers. Cocoa also contains stimulants caffeine and theobromine that cause a chocoolate "high."

What is the difference between MELTING AND TEMPERING CHOCOLATE?

To create perfect chocolate confections, it's worth mastering the chocolatiers' art of tempering.

Melted chocolate is suitable for use in desserts or baked goods that will be served warm, but chocolate intended for confectionery eaten at room temperature benefits from a process known as tempering. Tempering involves heating, cooling, and reheating chocolate to control fat crystal formation and improve the texture of solidified chocolate (see below). Tempering coaxes the fats in cocoa butter into setting correctly, creating solid chocolate that is glossy, snaps in the mouth, and melts without becoming greasy.

Remarkably, the fat molecules in cocoa butter solidify into six different types of "crystals": I, II, III, IV, V, and VI, each with different densities and melting points. If molten chocolate is allowed to cool naturally, it sets into a mixture of these crystal types (other than type VI, which forms only several months after the chocolate solidifies). Such chocolate will have a soft, crumbly texture and an oily aftertaste. Only crystal type V creates perfect solid chocolate, so the key is to prevent crystals I–IV from forming, as shown in the steps below.

#1 *#2* *#3* *#4*

Warming chocolate

Chocolate that has been poorly tempered will have a variety of fat crystals. When remelted it will need careful heating and cooling so that all the fat sets into type V crystals.

Melting fat crystals

Chocolate melts around 86–90°F (30–32°C), but must be heated to 113°F (45°C) to melt all of the fat crystals thoroughly. Stir the chocolate regularly and monitor the temperature closely.

Forming crystals IV and V

Cooling chocolate until it reaches 82°F (28°C) causes lots of type V fat crystals to form, alongside some IV. Traditionally spread on marble to cool, chocolate can also be cooled over a bowl of cold water.

Leaving crystal V

After cooling, the chocolate must be very gently reheated to 88°F (31°C), causing just the type IV crystals to melt away. This leaves only type V crystals, creating tempered chocolate.

The anatomy of chocolate "bloom"

Fat bloom occurs when fats within the chocolate liquefy and re-form into large, visible clusters. Sugar bloom is caused by sugar dissolving in surface moisture, which then evaporates to leave a thin, sugary crust.

BLOOMED CHOCOLATE

Fat clusters

Sugar crystal crust

Cocoa solids

Milk powder

Can I still use chocolate that's
TURNED WHITE?

The behavior of key ingredients in chocolate can cause it to develop a dusty white "bloom."

All types of chocolate—including bars, coatings, and confections—can develop white, mottled blemishes that are easy to mistake for mold. Your chocolate is likely to be safe to eat, cook, or bake with for two reasons. Firstly, chocolate has a very low moisture content, so microbes struggle to set up camp and grow, despite high quantities of sugar. Secondly, cocoa is packed with natural antioxidants that prevent fats from oxidizing and becoming rancid. Dark chocolate will last for at least two years; milk and white chocolate last about half that time, as they contain milk fats that turn rancid more quickly than cocoa butter fats. Powdery patches on chocolate are natural changes that develop over time in poorly tempered chocolate or due to storage in warm or moist conditions. This dusting, known as "bloom," is caused by fat or sugar deposits on the surface of the chocolate (see above).

How do I salvage melted chocolate that's
GOTTEN LUMPY?

With a little care and understanding of chocolate's composition, you can rescue any mishaps.

Lumpy melted chocolate is typically caused by contact with water or steam. Within moments, a mere drop or two will turn melted chocolate into a congealed mass. This is known as "seizing" and sugar is responsible for this transformation. Usually, minute sugar particles are evenly suspended throughout cocoa butter. When water enters, the sugar rapidly dissolves and clumps around the water droplets, stiffening into a syrupy paste. Taste is largely unchanged, but the texture is lumpy. Take care to prevent the melting chocolate from coming into contact with moisture, and try these ideas if it seizes (see below).

BEWARE WATER

AS LITTLE AS ½ TSP (2.5ML) OF WATER IS ENOUGH TO MAKE 3½OZ (100G) OF CHOCOLATE SEIZE.

Add more chocolate
If only a tiny quantity of water has made it into the chocolate, you can try adding more chocolate to the mix to dilute the water.

Add cream
Cream will turn the chocolate to a smooth liquid sauce. This works because cream is a mixture of water and milk-fat globules.

Add more water
At around 20 percent water, the sauce will "invert," converting it into a syrup, thickened by suspended cocoa and fat particles.

Double boiler

HOW TO SALVAGE LUMPY MELTED CHOCOLATE

How do I make a
CHOCOLATE GANACHE?

In spite of its association with professional bakeries, a chocolate ganache is easy to master.

A ganache is a delightfully simple mixture of cream and chocolate that can be adapted and used as a truffle filling, a flavored cake icing, or a decadent dessert in its own right.

Combining fats with water

Scientifically, a ganache is like a chocolate-flavored cream—an "emulsion" and a "suspension." Cream is an emulsion of milk-fat globules floating in water, into which all the components of chocolate are added: cocoa

EASY DOES IT

NEVER HEAT A GANACHE ABOVE 91°F (33°C), AS THIS WILL DISRUPT FATS IN THE CHOCOLATE AND CAUSE SPLITTING.

butter, cocoa particles, and sugar (plus any milk solids or other oils in the chocolate). The cocoa butter droplets are scattered in the liquid along with milk-fat globules; the sugar dissolves in the water, sweetening it to a syrup; while the solid cocoa particles swell as they absorb water to become dispersed within the liquid. Equal proportions of chocolate to double cream results in a smooth ganache, while increasing the chocolate or cocoa content (see below) thickens the consistency and intensifies flavor.

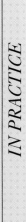

MAKING A CHOCOLATE GANACHE

A simple ganache is easy to master, and endlessly variable. You can use lower-fat cream for a thinner, less rich-tasting pouring ganache or glaze, or add more chocolate for a thicker ganache that's easy to roll into truffles or coat in melted chocolate. You can also add fruit powders or alcohol- or oil-based flavorings along with the chocolate.

#1

SCORCH MILK PROTEINS
Finely chop 7oz (200g) dark chocolate into evenly sized pieces. Heat 7fl oz (200ml) heavy cream in a saucepan over low heat, until it just begins to bubble. This "scorches" proteins in the milk, adding depth of flavor to the cream. Do not allow it to boil: this can destabilize fat globules and split the mix.

#2

COMBINE FATS AND WATER MOLECULES
Remove the saucepan from the heat. Add the finely chopped chocolate into the cream, and allow to melt for 30 seconds. The finer the chopped chocolate, the more quickly it will melt. Evenly sized pieces melt at a similar pace, reducing the likelihood of lumps.

#3

BEAT TO EMULSIFY
Stir with a spatula to combine the liquefied cocoa butter, cocoa, and sugar particles with the hot cream. The mixture will come together into a smooth ganache, with fats and water perfectly combined. Use hot as a sauce or pour into a shallow bowl and leave to cool for confectionery or tart fillings.

Can I make chocolate sauce that HARDENS ON ICE CREAM?

The science behind this trick is quite straightforward.

The magic behind the flavored sauces that harden the instant they're poured on ice cream is nothing more mysterious than coconut oil. Unlike most plant-based oils, coconut oil is high in saturated fat, so it sets solid at room temperature. The fats in coconut oil are less varied than the many types in animal fats, so coconut oil melts and sets abruptly. Blending with sugar and cooking it in a chocolate sauce makes it more difficult for the fat molecules to solidify, and the melting point of coconut oil is pushed below room temperature. To make your own sauce, place 4 tablespoons refined coconut oil, 3oz (85g) chopped dark chocolate, and a pinch of salt in a bowl, microwave for 2–4 minutes, stir, cool to room temperature, and then pour over ice cream.

Coconut oil quickly sets at room temperature.

ADDED BONUS

THE SHELL OF THE SAUCE INSULATES THE ICE CREAM FROM THE WARM AIR, SO THE ICE CREAM STAYS SOLID LONGER.

A solid oil
The ability of coconut oil to set so abruptly gives it the added "wow" factor.

How the soufflé rises

As it bakes, the air trapped in the semisolid egg foam expands, and moisture evaporates into steam, causing the pockets of air to inflate further. The egg yolk base forms walls between the egg white air bubbles.

Small air bubbles expand.

Proteins hold air bubbles in place.

PLAN AHEAD

EGG WHITE FOAMS DEFLATE SLOWLY OVER TIME, SO THE BASE SHOULD BE PREPARED BEFORE THE WHISKING STARTS.

RAW SOUFFLÉ MIX

How the soufflé sets

As the soufflé continues to rise, the proteins in the egg white and yolk coagulate, giving it a soft, gooey texture in the center, while the surface browns and crisps.

How do I master a CHOCOLATE SOUFFLÉ?

Sweet or savory, the principles hold: fatty yolks form a base into which whipped egg whites are added.

Beaten egg whites form the basis of any soufflé. Whipped into firm peaks, air bubbles caught in the meringue foam expand in the oven heat to make the soufflé puff up. The flavor comes from a fat-rich base made from egg yolks and, in this instance, cocoa and sugar. Mixing the two causes problems, however: the air bubbles in an egg white foam burst when they come into contact with fats, so it's essential to mix them carefully. Using twice the amount of egg white to yolk, folding is best done delicately in two or three batches with a rubber spatula. Cocoa and sugar thicken the base, stabilizing the bubble walls, but if the base is too dense, it will be too heavy for the expanding air and steam bubbles to lift.

The expanded air bubbles raise the mixture.

Proteins have coagulated.

"Egg whites are *whipped to soft peaks and combined* with the *yolks.*"

The surface sets and browns via the Maillard reaction (see pp.16–17).

(see pp.16–17)

DID YOU KNOW?

You can rebake sunken soufflés

All is not lost if your soufflés sink before diners start to eat.

A second rise

Putting soufflés back in the oven causes the air inside to expand once more and the soufflé will regain much of its former stature. You can also put cooked soufflés in a plastic bag and chill them overnight or freeze them. When you reheat them, the "double-baked" soufflés will rise slightly less, but have a more cake-like consistency.

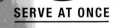

SERVE AT ONCE

AFTER RISING, A SOUFFLÉ INEVITABLY SINKS: HOT AIR CONTRACTS AND THE WEAK LOW-STARCH WALLS OFFER LITTLE SUPPORT.

SUNKEN SOUFFLÉ MIX

COOKED SOUFFLÉ MIX

INDEX

A

acetic acid 216, 224
acid
  ceviche 88
  Maillard reaction 16
adzuki beans, soaking 137
aging meat 49
aji limon 189
alanine 123
alcohol
  evaporation during cooking 199
  flambéing food 198, 199
  as food enhancer 198
alkaloids 150
allicin 184
almond milk 109
almonds 174
  harvesting 176
aluminum pans 24
amines 123
amino acids 123
amylopectin 128
amylose
  in rice 128, 129
  in waxy potatoes 161
anchovies 68
anthocyanins 160
antioxidants
  in bran 136
  in crab apples 148
  in fruit 148, 167
  in heirloom fruits and vegetables 148
  in popcorn 141
  in potatoes 161
  in tomatoes 150
  in vegetables 148, 151, 167
Anya potatoes 161
apples
  antioxidants 148
  choosing apples 171
  cooking apples vs. eaters 171
  pectin levels 171
ascorbic acid 170, 225
asparagus
  benefits of cooking 150
  griddling 157
  nutrient degradation 149

B

Aspergillus 205
astaxanthin 70, 90, 91
avocados 175
  ripening 149
  storing 149

Bacillus cereus 132
bacon, wet-cured 41
bacteria
  in blue cheese 122
  in cheese making 122–23, 124, 125
  effect of cooking on 12
  in fish 68
  in probiotic yogurt 119
  in rice 132
  salmonella 96, 97, 98
  in sashimi 88
  in sourdough starters 216
  in undercooked meat and poultry 63
  in yogurt making 118
baking
  adding salt to recipes 211
  bread 216–25
  cakes 210–15
  oven-baking process 222–23
  pastry 226–29
  sifting flour 210
  sugar 230, 231
  three stages of cake baking 214–15
  types of fats for 212–13
  with fruit 171
baking powder
  in bread 218
  in cakes 214
  double rise 211, 214
  self-rising flour 209
  using instead of baking soda 211
baking soda
  bread 218
  instead of baking powder 21

  Maillard reaction 46
balloon whisk 26

balsamic vinegar
  grades 200
  separated salad dressings 200
  traditional production 201
bananas
  production of 168
  ripeness 168–69
barbecuing *see* grilling
basil 181, 182
  how to prepare 182
  infusing oil 192
  storing 149
  when to add to cooking 183
basmati rice 129
  cooking basmati rice 130
basting 57
Bavaria Blu 121
bay 181, 182
  how to prepare 182
  when to add to cooking 183
beans
  bean size comparison 137
  gaseous side effects 140
  soaking 136–37, 140
beef 31
  best cuts 38–39
  color 34
  cooking the perfect steak 52–53
  effect of animal's feed on taste 37
  flavor pairings 18
  grilling beef 52
  purebred and heritage 36
  rare beef 53, 63
  testing for doneness 53
  Wagyu beef 39
beer
  flavor pairings 18
  as food enhancer 198
bell peppers *see* peppers
berries, freezing 170
betacarotene
  in carrots 150
  in peppers 155
bird's eye chiles 188
bitter taste 14, 15
black beans 137
black tea 18

blackberries, pectin content 235
blenders 166, 167
blind baking 228
bloom, chocolate 240
blue cheese 120, 122
blueberries, freezing 170
boiling vegetables 157
bouillon 62
bowls 27
bran 136, 208
Brazil nuts 175
bread 216–25
   adding salt to recipes 211
   baking bread 220–21
   bread dough basics 218–19
   flour 208
   gluten 208, 218–19, 220
   gluten-free bread 224–25
   homemade vs. store-bought 224–25
   improvers 225
   kneading bread dough 219, 226
   oven baking 222–23
   proofing dough before baking 220–21
   rising loaves 218, 219, 220–21
   sourdough starters 216–17
Brevibacterium 122
brie 122
   Brie de Meaux 122
brining
   olives 172
   poultry 56
brittle 234
broad beans, phytohemagglutinin 140
broccoli
   griddling 157
   nutrient degradation 149
   raw 150
   steaming 152
broiler chickens 36, 40
browning reaction *see* Maillard reaction
buffalo milk 120
burned food 17
butter 193
   baking with 212–13
   butter fat 112
   flaky pastry 226
   flavor pairings 18
   full-fat 111
   pastry 193, 226–27

pie crust 226
puff pastry 226, 227
using to improve flavor 111
using in pastry 226, 227, 228, 229
butter beans 137

C

cabbage, benefits of cooked 150
cakes 210–15
   adding salt to recipes 211
   baking powder 211
   cake pans 215
   flour 208
   food processors 210
   preheating ovens 213
   retrogradation 215
   sifting flour 210
   sunken cakes 213
   three stages of cake baking 214–15
   types of fats for 212–13
   why cakes get hard 215
calcium 124
calpains 39
camel milk 120
Camembert 120, 122
Campylobacter 63
cannellini beans
   phytohemagglutinin 140
   soaking 136, 137
capsaicin 188, 190–91
caramelization 230, 234
   wet caramel technique 234–35
carbohydrates
   pulses 136
   in ripe bananas 168
carbon steel
   knives 22
   pans 25
carotene 70
carotenoids
   in cabbage 150
   in carrots 157
   in eggs 96
carrots
   benefits of cooked 150
   boiling 157
   green tops 150
   nutrient degradation of 149
   raw 150
   roasting 156–57

skins 151
storing 149
water content 156
carving knife 23
cascabel chiles 189
casein proteins 118, 124, 125
cashews 174
casserole dishes 25
cast iron pans 25
caustic soda 172
caviar, flavor pairings 19
cellulose 157, 166
ceramic knives 22
cereals
   effect of cooking on cereal flours 12
   whole grains 136
ceviche 88
charcoal barbecues 44, 45
Charlotte potatoes 161
Cheddar 122
   cooking with 124
cheese 120–25
   alcohol to cook with 198
   Bavaria Blu 121
   blue cheese 120, 122
   brie 122
   Brie de Meaux 122
   Camembert 120, 122
   casein curds 124
   Cheddar 122, 124
   cheese-making process 120
   composition 120–21
   cooking with 121
   Danish Blue 122
   Emmental 121
   Epoisses 122
   feta 120
   Gorgonzola 122
   Gouda 122
   hard cheeses 121, 123, 124, 125
   Limburger 122
   making soft cheese 125
   Manchego 121
   mascarpone 125
   milk curds 108, 120, 123
   Monterey Jack 121
   mozzarella 120, 124
   Munster 122

paneer 120, 122, 125
Parmesan 122
Parmigiano-Reggiano 121
processed cheese 124
raw milk cheese 110
ricotta 125
ripening process 123
Roquefort 122
smelly cheeses 122–23
soft cheese 120–21, 124, 125
Stilton 122, 124
stringy cheese 124
types of cheese 120–21
types of milk used 120, 123
chef's knife 23
cherries, pectin content 235
chestnuts 177
chicken 30
  basting 57
  breeds 36
  broilers 36, 40
  checking for doneness 58
  chicken stock 62
  color 34
  corn-fed 40
  flavor 36
  free-range 40–41, 97
  grilling 58
  indoor reared 40–41, 97
  organic 40–41, 97
  preventing from drying out 56–57
  tenderizing 42
  undercooked 63
  water-plumped 41
chickpeas, soaking 137
chiles 184, 188–89
  aji limon 189
  bird's eye chiles 188
  capsaicin 188, 190–91
  cascabel chiles 189
  chipotles 189
  cooking 189
  cooking in oil 187, 188
  counteracting chile heat 190
  drying 189
  infusing oil 192
  jalapeño peppers 189
  pimiento chiles 189
  piri piri 188
  placenta 188, 189
  reducing chile burn 190–91

Scotch bonnet 188
Scoville Scale 188–89
seeds 188, 189
serrano peppers 189
Thai chiles 188
chipotles 189
chives
  how to prepare 182
  when to add to cooking 183
chlorophyll
  in olive oil 195
  in peppers 154, 155
chocolate 236–43
  100% cocoa chocolate 236
  bloom 240
  chemistry of cocoa 238
  chocolate ganache 241
  chocolate soufflés 242–43
  dark chocolate 236
  dark milk chocolate 237
  flavor variations 238
  ice-cream sauces 242
  lumpy melted chocolate 240
  melting 239
  milk chocolate 237
  origins 238
  shelf life 240
  tempering 236, 237, 239
  types of 236–37
  white chocolate 237
cholesterol
  absorption by the body 136
  in eggs 96
  and nuts 175
  in oils 192
choline 96
chopping board 27
chuck 39
cider, as food enhancer 198
cilantro 181, 182
  how to prepare 182
  when to add to cooking 183
citrus fruits
  lemons 47, 166, 192
  nutrient degradation 149
  reducing chile heat 190
clams
  eating raw safely 75
  effects of cooking on 74
clotted cream 112–13
cocoa beans 236, 238

chemistry of 238
varieties 238
cocoa butter 236, 238
  tempering chocolate 239
cocoa nibs 236
coconut milk 109
coconut oil 193, 242
cod 67
  curing 78
  pan-frying 82, 86
coffee, flavor pairings 18
cold-smoking meat 48
collagen 54, 55, 57, 60
condensed milk 109
connective tissue 30
contamination
  meat 63, 89
  milk 110
cookies
  hygroscopy 215
  using baking soda 211
  why cookies turn soft 215
cooking, why we cook 12–13
cooking methods
  boiling 152
  grilling 44–45
  microwaving 164–65
  oven baking 222–23
  pan-frying 76–77
  pressure cooking 134–35
  sous vide 84–85
  steaming 152–53
  stir-fries 158–59
cooling food 133
  rice 132
copper pans 24
corn 136
  popping popcorn 140–41
corn syrup 231
crab, color 90
crab apples 148
crackling, pork 50–51
cream 108
  chocolate ganache 241
  cooking with 113
  creamy sauces 61
  fat content 113
  full-fat 111
  overwhisking 113
  production 112
  types of 112–13

using to reduce chile heat 190
cream cheese, low-fat 111
crème fraîche 112–13
   adding to spicy dishes 119
   full-fat vs. low-fat 111
Criollo cocoa beans 238
crustaceans
   color 90
   crab 90
   lobster 90, 91
   prawns 72, 90
   shrimp 90
crustacyanin 90, 91
curdling
   milk 125
   yogurt in spicy dishes 119
curds
   cheese 120, 123, 124, 125
   milk 108, 114
   yogurt making 118
curing
   curing salt 203
   fish 78–79
curry, using yogurt in 119
custard 104–105
   preventing a skin from forming 114

D

dairy 108–25
   cheese 120–25
   full-fat vs. low-fat 111
   homemade yogurt 118–19
   ice cream 116–17
   milk 108–19
   reducing chile heat 190
Danish Blue 122
deep-fat fryers 196
deglazing pans 60
Desirée potatoes 161, 162
desserts, alcohol to cook with 198
diarrhea 119
digestion, and cooked food 12
dill
   how to prepare 182
   when to add to cooking 183
dough
   forming bread dough 218–19
   proofing before baking 220–21
Dover sole, cooking methods 82, 83
dressings, separated 200

dry-curing, fish 78–79
duck 30
   color 34
duck eggs 95, 96
durum wheat flour, pasta 142, 144

E

edamame, flavor pairings 19
eggs 94–107
   chicken eggs 95
   chocolate soufflés 242–43
   and cholesterol 96
   composition 94–95
   cooking at altitude 103
   cooking methods 100–105
   custard 104–105
   duck eggs 95, 96
   egg pasta 142, 144
   egg-washing pastry 228
   egg whites 46
   flavor pairings 19
   free-range eggs 97
   gauging freshness 99
   goose eggs 94, 96
   how many should you eat? 96
   mayonnaise 107
   nutrients in 96
   peeling hard-boiled eggs 102
   poaching 100–101
   quail eggs 95, 96
   raw eggs 97
   rotten eggs 98
   Salmonella 96, 97, 98
   scrambled eggs 104
   soft-boiled eggs 102
   storing 98
   types of 94–95
   whipping egg whites 106
elastin 55
Emmental 121
emulsifiers 61, 124, 200, 224
endosperm 128, 136, 208
enzymatic browning 166, 167
Epoisses 122
Escoffier, Auguste 62
ethylene gas 168, 169
evaporated milk 109
extra virgin olive oil 192, 194

F

fan ovens 222, 223
fats 192–93
   adding to poultry 57
   baking fats 212–13
   butter 193
   content in cream 112–13
   effect of cooking on meat fat 12, 30, 31, 38, 50
   fat bloom 240
   frying food 196
   full-fat vs. low-fat dairy products 111
   ghee 193
   lard 193
   marinades 47
   and meat flavor 38
   saturated fats 193
   tallow 193
   trimming off meat 50
   using in sauces 60, 61
fattiness taste 14, 15
fenugreek, flavor pairings 19
fermentation, yeast 220
ferrous gluconate 172
fertilizers 216
ferulic acid 150
feta 120
fiber
   bran 136
   potatoes 160
   pulses 136
fillet steak 38
fine sugar 230
fish 64–91
   achieving an "even" cook 82
   alcohol to cook with 198
   baking methods 80–81
   as brain food 68–69
   canned 68
   ceviche 88
   color of salmon 70
   composition 66–67
   cooking "*en Papillote*" 80–81
   cooking from frozen 80
   cooking methods 80–87, 88
   crispy golden skin 86–87
   dry-curing 78–79
   farmed fish vs. wild 71
   fresh vs. frozen 80
   freshness 68
   muscles 67, 82, 83, 87

oily fish 66–67, 68, 69
pan-frying 76–77, 82, 86–87
poaching 83
preserving at home 78–79
resting 87
retaining moisture while cooking 82–83
salt-baking 79
sashimi 88–89
smell 68
sous vide 82, 84–85
types of fish 66–67
white fish 67
flaky pastry 226
flambéing food 198, 199
flavor
   and chewing 167
   chickens 36
   chocolate flavor variations 238
   effect of cooking on 12, 31
   and flambéing 198
   garlic 184, 185
   grilling 44, 45
   herbs 180, 181, 183
   infusing oils 192
   marinating meat 46
   meat fat 30, 31, 38, 50
   oils 192, 195
   pairing flavors 18–19
   salt as an enhancer 47, 202, 203
   salting meat 47
   spices 186
flounder 87
flour 208–10
   00 flour 209
   composition 208
   effect of cooking on 12
   for fresh pasta 142
   gluten content 208, 226
   gluten-free flour 224
   high-protein flours 208
   ingredients 136
   medium-low protein 209
   multigrain flour 208
   nutrients 208
   organic 216
   plain white flour 209
   self-rising flour 209
   shelf life 209
   sifting flour 210
   storage 209

strong flour 208
types of 208–209
wheat flour 208, 224
whole-wheat flour 208
food poisoning
   eggs 96, 97, 98
   kidney beans 140
   oysters and clams 75
   rice 132
   Salmonella 96, 97, 98
   sashimi 88–89
   undercooked meat and poultry 63
food processors 210
Forestero cocoa beans 238
free-range chicken 40–41, 97
freezing food
   cooking fruit from frozen 170
   dried herbs 183
   fish 80
   freezer burn 42
   meat 42
   nuts 176
fried food
   calorie content 196
   cooking times 196
   pan-frying 76–77, 82, 86–87
   vegetables 157
fructose 231
fruit
   baking with 171
   bananas and ripening fruit 168
   cooking 170–71
   cooking from frozen 170
   enzymatic browning 166, 167
   heirloom 148
   juicing vs. whole fruit 166–67
   organic 148
   pectin content 235
   poaching 171
   purées 171
   ripeness 171
   sauces 171
   see also apples; bananas; *etc.*
frying
   calorie content of fried food 196
   cooking times 196
   pan-frying 76–77, 82, 86–87
   vegetables 157
frying pans 25
fungi 151

G

ganache, chocolate 241
garlic
   curing 185
   flavor 184, 185
   flavor pairings 19
   garlic breath 184
   garlic strength 184
   preparation and pungency 184
   raw 150
garnishes, herbs 181, 183
gas grills 44, 45
gelantinization 128, 131, 228
gelatin
   marshmallows 233
   in meat 30, 50, 54, 58
   and sauces 60
germ 136, 139, 208
ghee 193
gliadin 218, 224
glucose
   invert sugar 231
   marshmallows 233
glutamate 15, 74, 123
gluten
   in bread 218–19, 220, 222
   in flour 208
   gluten-free bread 224–5
   how gluten forms 224
   in pastry 226
   and sugar 211
glutenin 218, 224
gnocchi 143
goat's milk 108
   cheese made from 120, 123
goose eggs 94, 96
Gorgonzola 122
Gouda 122
grain-fed animals, effect on taste 37
grains
   anatomy of 136
   pearl barley 139
   quinoa 138–39
   whole grains 136
grass-fed animals
   effect on color 32
   effect on taste and flavor 35, 37
graters 26
gravy 57
Greek-style yogurt 119
griddling vegetables 157

grilling
  chicken 58
  meat 44–45
  process of grilling 44–45
  steaks 52

H

haddock 67
  cooking methods 82
Haematoccus algae 70
halibut
  pan-frying 82
  poaching 83
ham, wet-cured 41
Häning, D. P. 14
hazelnuts 175
heavy cream 112–13, 241
heirloom fruits and vegetables 148
hemicellulose 157
herbs 180–83
  basil 181, 182, 183
  bay 181, 182, 183
  chives 182, 183
  cilantro 181, 182, 183
  cooking 180, 181
  cooking in oil 192
  dill 182, 183
  dried herbs 183
  flat-leaved parsley 181
  flavor 180, 181, 183
  garnishes 181, 183
  hardy herbs 180–81, 182, 183
  marinades 47
  mint 181, 182, 183
  oil glands 180, 182
  oregano 182, 183
  parsley 182, 183
  preparing fresh herbs 182
  rosemary 180, 182, 183
  sage 180, 182, 183
  storing 181, 183
  tarragon 182, 183
  tender herbs 181, 182
  thyme 180, 182, 183
  when to add during cooking
    183
homogenized milk 108, 111, 112
honey
  hygroscopy 215
  invert sugar 231

marshmallows 233
  reducing chile heat 190
honing steel 27
hot-smoking meat 48
hydrocolloids 235
hydrogen sulphide 98
hygroscopy 47, 215

I J K

ice, reducing chile heat with 190
ice cream
  ice-cream makers 117
  making without an ice-cream maker
    116–17
  sugar in 230
improvers 225
invert sugar 230, 231
iodized salt 202
iron, content in popcorn 141
jalapeño peppers 189
jam, improving set 235
jugs, measuring 26
juicers 166, 167
juicing fruits and vegetables 166–67
jus, tasty 60–61
kale, storing 149
kidney beans
  phytohemagglutinin 12
  soaking 137
  uncooked 140
King Edward potatoes 160, 163
knives 22–23
Kraft, James L. 124

L

lachrymatory factor 154
lactic acid
  cheese 123, 125
  probiotic yogurt 119
  sourdough starters 216
  soy sauce 205
  yogurt making 118
Lactobacillus 125, 205, 216
  Lactobacillus delbrueckii 118
lactones 35
lactose 109, 114, 123
ladles 27
lager, as food enhancer 198
lamb 31

color 34
lard 193
  baking with 212–13
leafy greens 149
leavening agents 212
  bread 218
  cake baking 214
  double rise 211, 214
  self-rising flour 209
  using baking powder instead of
    baking soda 211
lecithin 94, 107, 116
lemon drop pepper 189
lemons
  and enzymatic browning of fruit 166
  infusing oil 192
  marinades 47
lenticels 161
lentils, soaking 136–37
light cream 112–13
lignin 48, 157, 166
Limburger 122
linoleic acid 96
liquids, for sauces 61
lobsters
  color 90
  killing kindly 91
longlife (UHT) milk 110–11
low-fat spread, baking with 212–13
lutein
  in eggs 96
  in peppers 154
lycopene 150
lye 172

M

macadamia nuts 175
mackerel 66
  omega-3 levels 68, 69
  pan-frying 82
magnesium chloride 203
Maillard, Louis-Camille 16–17
Maillard reaction 13, 16–17
  and basting 57
  meat 52
  milk 114
  nuts 175, 177
  pan-frying 86
  pastry 109, 228

slow cookers 54
spices 186
stir-fries 158
malt syrup 231
Manchego 121
marbling 36
    cooking marbled meat 31
    and flavor 32, 36
    grain-fed cows 36, 37
    steaks 52
    Wagyu beef 39
margarine, baking with 212–13
marinating
    ingredients 47
    meat 46–47
Maris Piper potatoes 160
marshmallow plant 233
marshmallows
    homemade 233
    toasting 232
mascarpone 125
mayonnaise 107
measuring cups 26
meat 30–63
    aging meat at home 49
    basting 57
    buying tips 32–33
    checking for doneness 58
    color 32, 33–35
    composition 30
    contamination 63, 89
    cooking from room temperature 52
    cutting 50
    dry-aged 33, 49
    effect of animal's feed on taste 37
    freezing 42, 43
    good quality 32
    grilling 44–45
    ground meat 47
    marbling 31, 32, 36, 37, 39, 52
    marinating 46–47
    muscle types 63
    organic 35
    overcooked 59
    pan-frying 76–77
    pounding 42
    purebred and heritage 36
    resting 59, 87
    salting 47
    searing 52
    slow cooking 54

smoking meat at home 48–49
sous vide 84
stock 62
taste 63
testing for doneness 53
trimming fat 50
types of 30–31
vacuum-packed meat 33
water-plumped meat 41
see also beef; lamb; *etc.*
melting chocolate 239
microbes
    blue cheese 122
    effect of cooking on 12
    pasteurization 110
    probiotic yogurt 119
microwaving 164–65
milk 108–19
    2% 108
    cheese making 120, 123
    composition 108–109
    condensed milk 109
    consistency 111
    curds 108, 114
    effects of cooking on 109
    evaporated milk 109
    flavor pairings 18
    goat's milk 108
    heating without a skin forming 114
    homogenized 108, 111, 112
    lactose 109, 114
    milkfats 108, 112
    milk skins 114–15
    pasteurization 109, 110–11, 120
    raw milk 110–11, 120
    sheep's milk 109
    skim milk 108
    types of milk 108
    UHT (longlife) 110–11
    unpasteurized raw milk 110–11, 120
    using to reduce chile heat 190
    whey proteins 114
    whole milk 108
    yuba 114
    see also cream
milks, nondairy 109
millet 139
minerals
    in bran 136
    effect of cooking on 12
mint 181, 182

how to prepare 182
    using to reduce chile heat 190
    when to add to cooking 183
mixing bowls 27
molasses 231
mold, on cheese 120, 122
molluscs
    clams 74, 75
    eating raw safely 75
    effects of cooking on 74
    mussels 91
    oysters 74, 75
monkfish 67
    sous vide 82
Monterey Jack 121
mozzarella 120
    casein curds 124
mucilage 200, 233
Muenster 122
muffins 212
multigrain flour 208
muscle 31
muscovado sugar 231
mushrooms, increasing vitamin D
        content 151
    flavor pairings 19
mussels
    cooking 91
    preparing 91
mustard seeds
    mucilage 200
    soaking 186
mutton, color 35
myoglobin 33, 34–35, 58

N

nutrients
    cooking vegetables to optimize 157
    effect of cooking on 12
    juicing vs. whole vegetables 166–67
    vegetable nutrient loss 149
nuts 174–77
    almonds 174
    Brazil nuts 175
    brittle 234
    cashews 174
    chestnuts 177
    composition 175
    cooking methods 177
    freezing 176

freshness 176
hazelnuts 175
macadamia 175
nut butters 174, 175
nut milks 175
nut pastes 174
oils 176
pecans 175
pistachios 174
roasting 175, 176, 177
storing 176
toasting 175, 177
types of 174–75
vacuum-packed 176
walnuts 175

O

oat milk 109
oats 136
octopus 82
oils 192–93
    adding to pasta cooking water 145
    baking with 212–13
    chilling 195
    coconut oil 193, 242
    cooking chiles in 188
    cooking spices in 187, 192
    cooking with 193
    extra virgin olive oil 192, 194
    flavor 195
    infusing 192
    molecular structure 195
    olive oil 192, 194–95
    peanut oil 193
    price of olive oil 194
    rapeseed (Canola) oil 192
    shelf life 195
    separated salad dressings 200
    storing 193, 195
    types of 192–93
    use in cooking 192
    using in sauces 60
oleosomes 177
oleuropein 172, 173
oligosaccharides 140
olive oil 192
    price 194
    separated salad dressings 200
    storing 195
olives 175, 189

black olives 172
brining 172
California olives 172
making olives edible 172–73
olive oil production 194
omega-3
    in eggs 96, 97
    in chickens 41
    in fish 68, 69
    in meat 37
    in nuts 174, 175
    in oils 192
omega-6, in oils 192
onions
    flavor pairings 19
    how to chop without crying 154
    raw 150
oregano
    how to prepare 182
    when to add to cooking 183
organic food
    chicken 40–41, 97
    fruits and vegetables 148
    meat 35
ovens
    cake baking temperatures 214
    convection ovens 222, 223
    oven baking 222–3
    preheating 213, 214, 227
oxidation, oils 195
oxygen, and meat color 33
oysters
    as aphrodisiacs 75
    best season for 75
    eating raw safely 75
    effects of cooking on 74
    oyster farming 75
    raw oysters 74–75
    species 74

P

paella rice 129
pan-frying 76–77
    fish 76–77, 82, 86–87
paneer 120, 122, 125
pans, cake 215
pans and pots 24–25
    deglazing 60
paprika 155
paring knife 23

Parmesan 122
Parmigiano-Reggiano 121
parsley
    flat-leaved 181
    how to prepare 182
    when to add to cooking 183
parsnips
    nutrient degradation of 149
    roasting 156–57
    storing 149
pasta
    adding oil to cooking water 145
    cooking methods 144–45
    flour 208, 209
    fresh vs. dried 144
    keeping pasta from sticking 145
    making fresh pasta 142–43
    pairing with sauces 143
    salting pasta water 144
pasta filata 124
pasteurization
    milk 109, 110–11, 120
pastries, flour for 208
pastry 226–29
    blind baking 228
    butter in pastry 193, 226–27
    chilling before rolling out 226–27
    flaky pastry 226
    gluten formation 226
    overworked pastry 226
    pie crust 226
    puff pastry 227
    resting 226–27
    soggy bottoms 228
    types of fats for 212–13, 229
peanut butter, flavor pairings 19
peanut oil 193
peanuts 175
pearl barley 139
pears, pectin content 235
pecans 175
pectin
    in apples 171
    in blackberries 235
    in cherries 235
    effects of cooking on 157
    and jam set 235
    in pears 235
    in peppers 154
pectin methylesterase 156, 171
Penicillium fungi 122

Penicillium glaucum 122
Penicillium roqueforti 122
penne 143
peppers
  color 154–55
  nutrient degradation of 149
  raw 150
  ripening 154
pesticides 151, 216
phenols 166, 172
phosphates 124
phytochemicals 151
phytohemagglutinin 12, 140
pie crust 226
pies
  pie dishes 228
  soggy bottoms 228
pimiento chiles 189
pinto beans, soaking 137
piri piri 188
pistachios 174
pizza "stones" 222
poaching 84
  eggs 100–101
  fish 82, 83
  fruit 171
polyphenoloxidase 182
pomme purée mashed potatoes 162
popcorn, popping 140–41
pork 31
  checking for doneness 58
  color 34
  pork crackling 50–51
  undercooked 63
potassium, in potatoes 160
potatoes
  adding to oversalted dishes 204
  antioxidants 161
  Anya 161
  blemishes and spots 161
  Charlotte 161
  color variations 160, 161
  composition 160–61
  creamy pomme purée mashed
    potatoes 162
  Desirée 161, 162
  fluffy mashed potatoes 163
  King Edward 160, 163
  Maris Piper 160
  mealy potatoes 160
  potato skins 160

Purple Majesty 161
roasting 156–57
Rooster 161
Russet 163
storing 149
varieties 160–61
water content 156
waxy potatoes 161
Yukon Gold 160
pots and pans 24–25
poultry 30–63
  alcohol to cook with 198
  basting 57
  color 34, 35
  good quality 32
  how to keep it from drying out
    56–57
  types of 30
  water-plumped 41
  see also chicken; duck; turkey
powdered sugar 230
PPO 166
preservatives, in bread 224
preserving fish 78–79
pressure cooking 134–35
probiotic yogurt 118, 119
processed cheese 124
proteins
  effect of cooking on 12, 30
  pulses 136, 140
pseudograins, quinoa 138–39
puff pastry 226–27
pulses 136–37, 140–41
  fiber 140
  protein 136, 140
  soaking 136–37
purées
  fruit 171
  thickening sauces with 61
Purple Majesty potatoes 161
putrescene 123
Puy lentils 137
pyrolysis 17

Q R

quail eggs 95, 96
quinoa 136, 138–39
  nutrients 139
  rinsing 139
rapeseed (Canola) oil 192

razor clams, effects of cooking on 74
red meat
  alcohol to cook with 198
  checking for doneness 58
  color 32, 33–35
  effect of animal's feed on taste 37
  good quality 32
  marbling 31, 32, 36, 37
  purebred and heritage 36
  resting 87
  taste 63
  types of 31
  see also beef; lamb; *etc.*
red wine, flavor pairings 18
rennet 120, 124, 125
resting
  fish 87
  meat 59, 87
retrogradation 163, 215
rib eye 39
rice 128–35, 136
  basmati rice 129, 130
  brown rice 128, 129, 130, 131
  composition 128–29
  cooking 128, 129, 130–35
  effects of cooking on 128
  fluffy rice 129, 130–31
  how much water to add 130
  paella rice 129
  pressure cooking 134–35
  reheating 132
  rinsing 130
  risotto rice 128
  sticky rice 128, 129
  types of 128–29
  white rice 128, 129, 131
  wild rice 129
ricotta 124
  making a ricotta-style cheese 125
ripening fruit 168, 171
risotto rice 128
roasting 222
rolling pins 26, 226
Rooster potatoes 161
root vegetables
  nutrient degradation of 149
  roasting 156–57
Roquefort 122
rosemary 180, 182
  how to prepare 182
  infusing oil 192

when to add to cooking 183
roux-based sauces 60, 62
rump roast 39
Russet potatoes 163

S

saffron, cost of 187
sage 180
  how to prepare 182
  when to add to cooking 183
salad dressings, separated 200
salad greens 149
salmon 66
  color 70
  cooking methods 82, 83, 84, 86
  dry-curing 78–79
  farmed salmon 70, 71
  omega-3 content 68
  pan-frying 82, 86
  poaching 83
  sous vide 82, 84
  wild salmon 70, 71
Salmonella
  chickens 63
  eggs 96, 97, 98
salt 202–204
  adding to baking recipes 211
  brines 202
  coarse salt 203
  colored salts 203
  cooking with 202
  curing salt 203
  dry-curing fish 78–79
  as flavor enhancer 202, 203
  formation 202
  granulated table salt 202
  iodized salt 202
  Maillard reaction 52
  marinades 47
  oversalted dishes 204
  refined salt 202–203
  rubs 202
  salt-baking fish 79
  salting meat 47
  salting pasta water 144
  salting vegetable water 157
  sea salt 203
  soaking beans 136
  structure of 202, 204
  types of 202–203

unrefined salt 203
salty taste 14, 15
saponins 139
sardines 68
sashimi 88–89
saucepans 25
sauces
  chocolate ice-cream sauces 242
  fruit sauces 171
  gelatin in 60
  lumpy chocolate sauces 240
  pairing with pasta 143
  preventing a skin from forming 114
  seizing 240
  tasty sauces 60–61
  thickening 54, 60, 61
sauté pans 25
sautéing 77
scales 26
Scotch bonnet chiles 188
Scoville Scale 188–89
sea bass 67
  pan-frying 82, 86
  salt-baking 79
sea bream, salt-baking 79
sea salt 203
seafood 64–91
  color 90
  salting 78
  see also fish; oysters; shrimp; *etc.*
searing meat 52
seasonings
  salt 202–204
  soy sauce 204–05
seeds
  calories 174
  cooking methods 177
seizing 240
serrano peppers 189
serrated knives 22
sheep's milk 109, 120
  cheese made from 120, 123
shell-shaped pasta 143
shellfish
  alcohol to cook with 198
  astaxanthin 70
  clams 74, 75
  color 90–91
  mussels 91
  oysters 74, 75
shrimp 73

buying tips 72
buying with their heads on 72
color 90
raw vs. precooked, fresh or
  frozen 72
sieves 26
sifting flour 210
sirloin steak 39
skillets 24, 52
slow cooking 54–55
  meat 30, 59
smoke point 192
smoking, meat 48–49
snapper
  pan-frying 86
  salt-baking 79
socialization 12
sodium 15, 157
sodium bicarbonate (baking soda) 209
soil quality 148, 149
soufflés
  chocolate 242–43
  rebaking 243
sour cream 112–13
sour taste 14, 15
sourdough starters 216–17
sous vide 84–85
  fish 82, 84–85
  meat 84
  poultry 56
  vegetables 157
soy flour 225
soy sauce
  "chemical" soy sauce 204
  light vs. dark 204–205
soy milk 109
soybeans 137
  soy sauce 205
spaghetti 143
spatchcocking 56
spatulas 26, 27
spices
  cooking 186
  cooking in oil 187, 192
  flavor 186
  ground spices 186
  Maillard reaction 186
  marinades 47
  saffron 187
  turmeric 187
  using yogurt in spicy dishes 119

whole spices 186
spinach, benefits of cooked 150
spit-roasting
    pork 51
    poultry 56
split peas, soaking 137, 140
spoons
    slotted 27
    wooden 27
squash, storing 149
squid 82
stainless steel
    knives 22
    pans 24
starches
    effect of cooking on 12
    in flour 209
    gluten-free flour 224
    in pasta 144, 145
    in potatoes 160, 163
    retrogradation 163
    in rice 128, 129, 130–31
    using in sauces 60
steaks
    cooking the perfect steak 52–53
    resting 59
    searing 52
    testing for doneness 53
steaming 152–53
    vegetables 157
steels, honing 26
Stilton 122
    cooking with 124
stir-fries, vegetable 158–59
stock 62
    chicken stock 62
    making in pressure
        cookers 134
    using in sauces 61
strawberries
    freezing 170
Streptococcus thermophilus 118
strong flour 208
sugar 230–35
    absorption by the body 136
    brown sugars 231
    caramelization 230, 234–35
    fine sugar 230
    hygroscopy 215
    icing sugar 230
    invert sugar 230, 231

marshmallows 233
reducing chile heat 190
sugar bloom 240
syrups 231
types of sugar 230–31
using in marinades 47
white sugar 230
sulphur 98
superfoods
    nuts 174
    quinoa 139
sweet potatoes 161
    nutrients in skin 151
    storing 149
sweet taste 14, 15
sweets 230
syrups 231

T

T-bone 39
tagliatelle 143
tallow 193
tannins 175, 198
tarragon
    how to prepare 182
    when to add to cooking 183
tarts
    pie dishes 228
    soggy bottoms 228
    using frozen fruit in 170
taste 14–17
    broiler chickens 36
    cattle breeds 36
    chocolate flavor variations 238
    effect of animal's feed on 37
    and ethically produced
        food 148
    frozen meat 42
    heirloom fruits and vegetables 148
    red meat 63
    white meat 63
teff 136
tempering chocolate 236, 237, 239
tenderizing meat 42
tenderloin 39
texture
    frozen meat 42
    salting meat 47
Thai chiles 188
thermometers 27, 58

thickening sauces 54, 60, 61
thyme 180
    how to prepare 182
    when to add to cooking 183
tomatoes
    alcohol to cook with 198
    cooked 150
    nutrient degradation of 149
    raw 150
    ripening 149
    storing 149
tongues, and taste 14–15
tooth decay 167
tørrfisk 78
triacylglycerol 195
trimethylamine oxide (TAMO)
    68
Trinitario cocoa beans 238
trout 67
    poaching 83
tryptophan 123
tuna 66
    omega-3 levels 68
    pan-frying 82
    poaching 83
    sashimi 88
turbot 83
turkey 30
    basting 57
    how to stop drying out 56–57
turmeric 187
turnips
    nutrient degradation of 149
    storing 149

U

UHT (longlife) milk 110–11
umami taste 14, 15
    and glutamate 123
    and mushrooms 151
    and salt 202, 211
utensils 26–27

V

vacuoles 166
vegetable shortening 212–13
vegetables
    adding salt to the water 157
    antioxidants 150, 151

boiling 152, 157
cooking to optimize nutrients 157
effect of cooking on 12
frying 157
green tops 150
griddling 157
heirloom 148
juicing vs. whole vegetables 166–67
nutrient loss 149
organic 148
peeling vs. scrubbing 151
raw 150
reducing chile heat 190
roasting 156–57
skins 151
sous vide 157
steaming 152–53, 157
stir-fries 158–59
stock 62
storage 149
venison 31
vinegar
  marinades 47
  reducing chile heat 190
  separated salad dressings 200
vitamin A 149
vitamin B
  in bran 136
  in carrots 150
  in flour 208
  in fruits and vegetables 149, 150, 160
  in potatoes 160
vitamin B3 175
vitamin B12 96, 151
vitamin C 15
  in bread 225
  in carrots 150
  in fruits and vegetables 149, 150, 167
  in juiced fruits and vegetables 167
  in potatoes 160
  in vegetable skins 151
vitamin D, increasing content in
    mushrooms 151
vitamin E
  in eggs 96, 97
  in fruits and vegetables 149
  in nuts 174
vitamins
  effect of cooking on 12
  vegetable nutrient loss 149

W

Wagyu beef 39
walnuts 175
water, using in sauces 61
watercress 150
wet-curing fish 78–79
wheat, flavor pairings 19
wheat berries 136
wheat flour 224
whey
  cheese 120, 121, 124, 125
  milk 114
whipping cream 112–13
whiskey, as food enhancer 198
whisks 26
white meat
  checking for doneness 58
  color 34, 35
  good quality 32
  preventing from drying out 56–57
  resting 87
  taste 63
  types of 30
  see also chicken; duck; turkey
whole grains
  whole grains vs. processed 136
  see also corn; oats; rice; etc.
whole-wheat flour 208
  appearance 209
  shelf life 209
wild rice 129
  cooking 130
wine
  as food enhancer 198
  marinades 47
  using in sauces 61
woks 24
  protecting nonstick 159
wooden spoons 27

X Y Z

xanthan gum 224
yeast
  fermentation 218, 220
  proofing bread dough 220
  sourdough starters 216
yogurt
  curdling 119
  Greek-style yogurt 119
  making your own 118–19

marinades 47
probiotic yogurt 118, 119
using to reduce chile heat 119, 190,
    191
yogurt starters 118
yuba 114
Yukon Gold potatoes 160
zeaxanthin 96
zinc 75
zucchini, griddling 157

ABOUT THE AUTHOR

Specializing in food science, Dr. Stuart Farrimond is a science and medical writer, and educator. He makes regular appearances on TV, on radio, and at public events, and his writing appears in international publications. A keen blogger, Stuart is also the founder and editor of online lifestyle-science magazine *Guru*, which is supported by the Wellcome Trust.

ACKNOWLEDGMENTS

Author's acknowledgments

Special thanks go to Chris Sannito, Seafood Technology Specialist at the Alaska Sea Grant Marine Advisory Program, who kindly taught me the finer points of salmon fishing, smoking, and storing; and Merrielle Macleod, Program Officer at World Wildlife Fund, who explained the reality of fish aquaculture in the world today, sinking some popular Internet scare stories along the way. Thanks go to Mary Vickers, Senior Beef & Sheep Scientist at the UK's Agriculture & Horticulture Development Board, for her expertise in cattle breeds around the world and the various factors that affect meat quality; and thanks to Kevin Coles of British Egg Information Service for his freshly laid stats. Louise and Matt Macdonald of New MacDonald Farm, Wiltshire, allowed me to get up close to their flock of egg-laying hens, and I am indebted to Geoff Bowles for satisfying my curiosity about the minutiae of milk, cream, and butter production and for taking me on a lengthy tour of Ivy House Farm Dairy, a dairy that I later learned provides milk to royalty. Kevin Jones, butcher at Hartley Farm, Wiltshire, UK, graciously took time away from his work to show me everything I need to know about knives and butchery, while Will Brown taught me how to select and age meat;

head chef Gary Says and culinary lecturer Steve Lloyd opened their kitchen doors to me to reveal how the "pros" practice their art, while Nathan Olive and Angie Brown, of The Oven Bakery, let me poke their sourdough and probe their ovens, answering my queries about the nuances of baking bread. No doubt there are many people whose contributions I have forgotten to mention, but I offer my thanks to Nathan Myhrvold, author of *Modernist Cuisine*, and Jim Davies, of UCL, London, who let me put various types of chocolate and cookies in his electron microscope so that I could study them in minute detail (insect parts and all).

I thank Dawn Henderson and the team at DK Books for inviting me to take part in this exciting project. Editors Claire Cross and Bob Bridle have been remarkably patient with my particular attention to scientific details; I am in awe of the beautiful imagery crafted by the artists and designers, while Claire has worked tirelessly to pare my work into a digestible tome. My literary agent, Jonathan Pegg, has been supportive from start to finish, and it would be wholly remiss of me not to offer my heartfelt thanks and love to my wife, family, and friends, who have supported me and kept me sane, despite the late nights and antisocial hours.

Publisher's acknowledgments

We would like to thank the author for his expertise and guidance throughout.

Photography Will Heap, William Reavell
Food stylists Kate Turner, Jane Lawrie
Design assistance Helen Garvey
Editorial assistance Alice Horne, Laura Bithell
Proofreading Corinne Masciocchi
Indexing Vanessa Bird

The publisher would like to thank the following for their kind permission to reproduce their photographs:

(Key: a-above; b-below/bottom; c-centre; f-far; l-left; r-right; t-top)
22 Dreamstime.com: Alina Yudina (ca); Demarco (ca/Stainless steel); Yurok Aleksandrovich (c). **24 Dreamstime.com:** Demarco (cr); Fotoschab (cr/Copper); James Steidl (crb). **25 Dreamstime.com:** Alina Yudina (cl); Liubomirt (clb). **27 123RF.com:** tobi (bl). **33 123RF.com:** Reinis Bigacs / bigacis (crb); Kyoungil Jeon (cla). **Dreamstime.com:** Erik Lam (c); Kingjon (c/Raw t-bone). **39 123RF. com:** Mr.Smith Chetanachan (br). **117 Alamy Stock Photo:** Huw Jones (tc). **124 Dreamstime. com:** Charlieaja (tl). **140-141 Dreamstime.com:** Coffeemill (cb). **145 Dreamstime.com:** Eyewave (l). **150 Depositphotos Inc:** Maks Narodenko (tr). **154 Dreamstime.com:** Buriy (bl). **188 Dreamstime.com:** Viovita (crb). **212 123RF.com:** foodandmore (bl). **233 123RF.com:** Oleksandr Prokopenko (cb)

All other images © Dorling Kindersley
For further information see: www.dkimages.com